AF769057

Charting Limitations on Trademark Rights

Charting Limitations on Trademark Rights

Edited by

HAOCHEN SUN
BARTON BEEBE

OXFORD
UNIVERSITY PRESS

OXFORD
UNIVERSITY PRESS

Great Clarendon Street, Oxford, OX2 6DP,
United Kingdom

Oxford University Press is a department of the University of Oxford.
It furthers the University's objective of excellence in research, scholarship,
and education by publishing worldwide. Oxford is a registered trade mark of
Oxford University Press in the UK and in certain other countries

© The many contributors 2023

The moral rights of the authors have been asserted

First Edition published in 2023

All rights reserved. No part of this publication may be reproduced, stored in
a retrieval system, or transmitted, in any form or by any means, without the
prior permission in writing of Oxford University Press, or as expressly permitted
by law, by licence or under terms agreed with the appropriate reprographics
rights organization. Enquiries concerning reproduction outside the scope of the
above should be sent to the Rights Department, Oxford University Press, at the
address above

You must not circulate this work in any other form
and you must impose this same condition on any acquirer

Public sector information reproduced under Open Government Licence v3.0
(http://www.nationalarchives.gov.uk/doc/open-government-licence/open-government-licence.htm)

Published in the United States of America by Oxford University Press
198 Madison Avenue, New York, NY 10016, United States of America

British Library Cataloguing in Publication Data

Data available

Library of Congress Control Number: 2023932986

ISBN 978–0–19–887124–8

DOI: 10.1093/oso/9780198871248.001.0001

Printed and bound in Great Britain by
CPI Group (UK) Ltd, Croydon, CR0 4YY

Links to third party websites are provided by Oxford in good faith and
for information only. Oxford disclaims any responsibility for the materials
contained in any third party website referenced in this work.

Contents

List of Contributors

Arpan Banerjee, Senior Intellectual Property Advisor, Authentix Inc; Assistant Professor (on leave), Jindal global Law School

Barton Beebe, John M. Desmarais Professor of Intellectual Property Law, New York University

Lionel Bently, Herchel Smith Professor of Intellectual Property and Deputy Director, Centre for Intellectual Property and Information Law, Faculty of Law, University of Cambridge

Robert G. Burrell, Professor of Intellectual Property and Information Technology Law, Faculty of Law, University of Oxford

Roberto Carapeto, Lecturer, Graduate School of Law, Nagoya University; Partner at Licks Attorneys

Carys J. Craig, Associate Professor of Law, Osgoode Hall Law School, York University

Jeanne C. Fromer, Walter J. Derenberg Professor of Intellectual Property Law, School of Law, New York University

Michael Handler, Professor, School of Private and Commercial Law, Faculty of Law & Justice, UNSW Sydney

Mark A. Lemley, William H. Neukom Professor, Stanford Law School; counsel, Lex Lumina PLLC

Kung-Chung Liu, Professor of Law, Singapore Management University

Mark P. McKenna, Professor of Law, UCLA School of Law; Faculty Co-Director, UCLA Institute for Technology, Law & Policy; Of Counsel, Lex Lumina PLLC

Christoph Rademacher, Professor of Law, School of Law, Waseda University

Martin Senftleben, Professor of Intellectual Property Law and Director of the Institute for Information Law (IViR), University of Amsterdam

Haochen Sun, Professor of Law, University of Hong Kong Faculty of Law

David Tan, Professor of Law, Faculty of Law, National University of Singapore

Introduction

Charting Limitations

*Haochen Sun**

In this day and age, virtually all goods and services are merchandized through trademarks. Trademarks are core assets for companies and a part of our daily lives, and thus have significant economic and cultural value. Trademark law recognizes that value, protecting the exclusive right to use a trademark and guarding against unauthorized uses that may mislead consumers or harm the mark's distinctiveness or reputation.[1]

Trademark law has also carved out limitations on trademark rights to protect the public interest.[2] Limitations such as descriptive and nominative uses promote freedom of commerce and healthy competition in the marketplace. The descriptive use limitation allows a company to, for instance, freely use the registered trademark MICRO COLOR to describe the color features of a cosmetic product without the trademark owner's permission.[3] Thanks to the nominative use limitation, magazines can launch cultural activities involving the use of registered entertainment trademarks,[4] and businesses can publicly advertise their repair and maintenance services involving the use of registered car trademarks.[5]

Limitations on trademark rights also promote freedom of expression. The Federal Trademark Dilution Act in the United States permits uses of trademarks for such purposes as parody, news reporting, and commentary.[6] The European Union (E.U.)

* Professor of Law, University of Hong Kong Faculty of Law.

[1] *See generally* Frank I. Schechter, *The Rational Basis of Trademark Protection*, 40 Harv. L. Rev. 813 (1927).

[2] *See, e.g.*, Ralph S. Brown, Jr., *Advertising and the Public Interest: Legal Protection of Trade Symbols*, 57 Yale L. J. 1165, 1202, 1204–05 (1948) ("That the trade-mark monopoly, like the patent monopoly, is confined by the policy of the anti-trust laws seems unquestionable. . . . Probably it is futile to recall that we are all imitators, and that our society is committed to the proposition that progress is advanced by the free use and adaptation of novel things and ideas.").

[3] *See* KP Permanent Make-Up, Inc. v. Lasting Impression I, Inc., 543 U.S. 111 (2004).

[4] *See* New Kids on the Block v. News America Publishing, Inc., 971 F.2d 302 (9th. Cir. 1992) (ruling that a magazine's use of a music band's name to solicit public opinion on that band constituted a nominative fair use).

[5] *See* Volkswagenwerk Aktiengesellschaft v. Church, 411 F.2d 350 (9th Cir. 1969); Toyota Motor Sales U.S.A., Inc. v. Tabari, 610 F.3d 1171 (9th Cir. 2010). Nominative use is known as informative use under E.U. Law. *See* Bayerische Motorenwerke AG (BMW) and BMW Nederland BV v. Ronald Karel Deenik, CJEU Case C-63/97, ¶ 54 (1999).

[6] 15 U.S.C.A. § 1125(c).

Haochen Sun, *Charting Limitations* In: *Charting Limitations on Trademark Rights*. Edited by: Haochen Sun and Barton Beebe, Oxford University Press. © Haochen Sun 2023. DOI: 10.1093/oso/9780198871248.003.0001

Trade Mark Regulation permits the use of trademarks by third parties in order to "ensure[] full respect for fundamental rights and freedoms, and in particular the freedom of expression."[7] These limitations allow social commentary and artistic speech to flourish, thereby enabling people to criticize or poke fun at brands and artists to come up with new works through their use of registered trademarks.

Despite the fundamental importance of such limitations, trademark scholarship has focused largely on the protection of trademark rights, studying areas such as consumer confusion and the dilution of trademarks. Studies of trademark rights limitations, meanwhile, have remained relatively peripheral, especially in jurisdictions outside of the United States.[8] We undertook this volume in the belief that much more research should be devoted to studying the following four aspects of trademark rights limitations.

Justifications for Limitations

According to conventional wisdom, free speech and competition justify limiting trademark rights.[9] Although these perspectives are theoretically insightful and practically important, there are emerging approaches to theorizing trademark law. Some scholars have attempted to entrench social and cultural theories such as linguistics[10] and semiotics[11] as an alternative to the natural rights and utilitarian visions of trademark rights that have a dominant position in the trademark scholarship.[12] However, these new approaches have yet to be systematically applied to study limitations on trademark rights.

We need to broaden the theoretical exploration of limitations on trademark rights to come up with more dynamic perspectives. This is an important undertaking because such limitations go to the heart of the social and cultural dimensions of contemporary society.[13] For example, the comparative advertising

[7] Regulation (EU) 2017/1001 of the European Parliament and of the Council of June 14, 2017 on the European Union Trade Mark, Recital 21.

[8] *See* Graeme B. Dinwoodie, *Developing Defenses in Trademark Law*, 13 LEWIS & CLARK L. REV. 99, 100 (2009) ("Trademark and unfair competition law pays insufficient attention to the articulation and development of defenses that immunize a defendant from liability for unauthorized use of a mark.").

[9] *See, e.g.*, Madhavi Sunder, *Intellectual Property in Experience*, 117 MICH. L. REV. 197, 247–49 (2018); Lisa P. Ramsey & Jens Schovsbo, *Mechanisms for Limiting Trade Mark Rights to Further Competition and Free Speech*, 44 INT'L REV. INTELL. PROP. & COMPETITION L. 671 (2013).

[10] *See, e.g.*, Rochelle C. Dreyfuss, *Expressive Genericity: Trademarks as Language in the Pepsi Generation*, 65 NOTRE DAME L. REV. 397 (1990).

[11] *See, e.g.*, Barton Beebe, *The Semiotic Analysis of Trademark Law*, 51 UCLA L. REV. 621 (2004). For other approaches drawing on sociology, anthropology, and geography, *see* TRADE MARKS AND BRANDS: AN INTERDISCIPLINARY CRITIQUE 140 (Lionel Bently et al., eds. 2008).

[12] *See* BARTON BEEBE, TRADEMARK LAW: AN OPEN-SOURCE CASEBOOK 22–24 (Version 9, 2022); William Fisher, *Theories of Intellectual Property*, *in* NEW ESSAYS IN THE LEGAL AND POLITICAL THEORY OF PROPERTY 168 (Stephen R. Munzer ed., 2001); Mark P. McKenna, *The Normative Foundations of Trademark Law*, 82 NOTRE DAME L. REV. 1839, 1844 (2007).

[13] *See* Haochen Sun, *Living Together in One Civilized World: How Luxury Companies and Consumers Can Fulfill Their Ethical Responsibilities to the Poor*, 46 UC DAVIS L. REV. 547, 557 (2013) ("Trademark

limitation may affect social justice. When a company's cheap fragrance products imitating expensive branded ones were ruled illegal, vehement concerns were voiced about poor consumers being deprived of an opportunity to enjoy the cheaper products as a result of this overly strict interpretation of the comparative advertising limitation.[14] Similarly, the parodic use limitation carries significant implications for the practice of cultural critique. Judicial interpretation of whether the Chewy Vuitton Dog Toy[15] and My Other Louis Vuitton Bag[16] constitute parodies will ultimately determine who has the power to poke fun at specific brands or open the door to meaningful discourse and reflection on consumerism.

Nature of Limitations

Traditionally, limitations are treated as defenses against allegations of trademark infringement. Courts routinely define the fair use of a trademark as a defense in cases involving descriptive use,[17] nominative use,[18] parodic use,[19] and so on. They shift the burden of proving fair use onto defendants and set out the factors for meeting the burden of proof.[20] Scholars have generally followed this judicial characterization of limitations as defenses.[21]

law should be empowered to inform both producers and consumers of the importance of ethical consumerism through the signs it protects."); Haochen Sun, *Can Louis Vuitton Dance with Hiphone? Rethinking the Idea of Social Justice in Intellectual Property Law*, 15 U. Pa. J. L. & Soc. Change 389 (2012); Sonia K. Katyal, *Stealth Marketing and Antibranding: The Love that Dare Not Speak Its Name*, 58 Buff. L. Rev. 795 (2010); Rosemary J. Coombe, The Cultural Life of Intellectual Properties: Authorship, Appropriation, and the Law 166–207 (1998).

[14] L'Oreal SA & Ors v. Bellure NV & Ors [2010] EWCA Civ 535, ¶ 14 (21 May 2010) ("The ECJ's decision in this case means that poor consumers are the losers. Only the poor would dream of buying the defendants' products. The real thing is beyond their wildest dreams. Yet they are denied their right to receive information which would give them a little bit of pleasure; the ability to buy a product for a euro or so which they know smells like a famous perfume.").

[15] Louis Vuitton Malletier S.A. v. Haute Diggity Dog, 507 F.3d 252 (4th Cir. 2007).

[16] Louis Vuitton Malletier, S.A. v. My Other Bag, Inc., 156 F. Supp. 3d 425 (S.D.N.Y. 2016).

[17] U.S. Shoe Corp. v. Brown Grp., 923 F.2d 844 (2d Cir. 1990) ("The purpose of the defense is to prevent the trademark rights of one party from being extended to preclude another party from the description of his product to the public.").

[18] New Kids on the Block v. News Am. Pub., Inc., 971 F.2d 302, 308 (9th Cir. 1992).

[19] Louis Vuitton Malletier S.A. v. Haute Diggity Dog, 507 F.3d 252, 266 (4th Cir. 2007).

[20] Kelly-Brown v. Winfrey, 717 F.3d 295, 303 (2d Cir. 2013) ("To gain its protection, a junior user must establish three elements: that it used the contested words '(1) other than as a mark, (2) in a descriptive sense, and (3) in good faith.' ").

[21] *See, e.g.*, Dinwoodie, *supra* note 8, at 100 ("I suggest that trademark would be better served if several of its limits were explicitly conceptualized as defenses to an action for infringement"); Deborah R. Gerhardt, *A Masterclass in Trademark's Descriptive Fair Use Defense*, 52 Akron L. Rev. 739, 794 (2018) ("Trademark law provides several fair use defenses for protecting businesses that use words which others have registered as trademarks.").

By contrast, in the copyright law arena, courts and scholars have reconsidered the definition of copyright fair use/dealing. The Canadian Supreme Court somewhat boldly redefined copyright fair dealing as "a user's right,"[22] holding that such a right is "an essential part of furthering the public interest objectives of the [Canadian] Copyright Act."[23] Some U.S. courts and many scholars[24] have made similar attempts to treat fair use as a user right. However, trademark law scholarship has been largely insulated from such a theoretical shift. Few have ventured to explore whether the purely procedural characterization of trademark rights limitations as defenses may prevent them from better protecting the public interest.[25] Against this backdrop, it is desirable for courts and scholars alike to consider the possibility of imbuing limitations on trademark rights with substantive values by dynamically redefining them as user rights. They may further examine how this redefinition would do justice to the wealth of public interests and protect them when trademark disputes arise.

Scope of Limitations

Existing scholarship focuses on delineating the scope of the limitations that are imposed upon proprietors after they have obtained trademark rights. Typically, these limitations refer specifically to fair use and the exhaustion of trademark rights. More desirable would be a broad-based approach to charting the scope of limitations. Generally speaking, there are *ex ante* limitations and *ex post* limitations, two categories of limitations divided by the timing of their carving out. *Ex post* limitations refer to limitations such as fair use and exhaustion that arise only after exclusive rights have been granted to trademark proprietors. By contrast, *ex ante* limitations deal with the conditions that trademark applicants must meet before they can be granted exclusive rights. They cover limitations on the granting of trademark rights such as genericide and prohibitions on the registration of disparaging, immoral, or scandalous marks.[26]

There are valid reasons for broadening the scope of limitations to include *ex ante* limitations, which serve as buffers against the undesirable expansion of

[22] CCH Canadian Ltd. v. Law Soc'y of Upper Can., [2004] 1 S.C.R. 399, para. 48 (Can.).

[23] Soc'y of Composers, Authors and Music Publishers of Canada v. Bell Canada, 2012 SCC 36, para. 27 (Can.).

[24] Haochen Sun, *Copyright Law as an Engine of Public Interest Protection*, 16 Nw. J. Tech. & Intell. Prop. 123, 167–69 (2019).

[25] *Cf.* Stacey L. Dogan & Mark A. Lemley, *Parody as Brand*, 47 U.C. Davis L. Rev. 473, 490 (2013) ("Lacking tools specifically designed for parody, courts treat it in an ad hoc way that reflects their own subjective assessment of the value or parody and the morality of free rides. The fact-intensive nature of the inquiry, moreover, means a long and costly process, which alone may deter parodies."); William McGeveran, *Rethinking Trademark Fair Use*, 94 Iowa L. Rev. 49, 52 (2008) ("The lethal combination of uncertain standards with lengthy and costly litigation creates a classic chilling effect upon the unlicensed use of trademarks to facilitate speech, even when such uses are perfectly lawful.").

[26] *Cf.* Matal v. Tam, 137 S. Ct. 1744 (2017); Iancu v. Brunetti, 139 S. Ct. 2294 (2019).

exclusive rights to symbols that should remain in the public domain free for others to use. Similar to *ex post* limitations, they also play the role of maintaining a robust public domain of symbols in which non-proprietors can freely use them without incurring legal liabilities.[27] This broad-based approach is also necessitated by the redefinition of limitations as user rights. Members of the public are not only entitled to use trademarked symbols as permitted by *ex post* limitations but should also be empowered to enjoy a robust public domain of untrademarked symbols through *ex ante* limitations. Such empowerment is critically important, as recent research has demonstrated the serious problem of the depletion and congestion of symbols caused by overzealous trademark registrations.[28]

Comparative Studies of Limitations

International intellectual property treaties set no minimum standards for limitations on trademark rights such as fair use and exhaustion. The Agreement on Trade-Related Aspects of Intellectual Property Rights (TRIPS Agreement)[29] affords member states considerable latitude in laying out such limitations as long as they "take account of the legitimate interests of the owner of the trademark and of third parties."[30] The TRIPS Agreement also does not regulate exhaustion of trademark rights.[31]

In the absence of international minimum standards, limitations on trademark rights vary significantly among jurisdictions. For instance, U.S. trademark law allows for the parodic use of trademarks, whereas China and the European Union have not yet explicitly adopted such a limitation. Even within jurisdictions, there are conflicting opinions on how to decide cases involving limitations such as nominative fair use.

Amid global trade growth and the rise of social media, it has become imperative to study variations in trademark rights limitations across jurisdictions.[32]

[27] *See* Jennifer Davis, *Protecting the Common: Delineating a Public Domain in Trademark Law, in* Trademark Law and Theory: A Handbook of Contemporary Research 345, 361 (Graeme Dinwoodie & Mark Janis eds., 2008) ("For the most part, the public domain has been defined very broadly.").

[28] *See* Barton Beebe & Jeanne C. Fromer, *Are We Running Out of Trademarks? An Empirical Study of Trademark. Depletion and Congestion*, 131 Harv. L. Rev. 945 (2018).

[29] Agreement on Trade-Related Agreements of Intellectual Property Rights art. 13, Apr. 15, 1994, Marrakesh Agreement Establishing the World Trade Organization, Annex 1C, 1869 U.N.T.S. 299 (1994).

[30] *Id.* art. 17.

[31] *Id.* art. 6 ("For the purposes of dispute settlement under this Agreement, subject to the provisions of Articles 3 and 4 nothing in this Agreement shall be used to address the issue of the exhaustion of intellectual property rights.").

[32] *See, e.g.*, The Cambridge Handbook of International and Comparative Trademark Law (Irene Calboli, & Jane C. Ginsburg eds. 2020) (containing a few chapters about comparative studies of limitations).

Comparative studies are useful for elucidating these differing legal standards, which have profound implications for global trade and cultural exchange.

Against this backdrop, we have developed this volume as the first academic book dealing comprehensively with limitations on trademark rights from the theoretical and comparative perspectives. In particular the volume tackles each of the four major areas of scholarly research identified earlier.

Part I of this volume presents new theoretical perspectives to justify trademark rights limitations. Mark McKenna aptly divides limitations into two categories: those needed internally to deal with trademark law's functions in guarding against confusion and dealing with exhaustion of rights and those imposed externally by values relevant to trademark protection such as freedom of expression. Building on her previous theoretical work, Jeanne Fromer examines the extent to which creativity can shed new light on distinctiveness and allow a reassessment of trademark rights expansion. From a cultural studies stance, David Tan explores the semiotic importance of fashion and luxury brand parodies, arguing that such parodic uses should be encouraged given their power to motivate audiences to engage in contestations of those brands.

Part II re-examines the nature of trademark rights limitations. Through the lens of the Canadian case of *United Airlines, Inc. v. Cooperstock*, Carys Craig argues that limitations on trademark rights should be redefined as user rights. This new characterization, she contends, would help the law to better serve trademarks' communicative and dialogic functions. Mark Lemley criticizes trademark owners' overzealous use of litigation against users of their trademarks. He contends that to better align free speech values with trademark owners' own enforcement incentives, U.S. courts should consider the extent to which a mark is the subject of unauthorized parodies, satires, or other referential uses as part of their assessment of the strength and fame of a mark. Martin Senftleben reveals problems with the protection of artistic use in the E.U., and proposes a novel solution for the legal presumption of fair use under E.U. trademark law.

Part III deals with the scope of trademark rights limitations. Based on a thorough historical review of the treatment of pharmaceutical trademarks in Britain, Lionel Bently explores how genericide promotes public health as a limitation on trademark rights. Robert Burrell discusses the role of limitations on the right to control trademark use in advertising, and further examines how the scope of such limitations should be properly determined. Michael Handler considers the scope of exhaustion, another major limitation on trademark rights. He argues that Australia's recent legislative reform broadening the scope of exhaustion can provide useful lessons for other jurisdictions on how to deal with the scope of this limitation.

Finally, Part IV focuses on comparative studies of limitations on trademark rights. In my own contribution, I first explore the differing ways in which such limitations are applied in common law and civil law jurisdictions. I then discuss

Chinese judges' creative deviation from the civil law tradition that China follows and considers how such judicial activism protects the public interest. Kung-Chung Liu compares the similarities and differences in the limitations adopted in major Asian jurisdictions, covering international exhaustion, prohibitions on the abuse of trademark rights, fair use, and unique defenses against the award of damages, as well as the new limitations adopted in these jurisdictions. Through examination of leading trademarks cases involving parodies, Arpan Banerjee explores the constitutional basis for parodic use in India and South Africa and how the courts in these two jurisdictions have tackled the thorny issue of protecting parodists' free speech rights. Christoph Rademacher and Roberto Carapeto delve into the growing body of Japanese case law dealing with parodies and discuss how Japan's courts and Patent Office have developed legal standards for determining the legality of the parodic use of trademarks.

PART I

JUSTIFICATIONS FOR LIMITATIONS

1

Externalizing Trademark's Limits

*Mark P. McKenna**

Courts and scholars alike conventionally describe trademark rights as inherently limited. By "inherently limited," they mean that the boundaries of trademark rights can be derived from the justifications for those rights, without resort to other competing values. That description is important to both trademark maximalists and minimalists. For the former, appeals to the inherent limits are meant to downplay concerns about broad rights; for the latter, they are meant to reinvigorate the limits.

The claim that trademark rights are inherently limited is undeniably correct in important ways. Nothing is more foundational to trademark law than the notion that trademark rights are not rights in gross—the rights arise out of use in connection with particular goods or services, and they exist only in relation to those goods or services. For that reason, eligibility for trademark protection depends on a claimed mark's relationship to the goods and services. We determine whether a party has a valid mark by asking how much and what kind of information the purported mark provides about the relevant goods or services.[1]

But the question of how limited trademark rights really are depends not only on how we determine the existence of rights, but also critically on the *scope* of those rights.[2] And in that respect, modern trademark law is very different from its former self. Once upon a time, trademark owners could enforce their rights only against those in direct competition, so it was literally true that trademark rights existed only in relation to the goods or services with which they were used. But that is history now. For many decades it has been more accurate to say that a party's rights grow out of its own use but extend to any other uses that are close enough to cause confusion. As a result, the scope of trademark rights has long been dependent on the meaning of likelihood of confusion.

* Thanks to Barton Beebe, Graeme Dinwoodie, Haochen Sun, and Rebecca Tushnet for helpful comments on earlier drafts of this chapter.

[1] For word marks, we do this in American trademark law by placing a claimed word mark along the *Abercrombie* spectrum. Abercrombie & Fitch Co. v. Hunting World, Inc., 537 F.2d 4 (2d Cir. 1976). That spectrum, as I have previously explained, really mashes up the traditional rules for determining trademark status with conditions for granting limited unfair competition relief. *See* Mark P. McKenna, *Property and Equity in Trademark Law*, 23 MARQ. INTELL. PROP. L. REV. 117 (2019). But *Abercrombie* is now the well-accepted framework for determining the distinctiveness of all claimed word marks.

[2] See Mark A. Lemley & Mark P. McKenna, *Scope*, 57 WM. & MARY L. REV. 2197 (2016).

Mark P. McKenna, *Externalizing Trademark's Limits* In: *Charting Limitations on Trademark Rights.* Edited by: Haochen Sun and Barton Beebe, Oxford University Press. © Mark P. McKenna 2023. DOI: 10.1093/oso/9780198871248.003.0002

And, of course, the concept of likelihood of confusion has expanded dramatically over time. Modern trademark law recognizes many forms of confusion, in many contexts, about many types of relationships, and at several points in time.[3] Dilution goes even further, giving a cause of action even when there is no plausible argument about confusion of any kind.[4] For many marks, and especially those that are most well known, the claim that trademark rights exist only in relation to certain goods or services is much more of a slogan than a reality.

That doesn't mean that trademark rights have become rights in gross in every sense. Courts continue to enforce several important limits, some of which have taken on even greater significance in recent years. But those limits often have a different character than they used to, especially in the United States, as courts have struggled to articulate the limits of likelihood of confusion. The consequence is that the former internal limits are less reliable and harder to apply, and some things that used to be easily understood as "internal" limits now look like "defenses" that really take the form of balancing tests.

Increasingly, trademark law's most important and hardest-edged limits are "external," in the sense that they are superimposed on trademark rights because of concerns that enforcement of those rights will tread on other interests. In particular, courts have imposed limits to protect broader competition values, free speech, and the operation of other intellectual property regimes. To put it somewhat differently, courts are now primarily policing whether trademark law, unconstrained by its own purposes, is encroaching on some other recognizable values. Trademark's bucket runneth over, and now it seems that all we can do is guard the other buckets.

I. Previously Internal Limits

As the Supreme Court famously said more than a century ago in *United Drug Co. v. Theodore Rectanus Co.*, "[t]here is no such thing as property in a trade-mark except as a right appurtenant to an established business or trade in connection with which the mark is employed."[5] Trademark rights are defined by and inseparable from their use in connection with particular goods or services, and as a result, they are naturally limited. Those limits have traditionally manifested in an infringement standard that requires likelihood of confusion, and in defensive doctrines that reflect the limited purposes of trademark rights.

[3] For a discussion of the overbreadth of modern confusion doctrine, *see* Mark A. Lemley & Mark McKenna, *Irrelevant Confusion*, 62 STAN. L. REV. 413 (2010); Mark P. McKenna, *A Consumer Decision-Making Theory of Trademark Law*, 98 VA. L. REV. 67 (2012).

[4] Dilution is based on the notion that even non-confusing uses might impair the distinctiveness of a mark or harm its reputation. *See* 15 U.S.C. § 1125(d).

[5] 248 U.S. 90, 97 (1918).

A. Tighter Likelihood of Confusion Rules

The primary way in which trademark rights have naturally been limited has been through use of an infringement standard that requires evidence that the defendant's use is likely to cause consumer confusion.[6] At the time the Supreme Court decided *United Drug*, the infringement standard was very strict, so the Court's confidence that trademark rights were tightly connected to the goods or services with which they were used was warranted.

Trademark law traditionally was concerned only with preventing passing off—acts that deceive consumers into purchasing the defendant's products believing that those products come from the mark owner.[7] Because courts could only be confident that the defendant's deception would divert consumers who otherwise would have gone to the plaintiff when the parties sold the same kinds of goods, only directly competing uses were deemed infringing. In one prototypical case, *Borden Ice Cream Co. v. Borden's Condensed Milk Co.*,[8] the court rejected the plaintiff's claim that use of the BORDEN mark for ice cream infringed its rights in BORDEN for milk and related products.[9] The court acknowledged that consumers might be confused by simultaneous use of BORDEN for milk and for ice cream, but it nevertheless denied the claim because the plaintiff could not show the defendant's use of the same mark for noncompetitive products would divert consumers who otherwise would have bought from it (the plaintiff). People who want milk don't buy ice cream by mistake.

But confusion is now much more broadly construed. First, courts rejected the requirement of direct competition, counting as "source" confusion the mistaken belief that the defendant's goods also come from the plaintiff, even if the parties' goods were not the same. In *Aunt Jemima Mills Co. v. Rigney & Co.*,[10] for example, the plaintiff, which had used the AUNT JEMIMA mark for syrup, alleged that Rigney's use of the AUNT JEMIMA mark for flour infringed its rights in the mark. Under the traditional standard, Aunt Jemima should have lost the case. As the court admitted, "no one wanting syrup could possibly be made to take flour."[11] But the court found infringement anyway, on the ground the products were "so related as to fall within the mischief which equity should prevent."[12] Similarly in *Yale Electric*

[6] Courts used to focused on deception rather than confusion, to emphasize that only dishonest diversion of trade was actionable. Deception is a higher standard, and it typically implies a requirement of materiality. *See* McKenna, *supra* note 3.

[7] *See* Coats v. Holbrook, 7 N.Y. Ch. Ann. 713, 717 (1845) (noting trademark law's purpose of preventing a defendant from "attract[ing] to himself the patronage that without such deceptive use of such names . . . would have inured to the benefit of [the plaintiff]"). For a longer discussion of traditional trademark law principles, see generally Mark P. McKenna, *The Normative Foundations of Trademark Law*, 82 NOTRE DAME L. REV. 1839 (2007).

[8] 201 F. 510 (7th Cir. 1912).

[9] *Id.* at 515.

[10] 247 F. 407, 408 (2d Cir. 1917).

[11] *Id.* at 409.

[12] *Id.* at 409–10.

Corp. v. Robertson,[13] the court refused to allow registration of YALE for flashlights and batteries, finding that use likely to cause confusion with the plaintiff's prior use of the YALE mark for locks. The court acknowledged that the decision "[did] some violence to the language" of the Trademark Act of 1905, which made use of a mark actionable when it was for goods "of the same descriptive properties" as those for which the mark was registered.[14] But, according to the *Aunt Jemima* court, "it ha[d] come to be recognized that, unless the borrower's use is so foreign to the owner's as to insure against any identification of the two, it is unlawful."[15]

Courts have further expanded the range of actionable confusion by accepting that a defendant infringes if consumers might believe the plaintiff "sponsors" or is "affiliated" with the defendant or its goods. In one early example, *Vogue Co. v. Thompson-Hudson Co.*,[16] the court held that the defendant's use of "The Vogue Hat Company" to sell hats infringed Vogue's rights in the VOGUE mark for magazines because "[the] course of conduct by the defendant manufacturer and its retailers created a very common alternative impression—first, that these hats were manufactured by the plaintiff; or, second, that, although some knew that plaintiff was not manufacturing, yet these hats were in some way vouched for or sponsored or approved by the plaintiff."[17] In another case, the court found that the defendant's use of ESQUIRE for a bar infringed a magazine publisher's rights in the same mark.

> The Court finds from the evidence that the defendant's use of plaintiff's name 'Esquire' is calculated to, and does, cause the public (not otherwise fully informed) to believe there is some connection between the two, either that the plaintiff owns or controls the business of the defendant, or sponsors it, or has given leave to conduct the business under some contract, and that the defendant's business has the approval of plaintiff, or that the defendant's business is in some manner related to the plaintiff's business, Esquire, Inc., and thereby constitutes unfair competition in violation of plaintiff's rights.[18]

The concept of "sponsorship" or "affiliation" confusion is now codified in § 43(a) of the Lanham Act,[19] though it remains unclear precisely what "sponsorship" and

[13] 26 F.2d 972 (2d Cir. 1928).

[14] *Id.* at 974.

[15] *Id.*

[16] 300 F. 509 (6th Cir. 1924).

[17] *Id.* at 511. *See also* Triangle Publ'ns, Inc. v. Rohrlich, 167 F.2d 969, 972 (2d Cir. 1948) ("the defendants' use of 'Seventeen' created a likelihood that the public would erroneously believe that defendants' dresses were advertised in or sponsored by the magazine and that the plaintiff's reputation and good will would thereby be injured.").

[18] Esquire, Inc. v. Esquire Bar, 37 F. Supp. 875, 876 (S.D. Fla. 1941). Magazine cases remain an active part of the trademark docket. *See, e.g.*, PRL USA Holdings, Inc. v. U.S. Polo Ass'n, Inc., 520 F.3d 109 (2d Cir. 2008); Entrepreneur Media, Inc. v. Smith, 279 F.3d 1135 (9th Cir. 2002); Westchester Media v. PRL USA Holdings, Inc., 214 F.3d 658 (5th Cir. 2000).

[19] 15 U.S.C. § 1125(a)(1)(A) (2006) (providing a civil cause of action against anyone who "uses in commerce any word, term, name, symbol, or device, or any combination thereof, or any false

"affiliation" mean. Lack of terminological clarity is a problem because those terms could refer to virtually any relationship between the parties,[20] and in fact courts have readily embraced new ways of characterizing the relationships about which consumers might be confused.[21] The more recent promotional goods cases foreshadowed even greater expansion in the social media context, where any mention is plausibly portrayed as endorsement.

These expansions have enabled parties to successfully assert their rights against a wide range of uses far removed from the mark owner's original use. The breadth is even more striking when we account not just for the range of new relationships about which confusion might be relevant, but also the variety of new types of confusion courts have recognized, including reverse confusion,[22] initial interest confusion,[23] and post-sale confusion.[24] Those doctrines treat as legally relevant "confusion" at various points in time and among various different groups (sometimes including people who aren't, and likely won't ever be, consumers).[25]

designation of origin, false or misleading description of fact, or false or misleading representation of fact, which . . . is likely to cause confusion, or to cause mistake, or to deceive as to the affiliation, connection, or association of such person with another person, or as to the origin, sponsorship, or approval of his or her goods, services, or commercial activities by another person").

[20] *See* James Gibson, *Risk Aversion and Rights Accretion in Intellectual Property Law*, 116 YALE L. J. 882, 907 (2007) ("The definitions of sponsorship and approval, however, are notoriously broad and ambiguous, making liability a significant possibility for any use of a mark from which consumers might infer acquiescence by the mark owner.").

[21] *See* Adolph Kastor & Bros. v. FTC, 138 F.2d 824, 825 (2d Cir. 1943) ("At the outset we hold therefore that the word, 'Scout,' when applied to a boy's pocket knife, suggests, if indeed it does not actually indicate, that the knife is in some way sponsored by the Boy Scouts of America."); Copacabana, Inc. v. Breslauer, 101 U.S.P.Q. 467, 468 (Dec. Comm'r Pat. 1954) (rejecting an application to register Copacabana for cosmetics in light of the prior use of Copacabana for a nightclub and restaurant despite the finding that cosmetics are "entirely different" from the nightclub and restaurant because customers may assume that the cosmetics were "made by, sponsored by, or in some way connected with" Copacabana, Inc.).

[22] *See, e.g.*, A & H Sportswear, Inc. v. Victoria's Secret Stores, Inc., 237 F.3d 198, 228 (3d Cir. 2000) ("reverse confusion occurs when the junior user saturates the market with a similar trademark and overwhelms the senior user").

[23] Initial interest confusion has recently been limited to some extent, *see* Multi Time Machine, Inc. v. Amazon.com, Inc., 804 F.3d 930 (9th Cir. 2015), but it remains a viable theory of confusion in every circuit and in the registration context. *See, e.g.*, Brookfield Commc'ns v. W. Coast Ent. Corp., 174 F.3d 1036, 1057 (9th Cir. 1999); Elvis Presley Enters. v. Capece, 141 F.3d 188, 204 (5th Cir. 1998); Dorr-Oliver, Inc. v. Fluid-Quip, Inc., 94 F.3d 376, 382 (7th Cir. 1996); HRL Assocs. v. Weiss Assocs., 12 U.S.P.Q.2d (BNA) 1819, 1821–23 (T.T.A.B. 1989), aff'd on other grounds, 14 U.S.P.Q.2d (BNA) 1840 (Fed. Cir. 1990); Mobil Oil Corp. v. Pegasus Petroleum Corp., 818 F.2d 254, 259–60 (2d Cir. 1987); Commc'ns Satellite Corp. v. Comcet, Inc., 429 F.2d 1245, 1251 (4th Cir. 1970).

[24] Hermès Int'l v. Lederer de Paris Fifth Ave., Inc., 219 F.3d 104, 109 (2d Cir. 2000) ("[A] loss occurs when a sophisticated buyer purchases a knockoff and passes it off to the public as the genuine article, thereby confusing the viewing public and achieving the status of owning the genuine article at a knockoff price"); Ferrari S.P.A. Esercizio v. Roberts, 944 F.2d 1235, 1244–45 (6th Cir. 1991); Krueger Int'l. v. Nightingale, Inc., 915 F. Supp. 595, 610 (S.D.N.Y. 1996). Post-sale confusion has been heavily criticized, but it too remains a viable theory in every circuit. *See* Jeremy Sheff, *Veblen Brands*, 96 MINN. L. REV. 769 (2011–12); McKenna, *supra* note 3.

[25] *See* McKenna, *supra* note 3.

Collectively, these expansions of likelihood of confusion substantially qualify the claim that trademark rights are inherently limited, especially for strong marks.[26] At this point, it's hard to imagine *any* use of the Coca-Cola mark that couldn't plausibly be considered confusing, no matter how distant the goods. Indeed, the breathtaking scope of likelihood of confusion is the reason that dilution, which more flagrantly contradicts any internal limits, is practically unimportant. The owners of famous marks almost never need dilution claims because there are hardly any uses of their marks that would be dilutive but not infringing.

B. "Defenses"[27]

Because courts traditionally understood confusion so narrowly, there was little need for additional defenses aside from trans-substantive equitable defenses like laches and acquiescence.[28] When courts ruled for defendants, in most cases they did so by enforcing the inherent limits of trademark rights. To be sure, courts often invoked the value of competition when rejecting a plaintiff's claim, but they did so primarily to emphasize the reasons why trademark rights were so limited. Several doctrines we now tend to refer to as defenses illustrate the point.

1. Descriptive Fair Use

Take, for example, what we call descriptive fair use in American trademark law. That doctrine, now codified in the Lanham Act, precludes liability for use of an admittedly valid trademark if the defendant is using the term "fairly and in good faith," "otherwise than as a mark," and merely for the purposes of "describing the goods or services (or their geographic origin)."[29]

Descriptive fair use is an important doctrine, but it's also notoriously unclear because it is so bound up with likelihood of confusion.[30] Even as the Supreme Court in *KP Permanent* emphasized that some amount of confusion must be compatible

[26] Barton Beebe & C. Scott Hemphill, *The Scope of Strong Marks: Should Trademark Law Protect the Strong More than the Weak?*, 92 N.Y.U. L. Rev. 1339 (2017).

[27] This section is adapted in part from William McGeveran & Mark P. McKenna, *Confusion Isn't Everything*, 89 Notre Dame L. Rev. 253 (2013).

[28] Even those doctrines were not complete defenses—they applied to preclude damages from past infringement, but not to bar injunctions against future infringement. *See, e.g.*, McLean v. Fleming, 96 U.S. 245, 251 (1877) ("Unreasonable delay in bringing a suit is always a serious objection to relief in equity; but cases arise in litigations of the kind before the court where the complainant may be entitled to an injunction to restrain the future use of a trade-mark, even when it becomes the duty of the court to deny the prayer of the bill of complaint for an account of past gains and profits.").

[29] 15 U.S.C. § 1115(b)(4). *See* Fortune Dynamic, Inc. v. Victoria's Secret Stores Brand Mgmt., Inc., 618 F.3d 1025 (9th Cir. 2010) (noting that all three are separate requirements of fair use).

[30] *See* McGeveran, *supra* note 28, at 82–97 (critiquing "classic" and nominative fair use doctrines and their entanglement with confusion prevention); Mark P. McKenna, *Trademark Use and the Problem of Source*, U. Ill. L. Rev. 773, 821–28 (2009) (critiquing ways in which constant reference to consumer understanding destabilizes trademark law).

with fair use,[31] it also told lower courts that the extent of confusion was relevant "in assessing whether a defendant's use is objectively fair."[32] Predictably, courts have continued to assess confusion, without any clear sense of how much or what kind of confusion disqualifies a use from being a descriptive fair use.[33]

A major part of the problem is that the descriptive fair use doctrine is now being asked to serve a very different purpose than the doctrines from which it was derived. What we now call descriptive fair use actually comes from an era in which descriptive terms (and geographic terms and surnames) were, by definition, *not* trademarks.[34] A plaintiff that wanted relief against another party that was using a descriptive term had to turn to unfair competition. Those unfair competition claims involved use of a term that might have had a legitimate explanation (the defendant might, for example, simply have been using the disputed term to describe characteristics of its goods). For that reason, courts couldn't presume the mere use of the term was illegitimate.[35] Instead, the plaintiff had to prove that the defendant was, in fact, using the descriptive term in a way that was designed to result in passing off its goods, rather than for some other innocent purpose.[36]

Trademark infringement claims necessarily involved terms for which the defendant had no legitimate need (because the only things that qualified as trademarks were words or symbols that provided no information about the nature or

[31] KP Permanent Make-Up, Inc. v. Lasting Impression I, Inc., 543 U.S. 111, 121 (2004) ("[S]ome possibility of consumer confusion must be compatible with fair use ").

[32] *Id.* at 123 ("It suffices to realize that our holding that fair use can occur along with some degree of confusion does not foreclose the relevance of the extent of any likely consumer confusion in assessing whether a defendant's use is objectively fair. Two Courts of Appeals have found it relevant to consider such scope, and commentators and amici here have urged us to say that the degree of likely consumer confusion bears not only on the fairness of using a term, but even on the further question whether an originally descriptive term has become so identified as a mark that a defendant's use of it cannot realistically be called descriptive.") quoting Shakespeare Co. v. Silstar Corp., 110 F.3d 234, 243 (4th Cir. 1997) ("[T]o the degree that confusion is likely, a use is less likely to be found fair ... "); Sunmark, Inc. v. Ocean Spray Cranberries, Inc., 64 F.3d 1055 (7th Cir. 1995).

[33] Indeed, on remand in that very case, the Ninth Circuit held that the degree of customer confusion remains a factor in determining fair use. KP Permanent Make-up, Inc. v. Lasting Impression I, Inc., 408 F.3d 596, 609 (9th Cir. 2005). Thus, having found a fact question on likelihood of confusion that precluded summary judgment for the defendant, the court found that summary judgment on the fair use defense also was inappropriate. *Id.* ("Among the relevant factors for consideration by the jury in determining the fairness of the use are the degree of likely confusion, the strength of the trademark, the descriptive nature of the term for the products or services being offered by [the defendant] and the availability of alternative descriptive terms, the extent of the use of the term prior to the registration of the trademark, and any differences among the times and contexts in which [the defendant] has used the term.").

[34] For a more complete description of the trademark/unfair competition distinction, *see* McKenna, *supra* note 1.

[35] *Cf.* Wm. A. Rogers, Ltd., v. Int'l Silver Co., 30 App. D.C. 97, 102 (D.C. Cir. 1907) ("As an ordinary surname cannot be appropriated as a trademark, to the exclusion of others of the same name, it follows that the rules of law relating to the similarity of technical trademarks cannot be applied to the use of such surname as a mark, notwithstanding the confusion that may result from its legitimate use by such others.").

[36] *See e.g.*, G. & C. Merriam Co. v. Saalfield, 198 F. 369, 375–76 (6th Cir.1912); Cook & Bernheimer Co. v. Ross, 73 F. 203, 205–06 (C.C.S.D.N.Y. 1896); *see also* McKenna, *supra* note 1, at 1862.

characteristics of the goods). As a result, trademark claimants were not required to prove either source indication or intent to pass off—both were presumed.[37] Prevailing plaintiffs in unfair competition cases also typically got more limited remedies—injunctions requiring defendants to modify their uses to prevent the passing off, but typically not prohibitions on use of the term altogether.[38]

In that bygone legal world, "descriptive fair use" was not a defense to trademark infringement—the considerations that are now parts of that defense were relevant only in a category of cases where the plaintiff, by definition, did not own a trademark. Courts in unfair competition cases considered whether a defendant was using a descriptive term "fairly, and in good faith" and "merely to describe the goods or their geographic origin" in order to differentiate legitimate uses of those terms from uses that enabled the defendant to pass off its goods as those of the plaintiff.

The modern descriptive fair use doctrine inverts this structure and presents "use otherwise than as a mark," "fairly, in good faith," and "merely to descri[be] the goods" as prerequisites for excusing use of the plaintiff's trademark.[39] The consequence is that we have a doctrine presented formally as a defense, but which really demands that courts balance the right of parties to describe their goods against likelihood of confusion, where "confusion" might take any of the variety of forms recognized under current law.

2. Nominative Fair Use and Comparative Advertising

Something very similar can be said about the so-called "nominative fair use doctrine." Under that doctrine, which typically is associated with the Ninth Circuit's *New Kids on the Block* decision, certain referential uses of a trademark are deemed

[37] *See e.g.*, Socony-Vacuum Oil Co. v. Oil City Refiners, 136 F.2d 470, 474 (6th Cir. 1943) ("In cases involving technical trademarks, the fraudulent intent to deceive is presumed, while in cases of unfair competition complainant must prove this intent or show facts and circumstances from which it may reasonably be inferred."); Goldsmith Silver Co. v. Savage, 229 F. 623, 627 (1st Cir. 1915) ("In the case of infringement of a technical trade-mark the intention of the infringer is immaterial, as the essence of the wrong lies in the injury to a property right; while in the case of unfair competition the intention is material, to establish fraud on the part of the defendant in the use of the imitative device to beguile the public into buying his goods as those of his rival."); *see also* McKenna, *supra* note 1, at 1862.

[38] *See, e.g.*, DuPont Cellophane Co. v. Waxed Prods. Co., 85 F.2d 75, 80, 82 (2d Cir. 1936) (holding "cellophane" generic for cellulose wrapping but requiring defendant to identify itself as the source of goods to avoid confusion with plaintiff); Barton v. Rex-Oil Co, 2 F.2d 402, 404 (3d Cir. 1924) ("[T]he utmost that the courts can do for the relief of the first user [in a case of unfair competition] is to enjoin not the use of the trade-mark but the unfair method of its use."); *Saalfield*, 198 F. at 373–76 (allowing defendant to use the generic term "Webster's dictionary" so long as it explained that it was not the plaintiff); L.E. Waterman Co. v. Modern Pen Co., 197 F. 534, 535 (2d Cir. 1912) (allowing defendant to continue to use the surname "Waterman" but requiring a label that disclaimed connection with the plaintiff).

[39] Most courts treat these as distinct requirements, even though they obviously overlap in many cases. *See, e.g.*, Fortune Dynamic, Inc. v. Victoria's Secret Stores Brand Mgmt., Inc., 618 F.3d 1025 (9th Cir. 2010). *See also* McKenna, *supra* note 8, at 1867 n.122 (collecting cases).

not to be infringing.[40] As the nominative fair use doctrine was originally articulated, a use is not infringing when the following three conditions are met:

> First, the product or service in question must be one not readily identifiable without use of the trademark; second, only so much of the mark or marks may be used as is reasonably necessary to identify the product or service; and third, the user must do nothing that would, in conjunction with the mark, suggest sponsorship or endorsement by the trademark holder."[41]

In the Ninth Circuit's view, nominative fair use protects the ability to communicate effectively in situations where there aren't good alternatives to use of the mark.

> With many well-known trademarks, such as Jell–O, Scotch tape and Kleenex, there are equally informative non-trademark words describing the products (gelatin, cellophane tape and facial tissue). But sometimes there is no descriptive substitute, and a problem closely related to genericity and descriptiveness is presented when many goods and services are effectively identifiable only by their trademarks. For example, one might refer to "the two-time world champions" or "the professional basketball team from Chicago," but it's far simpler (and more likely to be understood) to refer to the Chicago Bulls. In those cases, use of the trademark does not imply sponsorship or endorsement of the product because the mark is used only to describe the thing, rather than to identify its source.[42]

Though the terminology of "nominative fair use" was new, the *New Kids* court was clear that the underlying concept was not. Indeed, the court used as an example its earlier decision in *Volkswagenwerk Aktiengesellschaft v. Church*, in which it "held that Volkswagen could not prevent an automobile repair shop from using" the Volkswagen mark to advertise the fact that it repaired Volkswagen vehicles.[43] As the earlier Ninth Circuit decision said, in "advertising [the repair of Volkswagens, it] would be difficult, if not impossible, for [Church] to avoid altogether the use of the word 'Volkswagen' or its abbreviation 'VW,' which are the normal terms which, to the public at large, signify appellant's cars."[44]

40 New Kids on the Block v. News Am. Publ'g, Inc., 971 F.2d 302 (9th Cir. 1992).

41 *Id.* at 308.

42 *Id.* at 306. See also *id.* at 306–07 ("Indeed, it is often virtually impossible to refer to a particular product for purposes of comparison, criticism, point of reference or any other such purpose without using the mark. For example, reference to a large automobile manufacturer based in Michigan would not differentiate among the Big Three; reference to a large Japanese manufacturer of home electronics would narrow the field to a dozen or more companies. Much useful social and commercial discourse would be all but impossible if speakers were under threat of an infringement lawsuit every time they made reference to a person, company or product by using its trademark.").

43 411 F.2d 350 (9th Cir. 1969).

44 *Id.*

Notably, the *New Kids* court described the result in *Volkswagenwerk* as simply reflecting the fact that the repair shop's use was not likely to cause confusion. "Church did not suggest to customers that he was part of the Volkswagen organization or that his repair shop was sponsored or authorized by VW; he merely used the words 'Volkswagen' and 'VW' to convey information about the types of cars he repaired. Therefore, his use of the Volkswagen trademark was not an infringing use."[45]

The same was true in *WCBV-TV v. Boston Athletic Association*, another pre-*New Kids* case that the Ninth Circuit thought had applied the same principle when it permitted a news station to use the words "Boston Marathon" in connection with its broadcast of that event.[46] According to the First Circuit, the news station's use was permitted, not because of some special exemption, but simply because no reasonable consumer would have been confused by the use.

> [T]he words "Boston Marathon" ... do more than call attention to Channel 5's program; they also *describe* the event that Channel 5 will broadcast. Common sense suggests (consistent with the record here) that a viewer who sees those words flash upon the screen will believe simply that Channel 5 will show, or is showing, or has shown, the marathon, not that Channel 5 has some special approval from the [trademark holder] to do so.[47]

These cases, the Ninth Circuit said, "are best understood as involving a non-trademark use of a mark—a use to which the infringement laws simply do not apply."[48] So too with comparative advertising cases.[49] All of those cases are part of a "class of cases where the use of the trademark does not attempt to capitalize

[45] *New Kids*, 971 F.2d at 307.

[46] 926 F.2d 42 (1st Cir. 1991).

[47] *Id.* at 46 (emphasis in original). The First Circuit believed that, in "technical trademark jargon," this was merely a "use of words for descriptive purposes," which "is called a 'fair use,'" and that "the law usually permits it even if the words themselves also constitute a trademark." *Id.* It's true that, under the descriptive fair use doctrine, parties can use descriptive terms in some capacity even when those terms are protectable marks. But the news station's use in *Boston Marathon* was different than those at issue in descriptive fair use cases. Descriptive fair use involves use of a term with both descriptive and source-identifying meanings, and the defendant is simply using the primary, descriptive meaning rather than the trademark meaning—using "fish fry" to describe batter for frying fish, and *not* for the purpose of evoking the company that uses those words as its trademark. *See Zatarains, Inc. v. Oak Grove Smokehouse, Inc.*, 698 F.2d 786 (5th Cir. 1983). The news station in *Boston Marathon* was clearly referring to the actual Boston Marathon because that's the event it was broadcasting. The station was describing its broadcast, but by way of reference to a branded event.

[48] *New Kids*, 971 F.2d at 307–08.

[49] *See, e.g.*, Smith v. Chanel, 402 F.2d 562 (9th Cir. 1968) ("competitors may use a rival's trademark in advertising and other channels of communication if the use is not false or misleading"). *See also* Graeme B. Dinwoodie, *Lewis & Clark Law School Ninth Distinguished Ip Lecture: Developing Defenses in Trademark Law*, 13 Lewis & Clark L. Rev. 99, 109–10 (2009) ("although cast as a 'defense,' the protection of comparative advertising is in fact a rather routine application of the basic premise that, so long as consumers are not confused by the defendant's use of the plaintiff's mark, the concerns of trademark and unfair competition law are not engaged by such use.").

on consumer confusion or to appropriate the cachet of one product for a different one."[50] "Such *nominative use* of a mark—where the only word reasonably available to describe a particular thing is pressed into service—lies outside the strictures of trademark law: Because it does not implicate the source-identification function that is the purpose of trademark, it does not constitute unfair competition; such use is fair because it does not imply sponsorship or endorsement by the trademark holder."[51] Indeed, a number of later cases involving uses like the ones at issue in the cases the *New Kids* court highlighted have evaluated the challenged use entirely through the likelihood of confusion factors.[52]

Predictably, given the anchoring of nominative fair use in assertions about lack of confusion, courts have struggled to articulate the doctrine as a true defense.[53] As a result, courts have often rejected nominative fair use in cases where they perceived any risk of any type of confusion, or at least they have denied summary judgment in those cases because the possibility of such confusion creates a question of fact.[54]

Taken as a whole, nominative fair doctrine use is an unmitigated disaster. There are currently three different formulations of the doctrine, and they differ precisely in terms of the relationship between the nominative fair use considerations and the likelihood of confusion factors. After previously holding that a defendant asserting nominative fair use had the burden of proving lack of confusion,[55] the Ninth Circuit most recently held that the plaintiff in a nominative fair use case retains the burden of proving confusion, but that the *New Kids* factors substitute for

[50] *New Kids*, 971 F.2d at 307–08.

[51] *Id.* at 308. Of particular note, the court anchored that statement with a quote from *Prestonettes*: "When the mark is used in a way that does not deceive the public we see no such sanctity in the word as to prevent its being used to tell the truth." Prestonettes, Inc. v. Coty, 264 U.S. 359, 368 (1924). As we will see, the doctrine that descends from *Prestonettes* has exactly the same problems.

[52] *See, e.g.*, Scott Fetzer Co. v. House of Vacuums Inc., 381 F.3d 477, 484–88 (5th Cir. 2004) (applying typical multifactor confusion test to determine whether independent vacuum sale and repair business infringed on Kirby trademark in telephone book advertisement); Porsche Cars N. Am., Inc. v. Manny's Porshop, Inc., 972 F. Supp. 1128, 1130–32 (N.D. Ill. 1997) (applying standard test for likelihood of confusion to auto repair shop and finding for markholder); Bumble Bee Seafoods, L.L.C. v. UFS Indus., Inc., No. 04 Civ. 2105(SHS), 2004 WL 1637017, at *5 (S.D.N.Y. July 20, 2004) (allowing vendor to use Bumble Bee Tuna mark to describe main ingredient of its tuna salad in business-to-business communication because retail consumers would not see it and risk confusion).

[53] *See* Dinwoodie, *supra* note 50, at 110–12; McGeveran, *supra* note 28, at 95–97; Greg Lastowka, *Nominative Use Makes No Sense* (working paper) (https://papers.ssrn.com/sol3/papers.cfm?abstract_id=2338296).

[54] *See, e.g.*, Abdul-Jabbar v. Gen. Motors Corp., 85 F.3d 407, 412–13 (9th Cir. 1996) (denying summary judgment where the likelihood of confusion regarding an endorsement raised issues of fact); Standard Process, Inc. v. Total Health Disc., Inc., 559 F. Supp. 2d 932, 938, 942 (E.D. Wis. 2008) (rejecting nominative use and denying summary judgment on questions of fact grounds); State Farm Mut. Auto. Ins. Co. v. Sharon Woods Collision Ctr., Inc., No. 1:07cv457, 2007 WL 4207158, at *8–9 (S.D. Ohio Nov. 26, 2007) (denying summary judgment because the possibility of confusion raises issues of fact).

[55] Brother Recs., Inc. v. Jardine, 318 F.3d 900, 908 n.5, 909 (9th Cir. 2003) (shifting the burden to the defendant). *See* Century 21 Real Est. Corp. v. Lendingtree, Inc., 425 F.3d 211, 217–21 (3d Cir. 2005) (diagnosing this problem in other cases).

the ordinary likelihood of confusion factors—fixing the burden problem, but continuing to comingle nominative fair use and likelihood of confusion.[56] The Third Circuit requires the plaintiff to first prove that the defendant's use is likely to cause confusion and then, if the plaintiff succeeds, puts the burden on the defendant to show that its nominative use is nonetheless fair.[57] That court acknowledged, however, that nominative fair use and likelihood of confusion can't be completely disentangled, and it suggested "eliminating those factors used to establish confusion in other trademark infringement cases that do not 'fit' in the nominative use context."[58] The Second Circuit rejected the idea that nominative fair use is a defense, collapsing it entirely into consideration of likelihood of confusion and *adding* both the Ninth and Third Circuit's nominative fair use factors to the multifactor likelihood of confusion test.[59]

3. First Sale/Exhaustion

The same pattern is evident with respect to what we now call the first sale doctrine—which also wasn't born as a "defense" to trademark infringement but instead as an explication of the inherent limitations on trademark rights. In *Prestonettes, Inc. v. Coty*,[60] Prestonettes purchased genuine Coty toilet powder, "subject[ed] [it] to pressure, add[ed] a binder to give it coherence and [sold] the compact in a metal case."[61] Prestonettes also rebottled genuine Coty perfume in smaller containers.[62] The district court had issued, and Prestonettes agreed to abide by, a decree that allowed Prestonettes

> to put upon the rebottled perfume "Prestonettes, Inc., not connected with Coty, state[] that the contents are Coty's—(giving the name of the article) independently rebottled in New York," every word to be in letters of the same size, color, type and general distinctiveness [and to] make compacts from the genuine loose powder of the plaintiff and to sell them with this label on the container: "Prestonettes, Inc., not connected with Coty, states that the compact of face powder herein was independently compounded by it from Coty's—(giving the name) loose powder

[56] Toyota Motor Sales, U.S.A., Inc. v. Tabari, 610 F.3d 1171, (9th Cir. 2010).
[57] Century 21 Real Estate Corp. v. Lendingtree, Inc., 425 F.3d 211, 222 (3d Cir. 2005). To demonstrate fairness, the Third Circuit requires the defendant to satisfy a three-pronged test "derived to a great extent from the one articulated by the Court of Appeals for the Ninth Circuit." *Id.* Under the Third Circuit's fairness test, "a defendant must show: (1) that the use of plaintiff's mark is necessary to describe both the plaintiff's product or service and the defendant's product or service; (2) that the defendant uses only so much of the plaintiff's mark as is necessary to describe plaintiff's product; and (3) that the defendant's conduct or language reflect the true and accurate relationship between plaintiff and defendant's products or services." *Id.*
[58] *Id.*
[59] Int'l Info. Sys. Sec. Cert. Consortium, Inc. v. Sec. Univ., LLC, 823 F.3d 153 (2d. Cir. 2016).
[60] 264 U.S. 359 (1924).
[61] *Id.* at 366.
[62] *Id.* at 367.

> and its own binder. Loose powder–per cent, Binder–per cent," every word to be in letters of the same size, color, type and general distinctiveness.[63]

The Court of Appeals rejected that decree and "issued an absolute preliminary injunction against the use of the [Coty] marks except on the original packages as marked and sold by [Coty], thinking that the defendant could not put upon the plaintiff the burden of keeping a constant watch."[64] But the Supreme Court reversed. To begin with, the Court thought that Prestonettes

> of course by virtue of its ownership had a right to compound or change what it bought, to divide either the original or the modified product, and to sell it so divided. The plaintiff could not prevent or complain of its stating the nature of the component parts and the source from which they were derived if it did not use the trade mark in doing so.[65]

Thus, the only question was whether Prestonettes's use of Coty's trademark in reference to the compounded product changed the result. And the answer to that question was clear once the Court focused on the limited nature of a trademark right.

> Then what new rights does the trade mark confer? It does not confer a right to prohibit the use of the word or words. It is not a copyright. The argument drawn from the language of the Trade Mark Act does not seem to us to need discussion. *A trade mark only gives the right to prohibit the use of it so far as to protect the owner's good will against the sale of another's product as his.... When the mark is used in a way that does not deceive the public we see no such sanctity in the word as to prevent its being used to tell the truth. It is not taboo.*[66]

Prestonettes did not carve out any special new "first sale" exemption from the scope of trademark rights. It simply reiterated that trademark law only provided a remedy against uses that deceived consumers into purchasing the defendant's product instead of the plaintiff's. Because Prestonettes's use of the Coty mark didn't risk passing off, at least with the limitations ordered by the district court, its use wasn't infringing.[67]

[63] *Id.*
[64] *Id.*
[65] *Id.* at 368 ("If the name of Coty were allowed to be printed in different letters from the rest of the inscription dictated by the District Court a casual purchaser might look no further and might be deceived. But when it in no way stands out from the statements of facts that unquestionably the defendant has a right to communicate in some form, we see no reason why it should not be used collaterally, not to indicate the goods, but to say that the trade-marked product is a constituent in the article now offered as new and changed. As a general proposition there can be no doubt that the word might be so used.").
[66] *Id.* (emphasis added) (citation omitted) (citing Canal Co. v. Clark, 80 U.S. 311, 327 (1872)).
[67] *Id.* at 368–369. Importantly, the Court noted that the case was only one of trademark infringement and not unfair competition.

Champion Spark Plug v. Sanders is similar, even though that case was decided in 1947, when trademark law had already begun to expand beyond passing off.[68] In that case, the district court found that the defendants had infringed Champion's trademark and engaged in unfair competition when they sold used Champion spark plugs without making clear that those plugs were repaired and reconditioned.[69] The district court therefore enjoined the defendants

> from offering or selling any of [Champion's] plugs which had been repaired or reconditioned unless (a) the trade mark and type and style marks were removed, (b) the plugs were repainted with a durable grey, brown, orange, or green paint, (c) the word "REPAIRED" was stamped into the plug in letters of such size and depth as to retain enough white paint to display distinctly each letter of the word, (d) the cartons in which the plugs were packed carried a legend indicating that they contained used spark plugs originally made by [Champion] and repaired and made fit for use up to 10,000 miles by [defendants].[70]

The Second Circuit affirmed the findings of trademark infringement and unfair competition, but it modified the injunction. First, it eliminated the provision requiring removal of the trademark and type and style marks from the repaired or reconditioned plugs.[71] Second, it substituted for the requirement that the word "REPAIRED" be stamped into the plug, etc., a provision that the word "REPAIRED" or "USED" be stamped and baked on the plug by an electrical hot press in a contrasting color so as to be clearly and distinctly visible, the plug having been completely covered by permanent aluminum paint or other paint or lacquer.[72] And third, it eliminated the provision specifying the precise legend to

> "The question therefore [was] not how far the court would go in aid of a plaintiff who showed ground for suspecting the defendant of making a dishonest use of his opportunities, but [was] whether the plaintiff ha[d] the naked right alleged to prohibit the defendant from making even a collateral reference to the plaintiff's mark."
>
> *Id.* at 369.

[68] Champion Spark Plug Co. v. Sanders, 331 U.S. 125 (1947).

[69] *Id.* at 126 ("The outside box or carton in which the plugs are packed has stamped on it the word 'Champion,' together with the letter and figure denoting the particular style or type. They also have printed on them 'Perfect Process Spark Plugs Guaranteed Dependable' and 'Perfect Process Renewed Spark Plugs.' Each carton contains smaller boxes in which the plugs are individually packed. These inside boxes also carry legends indicating that the plug has been renewed. But respondent company's business name or address is not printed on the cartons. It supplies customers with petitioner's charts containing recommendations for the use of Champion plugs. On each individual plug is stamped in small letters, blue on black, the word 'Renewed,' which at times is almost illegible." (footnote omitted)).

[70] *Id.* at 126–27.

[71] *Id.* at 127.

[72] *Id.*

be printed on the cartons and substituted a more general requirement for such a legend.[73]

On appeal to the Supreme Court, Champion argued that the Second Circuit had erred by allowing the defendant to keep the word "Champion" on the repaired or reconditioned spark plugs.[74] The Supreme Court rejected Champion's argument, holding that a party that adequately discloses the repaired or reconditioned status of authentic secondhand goods may use the original trademark to resell those goods.[75] Just as in *Prestonettes*, on which it relied extensively, the Court made clear that the defendant's use of the Champion mark with full disclosure of the goods' reconditioned status simply fell outside the limited scope of Champion's trademark rights.[76] The Court "put to one side the case of a manufacturer or distributor who markets new or used spark plugs of one make under the trade mark of another,"[77] and it limited relief to disclosure of the repaired spark plugs' repaired or reconditioned status, because there had been "no showing of fraud or palming off."[78]

The first sale doctrine remains important and has significant competitive consequences. Because of that doctrine, parties can compete in secondary markets, refurbishing and reselling everything from cars to handbags and golf balls, and they can sell those products using their original brand names.[79] But the first sale doctrine is also now harder to describe as a function of the inherent limitations of trademark rights. Vertical integration and official relationships with resellers (even "certified pre-owned" cars) have made plausible mark owners' contentions of possible confusion about relationships between the mark owner and anyone selling branded goods. When courts refuse to impose liability in the first sale cases, they are often simply refusing to consider those types of confusion in order to protect competition in secondary markets. There are good reasons for courts to do that, but the resulting limitations do not derive strictly from the justifications of trademark rights in the first place. They reflect judicial balancing of trademark rights and competition interests.

[73] *Id.* at 127–28.

[74] *Id.* at 128.

[75] *Id.* at 130.

[76] *Id.*

[77] *Id.* at 128.

[78] *Id.* at 130. There was fault, of course, in the defendant's original packaging, which the Court believed fell within the reach of unfair competition law because it did not adequately disclose that the spark plugs were used and were coming from a company other than Champion. *Id.*

[79] *See, e.g.*, Nitro Leisure Prods., L.L.C. v. Acushnet Co., 341 F.3d 1356, 1362 (Fed. Cir. 2003) (rejecting plaintiff's claim against defendant's use of original trademark on reconditioned golf balls); Swarovski Aktiengesellschaft v. Bldg. No. 19, Inc., 704 F.3d 44 (1st Cir. 2013) (per curiam) (requiring a clear showing of confusion against a reseller who advertised the availability of genuine Swarovski crystal using the Swarovski trademark); Tiffany (NJ) Inc. v. eBay, Inc., 600 F.3d 93, 103 (2d Cir. 2010) (rejecting Tiffany's claim against online seller eBay's use of the Tiffany mark for authentic Tiffany products).

II. Increasingly Important External Limits

The point here is not that descriptive fair use, nominative fair use, or the first sale doctrine no longer play important roles in trademark law. All of those doctrines continue to limit the scope of trademark rights in meaningful ways, at least at times. But they have been cast (or recast) as defenses that vindicate competing interests that must be balanced against trademark rights rather than manifestations of the inherent limits of those rights.

In other areas, limitations on trademark subject matter have been eroded and harder-edged categorical exclusions have been replaced with more limited doctrines that sometimes express different values. So, for example, rather than categorically excluding unpatented designs and limiting relief to labeling or packaging requirements, modern law has assimilated trade dress into trademark subject matter and developed a doctrine that excludes "functional" features.[80] Functionality is perhaps trademark law's most difficult and controversial doctrine, and despite periods of greater consensus, many important differences remain—most fundamentally, whether the doctrine primarily seeks to channel protection of useful features to utility patent law, or whether it primarily focuses on competitive need for the claimed features.

Courts have also created some new "defensive doctrines" to manage new types of conflicts that have arisen because of the breadth of modern confusion doctrine. Nowhere has that been more evident than in the context of so-called "expressive works." A series of related doctrines, including the one typically associated with the Second Circuit's decision in *Rogers v. Grimaldi*, deals with uses in so-called "expressive works." Under *Rogers*, use of a mark in an expressive work is not infringing so long as the use is "artistically relevant" to the work and is not "explicitly misleading."[81] That doctrine is essentially new in the last several decades, and it exists because trademark owners now routinely assert their rights against references to their marks in movies,[82] television shows,[83] songs,[84] video games,[85] and a wide range of other noncommercial speech.[86]

[80] *See* TrafFix Devices, Inc. v. Mktg. Displays, Inc., 532 U.S. 23 (2001). For a description of functionality as a replacement for the categorical exclusion of trade dress as trademark subject matter, *see* Mark P. McKenna & Caitlin P. Canahai, *The Case Against Product Configuration Trade Dress*, *in* Research Handbook on Trademark Law Reform 137 (Graeme Dinwoodie & Mark Janis, eds., 2021).

[81] Rogers v. Grimaldi, 875 F.2d 994, 999 (2d Cir. 1989); Twentieth Century Fox Television v. Empire, 875 F.3d 1192 (9th Cir. 2017).

[82] Louis Vuitton Malletier S.A. v. Warner Brothers Ent., Inc., 868 F.Supp.2d 172 (S.D.N.Y. 2012).

[83] *Empire*, 875 F.3d 1192.

[84] Parks v. LaFace Recs., 329 F.3d 437 (6th Cir. 2003).

[85] Brown v. Elec. Arts, Inc., 724 F3d 1235 (9th Cir. 2013); E.S.S. Ent. 2000, Inc. v. Rock Star Videos, Inc., 547 F.3d 1095 (9th Cir. 2008).

[86] As recently as 2004, distinguished Second Circuit judge Pierre Leval argued that trademark law's internal limits, grounded in likelihood of confusion, usually made it unnecessary to turn to the First Amendment to find for the defendant. Pierre N. Level, Trademark: Champion of Free Speech, 27 Colum. J.L. & Arts 187 (2004).

Precisely because it developed as a consistently strong defensive doctrine that, when applicable, nearly always insulated the user from liability, it has recently been invoked in a wider range of contexts. That has put increasing pressure on courts to delineate the doctrine's boundaries.[87]

The Ninth Circuit's decision in *Jack Daniel's v. VIP*, for example, applied *Rogers* to use of the "Bad Spaniels" name on dog toys that were made to resemble the Jack Daniel's whiskey bottle.[88] The court's conclusion that the name and design of the dog toys were protected under *Rogers* was controversial because it seemed to stretch the *Rogers* doctrine beyond the expressive *works* that were at issue in earlier cases to the defendant's expressive *use* of the marks on products that Jack Daniel's characterized as ordinary commercial products.[89] The boundaries of this doctrine will ultimately need to be reconciled with judicial approaches to trademark claims in other speech-implicating contexts, including claims against gripe sites and claims by and against religious organizations.[90]

Similarly, the U.S. Supreme Court's decision in *Dastar v. Twentieth Century Fox* does some work to prevent trademark from creeping into copyright's domain. Under the rule of *Dastar*, only uses that cause confusion about the origin of physical goods are actionable; uses that cause confusion about the origin of intangible content are not.[91] Because Twentieth Century Fox's claim against Dastar was for failing to attribute the content of its video series to Fox, not for falsely designating the origin of any tangible product, its claim was barred.[92] Courts applying *Dastar* have, for example, concluded that the Lanham Act does not provide a cause of action against uses alleged to cause confusion about the origin (authorship) of intangible karaoke tracks.[93] *Dastar* seems certain to be implicated by the recent flood of claims of trademark rights in relation to digital goods,[94] especially in the context of the metaverse.

[87] *See* Gordon v. Drape Creative, Inc., 909 F.3d 257 (9th Cir. 2018); Dr. Seuss Enters., L.P. v. ComicMix LLC, 983 F.3d 443 (9th Cir. 2020); *Empire*, 875 F.3d 1192.

[88] VIP Prods. LLC v. Jack Daniel's Props., Inc., 953 F.3d 1170 (9th Cir. 2020).

[89] Petition for a Writ of Certiorari, Jack Daniel's Props., Inc. v. VIP Prods. LLC at 23 (Sept. 15, 2020) (arguing that the Ninth Circuit "extended *Rogers*' heightened First Amendment standard beyond traditionally expressive or artistic works to any commercial product copying another's trademark to identify the source of the copier's own product in a humorous way"); Amicus Curiae Brief of the INTA in Support of Petitioner, VIP Prods. LLC v. Jack Daniel's Props., Inc., 953 F.3d 1170 (9th Cir. 2020) (No. 20-365).

[90] For a through discussion of the somewhat different approaches in these categories of cases, *see* Rebecca Tushnet, *Bad Spaniels, Lying Birds, and Tiny Hands: How Trademark Law Reinvented Strict Scrutiny* (draft on file with author). *Jack Daniels* has now been taken up by the Supreme Court, which has the opportunity to clarify the First Amendment limits on trademark rights. Jack Daniel's Properties, Inc. v. VIP Products LLC, 143 S.Ct. 476 (2022).

[91] Dastar Corp. v. Twentieth Century Fox Film Corp., 539 U.S. 23 (2003).

[92] *Id.*

[93] Phoenix Ent. Partners, LLC v. Rumsey, 829 F.3d 817 (7th Cir. 2016); Slep-Tone Entm't Corp. v. Wired for Sound Karaoke and DJ Servs., LLC, 845 F.3d 1246 (9th Cir. 2017).

[94] For a discussion of the legitimacy of trademark rights in digital goods, see Mark P. McKenna & Lucas Osborn, *Trademarks and Digital Goods*, 92 NOTRE DAME L. REV. 1425 (2017).

Taking these developments collectively, the limitations on the scope of trademark rights are, to a much greater extent than was once true, motivated by concerns about conflicting values. In particular, the primary limiting doctrines reflect broader competition concerns and concerns about trademark law's interference with other IP regimes or with free speech. Those limits, then, are increasingly "external" to trademark law in the sense that they apply, not because they reflect trademark's natural limits, but precisely because trademark law isn't limited enough to avoid conflict.

III. External vs. Internal Limits

There is, of course, nothing categorically wrong with external limits. Indeed, I have written extensively about those limits, many of which are important in a world of significantly overlapping IP rights.[95] Nor are external limits entirely new to trademark law—the functionality doctrine's concerns about interference with patent law are old, even if now differently implemented.[96]

But there are reasons to be concerned about *over*reliance on external limits. For one thing, the very fact that a limit is external means that it arises in a context in which there's a perceived conflict between the "ordinary" application of trademark principles and some other value outside of trademark law. The cases therefore always appear to involve a clash of values, and that means consensus is unlikely to develop, because one's views about the appropriate outcome depend on the relative importance of the conflicting values. We might see as an example here the pendulum swings regarding functionality—persistent debate about whether functionality is primarily about interference with patent law, or if it is instead about competitive need to use the claimed design features.[97]

Another reason to be concerned is that the sense that there are external "release valves" that preserve important values makes it easier for courts to accept expansive interpretations of the rights that have at least subtle and sometimes important effects. One analogy here comes from the recent *Booking.com* case, where the Supreme Court dismissed concerns about the scope of rights in marks that consist of generic terms plus the .com top-level domain (TLD).[98] It did so by emphasizing trademark law's limits, including the descriptive fair use doctrine.

[95] Mark P. McKenna & Katherine J. Strandburg, *Progress and Competition in Design*, 17 STAN. TECH. L. REV. 1 (2014); Mark P. McKenna, *(Dys)Functionality*, 48 HOUS. L. REV. 823 (2012) (hereinafter McKenna, *(Dys)Functionality*); Mark P. McKenna, *Dastar's Next Stand*, 19 J. INTELL. PROP. L. 357 (2012).

[96] McKenna & Canahai, *supra* note 80; McKenna, *(Dys)Functionality*, *supra* note 95.

[97] McKenna, *(Dys)functionality*, *supra* note 91; McKenna & Canahai, *supra* note 80.

[98] U.S. Pat. & Trademark Off. v. Booking.com B.V., 140 S.Ct. 2298 (2020).

According to the Court, we need not worry that "trademark protection for 'Booking.com' could exclude or inhibit competitors from using the term 'booking' or adopting domain names like 'ebooking.com' or 'hotel-booking.com,'" because trademark law "hems in the scope of such marks short of denying trademark protection altogether."[99] It does so by taking into account a mark's distinctiveness as part of the likelihood of confusion analysis: "the weaker the mark, the fewer are the junior uses that will trigger a likelihood of confusion."[100] Specifically, the Court insisted that ["w]hen a mark incorporates generic or highly descriptive components, consumers are less likely to think that other uses of the common element emanate from the mark's owner."[101] The Court was further convinced that "[i]n a 'crowded' field of look-alike marks" (*e.g.*, hotel names including the word "grand"), consumers "may have learned to carefully pick out" one mark from another."[102] And, finally, "even where some consumer confusion exists, the doctrine known as classic fair use, protects from liability anyone who uses a descriptive term, 'fairly and in good faith' and 'otherwise than as a mark,' merely to describe her own goods."[103]

But the Court's assurances notwithstanding, in fact courts police scope very inconsistently, at best. To take one recent example, the owner of the VAGISIL mark, which it registered for various vaginal-health products, was able to prevent registration of VAGISAN for various similar pharmaceutical preparations.[104] It prevailed despite the highly descriptive nature of the "vagi" component of the marks. Indeed, the court specifically rejected the applicant's contention that greater emphasis should be placed on the other parts of the respective marks ("SIL" and "SAN").[105] According to the Fourth Circuit, courts should not focus on dominant portions of single word marks; for those marks, "the proper analysis compares whole words, not parts."[106] Then the court concluded that the district court correctly determined that the marks were very similar—emphasizing the similarity of the generic components.[107]

That case did not involve "external" release valves, but it demonstrates a similar point. When courts persuade themselves that limits are not needed because there are other doctrines that can save the day, they often fail to limit rights appropriately because their confidence in those other doctrines turns out to be misplaced. That is an especially serious problem when courts rely on the availability of external values that aren't implicated in every case to which the expansive rights will apply.

[99] *Id.* at 2307.
[100] *Id.* quoting 4 McCarthy § 11:76
[101] *Id.*
[102] *Id.*
[103] *Id.* at 2307–08
[104] Combe Inc. v. Dr. August Wolff GMBH & Co. KG Arzneimittel, No. 19-1674, 2021 U.S. App. LEXIS 10536, *357 (4th Cir. Apr. 13, 2021).
[105] *Id.* at *364.
[106] *Id.*
[107] *Id.*

If nothing else, increasing emphasis on external limits has consequences in terms of the frequency and types of balancing that are necessary. It's one thing to balance concerns about undermining patent law's limits against a genuine concern about passing off, as courts did in the unfair competition era.[108] It's quite another to balance concerns about patent's limits against vague and undifferentiated concerns about "confusion" in the many forms in which it's now recognized.

Finally, and perhaps most importantly, relying on external values as the limiting principles makes it critical that trademark law correctly interpret the policy judgments in the other areas from which it purports to be drawing. If, for example, functionality doctrine is intended to keep trademark law from encroaching on patent law's domain, then courts need to understand patent law's actual domain. In reality, trademark law makes implicit (and sometimes explicit) judgments about the importance of access to certain features, which reflects judgments about competitive significance more than an honest approximation of the boundaries of patent law.[109] That manifests in trademark law's definition of function, and more specifically its understanding of "utilitarian" function), which does not match utility patent's more capacious understanding of "utility."[110] It also reflects in different rules for "utilitarian" and "aesthetic" features—the former typically presumed to be more competitively significant and therefore more important to be available to competitors, notwithstanding the fact that we have a patent system devoted to protecting ornamental designs.[111]

None of this is to say that external limits don't have an important role to play in trademark law, or that courts shouldn't work to better define those limits and implement them in more effective ways. But external limits can't do all the work, we can and should take pressure off of these doctrines by doing more work to identify real internal limits to trademark rights.

[108] Courts' remedial flexibility also helped a lot here. *See* Mark P. McKenna, *Back to the Future: Rediscovering Equitable Discretion in Trademark Cases*, 14 Lewis & Clark L. Rev. 537 (2010).

[109] *See* Mark P. McKenna & Christopher Jon Sprigman, *What's In and What's Out: How IP's Boundary Rules Shape Innovation*, 30 Harv. J. L. & Tech. 491 (2017).

[110] *Id.*

[111] McKenna, *(Dys)Functionality*, *supra* note 91.

2

The Role of Creativity in Granting and Limiting Trademark Rights

*Jeanne C. Fromer**

This chapter explores the role of creativity in trademark law's grant and limitation of rights. Trademark law—unlike patent and copyright law, its intellectual property cousins—is not structured to reward creators for producing particular content.[1] That is unsurprising because trademark law and theory—as discussed in Section I—is significantly different than that of patent and copyright. As the U.S. Supreme Court has remarked, trademark law was "not designed to protect originality or creativity," while patent and copyright law were.[2] Nonetheless, as Section II analyzes, there are critical ways in which trademark law, like patent and copyright law, seeks to encourage creative activity, even without directly rewarding marks' creators. At the same time, trademark law discourages certain types of activity thought to lack creativity, which are deemed to be less deserving of protection. This underappreciated current of incentive to be creative in certain ways courses through trademark law in ways that complement trademark law's basic purposes. At the same time, however, trademark law has a particular vision of creativity that might or might not align with society's. In addition, the law's drive to reward creativity has also paradoxically helped justify its expansion in certain ways unmoored from core trademark theory.

I. Trademark Law

As a springboard for analysis of the role of creativity in trademark law, this section recounts fundamental aspects of U.S. trademark law, starting with its current implementation and followed by a discussion of the principles understood to be animating the law.

* This book chapter is based on Jeanne C. Fromer, *The Role of Creativity in Trademark Law*, 86 Notre Dame L. Rev. 1885 (2011).

[1] *See generally*, Jeanne C. Fromer, *A Psychology of Intellectual Property*, 104 Nw. U. L. Rev. 1441 (2010) (exploring the central role of creativity in patent and copyright law).

[2] Dastar Corp. v. Twentieth Century Fox Film Corp., 539 U.S. 23, 37 (2003) (emphasis omitted).

Jeanne C. Fromer, *The Role of Creativity in Granting and Limiting Trademark Rights* In: *Charting Limitations on Trademark Rights*. Edited by: Haochen Sun and Barton Beebe, Oxford University Press. © Jeanne C. Fromer 2023.
DOI: 10.1093/oso/9780198871248.003.0003

A. Implementation

Words, symbols, logos, and sometimes a product's design or packaging may be protected under American trademark law.[3] According to the Lanham Act, these are protectable under federal law so long as they are "used by a person" in commerce in a distinctive way "to identify and distinguish his or her goods ... from those manufactured or sold by others and to indicate the source of the goods, even if that source is unknown."[4] Federal law similarly protects marks that designate services.[5]

There are two ways in which a mark can qualify as distinctive. First, certain marks are inherently distinctive, in that at the moment of first use in conjunction with a good or service, they are already capable of identifying a unique source of that good or service.[6] Marks are considered to be inherently distinctive if they are arbitrary, fanciful, or suggestive.[7] As one court has explained, "[a]rbitrary or fanciful terms bear no relationship to the products or services to which they are applied."[8] While fanciful terms—like KODAK for photographic goods—are new coinages, arbitrary terms—such as APPLE for computers—are not.[9] A suggestive mark, such as POLAR to signify air conditioners, "requires imagination, thought and perception to reach a conclusion as to the nature of goods."[10] Although POLAR connotes coldness, it is not a mere description of air conditioners or one of their qualities.[11]

Alternatively, marks that are not inherently distinctive, but are descriptive of the particular good or service, can become distinctive with proof of secondary meaning.[12] A descriptive term, such as VISION CENTER for a store offering eyeglasses, directly " 'identifies a characteristic or quality of an article or service,' such as its color, odor, function, dimensions, or ingredients."[13] Secondary meaning

[3] 15 U.S.C. § 1127 (defining trademarks to include certain "word[s], name[s], symbol[s], or device[s], or any combination thereof"); Wal-Mart Stores, Inc. v. Samara Bros., 529 U.S. 205, 209–16 (2000) (holding that product design or packaging might constitute a protectable trademark).

[4] 15 U.S.C. § 1127. Likewise, under a more recent addition to the law, they are protectable if a person has a "bona fide intention to use [them] in commerce and applies to register [them] on the principal register established by [federal law]." *Id.*

[5] *Id.*

[6] *See* Barton Beebe, The Semiotic Analysis of Trademark Law, 51 U.C.L.A. L. REV. 621, 671 (2004).

[7] Zatarains, Inc. v. Oak Grove Smokehouse, Inc., 698 F.2d 786, 791 (5th Cir. 1983).

[8] *Id.* (emphasis omitted).

[9] *See* Abercrombie & Fitch Co. v. Hunting World, Inc., 537 F.2d 4, 11 n.12 (2d Cir. 1976) (distinguishing arbitrary from fanciful marks).

[10] *Id.* at 11 (quoting Stix Prods., Inc. v. United Merchs. & Mfrs., Inc., 295 F. Supp. 479, 488 (S.D.N.Y. 1968)).

[11] A suggestive mark lies on the distinctiveness spectrum between descriptive on the one hand and arbitrary or fanciful on the other. *Id.*

[12] 15 U.S.C. § 1052(f); Zatarains, 698 F.2d at 790. Under the common law and until the Lanham Act's enactment, descriptive marks were not protectable even in the presence of significant secondary meaning. *Abercrombie & Fitch Co.*, 537 F.2d at 9.

[13] *Zatarains*, 698 F.2d at 790 (quoting Vision Ctr. v. Opticks, Inc., 596 F.2d 111, 115 (5th Cir. 1979) and citing Am. Heritage Life Ins. Co. v. Heritage Life Ins. Co., 494 F.2d 3, 11 (5th Cir. 1974)); *accord Abercrombie & Fitch Co.*, 537 F.2d at 11.

arises once "the primary significance of the term in the minds of the consuming public is not the product but the [particular] producer" of it.[14] When registering a mark, the U.S. Patent and Trademark Office (PTO) "may accept as prima facie evidence that the mark has become distinctive ... proof of substantially exclusive and continuous use thereof as a mark by the applicant in commerce for the five years before the date on which the claim of distinctiveness is made."[15]

Terms that are (or become) generic—which can happen by "nam[ing] ... a particular genus or class of which an individual article or service is but a member,"[16] such as COMPUTER as a mark for computers or ASPIRIN for the pain relief medication—cannot receive trademark protection, even if secondary meaning has been established.[17]

> Federal law protects registrants of distinctive trademarks against another's
>
> use in commerce [of] any reproduction, counterfeit, copy, or colorable imitation of [their] registered mark in connection with the sale, offering for sale, distribution, or advertising of any goods or services on or in connection with which such use is likely to cause confusion, or to cause mistake, or to deceive.[18]

Unregistered marks are similarly protected.[19] In judging the likelihood of consumer confusion between two marks, courts typically look to the following factors: the strength of the plaintiff's mark, the proximity of the goods with which the marks are associated, the marks' similarity, evidence of actual confusion, the marketing channels used with each mark, the type of goods at issue (including how much care a purchaser would typically use before buying), the defendant's intent in using the mark, and the likelihood of expansion into other products.[20]

Even though protection against infringement is provided in the United States whether or not the mark is registered, there are significant advantages to registration. Among the advantages conferred are nationwide constructive use conferring priority over most users of the same or similar marks,[21] enhanced remedies in federal court,[22] and the possibility of the mark becoming incontestable in many ways after five years.[23]

With this primer on the contours of current U.S. trademark law, it is instructive to turn to the law's theoretical foundations.

[14] *Zatarains*, 698 F.2d at 791 (quoting Kellogg Co. v. Nat'l Biscuit Co., 305 U.S. 111, 118 (1938)).
[15] 15 U.S.C. § 1052(f).
[16] *Zatarains*, 698 F.2d at 790 (quoting Vision Ctr., 596 F.2d at 115).
[17] *Id.* at 790–91.
[18] 15 U.S.C. § 1114(1)(a).
[19] *Id.* § 1125(a)(1).
[20] *E.g.*, AMF Inc. v. Sleekcraft Boats, 599 F.2d 341, 348–49 (9th Cir. 1979).
[21] 15 U.S.C. §§ 1057(c), 1072.
[22] *Id.* § 1117(b).
[23] *Id.* § 1065.

B. Theory

Trademark law originated to protect indications of an article's source, but only in the strictest sense. As Beverly Pattishall explains of nineteenth-century trademark law, "Even though an article may have become well known under an arbitrary mark, if that mark did not directly denote the article's source, another was free to use it."[24] This rule stemmed from two historical uses of marks: the proprietary mark affixed by owners so that they would be able to identify and retrieve their own goods after shipping,[25] and the regulatory production mark required by law or guilds to be affixed to certain goods so that defective or illegal work might be traced to the goods' originator for varied punishments.[26] Rights in these marks focused primarily on protecting producers from competitors' illegitimate interference with their trade rather than on the consumer.[27]

As suggested by current trademark law,[28] the law has broadened beyond these narrow, early purposes. Trademark law came to emphasize protecting consumers from confusion to foster fair competition and used that reasoning to justify a more extensive right.[29] The increased production capacity for goods ushered in by the industrial revolution intensified the use of advertising to the public to distinguish between these goods, which in turn popularized trademarks as identifiers of the source of goods.[30] As time marched on, consumers began to know less and less about the specific source of particular goods.[31] Nonetheless, a trademark affixed to goods would help consumers know that those goods originated from the same source, whatever that source was.[32] Relatedly, a trademark would distinguish a product from others with different marks.[33]

Trademark theory also suggests that marks, even without signifying a specific source, bolster trade by "identify[ing] a product as satisfactory and thereby ... stimulat[ing] further purchases by the consuming public."[34] Scholars theorize that producers of trademarked goods will have the incentive to invest in

[24] Beverly W. Pattishall, *Two Hundred Years of American Trademark Law*, 68 TRADEMARK REP. 121, 128 (1978).

[25] Frank I. Schechter, *The Rational Basis of Trademark Protection*, 40 HARV. L. REV. 813, 814 (1927); *accord* Sidney A. Diamond, *The Historical Development of Trademarks*, 65 TRADEMARK REP. 265, 270 (1975) (tracing the use of proprietary marks to before the Common Era).

[26] Schechter, *supra* note 25, at 814.

[27] Mark P. McKenna, *The Normative Foundations of Trademark Law*, 82 NOTRE DAME L. REV. 1839, 1841 (2007); Schechter, *supra* note 25, at 819.

[28] *Supra* Section I.A.

[29] *See* Park 'N Fly, Inc. v. Dollar Park & Fly, Inc., 469 U.S. 189, 198 (1985); McKenna, *supra* note 27, at 1843. *See generally* Schechter, *supra* note 25, at 814–19 (tracing the development of trademark law from its original purposes to broadened modern aims).

[30] Diamond, *supra* note 25, at 280–81.

[31] Schechter, *supra* note 25, at 814–15.

[32] *Id.* at 817.

[33] Beebe, *supra* note 6, at 677, 682.

[34] Schechter, *supra* note 25, at 818.

the goods' quality.[35] They suggest that this investment ought to occur because consumers will use the trademark as a way to identify a desirable good only if their past experiences reliably forecast the good's worth.[36] Protecting against trademark infringement, from this vantage point, thus prevents others from trading on the goodwill that is represented by the trademark.[37] Producers might then leverage the goodwill engendered by consumers' association of a particular mark for their goods or services with positive value and meaning by using the mark for an ever wider range of products and services.[38]

In all of these ways, trademarks are thought to reduce consumers' search costs—the expenditures they must make to discern important qualities of goods or services, which are frequently hard to measure.[39] On this thinking, trademarks promote trade and enable consumer decision-making. Trademark protection thus guards against use of a too-similar mark that causes consumer confusion as to goods' or services' origin.[40]

Rochelle Dreyfuss observes that, in recent decades, trademarks have begun to serve an additional purpose, of "becom[ing] products in their own right, valued as indicators of the status, preferences, and aspirations of those who use them."[41] To take one heavily litigated instance, a band sings a song entitled *Barbie Girl* to offer commentary on the values a Barbie doll represents: "I'm a blond bimbo girl, in a fantasy world/Dress me up, make it tight, I'm your dolly."[42] As a federal court adjudicating the case put it:

> Some trademarks enter our public discourse and become an integral part of our vocabulary. How else do you say that something's "the Rolls Royce of its class"? What else is a quick fix, but a Band-Aid? Does the average consumer know to ask for aspirin as "acetyl salicylic acid"? Trademarks often fill in gaps in our vocabulary and add a contemporary flavor to our expressions. Once imbued with such

[35] *E.g.*, William M. Landes & Richard A. Posner, *Trademark Law: An Economic Perspective*, 30 J.L. & Econ. 265, 269–70 (1987).

[36] William M. Landes & Richard A. Posner, *The Economics of Trademark Law*, 78 Trademark Rep. 267, 271 (1988). There has been a good deal of debate among trademark scholars about whether the law ought to view the consumer as a free individual making a choice to pay more for intangible values conveyed through advertising or as a person to be protected from the irrational encouragement that advertising and trademarks provide, beyond the underlying goods' quality. *See generally* Ralph S. Brown, Jr., *Advertising and the Public Interest: Legal Protection of Trade Symbols*, 57 Yale L.J. 1165 (1948) (describing this debate).

[37] Robert G. Bone, *Hunting Goodwill: A History of the Concept of Goodwill in Trademark Law*, 86 B.U. L. Rev. 547, 549 (2006).

[38] McKenna, *supra* note 27, at 1843.

[39] Beebe, *supra* note 6, at 623.

[40] Graeme B. Dinwoodie, *The Death of Ontology: A Teleological Approach to Trademark Law*, 84 Iowa L. Rev. 611, 614 (1999).

[41] Rochelle Cooper Dreyfuss, *Expressive Genericity: Trademarks as Language in the Pepsi Generation*, 65 Notre Dame L. Rev. 397, 397 (1990); *accord* Beebe, *supra* note 6, at 624, 656.

[42] Mattel, Inc. v. MCA Records, Inc., 296 F.3d 894, 901 (9th Cir. 2002) (quoting Aqua's song, *Barbie Girl*).

expressive value, the trademark becomes a word in our language and assumes a role outside the bounds of trademark law.[43]

In light of this shift in the use of trademarks, scholars suggest circumscribing trademark law's reach to prevent it from reaching communicative uses, which enrich society's conversations.[44]

These theories show that trademarks are useful in more expansive ways than in their earliest incarnations: to lower consumer search costs, encourage quality in the underlying goods or services, foster trade, and serve as status and communicative indicators. With this background, I now turn to the role of creativity in trademark law's grant and limitation of rights.

II. Creativity in Trademark Law

Most people take it as a given that patent and copyright laws—trademark's cousins—have the encouragement of creative activity as a central motivator.[45] That much seems to follow from the U.S. Constitution, which seeks to "promote the Progress of Science and useful Arts" by providing Congress with the power to "secur[e] for limited Times to Authors and Inventors the exclusive Right to their respective Writings and Discoveries."[46]

Yet trademarks, which are described as "intellectual property" much like patents and copyrights,[47] have been treated differently. In 1879, the U.S. Supreme Court ruled that Congress could not enact a trademark law under the same constitutional power as for patent and copyright law, suggesting instead that any federal trademark law would have to be passed under the power of the Commerce Clause.[48] The Supreme Court, in that decision, reasoned that "[t]he ordinary trade-mark has no necessary relation to invention or discovery," especially because it need not be original.[49] Instead, the Supreme Court reasoned, "The trade-mark may be, and generally is, the adoption of something already in existence as the distinctive symbol of the party using it."[50]

This section explores whether these differences between trademark law on the one hand and patent and copyright law on the other hand are as vast as suggested

[43] *Id.* at 900 (citation omitted).
[44] *E.g.*, Dreyfuss, *supra* note 41, at 418.
[45] *E.g.*, Dastar Corp. v. Twentieth Century Fox Film Corp., 539 U.S. 23, 37 (2003); Fromer, *supra* note 1, at 1457–59.
[46] U.S. CONST. art. I, § 8, cl. 8.
[47] *See*BRAD SHERMAN & LIONEL BENTLY, THE MAKING OF MODERN INTELLECTUAL PROPERTY LAW 168 (1999); Sonia K. Katyal, *Trademark Intersectionality*, 57 UCLA L. REV. 1601, 1602 (2010) (grouping the three).
[48] Trade-Mark Cases, 100 U.S. 82, 92–97 (1879).
[49] *Id.* at 94.
[50] *Id.*

by this ruling and the subsequent reenactment of federal trademark laws under the Commerce Clause. In particular it focuses on the role of creativity in trademark law, arguing that it is more central to this body of law than has been commonly appreciated, both in granting and limiting trademark rights. This section concludes by showing that this encouragement of creativity is central to trademark theory, but that it has likely helped drive the expansion of trademark protection in recent years in ways only weakly connected to trademark law's fundamental goals.

Unlike creators, who receive no special cognizance under trademark law,[51] creativity itself is strongly encouraged. In fact, in spite of Supreme Court and other pronunciations to the contrary,[52] encouraging creativity lies at the heart of trademark law and theory.

In previous work, I explore the role that creativity plays in patent and copyright laws, through the lens of their differing protectability standards.[53] I explain how the creative process "includes as important steps both 'problem finding' (formulating and constraining a problem) and 'problem solving' (achieving a goal by removing any obstacles in the way)."[54] I find that "the general structure of the creative process looks similar for scientists and engineers ultimately protected by patent and for artists ultimately protected by copyright."[55] That said, society values different aspects of the creative process for scientific works and artistic works.

> For scientific and technological inventions, society emphasizes problem solving over problem finding, while for artistic works, it stresses problem finding over problem solving. Moreover, while it is often acceptable for scientific and technological inventions to be more groundbreaking, it is psychologically preferable that artistic works be new, but not be too new.[56]

I suggest that these differences mostly parallel the different protectability standards in patent and copyright laws. The protectability standards of patent law—which principally protects scientific and technological inventions—emphasize how well the inventor solved a particular problem, as well as establish a high threshold for qualification.[57] By contrast, the protectability standards of copyright law—which mainly grant rights with regard to artistic works—dwell on an author's finding of a problem, as well as set a low threshold for qualification, thereby encouraging the creation of works that are not too new.[58]

[51] Fromer, *supra* note *, at 1894–1902.
[52] *See supra* text accompanying note 2.
[53] Fromer, *supra* note 1, at 1445–56.
[54] *Id.* at 1444.
[55] *Id.*
[56] *Id.* (footnote omitted).
[57] *Id.* at 1484–92.
[58] *Id.* at 1492–98.

Creativity is something central that patent and copyright laws each seeks to encourage, which is why it is vital to ensure that these laws actually encourage creative work in their respective purviews.[59] With patent and copyright, the law seeks to encourage the creator to craft something valuable. According to Rochelle Dreyfuss, "Exclusivity is therefore necessary to assure the creator freedom from those who did not make the creative effort and thus would undercut the price at which the creator could profitably sell the work."[60]

Trademark law is different to Dreyfuss, in that "the owner of a trademark is [primarily] in the business of selling a *different* product," the product with which the mark is associated.[61] In this regard, creativity does not seem to be the sine qua non of trademark law. Rather, well-established theory suggests that trademark law is designed to promote trade, by protecting consumers from source confusion, so as to minimize unfair competition, reduce consumer search costs, and promote quality in goods and services.[62] This section establishes, nonetheless, that creativity is something central that trademark law seeks to encourage and this encouragement is desirable to promoting trademark's fundamental goals.[63] I focus on how trademark law subtly encourages creativity in choosing distinctive marks. Its particular notion of creativity is essential to the grant and limitation of trademark rights. (I do not, however, dwell on the well-explored terrain of a connected situation: of society—such as everyday speakers and makers of parodies, commentaries, and comparative advertising—using already existing marks for creative purposes beyond signifying goods or services.[64]) Nonetheless, the important role of creativity in trademark law has perhaps also promoted trademark's expansion in ways only tenuously linked to trademark law's underlying goals.

Creativity made its way into trademark law once trademark law moved from protecting significations of a single known source to marks signaling a single, but typically unknown, source.[65] As Frank Schechter observes, this shift "brings

[59] *Id.* at 1457–59.

[60] Dreyfuss, *supra* note 41, at 408.

[61] *Id.* Rochelle Dreyfuss therefore worries about awarding strong rights to a mark's owner when "the public … enjoy[s] the expressive dimensions of [the] trademark more than it values the underlying product." *Id.*

[62] *Supra* Section I.B; *cf.* Am. Express Co. v. Goetz, 515 F.3d 156, 159 (2d Cir. 2008) (per curiam) ("While copyright law protects the content of a creative work itself, it is trademark law that protects those symbols, elements or devices which identify the work in the marketplace and prevent confusion as to its source" (citations omitted).)

[63] *But cf.* Stephen L. Carter, *The Trouble with Trademark*, 99 YALE L.J. 759, 768 (1990) ("Trademark law … provides no incentive to create new marks. A firm might well develop an idea for a mark that has some special charm and seems to be appealing, but its appeal has nothing to do with the reason that marks receive protection. Indeed, trademark law may be described as indifferent to the creation of marks, in the sense that the number of marks makes no difference. One might conceive of an optimal supply of copyrighted works or patented inventions").

[64] *E.g., id.* at 763; Wendy J. Gordon, *A Property Right in Self-Expression: Equality and Individualism in the Natural Law of Intellectual Property*, 102 YALE L.J. 1533, 1585 (1993); Sonia K. Katyal, *Semiotic Disobedience*, 84 WASH. U. L. REV. 489, 498, 554–68 (2006); *supra* notes 41–44 and accompanying text (discussing this shift in use of trademarks).

[65] *Supra* text accompanying notes 24–33.

out ... the creative and not merely symbolic nature of the modern trademark."[66] With this change, a mark no longer needs to identify a specified provider but (typically) a single provider. Therefore, it must be sufficiently linked—frequently via creativity, although sometimes via repetition—to the underlying good or service to stick in consumers' minds.

As the development of trademark law shows, the structure of trademark law indicates that it is protecting this linkage between signifier and business, not just the signifier on its own.[67] Most importantly, trademark rights arise only when a mark is used to signify a good or service.[68] Moreover, historically, the scope of trademark protection was keyed to the particular goods or services to which a mark was linked.[69]

Although our intuitive understanding of creativity typically emphasizes the works protected by copyright and patent laws (such as novels and drugs), establishing that link is also an exercise of creativity. In addition to the prototypical forms of creativity in the arts and sciences, "[c]reativity courses through so many different domains, ... [including] everyday activities—whether writing in a journal or figuring out an ingenious way to attain an object beyond one's reach."[70] According to psychologists, creativity is "a process that generates a product or idea and possesses two qualities: newness and appropriateness—appropriate in the sense that some community recognizes it as socially valuable."[71] Trademark creation fits this schema of creativity. The creator here is, by definition, building something new: a link between a mark and goods and services that has not previously existed. In the abstract, this link creation is socially appropriate, in that trademark law seeks to benefit consumers and trade in innumerable ways.[72] Furthermore, trademark creators strive, as a practical matter, for social appropriateness. Trademark creation typically involves extensive market research to determine how

[66] Schechter, *supra* note 25, at 817.

[67] *Supra* text accompanying notes 28–33; *cf.* Katyal, *supra* note 64, at 522 ("Since a product, at least initially, has no 'meaning,' it must acquire value through an association with a person or object that already has some meaning to the consumer. To protect this association, then, advertising uses intellectual property—trademarks, copyrighted works, and the like—as a visual vehicle or code to evoke common threads of emotions and thereby connect consumers to the psychological essence at hand" (footnote omitted)).

[68] McKenna, *supra* note 27, at 1887; *supra* text accompanying notes 13–15.

[69] McKenna, *supra* note 27, at 1888. Traditionally, one could license or assign a mark to a third party only if the underlying business was sold to the third party as well. *Id.* at 1893–94. Over time, however, reflecting the notion that trademarks are repositories of goodwill, the courts began to allow trademarks to be licensed "as long as the mark owner ensured a consistent level of quality in the products or services offered under its mark." *Id.* at 1910–11.

[70] Fromer, *supra* note 1, at 1461; *see also* Richard E. Ripple, *Ordinary Creativity*, 14 CONTEMP. EDUC. PSYCHOL. 189, 189 (1989) ("Ordinary creative thinking is proposed as a point of view in which creativity results from ordinary people thinking in identifiably unique ways when they meet everyday problems in real-life situations.").

[71] Fromer, *supra* note 1, at 1459–60 (footnote omitted) (expanding on this psychological understanding of creativity).

[72] *Supra* Section I.B.

best to appeal to consumers through branding.[73] By seeking to appeal to a relevant community—the intended consumers of a product or service—trademark creation is occupied with selecting or creating a mark that is socially appropriate. Once a mark is selected and used, society will find it either helpful and it will be a successful—and thus appropriate—mark or unhelpful as a source indicator. In the latter case, as discussed later, trademark law frequently steps in to deny protection for the link.

In a fundamental way, then, trademark law rewards those providers of goods or services who have established a sufficiently strong link between a mark and their goods or services.[74] In trademark parlance, this sufficiently strong link comes about by employing a mark that is distinctive.[75] As this section elaborates, developing this distinctiveness—this strong link—typically requires much creativity. (I focus primarily on the ways in which trademark law encourages the newness component of creativity, because it is natural, regardless of trademark law, for trademark creators to seek social appropriateness.[76]) As such, even though encouragement of creativity is not asserted as a basis for trademark law, it is typically central to accomplishing trademark law's principal goals.

Foundational work by Frank Schechter in trademark theory suggests that distinctiveness is a goal for which trademark originators should strive, in that more distinctive marks have "more effective ... selling power" than less distinctive ones.[77] In his view, the desirability of distinctive marks hinges on their typically strong impact on consumers.[78]

> [A] firm of fruitgrowers has recently popularized as its mark another animal of no well known or commonplace characteristics, the "blue goose." When the public hears or sees the phrase "Blue Goose" it thinks, not of "a North American wild goose having a grayish plumage resembling that of the young snow goose found chiefly during its migrations in the Mississippi Valley," but of oranges or grapefruit with a certain trademark and certain meritorious qualities.[79]

Distinctive marks therefore arguably deserve greater protection against appropriation by sellers of other goods and services, to guard against "los[ing their]

[73] *See, e.g.*, A. Samuel Oddi, *Product Simulation: From Tort to Intellectual Property*, 88 TRADEMARK REP. 101, 120 (1998).

[74] *See* FRANCIS H. UPTON, A TREATISE ON THE LAW OF TRADE MARKS, WITH A DIGEST AND REVIEW OF THE ENGLISH AND AMERICAN AUTHORITIES 23 (1860); Graeme B. Dinwoodie & Mark D. Janis, *Confusion over Use: Contextualism in Trademark Law*, 92 IOWA L. REV. 1597, 1612–13 (2007); Stacey L. Dogan & Mark A. Lemley, *Grounding Trademark Law Through Trademark Use*, 92 IOWA L. REV. 1669, 1689 (2007).

[75] *Supra* text accompanying notes 4–17.

[76] *Supra* text accompanying notes 72–73.

[77] Schechter, *supra* note 25, at 819.

[78] *See id.* at 825.

[79] *Id.* at 830.

arresting uniqueness and hence . . . selling power."[80] Schechter goes so far as to say that preserving a mark's uniqueness is the only rational reason to protect it.[81]

In this sense, the benefit of protecting an inherently distinctive mark is high. The cost of protecting it as against a confusing commercial use is typically low. As William Landes and Richard Posner observe, "[t]hese costs [of legally enforceable trademarks] are modest, at least in the simple care [sic] of the 'fanciful' mark, such as 'Exxon' and 'Kodak,' which has no information content except to denote a specific producer or brand."[82] Giving rights in fanciful marks, then, will not typically hurt trade—that which trademark law seeks to promote—because there was and is no need for competitors to use these marks to describe or even promote their competing products or services. Similarly, using an arbitrary mark like BLUE GOOSE to signify fruit products will not usually be harmful to trade, because it is not necessary for competing fruit producers to use BLUE GOOSE and other arbitrary marks to promote their products. (The cost–benefit analysis is the opposite for marks that are not inherently distinctive, in that their informational content beyond their use as a mark for one particular source of goods or services is strong, therefore suggesting that the cost of protecting these marks is high and the benefit is low.)

Trademark law grasps the high benefit and low cost of inherent distinctiveness by awarding valuable protection, without much more, to those marks that are inherently distinctive.[83] In doing so, the law provides an incentive to be creative in choosing trademarks, by coining new words or associating known words in an unexpected way with a good or service to gain trademark protection easily.[84] That is, to refer to one's computer products, trademark law offers the incentive of immediate protection for a business choosing a suggestive, arbitrary, or fanciful term like APPLE for computer products.[85] By contrast, were it to choose the unsurprising COMPUTER COMPANY, it would never receive trademark protection for this generic mark. Similarly, DIGITAL COMPANY would not easily get protection as a descriptive mark unless secondary meaning were to be established.

[80] *Id.*
[81] *See id.* at 831.
[82] Landes & Posner, *supra* note 35, at 273.
[83] *Supra* text accompanying notes 4–9.
[84] *Cf.* Beebe, *supra* note 6, at 673–74 ("One reason why trademark law has traditionally granted broader protection to inherently distinctive marks is to provide an incentive to trademark producers to generate new words rather than appropriate from the language preexisting words for commercial purposes."). Stephen Carter disputes that trademark law provides an incentive to be creative in choosing a mark. *See* Carter, *supra* note 63, at 768 ("[T]rademark law has never provided incentives to be clever in selecting a mark. Instead, the law encourages the development of goodwill and the association of that goodwill with a mark. The charming, attractive mark not yet associated with any goodwill simply does not carry any information, and, consequently, cannot possibly economize on it" (footnote omitted)).
[85] According to lore, the etymology of Apple Computers is co-founder Steve Jobs's earlier work in orchards. *Video: Steve Wozniak Explains Apple Company Name*, Obama Pacman (Nov. 21, 2010).

Standing alone this foregoing analysis would suggest that trademark law gives an incentive to be ever creative in choosing trademarks that are inherently distinctive, to the redounding benefit of trademark law's goals. In fact, the U.S. Supreme Court has intimated as much by highlighting that small and new companies can benefit by competing more readily in a marketplace with larger and more established competitors by choosing inherently distinctive marks and not needing to bear the expensive burden of cultivating secondary meaning.[86] In this way, trademark law's rule of inherent distinctiveness ultimately helps level and enhance competition to the benefit of consumers.

But this picture is not complete. As discussed above, trademark law treats suggestive marks as inherently protectable just as much as arbitrary and fanciful ones. It is genuinely open for debate whether suggestive marks are as creative as arbitrary or fanciful marks. On the one hand, originating suggestive marks generally entails less creativity than for arbitrary or fanciful marks like APPLE for computer products, BLUE GOOSE for fruits, and EXXON for oil products. As examples, consider the following marks that courts or administrative agencies have found to be suggestive, and thus inherently distinctive and protectable as trademarks: CITIBANK for urban banks,[87] DIAL-A-MATTRESS for telephonic mattress sales,[88] WET/DRY BROOM for electric vacuum cleaners,[89] and SPRAY 'N VAC for aerosol rug cleaners.[90] There is—by definition—a relatively closer and more direct link between these suggestive marks and the underlying goods and services they signify than between arbitrary or fanciful marks and their signified goods and services. All of these suggestive marks seem like somewhat obvious choices to associate with the respective goods or services. In fact, psychologists regularly find that one of the most important features of creativity is the ability to make connections between remote concepts.[91] That is precisely what creators and consumers of arbitrary or fanciful marks are doing, but creators and consumers of suggestive marks are doing to a lesser extent, if at all, given the very close connections between marks like DIAL-A-MATTRESS and the service of mattress sales over the telephone.

[86] *See* Two Pesos, Inc. v. Taco Cabana, Inc., 505 U.S. 763, 775 (1992) ("[A]dding a secondary meaning requirement [for inherently distinctive trade dress] could have anticompetitive effects, creating particular burdens on the startup of small companies. It would present special difficulties for a business ... that seeks to start a new product in a limited area and then expand into new markets. Denying protection for inherently distinctive nonfunctional trade dress until after secondary meaning has been established would allow a competitor, which has not adopted a distinctive trade dress of its own, to appropriate the originator's dress in other markets and to deter the originator from expanding into and competing in these areas.").

[87] *See* Citibank, N.A. v. Citibanc Grp., Inc., 724 F.2d 1540, 1545 (11th Cir. 1984).

[88] *See* Dial-A-Mattress Operating Corp. v. Mattress Madness, Inc., 841 F. Supp. 1339, 1347–48 (E.D.N.Y. 1994).

[89] *See In re* Shop-Vac Corp., 219 U.S.P.Q. (BNA) 470, 471–72 (T.T.A.B. 1983).

[90] *See* Glamorene Prods. Corp. v. Boyle-Midway, Inc., 188 U.S.P.Q. (BNA) 145, 164–65 (S.D.N.Y. 1975).

[91] *See* Fromer, *supra* note 1, at 1462 (citing psychological research).

On another view, suggestive marks may be seen as just as creative as arbitrary or fanciful ones, if not more so. A suggestive mark, it might be argued, walks the fine line between invoking the underlying good or service to which it is linked, yet without describing or naming it. As such, it could prove to be very memorable to consumers of the relevant good or service. Under this view, trademark law seeks to promote creativity, by encouraging the adoption of suggestive marks as inherently distinctive marks.

To the extent that one understands suggestive marks to be creatively chosen, trademark law seems to encourage creativity whichever category of inherently distinctive mark it encourages businesses to choose. Yet if one understands suggestive marks to be significantly less creative than arbitrary or fanciful ones, trademark law appears to encourage creativity to varying degrees in allowing easy protection for inherently distinctive marks.

If one adopts the latter view, one might find it perplexing that there seems to be no incentive in trademark law to produce marks that are more distinctive than suggestive because they pass the threshold for trademark protection just as arbitrary and fanciful marks do, something scholars and courts have suggested.[92] From this vantage point, trademark law encourages creativity in crafting distinctive marks but only up to a much less minimal point than that required to create arbitrary or fanciful marks.

Nonetheless, even if one believes that suggestive marks are less creative, trademark law in practice does not equally favor suggestive, arbitrary, and fanciful marks. Rather, it encourages the adoption of arbitrary or fanciful marks over suggestive ones in two ways. For one thing, a trademark holder will generally be entitled to a wider scope of protection against infringement when its mark is arbitrary or fanciful than when it is suggestive. Recall that courts balance multiple factors to determine whether a trademark has been infringed.[93] Two of these factors are more likely to weigh in a trademark holder's favor when the mark is arbitrary or fanciful than when it is suggestive. First, courts are more willing to find trademark infringement when a mark is strong,[94] which courts frequently measure by its distinctiveness.[95] As one court put it, more distinctive marks are "afforded the widest ambit of protection from infringing uses," with arbitrary or fanciful marks being favored in this way over suggestive marks.[96] One reason for this factor's weight could be to reward producers that choose marks that are unlikely to interfere with competitors' needs to describe their products and are directly helpful, by being

[92] *Abercrombie & Fitch Co.* 537 F.2d 4, 11 n.12 ("As terms of art, the distinctions between suggestive terms and fanciful or arbitrary terms may seem needlessly artificial."); Beebe, *supra* note 6, at 673–74.

[93] *Supra* text accompanying note 20.

[94] AMF Inc. v. Sleekcraft Boats, 599 F.2d 341, 349–50 (9th Cir. 1979).

[95] *See* McGregor-Doniger Inc. v. Drizzle Inc., 599 F.2d 1126, 1131 (2d Cir. 1979). Trademark strength is also related to its strength in consumers' minds. Kenner Parker Toys Inc. v. Rose Art Indus., Inc., 963 F.2d 350, 353 (Fed. Cir. 1992).

[96] *Sleekcraft Boats*, 599 F.2d at 349–50.

especially distinctive, to consumers. This factor thus provides an incentive to businesses to choose arbitrary or fanciful marks over suggestive (not to mention descriptive and generic) ones.

A second factor weighing in favor of trademark infringement is a defendant's bad intent in using the mark.[97] Courts reason that the presence of bad intent indicates infringement because "[w]hen the alleged infringer knowingly adopts a mark similar to another's, reviewing courts presume that the defendant can accomplish his purpose: that is, that the public will be deceived."[98] When a mark is arbitrary or fanciful, a competitor has no reasonable need to use the same or a very similar mark other than to benefit from consumer confusion by free-riding on the goodwill associated with the mark. Intentional use of such a mark thus tends to indicate trademark infringement. When a mark is suggestive or descriptive (or generic), it is easier to see how a competitor would intentionally use the mark without hoping to cause or actually causing consumer confusion. The competitor's use might merely be descriptive or suggestive of the competitor's goods or services without sufficiently confusing consumers. Through the lens of this likelihood-of-confusion factor, arbitrary or fanciful marks are more widely protected against intentional use by competitors than suggestive or descriptive ones.

In light of these two factors measuring likelihood of confusion, trademark infringement is more likely to be found for arbitrary or fanciful marks than for suggestive ones.[99] Thus, even though all three categories of marks are inherently distinctive and will receive trademark protection, trademark infringement doctrine encourages producers to adopt arbitrary or fanciful trademarks over suggestive ones.

An incentive to choose arbitrary or fanciful trademarks over suggestive ones also lies in trademark's protectability scheme. On the distinctiveness spectrum, the class of suggestive marks neighbors the class of descriptive ones.[100] In fact, it is widely thought that the borderline between suggestive marks, which are inherently distinctive, and descriptive ones, which require secondary meaning to be protectable,[101] is especially fuzzy.[102] Learned Hand went so far as to state that "[i]t is quite

[97] *Id.* at 354.

[98] *Id.*

[99] *See* Beebe, *supra* note 20, at 1637 ("[I]n the ninety dispositive opinions in which the court placed the plaintiff's mark in one of the five [distinctiveness] categories, the plaintiff multifactor test win rate steadily declined with the inherent strength of its mark: fanciful marks enjoyed the highest win rate, followed by arbitrary marks, suggestive marks, descriptive marks, and then generic marks.").

[100] *Cf.* 2 J. Thomas McCarthy, McCarthy on Trademarks and Unfair Competition § 11:63 (1996) (defining suggestive marks as those that are "subtly 'descriptive' ").

[101] *Supra* text accompanying notes 12–15.

[102] *See Abercrombie & Fitch Co.*, 537 F.2d 4, 9; Le Blume Import Co. v. Coty, 293 F. 344, 351 (2d Cir. 1923); 2 McCarthy, *supra* note 100, at § 11:64. The Second Circuit also notes that classifying marks' distinctiveness is made harder because a term that is in one category for a particular product may be in quite a different one for another, because a term may shift from one category to another in light of differences in usage through time, because a term may have one meaning to one group of users and a different one to others, and because the same term may be put to different uses with respect to a single product. *Abercrombie & Fitch Co.*, 537 F.2d at 9 (footnotes omitted).

impossible to get any rule out of the cases beyond this: That the validity of the mark ends where suggestion ends and description begins."[103] In his treatise on trademark law, Tom McCarthy notes that the "exact location in any given situation [between descriptive and suggestive marks] is hazy and only subjectively definable."[104]

It is thus unsurprising to find very similar—if not identical—marks for the same goods or services classified by one court as suggestive and by another as descriptive.[105] Examples abound. One court determined that L.A. as a mark for low alcohol beer was suggestive of it,[106] while another held that the same mark was descriptive of the beer's quality.[107] And while one court held that FAMILY MARKET as a mark for a retail store was suggestive,[108] other courts found SHOPPERS FAIR and FOOD FAIR to be descriptive marks for retail stores.[109]

The fuzziness of the boundary between suggestive and descriptive marks implies that producers of goods and services would typically prefer to avoid suggestive marks entirely, instead using arbitrary or fanciful marks. If a mark that seems plausibly suggestive is chosen, a court or administrative agency might nonetheless also reasonably decide that the mark is descriptive. As such, the mark would be protectable only if secondary meaning is shown. The uncertainty and a possible necessity of showing secondary meaning—which might not be possible in a significant number of cases—should deter some businesses from using suggestive marks in favor of arbitrary or fanciful marks. Even cautious types might not want to use a mark that is likely—but not certain—to be found to be suggestive, because they may have to invest significant sums and time in developing secondary meaning out of risk aversion.[110]

Just as trademark law pushes businesses away from suggestive marks in favor of arbitrary or fanciful marks, it grants significant incentive to entities not to use descriptive marks when they might use a more distinctive mark. For one thing, due to the same two factors discussed above, trademark infringement is more likely to be found for suggestive marks than for descriptive ones.[111] Moreover, the borderline between descriptive and generic marks is just as fuzzy as that between suggestive and descriptive marks.[112] Although descriptive marks are protectable as

[103] Franklin Knitting Mills, Inc. v. Fashionit Sweater Mills, Inc., 297 F. 247, 248 (S.D.N.Y. 1923).
[104] 2 McCarthy, *supra* note 100, at § 11:66.
[105] *See id.* at § 11:70 (citing illustrative cases).
[106] Anheuser-Busch Inc. v. Stroh Brewery Co., 750 F.2d 631, 633 (8th Cir. 1984).
[107] G. Heileman Brewing Co. v. Anheuser-Busch, Inc., 873 F.2d 985, 1000 (7th Cir. 1989).
[108] Tradewell Stores, Inc. v. T.B. & M., Inc., 500 P.2d 1290, 1294 (Wash. Ct. App. 1972).
[109] Shoppers Fair of Ark., Inc. v. Sanders Co., 328 F.2d 496, 499 (8th Cir. 1964); Food Fair Stores, Inc. v. Lakeland Grocery Corp., 301 F.2d 156, 160–61 (4th Cir. 1962).
[110] *Cf.* Dreyfus Fund Inc. v. Royal Bank of Can., 525 F. Supp. 1108, 1115 (S.D.N.Y. 1981) ("One of the benefits of a strong mark—and an aspect of its value—is the owner's well-earned capacity to achieve a high degree of consumer recognition (and response) with less costly forms of advertising than had been necessary to establish the mark's strength.").
[111] *Supra* text accompanying notes 93–98.
[112] 2 McCarthy, *supra* note 100, at § 12:20; *see also In re* Merrill Lynch, Pierce, Fenner, & Smith, Inc., 828 F.2d 1567, 1569 (Fed. Cir. 1987).

trademarks so long as secondary meaning has been established, generic marks are never protectable under trademark law.[113] Just as there are numerous cases at the suggestive–descriptive border, there are many at the descriptive–generic boundary. For example, while the Seventh Circuit held that ALO for cream of the aloe vera plant was generic,[114] the Fifth Circuit held that the same mark for the same product was descriptive.[115] Similarly, one court held FIRST NATIONAL BANK to be a generic mark for the first national bank in a certain geographic area,[116] while another held FIRST FEDERAL to be merely descriptive of the first federally chartered savings and loan organization in a specific geographic region.[117] A reasonable business might avoid descriptive terms, as courts and administrative agencies could label them generic and consequently unprotectable—a harsh result.

Even if a mark is squarely descriptive—or a business is willing to take a risk on what a court or administrative agency might conclude—the business must invest significant labor in establishing secondary meaning for the mark for it to be protectable.[118] The requisite expense and time that investment entails ought to encourage many businesses toward inherently distinctive marks. The business must develop a context in which enough consumers establish a link between the descriptive mark and only that business's goods or services, rather than the class of goods or services with which consumers would otherwise associate the mark.[119]

This push toward ever more distinctiveness—away from generic, descriptive, and suggestive marks and in favor of arbitrary or fanciful ones—is beneficial for society and consumers because it engenders appropriate limitations in trademark law. With this push, existing words tend not to be removed from circulation in trade—via trademark law's protections—unless they have nothing to do with the underlying goods or services being offered.[120] Society, consumers, and competitors can readily absorb this loss. In particular, competitors are left free to describe their goods in intuitive ways and to originate and use their own highly distinctive marks to distinguish their goods and services, in ways that ultimately benefit

[113] *Supra* text accompanying notes 12–17.

[114] Am. Aloe Corp. v. Aloe Creme Labs., Inc., 420 F.2d 1248, 1256 (7th Cir. 1970).

[115] Aloe Creme Labs., Inc. v. Milsan, Inc., 423 F.2d 845, 849–50 (5th Cir. 1970).

[116] First Nat'l Bank & Trust Co. v. First Nationwide Bank, 15 U.S.P.Q.2d (BNA) 1457, 1461 (W.D. Mo. 1990).

[117] First Fed. Sav. & Loan Ass'n of Council Bluffs v. First Fed. Sav. & Loan Ass'n of Lincoln, 929 F.2d 382, 384 (8th Cir. 1991).

[118] *See* Keith Aoki, *Authors, Inventors and Trademark Owners: Private Intellectual Property and the Public Domain, Part II*, 18 COLUM.-VLA J.L. & ARTS 191, 241 (1994); Mark A. Lemley & Mark P. McKenna, *Owning Mark(et)s*, 109 MICH. L. REV. 137, 173 (2010). To the extent this investment barrier is set too low, businesses will be less sensitive in picking inherently distinctive marks over descriptive ones, something I explore in ongoing work. *See* Jeanne C. Fromer, *Overhauling Trademark Distinctiveness* (working paper).

[119] McKenna, *supra* note 27, at 1891–92; Mark P. McKenna, *Trademark Use and the Problem of Source* U. ILL. L. REV. 773, 783 (2009).

[120] *Supra* text accompanying notes 77–82.

consumers.[121] As the Second Circuit put it, "The English language has a wealth of synonyms and related words with which to describe the qualities which manufacturers may wish to claim for their products and the ingenuity of the public relations profession supplies new words and slogans as they are needed."[122]

This analysis also provides a useful framework through which to analyze the role of goodwill in trademark law. Robert Bone criticizes goodwill's place in trademark law. He asserts that "the information transmission model aims to prevent misleading representations, while the [goodwill] misappropriation model aims to prevent unauthorized appropriations."[123] It is the former, he insists, that we ought to protect in light of trademark's goals of protecting against consumer confusion.[124] Seen through the lens of creativity's role in trademark law, however, the two models are more in step than Bone views them to be. Protection against trademark infringement when there is consumer confusion is a way of maintaining a trademark's goodwill. Essentially, protection against run-of-the-mill trademark infringement by a competitor protects the goodwill situated in a mark—in other words, the link between the mark and the underlying product or good. In this way, trademark law protects a mark's distinctiveness from being eroded by competitors' use as a source indicator. Given that trademark law encourages creativity to achieve distinctiveness, guarding a trademark's distinctiveness by imposing liability for trademark infringement frequently also provides shelter for the creativity trademark law encourages.

Despite the significant benefit to trademark law's fundamental purposes of promoting creativity in choosing ever distinctive marks as a way to limit trademark scope appropriately, there is reason to suspect that rewarding creativity might paradoxically also have helped fuel trademark's ever expansive reach. As Keith Aoki puts it, "Traces of authorship have been ascribed to the trademark owner who has invested her 'sweat of the brow' to 'create' value in a mark, so that she is looked upon as being legally entitled and justified in 'reaping what she has sown.'"[125] Encouraging creativity in choosing a distinctive mark to link with an underlying good or service might incline the law to give robust rights to the business that has

[121] Of course, not all words—even arbitrary or fanciful ones—are equal. *See* Felix S. Cohen, *Transcendental Nonsense and the Functional Approach*, 35 COLUM. L. REV. 809, 815–16 (1935). Either "peculiar emotional contexts give one word more sales appeal than any other word suitable for the same product" from the moment it is first used for that product, or "all words are originally alike in commercial potentiality, but become differentiated by advertising and other forms of commercial exploitation." *Id.* at 817. For an exploration of what this insight ought to mean for trademark law, see Fromer, *supra* note 118.

[122] *Abercrombie & Fitch Co.*, 537 F.2d 4, 11 (2d Cir. 1976) (quoting Aluminum Fabricating Co. of Pittsburgh v. Season-All Window Corp., 259 F.2d 314, 317 (2d Cir. 1958)). *But see* Barton Beebe & Jeanne C. Fromer, *Are We Running Out of Trademarks? An Empirical Study of Trademark Depletion and Congestion*, 131 HARV. L. REV. 945 (2018).

[123] Bone, *supra* note 37, at 550.

[124] *Id.* at 549.

[125] Aoki, *supra* note 118, at 242.

made this link,[126] just as patent and copyright law give vigorous rights to reward creativity.[127]

Trademark protection has expanded over time, from protecting against competitive uses of a trademark holder's signifier to shielding holders from many noncompetitive uses of it.[128] Numerous scholars are skeptical of this development, in part because the marketing literature does not demonstrate that consumers derive information about the quality of a product from the use of a mark associated with a noncompetitive product.[129]

Others have already delved into these expansions. I touch upon some of them—anti-dilution, doctrine of initial interest confusion, rights against noncommercial speech, and rights for the mere possibility of market expansion—to note how rewarding creativity in trademark law might have contributed to this growth in protective scope, often in ways beyond the traditional justifications of trademark law.

Trademark anti-dilution allows certain trademark holders to guard against use of their mark to protect a mark's distinctiveness even when there is no consumer confusion.[130] Some states began protecting against dilution in the mid-twentieth century, and Congress passed an anti-dilution law in 1996.[131] The federal law currently protects marks that are sufficiently famous against dilution by blurring—such as how a car marked as COCA-COLA might blur the soft drink's mark—and by tarnishment—such as a Coca-Cola-style logo, "Enjoy Cocaine."[132] For holders of sufficiently famous marks, dilution laws guard those marks even when

[126] *Cf. id.* at 235 (critiquing "the recent trend towards conceiving of trademarks as property-equivalents coupled with the growth of state anti-dilution ... [which] suggest[s] that trademark owners have been reconceived as quasi-authors, who by creating a set of meanings in the minds of consumers, are rewarded with judicial recognition of increasingly exclusive rights to prevent others from 'misappropriating' this quasi-property" (footnote omitted)).

[127] *See generally* Fromer, *supra* note 1 (examining creativity in the patent and copyright arenas); *supra* text accompanying notes 53–60 (recounting the central role of creativity in intellectual property law).

[128] Mark P. McKenna, *Testing Modern Trademark Law's Theory of Harm*, 95 Iowa L. Rev. 63, 67–68 (2009); *see also* Greg Lastowka, *Google's Law*, 73 Brook. L. Rev. 1327, 1367–71 (2008) (describing how trademark dilution and the doctrine of initial interest confusion have grown); Lisa P. Ramsey, *Free Speech and International Obligations to Protect Trademarks*, 35 Yale J. Int'l L. 405, 407 (2010) (discussing how trademark law has been applied to prohibit some forms of noncommercial speech, as well as commercial speech that is not misleading).

[129] McKenna, *supra* note 128, at 70–71. The same critique might be leveled against the Lanham Act's constructive protection of marks nationwide, even if they are used in a limited subset of the United States. Carter, *supra* note 63, at 760.

[130] Lastowka, *supra* note 128, at 1367.

[131] *Id.* (citing Federal Trademark Dilution Act of 1995, Pub. L. No. 104-98, § 3(a), 109 Stat. 985, 985–96 (codified at 15 U.S.C. § 1125(c))). Congress revised the law in 2006. Trademark Dilution Revision Act of 2006, Pub. L. No. 109-312, 120 Stat. 1730 (codified as amended at 15 U.S.C. §§ 1052, 1063, 1064, 1092, 1125, 1127).

[132] *See* 15 U.S.C. § 1125(c)(2)(B)–(C) (2006) (defining dilution by blurring as an "association arising from the similarity between a mark or trade name and a famous mark that impairs the distinctiveness of the famous mark," and dilution by tarnishment as an "association arising from the similarity between a mark or trade name and a famous mark that harms the reputation of the famous mark"). The second Coca-Cola example derives from Coca-Cola Co. v. Gemini Rising, Inc., 346 F. Supp. 1183, 1188 (E.D.N.Y. 1972).

consumers do not think that the Coca-Cola Company offered up a COCA-COLA car or an "Enjoy Cocaine" logo. Some commentators criticize anti-dilution laws as thereby being unmoored from trademark law's basic purpose of promoting trade by protecting against consumer confusion.[133] As such, the underpinning notion of protecting creativity in choosing distinctive marks might have, in part, motivated anti-dilution laws' aim of guarding distinctiveness standing alone. This goal, however, is at most weakly connected to the essential role of promoting creativity in trademark law, so as to ensure a strong link between a chosen mark and the actual goods or services the mark signifies.

Another expansion of trademark law is the range of actionable consumer confusion. Frequently noted is the doctrine of initial interest confusion, by which consumers who were at some point confused by a mark's source are no longer confused by the time of purchase.[134] For example, this doctrine might be employed to find trademark infringement when a goods provider puts up a highway a billboard advertising a competitor's store at a particular exit, when only the first provider has a store there.[135] Any consumer who goes to the store will not be confused as to the goods' source by the time of purchase, yet the Ninth Circuit has stated that this scenario can constitute trademark infringement.[136] A similar—and more common—situation is when consumers searching on the internet for a particular mark are misdirected to a competitor's; any consumer confusion is usually dispelled upon reaching the competitor's site. As with dilution law, given the lack of consumer confusion at any critical juncture—here, the point of sale—this doctrine arguably extends beyond the fundamental purposes of trademark law.[137] The promotion of creativity in trademark law might again have played a role in this expansion of actionable confusion, by trying to protect the goodwill developed in linking distinctive marks to goods and services. Just as with dilution law, however, this protection has a tenuous connection to the creativity that trademark law seeks to foster between linking marks to goods or services to promote trade.

A similar analysis might be applied to courts' findings of trademark infringement for use of a mark in noncommercial speech. In one notorious case, People for the Ethical Treatment of Animals (PETA) sued a person who had registered the website *peta.org* and hosted there a parody about "People Eating Tasty Animals."[138]

[133] *See, e.g.*, Lastowka, *supra* note 128, at 1369; Rebecca Tushnet, *Gone in Sixty Milliseconds: Trademark Law and Cognitive Science*, 86 TEX. L. REV. 507, 508–11 (2008). *But cf.* Barton Beebe, *A Defense of the New Federal Trademark Antidilution Law*, 16 FORDHAM INTELL. PROP. MEDIA & ENT. L. J. 1143, 1174 (2006) (arguing that the current federal law is relatively narrower than dilution theory); Clarisa Long, *Dilution*, 106 COLUM. L. REV. 1029, 1029–33 (2006) (sifting through judicial decisions on federal dilution, and finding that dilution is narrowly interpreted and not easily found).

[134] Lastowka, *supra* note 128, at 1369–71; Jennifer E. Rothman, *Initial Interest Confusion: Standing at the Crossroads of Trademark Law*, 27 CARDOZO L. REV. 105, 106–14 (2005).

[135] Brookfield Commc'ns, Inc. v. W. Coast Entm't Corp., 174 F.3d 1036, 1064 (9th Cir. 1999).

[136] *Id. But cf.* MultiTime Machine, Inc. v. Amazon.com, Inc., 804 F.3d 930 (9th Cir. 2015) (finding no initial interest confusion, though at least formally finding it actionable).

[137] *Brookfield*, 174 F.3d at 106–14.

[138] PETA v. Doughney, 263 F.3d 359, 362–63 (4th Cir. 2001).

In that case, the Fourth Circuit rejected a parody defense[139] and found trademark infringement because the operation of *peta.org* "prevented users from obtaining or using PETA's goods or services" and "provide[d] links to more than 30 commercial operations offering goods and services."[140] Putting aside that this case might also be an application of the doctrine of initial interest confusion, it seems to impose a prohibition on many forms of noncommercial speech. Again, by rewarding creativity in choosing distinctive marks, trademark doctrine might be making a leap toward the propertization of these marks, even when the allegedly infringing use is not in commerce.

As a final example, Mark Lemley and Mark McKenna express skepticism with protecting the possibility of market expansion via trademark law. They discuss the practice of finding trademark infringement as to a class of goods or services in which the trademark holder is not currently engaged on the basis that the holder might expand their market.[141] They reason that:

> [I]t's not clear why we would give ownership of the term ("Exxon" as applied to gloves, for example) to the first user of that mark in a different market (Exxon Oil company) rather than the first user in the new market (the company that had first used the term for gloves). Indeed, trademark law has always assumed the opposite: trademark rights are awarded on the basis of first use of a mark in a particular geographic and product market.[142]

A basis to shield trademark holders from noncompetitive uses by others may be to protect their opportunities for market expansion down the road and against free-riding.[143] Assuming some marks for particular goods or services are more attractive intrinsically than others, then, allowing expansive protection of a mark can raise barriers to entry in ways that undermine competition, precisely contrary to trademark law's purposes.[144] Again, rewarding creativity in choosing distinctive marks to link to one's goods or services might cause courts to award rights in the distinctive marks unlinked from those goods or services.

The important role of creativity in trademark law stems from building up a link between a mark and a particular set of goods and services.[145] Rewarding creativity

[139] *Id.* at 366–67.
[140] *Id.* at 365–66.
[141] *See* Lemley & McKenna, *supra* note 118, at 179.
[142] *Id.*
[143] *Id.* at 187.
[144] Beebe & Fromer, *supra* note 122.
[145] *Cf.* Aoki, *supra* note 118, at 241 ("Anti-dilution and misappropriation law to the contrary, it does not necessarily follow that property in a set of meanings that extend beyond a mark's signalling function should be allocated exclusively to the trademark owner."); Lemley & McKenna, Aoki, *supra* note 118, at 172 ("Whether or not we need to allocate additional markets to authors and playwrights in order to motivate them to create books and plays, it seems implausible to think that we need to award rights in words themselves in order to motivate the creation and use of new trademarks.").

in choosing a distinctive mark divorced from that particular set of goods and services or from trademark law's fundamental goals seems to move away from the precise (and derivative) role of creativity in trademark law in the first place. There is good reason to think that the narrow role of creativity in trademark law ought to inform trademark law's scope in granting and limiting rights.[146] Trademark law ought to encourage businesses that act creatively by building a link between a mark and its goods or services. In this vein, trademark law encourages businesses to use a mark that is highly distinctive of its goods and services, thereby promoting the role of creativity in trademark law to advance the goals of trade, reduction of consumer confusion, and promotion of quality in underlying goods and services. In this way, the role of creativity is essential to trademark law's goals. It steers businesses toward certain marks and away from others as a way to control grants and limitations of rights. However, trademark law should be wary of rewarding creativity in choosing distinctive marks in and of themselves, unmoored from their use on particular goods or services in commerce and their role in causing consumer confusion.

[146] *Cf.* Aoki, *supra* note 118, at 247 ("Anti-dilution theory, however, is all the more curious because of the complete absence of an explicit authorial figure in trademark law, whose personal (as opposed to economic) interests would be served by protecting a mark from 'unauthorized' downstream modifications by non-competing users.").

3

Logo Hacking, Downmarket Irony, and Counterfeit Chic

A Study of Contemporary Fashion Trends and Their Implications for Trademark Laws

David Tan

Introduction

Fashion is a whimsical creature, but at the same time it is a lucrative industry. In *The State of Fashion 2019* report jointly released by The Business of Fashion and McKinsey & Company, it was observed that:

> The ones who will succeed will have to come to terms with the fact that in the new paradigm that is taking shape around them, some of the old rules simply don't work ... They need to ... have the courage to 'self-disrupt' their own identity and the sources of their old success in order to realize these changes and win new generations of customers.[1]

Established luxury or heritage fashion houses such as Gucci, Louis Vuitton, and Balenciaga are doing precisely that: hiring irreverent designers to revamp their brands, inventing a new vernacular in fashion vocabulary that introduces terms like "logo hacking" and "downmarket irony," and capturing the attention and pockets of the mobile-obsessed millennial generation with Instagram-worthy designs. Even Donatella Versace herself has resorted to reproducing the Ford Motor Company's logo as a recurring motif on shirts and sportswear for the iconic Versace brand in the Fall–Winter 2019 runway collection unveiled in Milan.[2]

Self-disruption is the top-ranked trend that fashion executives predict will shape the fashion industry in the immediate future,[3] and this is epitomized by logo

[1] The Business of Fashion & McKinsey & Company, The State of Fashion 2019 11 (2019) https://www.mckinsey.com/~/media/McKinsey/Industries/Retail/Our%20Insights/The%20state%20of%20fashion%202020%20Navigating%20uncertainty/The-State-of-Fashion-2020-final.ashx.

[2] Luke Leitch, *Fall 2019: Menswear*, Vogue (Jan. 13, 2019), https://www.vogue.com/fashion-shows/fall-2019-menswear/versace. Leitch commented: "The logo-heavy interaction with Ford was a little strange, especially in the context of an Italian thoroughbred asserting its aristocracy, but deals are deals."

[3] *Id.* at 17.

David Tan, *Logo Hacking, Downmarket Irony, and Counterfeit Chic* In: *Charting Limitations on Trademark Rights.* Edited by: Haochen Sun and Barton Beebe, Oxford University Press. © David Tan 2023.
DOI: 10.1093/oso/9780198871248.003.0004

hacking, downmarket irony, and counterfeit chic. This is unsurprising since heritage brands like Gucci and Balenciaga are enjoying soaring profits by paradoxically selling merchandise bearing misspellings of their famous marks (e.g., GUCCY) and ill-fitting ugly clothes.[4] As these brands gravitate toward new logos, social causes, streetwear, and celebrity collaborations to create a cooler image among a younger demographic, some of these developments also present specific challenges to the established doctrines of trademark law. Fashion does not refer simply to clothes, but to clothes in relation to identity, society, and politics. It can be regarded as a "manufactured cultural object... [and] as a set social relations and communicative systems."[5] Essentially, dressed bodies become texts, creating "spaces of uniformity and conformity as well as spaces of conflict... in which vestimentary signs and individual and social identity dialogue and translate each other."[6] This chapter critically evaluates the prevailing trends in luxury fashion and their potential impact on our current understanding of trademark infringement and dilution laws.

I. Understanding a New Fashion Vocabulary

Fashion today has moved out of well-established formats and into new tightly interwoven digital cross-media multiplatform genres.[7] Intellectual property laws have not begun to contemplate how fashion studies as a field can bring valuable interdisciplinary insights to the legal domain of copyright and trademarks. Within fashion studies, fashion scholars are looking increasingly to media and communication studies for theoretical concepts and methodologies so as to comprehend more fully "a domain characterized by finely attuned signs and semiotic distinction."[8]

Vetements (meaning "clothing" in French), the contemporary fashion hackers *par excellence*, have proven themselves to be the experts at creating "viral" garments, items that have the irony and popularity of Internet memes, with as much life online as off.[9] The brand's phenomenal success is intimately tied to its deep

[4] Dhani Mau, *Millennials Bought a Lot of Gucci in 2018*, Fashionista (Feb. 12, 2019), https://fashionista.com/2019/02/gucci-kering-revenue-profits-fy-2018; Dhani Mau, *Balenciaga is about to Hit a Major Revenue Milestone*, Fashionista (Apr. 24, 2019), https://fashionista.com/2019/04/balenciaga-sales-growth-1-billion-euros. *See also* Andrea Cheng, *Why Everyone is into Ugly Fashion: An Explainer*, Fashionista (Nov. 14, 2017), https://fashionista.com/2017/06/ugly-fashion-mainstream-trend; *Does Gucci's £1,800 Shell Suit Signal the Return of the 1980s' Worst Look?*, The Guardian (June 25, 2019), https://www.theguardian.com/fashion/shortcuts/2019/jun/25/gucci-1800-pound-shell-suit-return-1980s-worst-look?.

[5] Chiara Battisti & Leif Dahlberg, *Focus: Law, Fashion and Identities*, 10 Pólemos 1, 2 (2006).

[6] *Id.* at 4.

[7] Synne Skjulstad, *Vetements, Memes, and Connectivity: Fashion Media in the Era of Instagram*, 24 Fashion Theory 181, 184 (2018).

[8] *Id.* at 6.

[9] Emma Hope Allwood, *The Fashion Meme: How Clothes Went Viral*, Dazed (Mar. 30, 2016), https://www.dazeddigital.com/fashion/article/30561/1/the-fashion-meme-vetements-vetememes-viral-clothes-dhl.

understanding of contemporary digital media culture and its adroit social media practices. A "fashion meme" refers to "fashion designed for prospective and collaborative mediation and design practices" and is thus "a product or a garment designed like an Internet meme, for being *copied, changed, modified, shared, spread, and commented*."[10] This approach, with fashion brands Vetements and Balenciaga under the creative direction of Demna Gvasalia being paradigmatic examples, situates the brands in the center of discursive activity in the community, as audiences and consumers are invited to actively participate in commentary, debate, parody, satire, and pastiche. As *Dazed Digital*'s Head of Fashion, Emma Hope Allwood commented, "[w]hile once being transformed into meme was a mark of derision, now it's a signifier of cultural relevance, to be encouraged rather than feared."[11] This trend stands in stark contrast to a design or a trademark traditionally conceived of as an original and not to be tampered with—one that exists in a reverential rights-based system that frowns against copying and imitation.

As the creative director for Vetements and Balenciaga, Demna Gvasalia's present cult status within the fashion industry can be polarizing. His appeal to an increasingly affluent younger generation obsessed with social media and a quest to appear "authentic" is legendary, but others who desire elegantly tailored clothes will naturally find his antics to be repellent and view his fame as transitory. Regardless, in the latter half of the 2010s, the "Vetements aesthetic" has spread like a virus across the world of luxury high fashion. His runway show models were scouted almost entirely from Instagram and Facebook. Gvasalia continues in the tradition of fashion hackers like Martin Margiela and Rei Kawakubo for Comme des Garçons (who will deconstruct clothes from the way they are traditionally worn and reconstruct them into a new shape or volume) and logo hackers like Moschino (who will appropriate famous logos and subvert them in a playful manner). Hacking in the fashion world is neither sinister nor destructive. Although it is often done to prove a point, share information, and subvert prevailing codes to create something new, clever, and elegant,[12] it is undeniably lucrative for the fashion brands, and especially for Gucci and Vetements.

"Logo hacking" was taken perhaps to the extreme by Gucci under the creative direction of Alessandro Michele who possibly started the trend of "self-hacking" among the luxury fashion brands.[13] When graffiti artist Trevor Andrew, a.k.a.

[10] Skjulstad, *supra* note 7, at 8. On Internet memes, *see, e.g.*, Limor Shifman, *The Cultural Logic of Photo-Based Meme Genres*, 13(3) J. VISUAL CULTURE 340 (2014).

[11] Allwood, *supra* note 9.

[12] Clara Yong, *What Fashion Hacking is and How It's Redefining the Industry*, FASHION MAGAZINE (May 3, 2017), https://fashionmagazine.com/fashion/fashion-hacking/.

[13] *See also* Steff Yotka, *Louis Vuitton's Stephen Sprouse Collaboration Turns 20—And Is Still One of the Best Logo Hacks Around*, VOGUE (May 6, 2021), https://www.vogue.com/article/louis-vuitton-stephen-sprouse-collaboration-20-years-later; Andrea Saadan, *Gucci "Hacked" Balenciaga For New Aria Collection and the Internet Went Wild*, TATLER (Apr. 16, 2021), https://www.tatlerasia.com/style/fashion/hk-gucci-balenciaga-aria-collection-2021; Helen Yu, *Balenciaga "Hacked" Gucci Back for Its SS22 Collection*, TATLER (June 7, 2021), https://www.tatlerasia.com/style/fashion/hk-balenciaga-gucci-hack-ss22-collection.

GucciGhost, who in late 2013 and 2014 scrawled the label's signatures all over Brooklyn and Manhattan, Gucci did not respond with a copyright-infringement suit or a cease-and-desist order. Instead Michele extended an invitation to Andrew to make clothes together, and the collaboration was presented in the Fall–Winter 2016 collection.[14] Logo hacking was taken to the next level when in the Gucci Cruise 2018 collection, Michele unveiled the "GUCCY" motif—which created a frenzy on social media—that was a deliberate mocking of poorly made Gucci knock-offs. Indeed Gucci has reclaimed "GUCCY" from the counterfeiters and have turned it into an asset for the brand as it continues to develop clothing, bags, and accessories with the "GUCCY" motif alongside its official "GUCCI" logo. In a surprising postmodern turn, Gucci has articulated its own countercultural statement by parodying its own bootlegs by selling, among other merchandise, a sweater that resembles a bad counterfeit, with Gucci replaced by "GUCCY," for £950.[15] It seems that this decision to sell a line of "GUCCY" products, a logo that parodied the luxury industry's problem with counterfeits and *shanzhai* products,[16] was perceived to be witty by Chinese consumers who made up 30% of Gucci's worldwide sales of US$7.2 billion in 2017.[17] It was a gambit that paid off handsomely. Scottish artist/art director Hey Reilly commented that

> the best or most powerful fashion labels can play with their icons because the message is still about them. It appears that the message and meaning of brands and logos can still operate even when disturbed: they continue to transmit powerful statements of status and identity, even when presented in bastardized form.[18]

The semiotic sign of "GUCCI" when subverted by its very brand owner to become "GUCCY" is communicating a message that the luxury symbol is cool, hip, irreverent, and, most importantly, relevant to the millennial generation.

Fashion journalist Sarah Mower writing for *Vogue* called this form of brandalism—a portmanteau of brand and vandalism—"conscious self-parody."[19] It was commented that:

[14] Frank Bruni, *Alessandro Michele, Fashion's Modern Mastermind*, N.Y. Times Style Magazine (Oct. 15, 2018), https://www.nytimes.com/2018/10/15/t-magazine/alessandro-michele-gucci-interview.html.

[15] *Id.*

[16] *See* Section II.

[17] Susanna Nicoletti, *The New Logo-Restyling Mania. A Risk or an Opportunity in China?*, Jing Daily (Jan. 8, 2019), https://jingdaily.com/logo-restyling-mania/; Faith Cooper, *Gucci Strikes Red: China's Love Affair with Gucci*, Fashion History Timeline (Mar. 8, 2019), https://fashionhistory.fitnyc.edu/gucci-strikes-red/.

[18] Katie Baron, *Why Brandalism Has Become a Luxury Brand's New Best Friend*, Forbes (June 4, 2018), https://www.forbes.com/sites/katiebaron/2018/06/04/why-brandalism-has-become-a-luxury-brands-new-best-friend/#2a88c81949cf.

[19] Sarah Mower, *Gucci: Resort 2018*, Vogue (May 30, 2017), https://www.vogue.com/fashion-shows/resort-2018/gucci.

> While it arguably looks somewhat like a spelling mistake, the primitive spelling of the name is an ironic jab at the momentous presence of knock-offs that are sold in droves—both from physical retailers and online – around the world. This particular spelling of the name was incredibly popular with counterfeit retailers in the 1980s.[20]

This "counterfeit chic" movement does not remain exclusively within the domain of luxury fashion brands to re-appropriate *shanzhai* and counterfeit practices for themselves by designing and selling what appears to be cheap and poor copies for the usual designer premium prices. In 2018, Diesel created a pop-up store on Canal Street in SoHo New York that sold official "DEISEL" clothing, with Renzo Rosso, the founder of Diesel, commenting that a brand can create its own fakes and embrace its own imitation.[21] This "self-hacking" trend, while popular with customers willing to pay top dollar for fake-looking authentic products, is likely to result in problems for enforcement of intellectual property rights in the future. Some questions have already been raised:

> Will high fashion's whirlwind upside-down, inside-out, love/hate relationship with bootlegging create consumer confusion and what are the long-term repercussions? ... Will Gucci to "Guccy" lessen the stigma and condition shoppers to view counterfeit goods as socially acceptable?[22]

The fashion brand Vetements is organized as a creative collective by seven designers who initially remained anonymous, but subsequently Georgian creative director Demna Gvasalia became the most profiled designer and was synonymous with the brand. Gvasalia had arguably brought anti-fashion back to fashion in its Spring–Summer 2016 runway collection when Vetements paraded a DHL T-shirt with a price tag of £185.[23] According to trends analyst Aleksandra Szymanska of the Future Laboratory: "They are hacking the fashion system ... and they're credible [enough] to make these statements of capitalist kitsch."[24] Szymanska also believes that unlike the logomania phenomenon in the 2000s, when a luxury brand's logo—Louis Vuitton's LV or Chanel's double-C—was an ostentatious symbol of the wealth of the wearer, fashion brands today use non-fashion logos that plug into the

[20] Emma Portelli Bonnici, *Putting the "Y" in Gucci*, Times of Malta (Nov. 24, 2018), https://timesofmalta.com/articles/view/putting-the-y-in-gucci.695003.

[21] Matthew Schneier, *To Knock Out Knockoffs, Knock Off Knockoffs*, N.Y. Times (Feb. 11, 2018), https://www.nytimes.com/2018/02/11/fashion/diesel-deisel-new-york-fashion-week-pop-up.html.

[22] J'Net Nguyen, *Fake Gucci to Real Guccy: Fashion's Identity Crisis or Alter Ego?*, The Right Brain Studio (Feb. 8, 2018), https://www.therightbrainstudio.com/fake-gucci-real-guccy-fashions-identity-crisis-alter-ego/.

[23] Lauren Cochrane, *Scam or Subversion? How a DHL T-shirt Became this Year's Must-Have*, The Guardian (Apr. 20, 2016), https://www.theguardian.com/fashion/2016/apr/19/dhl-t-shirt-vetements-fashion-paris-catwalk.

[24] *Id.*

cool vibe of the millennial generation, "because they are catnip on social media, where visual gags rule."[25] Synne Skjulstad observes that it is "achieved by way of a distinctive blend of unexpected moves, humor, irony, and contradictory intellectual anti-conceptualism, one which permeates both [Vetements'] collections and public profile."[26] The Vetements line of clothing is carried in more than 200 stores worldwide in 2016, and Guram Gvasalia, Demna's brother and Vetements' chief executive, cites sales in the eight figures.[27] The Vetements aesthetic is characterized by a "calculated disruption and assault on the status quo" and essentially "taking the products that each individual label is known for or does best (T-shirts for Hanes, heels for Manolo Blahnik) and reworking it à la Vetements, which often amounts to a sort of creative defacement,"[28] and then charging customers a high price for these. Although not all the brands initially gave their permission, for many of the globally recognized companies that Gvasalia approached, the opportunity to be part of the Vetements aesthetic—and consequently garnering widespread attention on social media—was simply irresistible. The phrase "to Vetementize" was born.[29] Skjulstad astutely notes that:

> Vetements has become a key player in the advancement of a distinctive stylistic universe where a nostalgic aestheticization of post-Soviet visual culture clearly breaks with the glamorous representations tided to a semiotic system of high-culture, which historically have been central to the mediation of major fashion brands. However, Vetements means business, and may laugh all the way to the bank.[30]

These "hackings" or reworkings of popular yet often inexpensive products sold by renowned streetwear brands such as Hanes t-shirts, Champion hoodies, and Levi's denim jeans, and the ubiquitous bright yellow DHL logo t-shirts, have also been referred to as the "downmarket irony": the trend for luxury fashion brands to create designs that have the look of bootleg creations found at cheap market stalls.[31] The

[25] *Id.*

[26] Skjulstad, *supra* note 7, at 9.

[27] Matthew Schneier, *Vetements Bring Its Brand of Disruption to Couture*, N.Y. Times (July 1, 2016), https://www.nytimes.com/2016/07/03/fashion/vetements-couture.html?searchResultPosition=6.

[28] *Id.*

[29] *Id.*

[30] Skjulstad, *supra* note 7, at 9. Gvasalia himself said: "I wanted to take an expensive silhouette and deliberately subvert the purpose of the garment by using a tacky material." Elizabeth Paton, *Who is Demna Gvasalia, Balenciaga's New Designer?*, N.Y. Times (Oct. 7, 2015), https://www.nytimes.com/2015/10/08/fashion/demna-gvasalia-balenciaga-new-artistic-director.html.

[31] Lauren Cochrane, *It's a Rip-Off: Now Bootleg Logos are a Fashion Must-Have*, The Guardian (Dec. 30, 2017), https://www.theguardian.com/fashion/2017/dec/30/bootleg-logos-designers-copyright-fashion. In October 2006, fashion designer Marc Jacobs shocked the world of high fashion by sending models down the runway for Louis Vuitton carrying cheap-looking checked tote bags reminiscent of the ugly plaid nylon canvas ones which are ubiquitous in Chinatown and carried by rural workers in the People's Republic of China. Perceived then to be a marketing gimmick, established fashion brands nonetheless adhered to more traditional aesthetics, albeit with sporadic deviations, until designers

present aesthetic objectives for brands like Gucci and Balenciaga appear to be to make their logos look as cheap and as ugly as possible on their clothing, and then charge a high price for these products.

In her analysis of semiotic disobedience, Sonia Katyal explains that a reader may choose to adopt the preferred reading of a particular "text," but also might "resist and modify the code to reflect his or her 'own positions, experiences, and interests.'"[32] While some antibranding projects adopt an oppositional framework to a certain brand, the more complex commentaries such as Gvasalia's, however, adopt Stuart Hall's tactic of negotiation, perhaps "seeking to both decode and recode particular images in ways that subtly reveal the need for consumers to actively 'talk back' to the hidden codes."[33] However, Demna Gvasalia announced his departure from Vetements in September 2019,[34] and it remains to be seen if Vetements will continue to exert its disproportionate influence in the fashion world, but it seems certain that Gvasalia's individual stardom—especially with his continuation of the Vetements aesthetic at the couture house of Balenciaga in Paris—will be a force to be reckoned with.

Even Versace, a brand that emphasizes glamour, sexiness, and celebrity star power, has recently fallen victim to these trends by collaborating with Ford Motor Company to reproduce the Ford logo on hoodies, t-shirts, and track pants in its Fall–Winter 2019 men's runway collection.[35] As fashion journalist Luke Leitch noted, such partnerships are not always successful: "The logo-heavy interaction with Ford was a little strange, especially in the context of an Italian thoroughbred asserting its aristocracy."[36] In 2017, David Fischer observed, "I was meeting with a luxury brand recently, and they were talking about not being exclusive anymore—about being inclusive. And I thought that was pretty interesting, because I know they wouldn't have said that a year ago."[37] Fischer is entirely accurate that luxury and exclusivity are at this point in time no longer synonymous.

In summary, the overarching theme of self-disruption that underpins the fashionable vernacular of logo hacking, downmarket irony, and counterfeit chic is

Alessandro Michele and Demna Gvasalia shattered the mold in 2015 when they were appointed creative directors of the heritage luxury houses of Gucci and Balenciaga. *See* MARIA MACKINNEY-VALENTIN, FASHIONING IDENTITY: STATUS AMBIVALENCE IN CONTEMPORARY FASHION (2017) 54–56.

[32] Sonia Katyal, *Stealth Marketing and Antibranding: The Love that Dare Not Speak Its Name*, 58 BUFFALO L. REV. 796, 806 (2010).

[33] *Id.* at 806.

[34] Miles Socha, *Exclusive: Demna Gvasalia Exits Vetements*, WWD (Sept. 16, 2019), https://wwd.com/fashion-news/designer-luxury/demna-gvasalia-exits-vetements-exclusive-1203283590/.

[35] Luke Leitch, *Versace: Fall 2019 Menswear*, VOGUE (Jan. 13, 2019), https://www.vogue.com/fashion-shows/fall-2019-menswear/versace.

[36] *Id.*

[37] Eugene Rabkin, *Op Ed: How Luxury Fashion is Reduced to Logomania*, HIGHSNOBIETY (Aug. 27, 2019), https://www.highsnobiety.com/p/luxury-fashion-appeal-lost-today/.

likely to have significant implications for trademark laws as applied to the world of fashion. The rest of this chapter will explore some possible influences.

II. Trademarks, Fashion, and Cultural Symbolism

A trademark is as symbolic as it is functional: it does much more than designate source or origin of goods. Judicial and scholarly treatment of trademark law are increasingly referring to the semiotic nature of trademarks. Umberto Eco describes semiotics as a social science discipline that studies "everything that can be taken as a sign."[38] A sign is simply a thing that stands for something else. Although it has its origins in the study of language, semiotic analysis is a trans-linguistic activity[39] that can be applied to the inquiry of "[a system] of structural codes ... that engages with culture, consumption, and communication in the marketplace."[40] The Swiss linguist, Ferdinand de Saussure is widely credited as the most influential scholar in the field of semiotics. He emphasized the nature of the sign as the coded association of a material *signifier*, such as the sound of a word, with a *signified* or preconceived meaning.[41] In his oft-cited work on the semiotic analyses of consumer cultures, *Mythologies*, Roland Barthes explains that "any semiology postulates a relation between two terms, a signifier and a signified"[42] and that a sign "is the associative total of the first two terms."[43]

In particular the application of semiotics to assist the development of intellectual property laws relating to logos, images, and literary works has received significant scholarly attention. For example, Barton Beebe, in his seminal works on a semiotic account of trademark doctrine,[44] has persuasively demonstrated that "semiotic concepts can be applied to clarify and ameliorate fundamental areas of trademark doctrine and policy."[45] I have also investigated the influence of semiotics on the laws relating to works of copyright,[46] famous

[38] UMBERTO ECO, THE THEORY OF SIGNS 7 (1979).

[39] ROLAND BARTHES, ELEMENTS OF SEMIOLOGY 11 (Annette Lavers & Colin Smith trans., 2000) (1964).

[40] LAURA R. OSWALD, MARKETING SEMIOTICS: SIGNS, STRATEGIES, AND BRAND VALUES 47 (2012).

[41] *See generally* FERDINAND DE SAUSURRE, THE COURSE IN GENERAL LINGUISTICS (COURS DE LINIGUISTIQUE GÉNÉRALE) (Roy Harris trans., 1983) (1916).

[42] ROLAND BARTHES, MYTHOLOGIES 111 (Annette Lavers trans., 1972) (1957).

[43] *Id.*

[44] *See, e.g.*, Barton Beebe, *The Semiotic Account of Trademark Doctrine and Trademark Culture*, *in* TRADEMARK LAW AND THEORY: A HANDBOOK OF CONTEMPORARY RESEARCH 42 (Graeme B. Dinwoodie & Mark D. Janis eds., 2008) (hereinafter Beebe, *Semiotic Account*); Barton Beebe, *The Semiotic Analysis of Trademark Law*, 51 U.C.L.A. L. REV. 621 (2004) (hereinafter Beebe, *Semiotic Analysis*).

[45] Beebe, *Semiotic Account*, *supra* note 44, at 42.

[46] David Tan, *The Lost Language of the First Amendment in Copyright Fair Use: A Semiotic Perspective of the "Transformative Use" Doctrine Twenty-Five Years On*, 26 FORDHAM IP, MEDIA & ENT. L. J. 311 (2016).

marks,[47] and the commercial appropriation of the celebrity personality in the right of publicity.[48]

It has been said that famous marks or well-known brands like Louis Vuitton, Apple, and Nike are *alpha brands* that carry significant "semiotic freight," and they possess particular configurations of meanings and can "offer peculiarly powerful affirmations of belonging, recognition, and meaning in the midst of the lives of their [consumers]."[49] It is precisely this symbolic nature of the Saussurean sign which "embeds structural semiotics in the culture of consumers"[50] that will drive consumption behavior in modern society. Oswald contends that semiotics

> does not stop with a structural analysis, but identifies ways brand meanings are embedded in broad cultural myths, social organization, and beliefs of the target market. The brand system resembles *la langue*, the term that Saussure gives to the system of linguistic codes that defines the range of possibilities for producing discourses.[51]

For famous marks, the brand signifier–signified relationship would have become universally codified for the consuming public; these consumers will automatically and consistently think of the coded brand meanings and values (the signified) when they are exposed to the signifiers such as the logo. Thus, the brand logo or trademark becomes a sign for a predetermined set of cultural codes and consumer experiences associated with the brand. But the relationship between the individual consumer and the brand (as represented by the trademark) is not "a unidirectional flow of information from good to buyer, but rather a dialogic process bordering on co-authorship,"[52] and brands are ultimately valuable to the consumer because of the "identity performances" they enable.[53] Thus, when Gucci introduces the subverted sign "GUCCY" alongside the ubiquitous well-loved "GUCCI," it is drawing on the consuming public's familiarity with the affective encoded meanings associated with "GUCCI," and advancing a new cultural narrative that resonates better with the millennial generation evident by the increased sales.

The U.S. Supreme Court in the twin decisions of *Matal v. Tam*[54] and *Iancu v. Brunetti*[55] emphatically recognized that trademarks "have an expressive

[47] David Tan, *The Semiotics of Alpha Brands: Encoding/Decoding/Recoding/Transcoding of Louis Vuitton and Implications for Trademark Laws*, 32 Cardozo Arts & Ent. L. J. 221 (2013).

[48] David Tan, The Commercial Appropriation of Fame: A Cultural Analysis of the Right of Publicity and Passing Off (2007); David Tan, *Political Recoding of the Contemporary Celebrity and the First Amendment*, 2 Harv. J. Sp. & Ent. L. 1 (2011); David Tan, *Affective Transfer & the Appropriation of Commercial Value: A Cultural Analysis of the Right of Publicity*, 9 Va. Sp. & Ent. L. J. 272 (2010).

[49] Tan, *supra* note 47, at 224.

[50] Oswald, *supra* note 40, at 48.

[51] *Id.* at 50.

[52] Mario Biagioli et al., *Brands R Us*, *in* The Luxury Economy and Intellectual Property: Critical Reflections 79 (Haochen Sun et al. eds., 2015).

[53] *Id.* at 81.

[54] Matal v. Tam, 137 S.Ct. 1744 (2017).

[55] Iancu v. Brunetti, 139 S.Ct. 2294 (2019).

component in addition to a commercial one."[56] In *Matal v. Tam*, a 2017 Supreme Court decision which declared that the disparagement clause of the Lanham Act[57] violated the First Amendment, Justice Alito held that trademarks are private speech,[58] and the prohibition of the registration of such offensive trademarks constituted constitutionally impermissible viewpoint discrimination.[59] The case concerned a dance-rock band's application for federal trademark registration of the band's name, "THE SLANTS." "Slants" is perceived to be a derogatory term for persons of Asian descent, and members of the band are Asian-Americans. But the band members believed that "by taking that slur as the name of their group, they will help to 'reclaim' the term and drain its denigrating force."[60] The eight-justice court was divided evenly between two opinions and could not agree on the overall framework for deciding the case. But all the justices agreed on two propositions: (i) if a trademark registration bar is viewpoint based, it is unconstitutional; and (ii) the disparagement bar was viewpoint based. All eight justices agreed that the provision violated the First Amendment because it discriminated on the basis of viewpoint. More explicitly, in a separate judgment by Justice Kennedy, with whom Justices Ginsburg, Sotomayor, and Kagan joined, it was noted that

> [i]n the realm of trademarks, the metaphorical marketplace of ideas becomes a tangible, powerful reality... These marks make up the expression of everyday life, as with the names of entertainment groups, broadcast networks, *designer clothing*, newspapers, automobiles, candy bars, toys, and so on.[61]

This view of the *expressive* cultural symbolism of trademarks was affirmed in *Iancu* where a majority of the Supreme Court in 2019 found that the Lanham Act's prohibition on the registration of immoral or scandalous trademarks[62] was viewpoint based and hence unconstitutional. In the plurality opinion delivered by Justice Kagan, in which Justices Thomas, Ginsburg, Alito, Gorsuch, and Kavanaugh joined, it was essentially an affirmation of the central tenet in *Matal*, that "[t]he

56 *Id.* at 2305.

57 Lanham Act 15 U.S.C. § 1052(a). The disparagement clause prohibits the registration of trademarks that may disparage or bring into contempt or disrepute any persons, living or dead.

58 *Matal*, 137 S.Ct. at 1760.

59 *Id.* at 1763.

60 *Id.* at 1750.

61 *Id.* at 1768 (emphasis added). The applicant Simon Tam has argued that he wanted to use "The Slants" to "supplant a racial epithet, using new insights, musical talents, and wry humor to make it a badge of pride," thus subverting "an offensive term for the positive purpose of celebrating all that Asian-Americans can and do contribute to our diverse Nation." *Id.* at 1766–67. The First Circuit has also pointed out that "[f]amous trademarks offer a particularly powerful means of conjuring up the image of their owners, and thus become an important, perhaps at times indispensable, part of the public vocabulary. Rules restricting the use of well-known trademarks may therefore restrict the communication of ideas." LL Bean, Inc. v. Drake Publishers, Inc., 811 F.2d 26, 30 (1st Cir. 1987).

62 Lanham Act 15 U.S.C. § 1052(a).

government may not discriminate against speech based on the ideas or opinions it conveys."[63]

Although *Iancu* was concerned with how the public may use the communicative function of trademarks to convey ideas and *Matal* dealt with how the government may not censor speech by denying registration of particular categories of marks, what is important here is the unequivocal declaration by the U.S. Supreme Court that trademarks can have an *expressive purpose* that triggers First Amendment protection, in addition to their traditional source-designating function. It follows that the social agenda of brand renegades, counterpublics, or subaltern groups therefore can be communicated to mainstream society through the use of widely recognized trademarks—as semiotic signs—to which the public have ascribed particular representative values or characteristics. Even the public act of "consuming" a brand can in itself be a form of commentary on or critique of the coded social meanings in that brand thus rendering it an "expressive" act. The expressive function of trademarks had been foreshadowed by Kozinski J in the Ninth Circuit in *Mattel Inc. v. MCA Records, Inc.*, who opined that

> [t]rademarks often fill in gaps in our vocabulary and add a contemporary flavor to our expressions. Once imbued with such expressive value, the trademark becomes a word in our language and assumes a role outside the bounds of trademark law ... Were we to ignore the expressive value that some marks assume, trademark rights would grow to encroach upon the zone protected by the First Amendment. Simply put, the trademark owner does not have the right to control public discourse whenever the public imbues his mark with a meaning beyond its source-identifying function.[64]

A famous luxury fashion brand, such as Louis Vuitton or Hermes, transcends clothing, bags, and accessories to take on political, pedagogical, and cultural meanings, much in the same way that McDonald's transcends ground beef and potatoes.[65] Beebe points out that *shanzhai* (山寨) practices—the term given to "a wide array of sometimes licit but usually illicit copying and appropriationist practices in China"—can openly challenge the inequalities in power and wealth that establishment culture perpetuates or work to reinforce established hierarchies.[66] The word *shanzhai* originates from Guangdong dialect in China and was initially used

[63] Iancu v. Brunetti, 139 S.Ct. 2294, 2299 (2019). Justice Sotomayor's disagreement was not based on whether trademarks also have a symbolic expressive function, but rather that "[p]rohibiting the registration of obscene, profane, or vulgar marks qualifies as reasonable, viewpoint-neutral, content-based regulation" and that "scandalous" in § 1052(a) "can reasonably be read to bar the registration of only those marks that are obscene, vulgar, or profane." *Id.* at 2317-8.

[64] Mattel, Inc. v. MCA Records, Inc., 296 F.3d 894, 900 (9th Cir. 2002).

[65] Tan, *supra* note 47, at 227.

[66] Barton Beebe, *Shanzhai, Sumptuary Law, and Intellectual Property Law in Contemporary China*, 47 UC Davis L. Rev. 849, 852, 862–63 (2014).

to describe the copycat phenomenon in the information technology industry. Used in the fashion context, *shanzhai* designers redesign a fashion item that is not necessarily an exact copy of the real product; they offer customers a taste of luxury at cut-rate prices. Luxury brands are often the target of such *shanzhai* practices.[67] *Shanzhai* practices often fall short of the level of outright identical-mark-on-identical-goods counterfeiting; for example, shoes bearing something resembling the Nike swoosh and the word mark "Like," the marks "Channel," "Guccy," "Dolce & Banana," "Prapa," and "Rurrebry" written in the same typeface as the original marks Chanel, Gucci, Dolce & Gabbana, Prada, and Burberry.[68] Haochen Sun explains that

> [i]n general, shanzhai producers routinely imitate the looks of branded products. Their products bear strong resemblance to the products of popular brands in well-established markets. Consumers might not be misled to believe that these shanzhai products are made by manufacturers of brand name products, but they can figure out that they have features that resemble those of the branded products.[69]

Indeed it is highly unlikely that more sophisticated consumers of expensive products offered by luxury brands would be confused as to the association between the patently inauthentic "Channel" and the well-recognized "Chanel." In this kind of recoding,

> the widespread propagation of, for example, inauthentic Louis Vuitton bags creates widespread desire for the authentic. In this way, shanzhai status goods simply promulgate the new sumptuary code, and *as Chinese consumers grow wealthier, they will shift their consumption from the simulation to the real.*[70]

There was even a Shanzhai Biennial which debuted in 2012 at Beijing Design Week as a countercultural critique of the contemporary art biennials, which is actually a

[67] Luxury brands are often referred to as "Veblen brands" derived from Thorstein Veblen's iconic work on conspicuous consumption. *See* <Jeremy N. Sheff, *Velben Brands*, 96 MINNESOTA L. REV. 769, 772–76 (2012). For an excellent account of *shanzhai* practices and their cultural significance, *see* Haochen Sun, *Can Louis Vuitton Dance with Hiphone? Rethinking the Idea of Social Justice in Intellectual Property Law*, 15 U. PA. J. L. & SOC. CHANGE 389 (2012).

[68] Brand owners are nonetheless frequently intolerant of such practices. According to Beebe, "[t]he persuasive imitation of distinctive goods has proved to be especially threatening to the sumptuary order because the circulation of such imitations impairs the ability of the imitated goods to yield relative utility, which in many cases is the only form of utility that they have to offer." Barton Beebe, *Intellectual Property Law and the Sumptuary Code*, 123 HARV. L. REV. 809, 833 (2010).

[69] Sun, *supra* note 67, at 397.

[70] Beebe, *supra* note 66, at 863 (emphasis added). Sun has also poetically noted that the "symbolic value of the shanzhai phenomenon lies in its power to signal the need for civil disobedience to the economically poor, the politically marginalized, and the culturally weak." Sun, *supra* note 67, at 432.

synthesis of an installation art project and a fashion label that defies conventional categorization.[71]

The U.S. decisions have demonstrated a willingness on the part of the courts to accept a semiotic reading of trademarks as cultural signs when assessing likelihood of confusion for trademark infringement or evaluating the availability of the noncommercial use exception in a trademark dilution claim for the purposes of parody, satire, or political speech. U.S. Circuit Courts of Appeals have consistently declined to find liability against defendants who engaged in non-illegal cultural jamming: Aqua's "Barbie Girl,"[72] Thomas Forsythe's Barbie photographs,[73] Haute Diggity Dog's Chewy Vuiton dog toy,[74] and My Other Bag's tote bags depicting drawings of Louis Vuitton bags.[75] But this evolving judicial attitude toward embracing a more expansive reading of the noncommercial use exception under the U.S. Lanham Act (15 U.S.C. § 1125(c)(3)(C)) has the effect of *overprotecting* so-called expressive uses which nonetheless take advantage of the commercial success of famous marks. Examining the action of dilution by tarnishment, Alexandra Olson cautions that the free speech rights of artists tend to trump the property rights of the mark holder as the noncommercial use and nominative fair-use/parody defenses under the Trademark Dilution Revision Act will immediately shield defendants when applied to artistic works.[76] But protecting a trademark against dilution can be said to mimic patent and copyright-infringement protection in the sense that it is aimed at protecting the mark owner's rights regardless of consumer confusion, and more robust statutory defenses would have to be enacted to balance this powerful protection.[77] In *L.L. Bean v. Drake Publishers*, the First Circuit Court of Appeals noted that such anti-dilution statutes may provide legitimate regulations on speech when the expression relates "*solely* to the economic interests of the speaker and its audience."[78]

When the commercial parodist draws on the semiotic meanings encoded in a famous mark to disrupt their perpetuated myths or provide social commentary, the U.S. courts appear willing to construe the defenses (such as the noncommercial

[71] Nate Cohan, *Corporate Aesthetics: Shanzhai Biennial*, Art in America (Apr. 30, 2014) https://www.artinamericamagazine.com/news-features/interviews/corporate-aesthetics-shanzhai-biennial/; Kevin McGarry, *Shanzhai Biennial*, Kaleidoscope (Issue 18, Summer 2013), http://kaleidoscope.media/shanzhai-biennial/.

[72] *Mattel*, 296 F.3d 894.

[73] Mattel, Inc. v Walking Mountain Productions, 353 F.3d 792 (9th Cir. 2003).

[74] Louis Vuitton Malletier, SA v. Haute Diggity Dog LLC, 507 F.3d 252 (4th Cir. 2007).

[75] Louis Vuitton Malletier, SA v. My Other Bag Inc., 674 Fed. Appx. 16 (2d Cir. 2016).

[76] Alexandra E. Olson, *Dilution by Tarnishment: An Unworkable Cause of Action in Cases of Artistic Expression*, 53 Boston College L. Rev. 693 (2012).

[77] Justin J. Gunnell, *Evaluation of the Dilution-Parody Paradox in the Wake of the Trademark Dilution Revision Act of 2006*, 26 Cardozo Arts & Ent. L. J. 441, 450 (2008).

[78] *L.L. Bean*, 811 F.2d 26, 32 (*quoting* Central Hudson Gas & Electricity v. Public Service Comm'n, 447 U.S. 557, 561 (1980)) (emphasis added). The "core notion of commercial speech is that it 'does no more than propose a commercial transaction."' Hoffman v. Capital Cities, 255 F.3d 1180, 1884 (9th Cir. 2001).

use exception or the parody defense) more generously. For instance, the Ninth Circuit Court of Appeals upheld a commercial song parody directed at Mattel's Barbie Doll observing that "with Barbie, Mattel created not just a toy but a cultural icon ... [and] with fame often comes unwanted attention."[79] In a number of culture jamming cases where the defendant engaged in semiotic recodings or playful disruptions of famous marks, such as in *Mattel v. MCA Records* and *Louis Vuitton Malletier SA v. Haute Diggity Dog, LLC* ("*Chewy Vuiton*"), the Circuit courts have found the defendant not to be liable; however, in some parody advertisements scenarios, the commercial defendant who was a *direct competitor* was found liable because the cases involved products and services that are similar and are in competition.[80]

III. The Fashionable First Amendment and Trademark Enforcement

A. Famous Fashion Brands Just Have to Put Up with Parodies

Courts generally are concerned that the enforcement of private rights, including intellectual property rights, does not have a "chilling effect"[81] on free speech. Trademark uses that tend to comment on or present a different way of viewing familiar iconography, societal archetypes, public obsessions, and majoritarian beliefs are likely to fall within the First Amendment categories of protected speech, such as political speech, art, entertainment, and matter of public interest. In trademark law, courts have often directly engaged with the First Amendment, whether in an infringement or a dilution claim, since trademark law does not have an in-built First Amendment safeguard.[82] Hence U.S. courts have resorted to accommodating the First Amendment within doctrinal grounds in trademark laws, primarily in the likelihood of confusion analysis for infringement and the noncommercial use and parody exceptions for dilution actions.[83] For instance, the Second Circuit noted

[79] *Mattel*, 296 F.3d 894, 898–99.

[80] *E.g.*, Deere & Co. v. MTD Products, Inc., 41 F.3d 39 (2d Cir. 1994); Harley Davidson, Inc. v. Grottanelli, 164 F.3d 806 (2d Cir. 1999); Conopco, Inc. v 3DO Co., 53 U.S.P.Q. 2d 1146 (S.D.N.Y. 1999).

[81] Dombrowski v. Pfister, 380 U.S. 479, 487 (1965). *See also* Eric Barendt, Freedom of Speech 38 (2d ed. 2005); Frederick Schauer, Free Speech: A Philosophical Enquiry 80–85 (1982).

[82] This is in contrast to copyright law which "contains built-in First Amendment accommodations" in the idea-expression dichotomy and the fair-use defense. Eldred v. Ashcroft, 537 U.S. 186, 219–20 (2003). *See also* Golan v. Holder, 132 S.Ct. 873, 890 (2012).

[83] The canon of constitutional avoidance dictates that courts should "construe the statute to avoid such problems unless such a construction is plainly contrary to the intent of Congress." Edward J. DeBartolo Corp. v. Fla. Gulf Coast Bldg. & Const. Trades Council, 485 U.S. 568, 575 (1988). Courts must first attempt to resolve any conflict between trademark law and the First Amendment by interpreting trademark claims narrowly and trademark defenses broadly in ways that protect expression. *See* Lisa P. Ramsey, *Increasing First Amendment Scrutiny of Trademark Law*, 61 S.M.U. L. Rev. 381, 448 (2008). *See generally* Tan, *supra* note 46.

that since the likelihood of confusion test "is at best awkward in the context of parody, which must evoke the original and constitutes artistic expression," courts should apply the factors "with proper weight given to First Amendment considerations."[84] The Ninth Circuit in *Mattel v. MCA Records* commented that when marks "transcend their identifying purpose" and "enter public discourse and become an integral part of our vocabulary," they assume "a role outside the bounds of trademark law."[85] Where a mark assumes such cultural significance, First Amendment protections come into play and the Circuit Courts have generally sided with the infringer as the trademark owner is perceived not to have the right to control public discourse whenever the mark has been imbued with a meaning beyond its source-identifying function.[86]

In the last two decades, luxury fashion brands, particularly Louis Vuitton, are traditionally notorious for aggressively sending cease-and-desist letters and filing claims against parodists, albeit with limited success.[87] A parody must invoke or copy a significant proportion of the primary mark in order for the parody to be effective; it will invariably satisfy the mark similarity factor in the likelihood of confusion analysis. The question that follows is whether the parody can nevertheless claim not to confuse customers. Parody enjoys an exalted protected status in intellectual property jurisprudence. The First Circuit Court of Appeals described parody as "a humorous form of social commentary and literary criticism ... [that] seeks to ridicule sacred verities and prevailing mores"[88] thus implicating First Amendment concerns. The Second Circuit noted "the broad scope permitted parody in First Amendment Law"[89] and that "in today's world of unrelieved solemnity, copyright law should be hospitable to the humor of parody."[90] In a more rigorous examination of the First Amendment's influence on the fair-use defense, the Ninth Circuit Court of Appeals has more overtly considered the status of parody under the Free Speech Clause in *Mattel v. Walking Mountain Productions*.[91] The court was of the view that parody has "socially significant value as free speech

[84] Cliffs Notes, Inc. v. Bantam Doubleday Dell Publ'g Group, 886 F.2d 490, 495 n.3 (2d Cir. 1989).

[85] *Mattel*,296 F.3d 894, 900. In 1997, Aqua produced the parody song "Barbie Girl" on the album *Aquarium* and the song made it onto Top 40 music charts. The defendants, MCA Records and a number of other music companies, produced, marketed, and sold "Barbie Girl."

[86] *Id.* at 900; New Kids on the Block v. News Am. Publ'g Inc., 971 F.2d 302, 307 (9th Cir.1992); *L.L. Bean*, 811 F.2d 26, 29.

[87] *See, e.g., My Other Bag*, 674 Fed. Appx. 16; Louis Vuitton Malletier, SA v. Hyundai Motor America, No. 10 Civ. 1611 (P.K.C.), 2012 WL 1022247 (S.D.N.Y. Mar. 22, 2012); Louis Vuitton Malletier, SA v. Akanoc Solutions, Inc., 591 F Supp. 2d 1098 (N.D. Cal. 2008); *Chewy Vuiton*, 507 F.3d 252; Louis Vuitton Malletier, SA v. Dooney & Bourke, Inc., 454 F.3d 108 (2d Cir. 2006); Plesner v. Louis Vuitton Malletier, SA, No.KG ZA 11-294 (Court of the Hague, July 21, 2011); Brian Farkas, Louis Vuitton v. U Penn, GS2LAW (Mar. 12, 2012).

[88] *L.L. Bean*, 811 F.2d at 29.

[89] Groucho Marx Productions v. Day and Night Co., 689 F.2d 317, 319 n.2 (2d Cir.1982).

[90] Elsmere Music v. National Broadcasting Co., 623 F.2d 252, 253 (2d Cir.1980).

[91] *Walking Mountain*, 353 F.3d 792, 801 (9th Cir. 2003).

under the First Amendment."[92] More importantly, the court ruled that while individuals may disagree on the success or extent of a parody, parodic elements that may "reasonably be perceived" in a work will often justify fair-use protection.[93] Parody may thus be seen as contributing valuable commentary and criticism to the marketplace of ideas, or advancing democratic debate on matters of public interest through the use of irreverent humor.

Parodies abound in the world of fashion. Louis Vuitton did not take kindly to a range of fluffy dog toys that evoked its "LV" and Monogram marks and took the manufacturer of Chewy Vuiton all the way to Fourth Circuit Court of Appeals; other brands, such as Prada, Chanel, and Tiffany & Co which were similarly parodied, chose to do nothing about it.[94] Louis Vuitton later argued that a tongue-in-cheek reference to its covetable status as a luxury brand in My Other Bag's canvas tote bags was not a type of recoding that should be deemed protectable parody; again the other brand owners did not sue, and naturally Louis Vuitton did not prevail before the Second Circuit Court of Appeals.[95] Stuart Hall has defined the taking of an existing meaning and reappropriating it for new meanings as "trans-coding"[96] and explained that repressed groups may use trans-coding strategies to reverse stereotypes, substitute negative portrayals with positive ones, or contest subordinate representations from within.[97] This notion of recoding is certainly relevant to the trademark infringement and dilution analysis, particularly when famous fashion marks have been employed as semiotic signs to communicate such messages. A countercultural or counterpublic agenda may be best communicated to mainstream society through the use of widely recognized semiotic signs to which the public have ascribed particular representative values or characteristics. Such uses are commonly seen in parodic merchandise or even more political ones such as Nadia Plesner's *Simple Living* painting of an emaciated African boy holding a Louis Vuitton handbag and a chihuahua to call attention to the horrific situation in Darfur by contrasting the starved boy and his obvious need for our attention, to the media's obsession with fashion and celebrity.[98] Employed in this manner, "re-coding, like flag burning, may advance an 'associative' type of discourse using the currency of symbolic referents … [realizing] its potential for promoting personal expression, self-government, and the pursuit of truth."[99]

92 *Id.* (*quoting* Dr. Seuss Enterprises, L.P. v. Penguin Books USA, Inc., 109 F.3d 1394, 1400 (9th Cir. 1997)).

93 *Id.*

94 *Chewy Vuiton*, 507 F.3d 252.

95 *My Other Bag*, 674 Fed. Appx. 16.

96 Stuart Hall, *The Spectacle of the "Other," in* REPRESENTATION: CULTURAL REPRESENTATIONS AND SIGNIFYING PRACTICES 223, 270 (Stuart Hall ed., 1997).

97 *Id.* at 270–75.

98 *See generally* Janis McCutcheon, *Designs, Parody and Artistic Expression—A Comparative Perspective of Plesner v. Louis Vuitton*, 41 MONASH U. L. REV. 192 (2015).

99 Note, *"Recoding" and the Derivative Works Entitlement: Addressing the First Amendment Challenge*, 119 HARV. L. REV. 1488, 1499 (2006).

The decision of the U.S. Fourth Circuit Court of Appeals in *Chewy Vuiton* sheds some light on how a fashion parody could be considered in the likelihood of confusion analysis.[100] In that case, the defendant Haute Diggity Dog manufactures, among other things, plush toys on which dogs can chew, which, it claims, parody famous trademarks on luxury products, including those of Louis Vuitton Malletier. The particular Haute Diggity Dog chew toys in question are small imitations of handbags that are labeled "Chewy Vuiton" and that mimic Louis Vuitton Malletier's distinctive monogram handbags.[101] They "undisputedly evoke Louis Vuitton handbags of similar shape, design, and color."[102]

The Fourth Circuit held that for trademark purposes, "[a] 'parody' is defined as a simple form of entertainment conveyed by juxtaposing the irreverent representation of the trademark with the idealized image created by the mark's owner."[103] In addition, the court explained that

> A parody must convey two simultaneous—and contradictory—messages: that it is the original, but also that it is *not* the original and is instead a parody. This second message must not only differentiate the alleged parody from the original but must also communicate some articulable element of satire, ridicule, joking, or amusement. Thus, [a] parody relies upon a difference from the original mark, presumably a humorous difference, in order to produce its desired effect.[104]

On the facts on the case, the court concluded that the Chewy Vuiton dog toys were successful recodings or parodies of the Louis Vuitton handbags. The court found that "the pet chew toy is obviously an irreverent, and indeed intentional, representation of an LVM handbag," and it "undoubtedly and deliberately conjures up the famous LVM marks and trade dress, but at the same time, it communicates that it is not the LVM product."[105] The court then proceeded to consider the *Pizzeria Uno* factors and held that there was on balance no likelihood of confusion. In particular, the court observed that "[d]espite Haute Diggity Dog's obvious intent to profit from its use of parodies, this action does not amount to a bad faith intent to

[100] *Chewy Vuiton*, 507 F.3d 252.

[101] In addition to Chewy Vuiton (a parody of Louis Vuitton), the company also produced Chewnel No. 5 (Chanel No. 5), Furcedes (Mercedes), Jimmy Chew (Jimmy Choo), Dog Perignonn (Dom Perignon), Sniffany & Co. (Tiffany & Co.), and Dogior (Dior). The chew toys and pet beds are plush, made of polyester, and have a shape and design that loosely imitate the signature product of the targeted brand. They are mostly distributed and sold through pet stores, although one or two Macy's stores in the United States carry Haute Diggity Dog's products. The products are also sold online. The dog toys are generally sold for less than US$20, although larger versions of the plush dog beds sell for more than US$100. *Chewy Vuiton*, 507 F.3d at 258.

[102] *Id.*

[103] *Id.* at 260 (*citing* People for the Ethical Treatment of Animals v. Doughney, 263 F.3d 359, 366 (4th Cir. 2001) ("*PETA*")).

[104] *Id.* (*citing PETA*, *id.*; Jordache Enterprises, Inc. v. Hogg Wyld Ltd., 828 F.2d 1482, 1486 (10th Cir. 1987)) (internal quotations omitted).

[105] *Id.*

create consumer confusion. To the contrary, the intent is to do just the opposite—to evoke a humorous, satirical association that *distinguishes* the products."[106]

The bar for tarnishment is a high one in U.S. law, particularly when First Amendment free speech concerns are triggered by a parody. The courts there have found that a trademark may be tarnished when it is "linked to products of shoddy quality, or is portrayed in an unwholesome or unsavory context," with the result that "the public will associate the lack of quality or lack of prestige in the defendant's goods with the plaintiff's unrelated goods."[107] In *V Secret Catalogue v. Moseley*, the Sixth Circuit observed that there have been "at least eight federal cases in six jurisdictions that conclude that a famous mark is tarnished when its mark is semantically associated with a new mark that is used to sell *sex-related products*."[108] In the United States, there appears to be a clearly emerging consensus in the case law that "a semantic 'association' is equivalent to a liability-creating mental 'association' of a junior mark ... with a famous mark ... that constitutes dilution by tarnishment when the junior mark is used to sell sexual toys, videos and similar soft-core pornographic products."[109] However, outside of this sex-related context, parodies, even where a semantic association is present, are accorded a different treatment. The *Chewy Vuiton* case is paradigmatic. Similarly, in *Hormel Foods Corp. v. Jim Henson Productions*, despite the obvious semantic association, the Second Circuit Court of Appeals rejected the argument that the image of the Muppet character Spa'am, as a grotesque, untidy wild boar will "inspire negative and unsavory associations with SPAM® luncheon meat."[110]

In *Chewy Vuiton*, the Fourth Circuit justified its consideration of a parody element in conducting the blurring analysis as follows:

> While a parody intentionally creates an association with the famous mark in order to be a parody, it also intentionally communicates, if it is successful, that it is not the famous mark, but rather a satire of the famous mark. That the defendant is using its mark as a parody is therefore relevant in the consideration of these statutory factors ... Indeed, by making the famous mark an object of the parody,

[106] *Id.* at 263.

[107] Hormel Foods Corp. v. Jim Henson Productions, 73 F.3d 497, 507 (2d Cir. 1996) (*citing* Deere & Co. v. MTD Productions, Inc., 41 F.3d 39, 43 (2d Cir. 1994)).

[108] V Secret Catalogue v. Moseley, 605 F.3d 382, 389 (6th Cir. 2010) (emphasis added). *See also* Pfizer, Inc. v. Sachs, 652 F.Supp.2d 512, 525 (S.D.N.Y. 2009) (defendants' display at an adult entertainment exhibition of two models riding a VIAGRA-branded missile and distributing condoms would likely harm the reputation of Pfizer's trademark); Mattel, Inc. v. Internet Dimensions, Inc., 2000 WL 973745, 55 USPQ 2d 1620, 1627 (S.D.N.Y. July 13, 2000) (linking BARBIE with pornography will adversely color the public's impressions of BARBIE); Polo Ralph Lauren, LP v. Schuman, 46 USPQ 2d 1046, 1048 (S.D. Tex. 1998) (defendants' use of "The Polo Club" or "Polo Executive Retreat" as an adult entertainment club tarnished POLO trademark).

[109] *V Secret*, 605 F.3d at 388.

[110] *Hormel Foods*, 73 F.3d at 507.

> a successful parody might actually enhance the famous mark's distinctiveness by making it an icon. The brunt of the joke becomes yet more famous.[111]

In 2016, Louis Vuitton was back in court again. The defendant My Other Bag, Inc. ("MOB") sells simple canvas tote bags with the text "My Other Bag ..." on one side and cartoonish drawings meant to evoke iconic handbags by luxury designers, such as Louis Vuitton, Chanel, and Hermes, on the other. These drawings depict easily recognizable handbags such as the Louis Vuitton Speedy and Hermes Birkin. The New York District Court acknowledged the presence of cultural commentary in MOB's totes as follows:

> its very name—are a play on the classic "my other car ..." novelty bumper stickers, which can be seen on inexpensive, beat up cars across the country informing passersby—with tongue firmly in cheek—that the driver's "other car" is a Mercedes (or some other luxury car brand). The "my other car" bumper stickers are, of course, a joke—a riff, if you will, on wealth, luxury brands, and the social expectations of who would be driving luxury and non-luxury cars. MOB's totes are just as obviously a joke[112]

Louis Vuitton's claims in trademark infringement, trademark dilution by blurring, and copyright infringement were all dismissed by the court. The court noted that "MOB markets its bags as '[e]co-friendly, sustainable tote bags playfully parodying the designer bags we love, but practical enough for everyday life' "[113] and found that the parody as "fair use" defense under 15 U.S.C. § 1125(c)(3) applied. Citing *Chewy Vuiton* and other Second Circuit precedents, the court held

> That joke—combined with the stylized, almost cartoonish renderings of Louis Vuitton's bags depicted on the totes—builds significant distance between MOB's inexpensive workhorse totes and the expensive handbags they are meant to evoke, and invites an amusing comparison between MOB and the luxury status of Louis Vuitton. Further, the image of exclusivity and refinery that Louis Vuitton has so carefully cultivated is, at least in part, the brunt of the joke: Whereas a Louis Vuitton handbag is something wealthy women may handle with reverent care and display to communicate a certain status, MOB's canvas totes are utilitarian bags "intended to be stuffed with produce at the supermarket, sweaty clothes at the gym, or towels at the beach."[114]

[111] *Chewy Vuiton*, 507 F.3d at 267. *See also* Starbucks Corp. v. Wolfe's Borough Coffee, Inc., 588 F.3d 97, 112–13 (2d Cir. 2009).
[112] Louis Vuitton Malletier, SA v. My Other Bag, Inc., 156 F.Supp.3d 425, 430 (S.D.N.Y. 2016).
[113] *Id.* at 431.
[114] *Id.* at 435.

Louis Vuitton argued that any humor present in MOB's totes is merely part of a larger social commentary, not a parody *directed toward* Louis Vuitton or its products, but the court adopted a generous interpretation of parody as applied to trademark law, and was of the view that "[t]he fact that MOB's totes convey a message about more than *just* Louis Vuitton bags is not fatal to a successful parody defense."[115] The court further held that even if MOB's use of Louis Vuitton's marks did not qualify as fair use under 15 U.S.C. § 1125(c)(3), the tote bags nevertheless pose no danger of impairing the distinctiveness of Louis Vuitton's marks.[116] On the infringement claim, the court found that applying the *Polaroid* factors, the claim fails for much the same reasons that the dilution claims failed. It was especially pertinent that "Louis Vuitton's marks are so well known that consumers are likely "both immediately to recognize the target of the joke and to appreciate the obvious changes to the marks that constitute the joke,"[117] and that even if a parody that evoked Louis Vuitton's marks was commercially successful "the intent is not necessarily to confuse the public but rather to amuse."[118] On appeal, the Second Circuit unanimously upheld the decision in a brief judgment that endorsed a broad definition of parody (which appears to encompass satire) in trademark law, commenting that the fact that "the joke on LV's luxury image is gentle, and possibly even complimentary to LV, does not preclude it from being a parody."[119] The court also found that because MOB's tote bags was parodic, it was entitled to the "fair use" exclusion from dilution liability under 15 U.S.C. § 1125(c)(3).

On April 5, 2019, MGA, a California corporation that develops and distributes children's toy, filed a complaint against Louis Vuitton seeking a declaratory judgment that MGA's toy product—and a "handbag shaped toy container" referred to as "Pooey Puitton"—in no way violates Louis Vuitton's intellectual property rights. The complaint additionally alleges that there is an actual controversy between the parties because Louis Vuitton "has a history of not respecting parody rights" and "filing vexatious lawsuits" related to its trademarks. On technical grounds, the California District Court held that Louis Vuitton's French lawsuit against MGA regarding E.U. trademark rights does not establish that an actual controversy exists under U.S. laws concerning the Pooey Product and Pooey Name and Louis Vuitton's marks in the United States.[120] While Louis Vuitton has not filed an action against MGA in the U.S., it is highly unlikely that it would succeed in its U.S. claim in light of the *Chewy Vuiton* and *My Other Bag* Circuit Court precedent. At the

[115] *Id.* at 436.
[116] *Id.* at 438–40.
[117] *Id.* at 443 (*citing* Tommy Hilfiger Licensing, Inc. v. Nature Labs, LLC, 221 F.Supp.2d 410, 416 (S.D.N.Y. 2002))
[118] *Id.* at 444 (*citing* Jordache Enterprises, Inc. v. Hogg Wyld Ltd., 828 F.2d 1482, 1486 (10th Cir. 1987)).
[119] *My Other Bag*, 674 Fed. Appx. 16, 18.
[120] MGA Entertainment, Inc. v. Louis Vuitton Malletier, SA, Case No. 2:18-cv-10758-JFW(RAOx) (C.D. Cal. May 14, 2019).

time of writing, irreverent fashion streetwear brand Off-White helmed by Virgil Abloh, known for subverting cultural icons, ironically has filed an action for trademark infringement by Afters Ice Cream for using the slogan "Off-Diet," which the defendant has argued was a word play on the calorie count of ice cream; it seems unlikely that Off-White will succeed.[121]

One of the few generalizations about the U.S. cases is that the defendant's use of parody or satire is not in itself a defense against trademark infringement or dilution. However, even when some commercial motive is present, the defendant is not liable merely because its satire or parody leads the public to think of the claimant's famous mark.[122] In the United States, "courts go to great lengths in weighing the interests of the public, the mark holder, and the parodist in determining whether to grant an injunction against a parody in the absence of confusion."[123] As the Tenth Circuit observed: "where a party chooses a mark as a parody of an existing mark, the intent is not necessarily to confuse the public but rather to amuse."[124] It should also be noted that not all parodies are unequivocally protected.[125]

B. Self-Disruption and Implications for Trademark Law

By reclaiming the counterfeit, heritage brands today are potentially extending their trademark rights into realms where consumers hitherto may not have been confused as to the origin. More recently, we are witnessing obvious efforts by Alessandro Michele (Gucci) and Demna Gvasalia (Balenciaga) to self-disrupt the image that the heritage brands have meticulously cultivated over the decades.[126]

There are two implications here: First, by selling authentic merchandise with shanzhai-inspired misspellings such as "GUCCY" or fake-looking logos which are different from the conventional font used to depict the word mark that consumers are accustomed to, these acts of self-disruption may result in enhancing a finding of a likelihood of confusion or actual confusion for the consumers of Gucci or Balenciaga when they are confronted with *shanzhai* products. If one accepts the view that the inauthenticity of *shanzhai* luxury fashion goods "strengthens the status hierarchies articulated by possession of 'real' luxury goods and makes those

[121] *See* Off-White LLC v. Afters Ice Cream, Inc., Case No. 8:20-cv-02121 (C.D. Cal.); *Afters Ice Cream Responds to Off-White Lawsuit, Claims "Off-Diet" Tees and Other Merch is Parody*, The Fashion Law (Jan. 4, 2021), https://www.thefashionlaw.com/afters-ice-cream-responds-to-off-white-lawsuit-claims-off-diet-and-other-merch-is-parody/.

[122] *See* LOUIS ALTMAN AND RUDOLF CALLMANN, Callmann on Unfair Competition, Trademarks and Monopolies § 22:61 (4th ed. 2003).

[123] Gunnell, *supra* note 74, 462.

[124] *Jordache*, 828 F.2d at 1486.

[125] *See supra* note 77.

[126] *E.g.*, *Balenciaga "Hacked" Gucci Back for Its SS22 Collection*, Tatler (June 7, 2021), https://www.tatlerasia.com/style/fashion/hk-balenciaga-gucci-hack-ss22-collection.

goods more desirable,"[127] then the disruption of this sumptuary code by brands like Gucci and Balenciaga will result in a blurring of the distinction.[128] Second, a luxury brand engaging in downmarket irony and playing with the cultural symbolism of the pedestrian logos such as Ford and DHL without a clear parodic message may expose *itself* to trademark infringement and dilution lawsuits.

It is not always the luxury fashion brands that sue the countercultural entrepreneur for trademark infringement and dilution. In a welcomed twist, Balenciaga under the creative direction of Demna Gvasalia was taken to court by Car-Freshner Corporation for copying its world-famous LITTLE TREES air fresheners tree design for a US$275 keychain "that are deliberately designed to replicate the plaintiffs' [trade dress-protected] Tree Design," which according to the statement of claim have become "staples of American culture, familiar to millions of consumers who encounter these products and marks in a wide variety of commercial contexts."[129] In particular the "Product Details" for Balenciaga's keychain leads with the statement that the products represent "Car fresheners inspiration," and the contours of the keychain track exactly the shape and dimensions of a genuine LITTLE TREES air freshener.[130] Balenciaga has even copied the specific colors associated with some of the popular scents in which the plaintiffs' LITTLE TREES air fresheners are offered.[131]

To the fashion cognoscenti, the Balenciaga "LITTLE TREES" keychain would belong comfortably in the self-disruptive aesthetic oeuvre of Gvasalia, who has sought to elevate the mundane and the pedestrian into the revered realm of high fashion through his collaboration with DHL, selling a leather lookalike of the IKEA iconic blue Frakta tote bag for over US$2000, and self-vandalizing the Balenciaga logo in graffiti-style. But to trademark lawyers, this may seem to be a commercial gimmick calculated to boost sales by simply appropriating well-known household marks and relying on the fame of the designer to assert that a parodic commentary undoubtedly exists. It would have been interesting to see how Balenciaga attempts to make use of the *Chewy Vuiton*, *My Other Bag*, and other precedents to argue that its high-fashion keychain is neither infringing nor dilutive, as the "joke" here

[127] Beebe, *supra* note 66, at 864 (*referring to* Rob Horning, *Shanzhai*, MARGINAL UTIL. ANNEX (June 23, 2013), http://marginalutilityannex.wordpress.com/2013/06/25/shanzhai/).

[128] *Shanzhai* fashion products may arguably be perceived as a commercial parody that is sufficiently robust to "prevent the confusion necessary for infringement under trade mark law, which requires the observer to be caused to wonder whether the infringing product originates from the registered owner." *See* Jani McCutcheon, *Designs, Parody and Artistic Expression—A Comparative Perspective of Plesner v Louis Vuitton*, 41 MONASH. U. L. REV. 191 at 241 (2015) (internal citations omitted) (discussing examples of two- and three-dimensional products parodying familiar trademarks). When luxury brands "appropriate" these *shanzhai* depictions for themselves, consumers may not be able to easily distinguish a self-parody and a *shanzhai* commercial parody.

[129] Car-Freshner Corp. v. Balenciaga America, Inc., Case No. 1:18-cv-09629, at [17] (S.D.N.Y., filed Oct. 19, 2018).

[130] *Id.* at [28]–[29].

[131] *Id.* at [30].

is not so obvious compared to the other cases. While self-logo hacking at Gucci and Balenciaga may contain valuable *expressive* messages about luxury fashion and consumerism, and irreverent merchandise—such as Chewy Vuiton dog toys, Pooey Puitton children toys, and My Other Bag tote bags—are clearly parodies, it is less certain that a court would rule in Balenciaga's favor that it can so easily appropriate famous marks to include in its cultural commentary about the world of fashion.

In respect of trademark infringement, the parodic commentary would be taken into account in the multifactorial test. However, the parody here is perhaps too subtle for the average consumer, and there is a real possibility of actual confusion. As Car-Freshner Corporation has entered into numerous licensing arrangements over the years, including with fashion brand Anya Hindmarch to use the Tree Design Marks as the configuration of high-quality hang tags for handbags,[132] an overall finding of a likelihood of confusion is likely. The noncommercial use exception and fair-use exclusion for a dilution claim, while successful for the defendants in *Chewy Vuiton* and *My Other Bag*, is a difficult one to argue as Balenciaga has not encouraged us "to laugh at the images and associations linked with the [LITTLE TREES] mark" or provided "entertainment conveyed by juxtaposing the irreverent representation of the [LITTLE TREES mark] with the idealized image created by the mark's owner."[133] As Reilly noted, when the most powerful fashion labels self-sabotage their lexicon or play with their own icons, the message is still *about* them.[134] In *My Other Bag*, the Second Circuit observed that: "a parody of LV's luxury image is the very point of MOB's plebian product. That distinguishes this case from ones cited by LV where a trademark was used merely to 'promote' or 'sell' goods and services, which is impermissible."[135] Is this a case of a parody of LITTLE TREES's plebian image that is the very point of Balenciaga's luxury product? This is indeed a novel case, but one will not know what the pronouncement of the court may be as the dispute has been settled out of court.[136] In 2018, Balenciaga was also sued for copyright infringement by City Merchandise for reproducing a New York City Skyline artwork ubiquitously seen on tourist souvenir bags as a kitschy leather tote bag priced around US$2000; again the suit was settled.[137]

[132] *Id.* at [16].
[133] *My Other Bag*, 674 Fed. Appx. 16, 18 (*citing L.L. Bean*, 811 F.2d 26, 34).
[134] Baron, *supra* note 16.
[135] *My Other Bag*, 674 Fed. Appx. at 18.
[136] *Balenciaga and Car-Freshner Corp. Settle Suit Over the Fashion Brand's $275 Copycat Keychains*, The Fashion Law (Mar. 20, 2019), https://www.thefashionlaw.com/home/balenciaga-and-car-freshner-corp-settle-suit-over-the-fashion-brands-copycat-keychains.
[137] City Merchandise, Inc., v. Balenciaga America, Inc., Case No. 1:18-cv-06748-JSR (S.D.N.Y.) (2018); *Balenciaga, City Merch Settle Lawsuit Over Copycat New York City Bags*, The Fashion Law (Dec. 10, 2018), https://www.thefashionlaw.com/home/balenciaga-city-merch-settle-copycat-bag-lawsuit.

Conclusion

Reading trademarks semiotically can reveal how such signs can "reproduce the existing social struggles in their images, spectacle, and narrative."[138] There is a significant emphasis in contemporary cultural studies on the notion of audience participation—be it their complicity or resistance—in the hegemony of cultural texts propagated by their authors or producers. It is in these studies of semiotic disruptions that one may find the relevant tools for understanding *expressive* uses of marks within trademark doctrine that addresses the countercultural agenda of the active audience.

When Haute Diggity Dog and My Other Bag appropriated the LOUIS VUITTON marks to comment on a societal obsession with luxury goods and status symbols, the defendants were relying on the public's understanding of the semiotic values of a fashion cultural icon in order to get the joke—and the critique—behind the merchandise.[139] However, the acts of self-disruption or self-brandalism by the luxury fashion brands such as Gucci and Balenciaga perhaps suggest an expressive commentary more about the brand *themselves* than about the other marks that they have invoked. It seems to be a tenuous argument to say that Balenciaga's appropriation of the LITTLE TREES mark was a joke or critique of Car-Freshner's products (or the semiotic meanings that they embody); it appears to be predominantly parasitic rather than primarily expressive.[140]

In First Amendment jurisprudence, certain recoded circulations can be viewed as a form of political activism akin characterized by their ability to "reverse perceptions of social devaluation or stigma, articulate alternative narratives of national understanding, and challenge exclusionary imaginaries of citizenship."[141] Propertizing signs as marks enables the owner to restrict speech, impede the free flow of ideas and control democratic dialogue. Trademark laws, especially when operating in the world of fashion, should ultimately aim to strike a balance between protecting, on the one hand, the proprietary right of brand owners to economically exploit the fruits of their labor, and on the other hand, the right of others to proffer alternative insights, create new understandings, and express political viewpoints through connotative recoded uses of the mark.

[138] DOUGLAS KELLNER, MEDIA CULTURE: CULTURAL STUDIES, IDENTITY AND POLITICS BETWEEN THE MODERN AND THE POSTMODERN 56 (1995).

[139] As Furman J so astutely observed: "In some cases, however, it is better to 'accept the implied compliment in [a] parody' and to smile or laugh than it is to sue ... MOB's use of Louis Vuitton's marks in service of what is an obvious attempt at humor is not likely to cause confusion or the blurring of the distinctiveness of Louis Vuitton's marks; if anything, it is likely only to reinforce and enhance the distinctiveness and notoriety of the famous brand." *My Other Bag*, 156 F.Supp.3d 425, 445 (S.D.N.Y. 2016).

[140] Tan, *supra* note 47, at 242.

[141] Raymen v. United Senior Association, Inc., 409 F.Supp.2d 15, 32 (D.D.C. 2006).

PART II
NATURE OF LIMITATIONS

4

Gripe Sites and Trademark User Rights

Lessons from Canada's *Cooperstock* Case

Carys J. Craig

Introduction

Readers may have heard it said that bad cases make bad law; but sometimes good cases can make bad law too—and when that happens, the bad law becomes a particularly ugly authority. So it is, I fear, with the Canadian case of *United Airlines v. Cooperstock*[1]—a case with the near-perfect set of facts to tee up a much-needed judicial statement defining the outer limits of trademark protection in Canada; but one that has, instead, trampled over those limits, reinforcing the fullest reach of trademark owners' rights. This chapter examines the unfortunate ruling with a view to identifying not only the obvious flaws in the Federal Court of Canada's doctrinal reasoning and the shortcomings of the statutory text that permitted them but also the deeper pathology of a decision that defies the principled limits of trademark protection. It means to present Canada's *United* case as paradigmatic example—and a cautionary tale—of what happens when owners' rights are overprotected, users' rights are disregarded, and trademark limits are irresolutely drawn.

Section I will provide the background and overview of the controversial case, pointing to the legal issues, arguments, and judicial interpretations that present cause for concern. From overly expansive conceptions of trademark use to tenuous claims of confusion, and from dubious dilution claims to a total disregard for free expression, we will see how the plaintiff prevailed at every point along the path toward a finding in its favor. Section II will dig a little deeper to draw some important lessons from the *United* case. The case has revealed the weakness of trademark law's so-called internal limits, which leaves them vulnerable and ultimately unfit for purpose, while external limits like the constitutional right of free expression failed to find any firm footing. The first lesson, then, is that trademark law requires explicit statutory exceptions, ideally in the form of a general fair-use defense, to circumscribe the reach of the trademark owner's rights. The second lesson is that such limits and exceptions need to be recognized as *user rights* (as they have been

[1] United Airlines, Inc. v. Cooperstock, 2017 FC 616, [2018] 1 F.C.R. 188 (Can.).

Carys J. Craig, *Gripe Sites and Trademark User Rights* In: *Charting Limitations on Trademark Rights.* Edited by: Haochen Sun and Barton Beebe, Oxford University Press. © Carys J. Craig 2023. DOI: 10.1093/oso/9780198871248.003.0005

in Canadian copyright jurisprudence) if they are to be an effective counterbalance against expanding owners' rights.

While such developments are sorely needed, however, they are likely insufficient to prevent similar rulings in the future. Underpinning the Court's reasoning throughout the judgment was an almost palpable disapproval of the defendant's critical engagement with the plaintiff's brand and the potential damage this posed to its economic value. As such, I will argue that what is really required—in Canada and elsewhere—is a departure from the loose proprietary logic that has, for too long, propped up trademark rights as intellectual *property* (IP) not to be trespassed upon. If the trademark system is to give adequate space to expressive uses of protected trade symbols (whether parodic, satirical, critical, or nominative), the infringement analysis needs to be reoriented away from proprietary entitlement and toward a concern with the communicative and dialogic nature of marks. It is in the expressive nature of commercial symbols as socially situated speech that we should find the reason for—and so the limits of—the rights that trademark law affords.

I. The Unfortunate Case of *United Airlines v. Cooperstock*

A. The Background

Jeremy Cooperstock was, like so many of us, a disgruntled customer of United Airlines. Following an unhappy trip from Toronto to Tokyo, Cooperstock, who is a professor of engineering at McGill University, wrote twice to United to complain about his seating. After finally receiving a form letter in response, he posted the written exchange to his personal website under the title "Poor Show." He soon began receiving letters from other unsatisfied travelers, which he added to the webpage. Within a year, he had launched UNTIED.com, a consumer criticism website (sometimes referred to as a "gripe site") where visitors could read and submit complaints about United Airlines. Starting in 1997, the site amassed roughly 32,000 complaints from disconsolate consumers and employees.

UNTIED.com was, of course, a play on the name UNITED, chosen by Cooperstock to suggest the disconnection and disorganization that he perceived in the company.[2] After news of a corporate merger and redesign of the United logo in 2011, Cooperstock redesigned his own website logo accordingly, adopting the same color and font for the lettering, and mimicking United's blue globe image but with the pointed addition of a sad frowny face. Next to this, playing on U.S. airlines' Star Alliance network, appeared the words: "AN EVIL ALLIANCE MEMBER."

[2] *Id.* para. 7.

Thereafter, Cooperstock received several communications from United demanding that changes be made to the appearance of the UNTIED.com website in order to reduce the potential for confusion in the minds of visitors. In response, he changed the color of the "TI" in UNTIED and the frown face from a matching blue to a more noticeable red, and added a disclaimer disavowing any connection with the official United Airlines website.

Unimpressed by these modifications, United commenced an action against Cooperstock in the Federal Court of Canada for trademark infringement, passing off, depreciation of goodwill, and copyright infringement. Thereafter, Cooperstock added a pop-up disclaimer to his site explaining that the site, which "is not the website of United Airlines," exists "only because of the airline's outright hostility toward its passengers and many of its employees," and requiring visitors to indicate their understanding or leave the page.[3]

Cooperstock represented himself and appeared as his sole fact witness at trial. Justice Phelan of the Federal Court ruled that Cooperstock had infringed United's trademarks and copyright, and issued an injunction restraining their use. An appeal of the decision, scheduled to be heard in December 2019, was discontinued after the parties reached a confidential settlement—one that presumably included taking down the gripe site. This was an unfortunate development. In the intervening period, recognizing the seriousness of the issues at stake, Cooperstock had been able to obtain pro bono legal representation, and the Federal Court of Appeal had granted intervenor status to the Canadian Civil Liberties Association and the Canadian Intellectual Property and Public Interest Clinic, each of which was prepared to argue in Cooperstock's favor, citing user rights, the public interest, and freedom of expression.[4]

It might be tempting to assume that the lower court ruling will now be of little consequence—that it can be brushed aside as a single case with a self-represented defendant and an overly censorious judge. But in Canada, trademark litigation is relatively rare, and Federal Court cases that directly address the interaction of trademark rights and free expression arise infrequently indeed. As such, there is a real risk that this judgment will set the stage for the use of trademarks in critical or parodic speech for many years to come.[5] And the unfortunate reality is that, in

[3] *See* Daniel R. Bereskin QC, *United Airlines, Inc. v. Jeremy Cooperstock: A Critical Review*, 33 INTELL. PROP. J. 91, 94 (2020).

[4] *See* Memorandum of Fact and Law of Samuelson-Glushko Canadian Internet Policy and Public Interest Clinic, Jeremy Cooperstock v. United Airlines, Inc. (Federal Court of Appeal File No. A-262-17), http://cippic.ca/sites/default/files/File/CIPPIC_memorandum_of_fact_and_law_-_FINAL_-_3_July_2018.pdf; Memorandum of Fact and Law of The Intervener, Canadian Civil Liberties Association, Jeremy Cooperstock v. United Airlines, Inc. (Federal Court of Appeal File No. A-262-17).

[5] I am thinking here of the unfortunate and longstanding authority of Cie Générale des Etablissements Michelin-Michelin & Cie v. C.A.W.-Canada, (1996) 71 C.P.R. (3d) 348 (Can. F.T.C.D.) (hereinafter *Michelin*), discussed *infra*.

many respects, the ruling, though wrong, is far from anomalous in the Canadian trademark terrain. Alas, there is good reason to be pessimistic.[6]

B. The Break Down

Before we embark on our overview of the ruling, readers should note some of trademark law's internal safety features. Trademark law in Canada contains very little in the way of explicit exceptions or defenses.[7] The limits of the trademark owner's rights are defined instead by the *scope* of the exclusive rights protected at common law or granted under the Trademarks Act,[8] and owners' overreach prevented only by the consistent recognition of those limits. A variety of key requirements must be met in order to establish infringement or passing off, which should, in combination, carefully circumscribe the boundaries of the trademark owner's claim against unauthorized users. These limiting requirements relate to the mark that is being used; the goods or services in association with which it is used; the nature of the use; and the function or effect of the use.

So, for example, trademark rights extend only to uses of a mark in connection with "goods" or "services," from which it is understood to follow that infringing uses must be *commercial* in nature[9]—a conclusion shored up in Canada by the grounding of federal jurisdiction over trademark law in the constitutional power to regulate "Trade and Commerce."[10] Noncommercial uses should therefore fall outside the scope of trademark protection. Nor do the trademark owner's rights extend to uses that fall outside of the technical definition of "use" under the Trademarks Act. This definition requires that a mark appears on the goods or is associated with them at the time of transfer, or that it is displayed in the performance or advertising of services.[11] For unauthorized use to infringe a registered owner's

[6] *Cf.* Teresa Scassa, *Trademarks Worth a Thousand Words: Freedom of Expression and the Use of the Trademarks of Others*, 53 LES CAHIERS DE DROIT 877, 896 (2012).

[7] Trademarks Act, R.S.C. 1985, c T-13, §§ 20(1.1), (1.2), (2) (Can.) (setting out limited exceptions for bona fide, non-depreciating use of personal and geographical names and descriptions, as well as exceptions for the use of utilitarian features and specific geographical indications). *See* David Vaver, *Towards a Distinctive Trademark Law for the 21st Century*, 30 INTELL. PROP. J. 183, 193 (2018) (aptly describing these as "two lonely subsections hidden away at the end of a long list of user taboos").

[8] Trademarks Act, R.S.C. 1985, c T-13, §§. 19, 20, 22 (Can.) (setting out the rights of registered trademark owners).

[9] Trademarks Act, R.S.C. 1985, c T-13, § 2 (Can.) (defining "trademark" as "a sign or combination of signs that is used or proposed to be used by a person for the purpose of distinguishing or so as to distinguish their goods or services from those of others"). *See also Michelin*, 71 C.P.R. (3d) 348, para. 40 (finding that "use" of the plaintiff's marks in a Union's campaign literature was not "use" in "advertising" because not in pursuit of profit).

[10] British North America Act, 1867, 30–31 Vict., c. 3, § 91(2) (U.K.). *See* Kirkbi AG v. Ritvik Holdings Inc., [2005] 3 S.C.R. 302, 2005 SCC 65.

[11] Trademarks Act, R.S.C. 1985, c T-13, § 4 (Can.). *See* Clairol International Corp. v. Thomas Supply & Equipment Co. Ltd., [1968] 2 Ex. C.R. 552 (Can. Ex. Ct.) (finding that only technical trademark uses within the meaning of section 4 could infringe the plaintiff's rights).

exclusive right, it is further required that the infringing use be use *as a trademark.*[12] Uses that are not for the purpose of, or likely to, identify the source of a product or service, are not uses *as* a trademark.[13] Arguably, such uses can still depreciate goodwill,[14] but they are otherwise beyond the reach of the owner's "exclusive right to the use throughout Canada of the mark,"[15] as well as the right to prevent use of a confusing mark.[16]

Other defining limits to trademark rights flow directly from the specific grounds of infringement. Section 19's "double-identity" infringement requires use of the same mark as registered and in association with the same goods or services.[17] Section 20's confusion infringement requires use of a "confusing" mark, of course, which means that the owner cannot prevent use of a mark unless it "would be likely to lead to the inference that the wares or services ... are manufactured, sold, leased hired or performed by the same person."[18] The owner's expansive rights under section 22 (Canada's counterpart to the U.S. "dilution" provisions)[19] extend only to uses of a "sufficiently well-known"[20] registered trademark "likely to have the effect of depreciating the value of the goodwill attaching thereto."[21] With or without registration, a passing off claim can extend only to uses of a mark with acquired reputation that amount to a misrepresentation likely to cause confusion and damage.[22]

These built-in limits are fundamental to defining the trademark owner's rights and ensuring the appropriate "balance between free competition and fair

[12] *See* MC Imports Ltd. v. Afod Ltd., 2014 FC 1161, para. 44 (Can. F.C.T.D), aff'd 2016 FCA 60 (Can. C.A.)

[13] *See, e.g.*, Bombardier Ltd. v. British Petroleum Co., 1971 CarswellNat 511 (Can. F.T.C.D.) (WL).

[14] Trademarks Act, R.S.C. 1985, c T-13, § 22 (Can.) (prohibiting the use of a registered trademark "in a manner that is likely to have the effect of depreciating the value of the goodwill attaching thereto"). *See* Clairol International Corp., [1968] 2 Ex. C.R. 552 (finding depreciation liability in respect of a hair color comparison chart that did not use plaintiff's mark as a trademark to identify source). *But see also* Daniel Bereskin, *Clairol Revisited: Trademark Rights v. Freedom of Expression and Competition in Canada*, 110(5) TRADEMARK REP. 809 (2020) (disputing the conclusion in *Clairol* that § 22 does not require use as a trademark); Venngo Inc. v. Concierge Connection Inc., [2017] 146 C.P.R. (4th) 182 (finding no violation of § 22 ostensibly because the "use" was not use as a trademark).

[15] Trademarks Act, R.S.C. 1985, c T-13, § 19 (Can.) (providing that registration "gives to the owner of the trademark the exclusive right to the use throughout Canada of the trademark in respect of those goods or services.").

[16] *Id.* § 20(a) ("The right of the owner of a registered trademark to its exclusive use is deemed to be infringed by a person ... who sells, distributes or advertises goods or services in association with a confusing trademark.").

[17] *Id.* § 19. *See, e.g.*, Mr. Submarine Ltd. v. Amandista Investments Ltd. (1987), [1988] 3 F.C. 91 (Can. C.A.) (holding that the extent of the exclusive right given by § 19 is defined by the mark "as registered").

[18] Trademarks Act, R.S.C. 1985, c T-13, § 6 (Can.) (defining when a mark or name is confusing).

[19] *Cf.* Lanham Act, 15 U.S.C. § 1125(c).

[20] Veuve Clicquot Ponsardin v. Boutiques Cliquot Ltée, 2006 SCC 23, [2006] 1 S.C.R. 824, para. 46 (Can.).

[21] Trademarks Act, R.S.C. 1985, c T-13, § 22 (Can.). *See also* Veuve Clicquot Ponsardin, 2006 SCC 23, para. 46.

[22] Ciba-Geigy Canada Ltd. v. Apotex Inc. [1992] 3 S.C.R. 120, 132 (Can.).

competition"[23]—but, as the *United* ruling demonstrates all too well, they are also frustratingly fragile and prone to malfunction.[24]

1. Use in Association with Services

Based on this brief catalogue of internal limits, Cooperstock's first argument in his own defense is an obvious one: he had not "used" the UNTIED marks in "the sale, distribution, or advertisement of 'services.'" While acknowledging that his website provided "services in the form of information delivery, advice on legal rights, and publication of complaints," he argued that these were not commercial services of the kind covered by the Trademarks Act.[25]

This argument, though quite clearly correct, was dismissed by Justice Phelan on the basis that "[t]here is no explicit requirement in the legislation of a monetary or commercial element to services."[26] In support of the proposition that "'services' should not be given a narrow interpretation," Justice Phelan cited a ruling in which a website that "offered services in the form of information and guidance to visitors" was found to be sufficient to establish "use" in Canada.[27] He neglected to note that the information offered in that case was specifically concerned with where to purchase a vast array of products being offered for sale in the United States by the second largest sporting goods retailer in the world. In that case, it was said that "the Act makes no distinction between primary, incidental or ancillary services. As long as some members of the public, consumers or purchasers, receive a benefit from the activity, it is a service."[28] Justice Phelan's reframing notably omits the mention of "consumers or purchasers" and concludes simply that "the key element of 'services' was the benefit to the public."[29] By providing information that could benefit the public, then, Cooperstock's free public service to disgruntled United customers (which the Court equated to a "consumer help line") was caught, notwithstanding that he offered the public no commercial goods or services to which these information services could be said to be "ancillary."

This finding, if followed, could extend trademark protection to cover informational and expressive uses of marks entirely untethered to any trade or commerce as such.[30] This is surely a startling development. Not only does it flout longstanding judicial recognition that "use" in association with "services" necessarily

[23] Mattel, Inc. v. 3894207 Canada Inc., 2006 SCC 22, [2006] 1 S.C.R. 772, para. 21 (Can.).

[24] *Cf.* Scassa, *supra* note 6, at 897 (2012) (describing the "fragility of the built-in limits on the scope of trademark rights" when it comes to protecting free expression).

[25] *United Airlines, Inc.*, 2017 FC 616, para. 32 (Can.).

[26] *Id.* para. 33.

[27] *Id.*

[28] Société Nationale des Chemins de fer Français SNCF v. Venice Simplon-Orient-Express Inc. (2000), 9 C.P.R. (4th) 443 (Can. F.T.C.D.) (finding that it is not necessary to show a ticket sale to an ultimate consumer in order to demonstrate use in association with "railway passenger services").

[29] *United Airlines, Inc.*, 2017 FC 616, para. 33.

[30] *But see id.* (Justice Phelan cautioning that "services" should not be cast so broadly as to cover "any provision of information" but only "in certain circumstances," which remained unspecified).

contemplates a commercial element,[31] but it also disregards the constitutional limits of trademark protection—both in terms of the limits of federal jurisdiction and the right of free expression (to which we shall return).[32]

Cooperstock further argued that he had not used the marks *as a trademark* to indicate the origin of goods or services. Justice Phelan was again unconvinced. Noting the similarity between the marks and their placement on the website, he found that the UNTIED marks would serve the purpose of indicating origin, bringing them within the ambit of the plaintiff's exclusive right. Cooperstock's explanation that he deliberately mimicked the appearance of the plaintiff's website for parodic effect was cited in the judgment as though it were a damning moment of self-incrimination.[33]

2. Confusion

Confusion among consumers is "the grave iniquity against which trademark laws and jurisprudence are intended to guard."[34] As the Supreme Court of Canada has stated, trademark law "is, in that sense, consumer protection legislation."[35] And so, in *United*, it was claimed that consumers must be protected from the misapprehension that Cooperstock's website was operated by or in association with the plaintiff—something that, in Cooperstock's raw assessment, "you'd have to be . . . , you know, cognitively challenged . . . to believe."[36]

[31] Clairol International Corp. v. Thomas Supply & Equipment Co. Ltd., [1968] 2 Ex. C.R. 55, para. 36 (Can.) (opining that "use" under § 4 is confined to "use in the course of trading . . . the statute being one relating to trade marks and unfair competition"); Les Rotisseries St.-Hubert Ltée v. Le Syndicat des Travailleurs(euses) de la Rotisserie St.-Hubert de Drummondville (C.S.N.) 1986 CarswellQue 91, para. 51 (Can. Qc Sup Ct) (WL) (finding that a trade union had not "used" a trademark because it was not engaged in the regular course of trade); *Michelin*, [1968] 71 C.P.R. (3d) 348, para. 40 (finding that a trade union had not "used" the employer's trademark because handing out leaflets to recruit members does not qualify as commercial activity).

[32] The constitutional significance of "wares or services" was hinted at in Bell ExpressVu Ltd. Partnership v. Tedmonds & Co. Inc., 2001 CanLII 28350, para. 43 (Can. Ont. Sup. Ct.) ("The website does not promote wares or services . . . Rather, the website promotes criticism of the plaintiff as a commercial enterprise. In that regard, its function could be characterized as the exercise of free speech"). *See also* British Columbia Automobile Assn. et al. v. Office and Professional Employees' Int. Union et al., 2001 BCSC 156, para. 153 (Can. B.C.) (finding that infringement requires a commercial element, the absence of which "would place an unwarranted restriction on free speech"). In the U.S. context, *see, e.g.*, Radiance Foundation, Inc. v. National Association for the Advancement of Colored People, 786 F.3d 316, 322 (4th Cir. 2015) (recognizing that a broad construction of "use in connection with goods or services" would "expose to liability a wide array of noncommercial expressive . . . activities" and thereby "push the Lanham Act close against a First Amendment wall"). *See also* Rogers v. Grimaldi, 875 F.2d 994, 998 (2d Cir. 1989); Taubman Co. v. Webfeats, 319 F.3d 770, 774 (6th Cir. 2003) (stating that the "Lanham Act is constitutional because it only regulates commercial speech").

[33] *United Airlines, Inc.*, 2017 FC 616, [2018] 1 F.C.R. 188, para. 40 (Cooperstock explaining, "I decided I could be far more effective in the parody by humorously mimicking the appearance, but with a twist on numerous elements of United's own website.").

[34] Ann Bartow, *Likelihood of Confusion*, 41 SAN DIEGO L. REV. 721, 722 (2004).

[35] Mattel, Inc. v. 3894207 Canada Inc., 2006 SCC 22, [2006] 1 S.C.R. 772, para. 2 (Can.).

[36] *United Airlines, Inc.*, 2017 FC 616, para. 46.

Once again, Justice Phelan regarded Cooperstock's stated intentions to be damning, noting that "the Defendant's obvious imitation of the United Marks and the United Website is meant to cause visitors to associate UNTIED.com with the Plaintiff."[37] Indeed, he emphasized, Cooperstock's "core purpose" was that the visitors to his website would identify his symbols and name with the Plaintiff, as "[h]is efforts serve no other useful purpose."[38] This is true; but it is also quite beside the point. Again, marks are confusing when their use "would be likely to lead to the inference that the goods or services associated with those trademarks are … performed by the same person."[39] The UNTIED marks were designed to make it abundantly clear that United was the target of the complaints collected there, and in this sense, consumers would "identify" or "associate" them with UNITED—but this kind of referential use is the opposite of confusing: it is pointing to the trademark owner not as the misrepresented source of the service but as the explicit object of critique.[40]

The multifactorial confusion analysis was off course from the outset, due to the mischaracterization of Cooperstock's "services," but the error compounded with each step. First, in what is supposed to be a comparison of the respective strength of plaintiff's and defendant's marks, Justice Phelan spoke only of the significant acquired distinctiveness and longstanding use of United's trademarks. Then, when comparing the nature of services offered, he found a direct overlap because both parties "provide information to prospective travellers as well as post-flight engagement with United customers."[41] Looking to the nature of the trade, he concluded that the character of the market for each was "identical" because consumers would reach both sites by searching online for "United" and "Complaints."[42] Regarding the resemblance of the marks, the analysis acquired a copyright hue, noting that Cooperstock "took a substantial majority of the UNITED Mark" and "took the entirety of the Globe Design," and "admitted that he was aware that the Globe Design was from the United Website when he appropriated it."[43] The language of "taking" and "appropriation" cast United's claim over its marks in proprietary terms, while the notion of an "admission" again gestures at some inherently wrongful act to which Cooperstock accidentally confessed.

[37] *Id.* para. 57.
[38] *Id.* para. 68.
[39] Trademarks Act, R.S.C. 1985, c T-13, § 6(2) (Can.).
[40] *See United Airlines, Inc.*, 2017 FC 616, para. 53 (noting "Defendant *admitted* he wanted visitors to UNTIED.com to 'recognize the similarities to the target of my criticism" [emphasis added]). *Cf.* Radiance Foundation, Inc. v. National Association for the Advancement of Colored People, 786 F.3d 316, 328 (4th Cir. 2015) ("It is not immediately apparent how someone would confuse an article which is strongly critical of an organization with the organization itself. The mark in this case was used primarily to identify … the object of criticism … albeit by employing a modified version of the name.").
[41] *Id.* para. 49.
[42] *Id.* para. 52.
[43] *Id. para. 55.*

In considering surrounding circumstances, evidence of actual confusion by one travel agent who submitted a customer complaint to Untied.com in error, together with examples of letters addressed to the attention of United, confirmed for Justice Phelan that confusion was likely. Cooperstock's motives weighed heavily: "Although the Defendant's intent is not determinative in an action under section 20(1), '[h]istorically, courts have been slow to conclude that a demonstrated piratical intent has failed to achieve its purpose.' "[44] To ascribe to the defendant a "piratical intent" is to cast the defendant in the role of pirate or thief, intent on taking away from the rightful owner something to which he can lay no lawful claim. Framed in this way, of course, the finding of infringement naturally follows.

Similar contortions animated the Court's passing off analysis. Justice Phelan again wrote at length of United's commercial success, noting its estimated brand value of $4.5 billion, the "significant resources" it devotes to its advertising and branding strategy, and how it "carefully controls the consumer experience of its branded spaces."[45] United was found to have proved the necessary likelihood of damage due to a loss of control over the brand, potential tarnishment of the UNITED mark, and depreciation of its acquired goodwill. Rather than an independent site for consumer information-sharing, Cooperstock's website was characterized as a "barrier" between United and its customers.[46] Thus, it was apparently assumed, the law must provide a remedy, in the form of an injunction, to protect the value of the brand by reinstating United's singular control over its marketing message.

A final argument advanced by Cooperstock was that the UNTIED marks were obvious "spoofs," which would be recognized as parody or satire in spite of the similarities. This was promptly dismissed as irrelevant: "As parody and satire are not defenses to trademark infringement, the addition of the frown to the Frowning Globe Design on UNTIED.com does not avoid trademark infringement or passing off."[47] In this respect, the ruling is regrettably consistent with the sparse Canadian jurisprudence on point. Cited in support is the Federal Court case of *Source Perrier S.A. v. Fira-Less Marketing Co.*, in which an interlocutory injunction was issued to restrain the defendant from marketing bottled water with the name PIERRE EH!—a spoof on PERRIER and a satirical reference to then Canadian Prime Minister Pierre Trudeau.[48] There, it was found that deliberate similarities in the marks and packaging were "obviously meant to cause confusion. Otherwise, the spoof would not be a spoof." Moreover, the fact that the defendant intended to produce a spoof did "not take away from the deception created in the minds of the customers";

44 *Id.* para. 68.
45 *Id.* para. 76.
46 *Id.* para. 87.
47 *Id.* para. 83.
48 Source Perrier S.A. v. Fira-Less Marketing Co., [1983] 2 F.C. 18 (Can. F.C.T.D.).

rather it was a "clear[] attempt[] to cash in on the well-established reputation of Perrier."[49] Also cited was a case involving a parody of the famous Canadian ROOTS clothing brand (featuring the name ROTS and a macabre looking beaver), where an injunction was granted because "notwithstanding that the defendant is obviously spoofing the plaintiff's trade mark he is also cashing in on the goodwill that the plaintiff has obtained for its trade mark."[50]

With this framing, parodic and satirical uses of a well-known trademark were reduced, in the eyes of the court, to an effort to benefit from the trademark owner's goodwill and misappropriate the fruits of the owner's investment in its brand. But if a spoof readily reveals itself as such to the ordinary consumer, then that consumer is not confused.[51] If trademark law is, as Canada's Supreme Court has stated, consumer protection law aimed at preventing confusion and "get[ting] the consumer where they want to go,"[52] then there is no reason to enjoin an obvious spoof. If anything, such an allusive use of the trademark reinforces the connection between the owner and the mark rather than undermining it.[53] But if trademark law is, alternatively, primarily concerned with protecting the owner's exclusive control over the meaning of the mark and preventing intrusions that might threaten the brand value in which it has invested, then such satirical uses take on the taint of misappropriation—and the law leaps to the rescue of the maligned trademark owner.[54]

3. Depreciation

Even if Justice Phelan had remained unconvinced of the likelihood of confusion, United had another promising route to the injunction: the controversial claim of depreciation of goodwill, to which we now turn. As mentioned above, section 22

[49] *Id.* para. 11.

[50] Green v. Schwarz (1986) 12 C.P.R. (3d) 84, para. 5 (Can. Ont. H.C.J.). *Cf.* Horn Abbott Ltd. et al. v. Thurston Hayes Developments Ltd. et al. (1985), 4 C.P.R. (3d) 376 (Can. F.T.C.D.) (granting a permanent injunction against the makers of SEXUAL PURSUIT board game for trading on the goodwill and commercial success of TRIVIAL PURSUIT); Subway IP LLC v. Budway, Cannabis & Wellness Store, 2021 FC 583 (Can. F.C.T.D.) (finding a likelihood of confusion between SUBWAY for sandwich restaurants and BUDWAY for a cannabis store, noting that "the respondents have adopted their mark by deliberately drawing on the famous mark of the applicant").

[51] *See, e.g.*, Tommy Hilfiger Licensing, Inc. v. Nature Labs, LLC, 221 F. Supp. 2d 410, 420 (S.D.N.Y. 2002) ("[D]efendant's use of the mark is an obvious parody or pun, readily so perceived, and unlikely to cause confusion among consumers."); Vuitton Malletier v. Haute Diggity, 507 F.3d 252, 261 (4th Cir. 2007) ("[The strength of a famous mark allows consumers immediately to perceive the target of the parody, while simultaneously allowing them to recognize the changes to the mark that make the parody funny or biting."); Louis Vuitton Malletier, S.A. v. My Other Bag, Inc., 156 F. Supp. 3d 425, 441–44 (S.D.N.Y. 2016).

[52] Mattel, Inc. v. 3894207 Canada Inc., 2006 SCC 22, [2006] 1 S.C.R. 772, para. 21 (Can.).

[53] *See* Michael Spence, *The Mark as Expression/The Mark as Property*, 58 CURRENT LEGAL PROBLEMS 491, 498 (2005).

[54] *See* Radiance Foundation, Inc. v. National Association for the Advancement of Colored People, 786 F.3d 316, 328 (4th Cir. 2015) ("Intemperate and worse as the commentary is, holding it actionable risks creating the paradox that criticism equals confusion, thereby permitting companies to shield themselves from adverse assessments.").

of Canada's Trademarks Act gives to the registered owner of a well-known mark the right to prevent another person from using it in a manner likely to depreciate the value of the goodwill, even where that use is not confusing. I have previously warned that the potential scope of this statutory right is enormous, and clearly capable of extending to restrict basic competitive practices as well as commercial (and other) speech unless its meaning is kept firmly in check[55]—fears that have now been realized in Cooperstock's case.

First, it should be underscored, the extension of section 22 to cover noncommercial expression requires deliberate disregard for the limiting concept of "use." A use need not be *as a trademark* in order to depreciate goodwill, but it must still be "use" *of a trademark*, in the technical sense: that is, use in association with goods or services in the course of trade. For this reason alone, Cooperstock's website and logos should have been beyond the reach of United's depreciation claim. As we have seen, however, the Court's expansive concept of "services" allowed United to crash straight through this barrier.[56]

According to the Supreme Court of Canada, in addition to use, a plaintiff pleading depreciation must also prove sufficient goodwill; a likely effect on that goodwill (i.e., a linkage or connection in the minds of consumers); and that the likely effect is depreciation of value (i.e., damage).[57] Justice Phelan had already found significant goodwill, of course, and once again quoted Cooperstock admitting his purpose ("to identify the target of [his] criticism as that of United.") In Justice Phelan's assessment, "[t]he Defendant therefore appropriated the goodwill associated with the United Marks."[58] "Goodwill" has been defined in Canadian jurisprudence as "the positive association that attracts customers toward [the trademark] owner's wares or services rather than those of its competitors."[59] Depreciation of its value can occur "through reduction of the esteem in which the mark itself is held or through the direct persuasion and enticing of customers who could otherwise be expected to buy or continue to buy goods bearing the trademark."[60] Drawing on U.S. "dilution" jurisprudence, Canada's Supreme Court of Canada has identified, as activities that could depreciate goodwill, "disparagement" or "tarnishing" of the mark through the creation of a negative association, as well

[55] *See* Carys Craig, *Perfume by Any Other Name May Smell as Sweet... But Who Can Say? A Comment on L'Oréal v. Bellure*, 22 I. P. J. 321, 332 (2010).

[56] *United Airlines, Inc.*, 2017 FC 616, [2018] 1 F.C.R. 188, para. 91 (restating the finding that "the Defendant has made use of the Plaintiff's registered trademarks on UNTIED.com").

[57] Veuve Clicquot Ponsardin v. Boutiques Cliquot Ltée, 2006 SCC 23, [2006] 1 S.C.R. 824, para. 46 (Can.).

[58] *United Airlines, Inc.*, 2017 FC 616, para. 96.

[59] *Veuve Clicquot Ponsardin*, 2006 SCC 23, para. 50. *See also* Clairol International Corp. v. Thomas Supply & Equipment Co. Ltd., [1968] 2 Ex. C.R. 552 at 573 (Can.) (Thurlow J. explaining that goodwill "consists of the whole advantage... of the reputation and connection, which may have been built up by years of honest work or gained by lavish expenditure of money and which is identified with the goods distributed by the owner in association with the trade mark").

[60] *Clairol International Corp.*, [1968] 2 Ex. C.R. 552, para. 42.

as "blurring" or "whittling away" its power to distinguish the owner's products.[61] Readers will not be surprised to learn that the requisite depreciation of goodwill was found in Cooperstock's treatment of United's marks, but may still be taken aback by the terms (and tone) in which this harm was described.

> The Defendant reproduces and disparages the Plaintiff's registered trademarks on UNTIED.com ... Further, the crudeness of UNTIED.com is likely to depreciate the goodwill of United's marks. ... The unprofessional nature of the Defendant's website ... tarnishes the goodwill attached to United's trademarks.
>
> Further, the Defendant's use ... decreases the distinctiveness of the United Marks. The similarities ... may discourage others from continuing their search for the Plaintiff's customer service website due to anger, frustration, or the mistaken belief that the Plaintiff does not have a "complaints" page.
>
> Therefore, I find that the Defendant has intentionally attempted to attract the Plaintiff's online consumers to his own website for notoriety. In doing so, he has depreciated the value of goodwill attached to the United Trademarks contrary to s 22.

Justice Phelan's disapproval is palpable. The defendant's critical commentary and the sharing of consumer information is reduced to a personal quest to attract "notoriety" (since attracting custom is not applicable),[62] and responsibility for anger or frustration felt by United's customers is placed onto Cooperstock's shoulders. Meanwhile, his efforts are diminished as "crude" and "unprofessional." Also worth noting is the continued creep of copyright morality. That the marks were "reproduced" should be of no concern to trademark law because the relevant wrong is not one of copying. Moreover, the notion that the distorted reproduction might "disparage" the rightholder has the rhetorical ring of a moral rights concern—except that here, the person claiming prejudice to their honor and reputation is a corporation, thereby implicating none of the relevant personhood concerns that underlie moral rights protections against reputational harm.[63] Cooperstock argued that the Court should distinguish between United's business reputation as a service provider and the goodwill attached to its marks: his website might harm the former, but it would be "ludicrous" to suggest it depreciated the latter.[64] With Justice Phelan's flat rejection of this distinction, the legal right to protect the value

[61] *Veuve Clicquot Ponsardin*, 2006 SCC 23, paras. 64–67.

[62] *See Clairol International Corp.*, [1968] 2 Ex. C.R. 552, para. 45 (finding a violation of § 22 because the defendants used the plaintiff's registered mark "for the express purpose of taking away custom enjoyed by competitors").

[63] *See* Copyright Act, R.S.C. 1985, c C-42, §§ 14, 28.2 (Can.) (providing for an author's right to prevent mutilations or distortions of their work that prejudice their honor or reputation).

[64] *United Airlines, Inc.* v., 2017 FC 616, [2018] 1 F.C.R. 188, para. 91 (Can.).

of goodwill in a trademark becomes the power to control corporate reputation by quashing critique.[65]

4. Freedom of Expression

By now, readers may be wondering whether there is a constitutional right to freedom of expression in Canada, and if so, whether it would have occurred to Cooperstock, self-represented as he was, to argue that his rights would be violated by an injunction. There is, and he did. Section 2(b) of the *Canadian Charter of Rights and Freedoms* guarantees to everyone "freedom of thought, belief, opinion and expression, including freedom of the press and other media of communication."[66] In two sentences, however, Justice Phelan dismissed Cooperstock's contention that an injunction would limit his freedom of speech, and rejected the suggestion that freedom of speech was even "at issue in this litigation."[67]

Unlike the U.S. First Amendment, Canada's Charter divides the question of whether free expression is being restricted (under section 2(b)) from the determination of whether the restriction is nonetheless reasonable and justified (under section 1): any activity that conveys or attempts to convey meaning *prima facie* comes within the scope of the section 2(b) right;[68] but a law that limits free expression might be constitutionally valid if it falls within "such reasonable limits prescribed by law as can be demonstrably justified in a free and democratic society."[69] To say that a law simply does not implicate the right of free expression, then, is to deny the expressive nature of the activity being enjoined, and so to sidestep the question of whether the law imposes a "justifiable" limit. It thereby avoids asking the question—an awkward one, to be sure, where section 22 is concerned[70]—of whether the limitation is rationally connected to the objective of the legislation and minimally impairs the right of free expression.

Disappointing as this detour around free expression was, Justice Phelan was on well-traveled Canadian terrain here. Canada's courts have, thus far, been derelict in

[65] *Cf.* Radiance Foundation, Inc. v. National Association for the Advancement of Colored People, 786 F.3d 316, 332 (4th Cir. 2015) ("Trademarks do not give their holders under the rubric of dilution the rights to stymie criticism"); New Kids on the Block v. News Am. Publ'g, Inc., 971 F.2d 302, 307 (9th Cir. 1992) ("Much useful social and commercial discourse would be all but impossible if speakers were under threat of an infringement lawsuit every time they made reference to a person, company or product by using its trademark.").

[66] Canadian Charter of Rights and Freedoms, Part I of the Constitution Act, 1982, *being* Schedule B to the Canada Act, 1982, c11, § 2(b) (U.K.) (hereinafter *Charter*).

[67] *United Airlines, Inc.*, 2017 FC 616, para. 16.

[68] Irwin Toy v. Quebec, [1989] 1 S.C.R. 927 (Can.).

[69] *Charter*, *supra* note 66, § 1. *See* R. v. Oakes, [1986] 1 S.C.R. 103 (Can.) (establishing as the criteria for satisfying § 1: a sufficiently important objective; a rational connection to the objective; impairing the right no more than necessary to accomplish the objective; and not having a disproportionately severe effect on persons to whom it applies).

[70] If the objective is to protect both consumers and traders by preventing confusion in the marketplace, then evidently § 22 impairs free expression more than is reasonably necessary. *See generally* Scassa, *supra* note 6.

their duty to examine IP laws through a constitutional lens.[71] In the *Source Perrier* case, when freedom of expression was raised in defense of the PIERRE EH parody, the court dismissed it, opining:

> [T]he most liberal interpretation of "freedom of expression" does not embrace the freedom to depreciate the goodwill of registered trade marks, nor does it afford licence to impair the business integrity of the owner of the marks merely to accommodate the creation of a spoof. It must be borne in mind that this application for an injunction does not originate from the targets of the parody . . . but from the owner of the trade marks[72]

Because it was the *owner* of a trademark who requested an injunction—someone trying to protect a property interest and not only to silence critique—section 2(b) was found not to be at issue. In other words, expression that might depreciate the goodwill of a registered trademark is not free expression: however broadly that freedom is construed, we are told, it could not possibly give the right to interfere with the value of IP. A familiar tone of moral disapproval pervades this passage, with the "business integrity of the owner" being juxtaposed against the defendant's mere "creation of a spoof." In this moral hierarchy, the injured corporate owner of IP is lauded as deserving rightsholder while the defendant's expressive efforts are trivialized and dismissed—predictably elevating property and diminishing speech.[73]

The assumptions embedded in this IP/speech hierarchy were made even more explicit in the controversial *Michelin* case.[74] There, the defendant trade union argued that prohibiting the use of an employer's trademark in a union organizing campaign would be an unconstitutional restriction on the Charter right of freedom of expression. The Federal Court correctly found no trademark infringement in the absence of commercial use; but issuing the injunction for copyright infringement, the Federal Court reasoned that the defendants' right to free expression was not restricted: "The *Charter* does not confer the right to use private property—the Plaintiff's copyright - in the service of freedom of expression."[75] The same

[71] See Bita Amani & Carys Craig, *The "Jus" of Use: Trademarks in Transition*, 30(2) Intell. Prop. J. 217, 255–57 (2018). In contrast, U.S. courts have explicitly recognized and grappled with the potential clash between trademark and free speech protections. *See, e.g.*, Radiance Foundation, Inc. v. National Association for the Advancement of Colored People, 786 F.3d 316, 319 (4th Cir. 2015) ("Courts have taken care to avoid Lanham Act interpretations that gratuitously court grave constitutional concerns"); Lamparello v. Falwell, 420 F.3d 309, 313 (4th Cir. 2005) ("Congress "did not intend for trademark laws to impinge the First Amendment rights of critics and commentators"); Mattel, Inc. v. MCA Records, Inc., 296 F.3d 894, 900 (9th Cir. 2002); Rogers v. Grimaldi, 875 F.2d 994, 998 (2d Cir. 1989).

[72] *Source Perrier S.A.* (1983), 70 C.P.R. (2d) 61, 67 (Can. F.T.C.D.).

[73] *Cf.* Carys Craig, Copyright, Communication and Culture: Towards A Relational Theory of Copyright Law 211 (2011).

[74] *Michelin*, [1996] 71 C.P.R. (3d) 348.

[75] *Id.* para. 85. Justice Teitelbaum explicitly stated that the conclusion would apply equally to the infringement provisions of the Trade-marks Act, at para. 82: "if I am incorrect in holding that there

principles would have applied, the Court made clear, if trademark infringement had occurred: the right to freedom of expression cedes to the protection of IP.

The *Michelin* ruling is over twenty years old and yet it continues to loom large at the intersection of freedom of expression and IP in Canada.[76] I have argued elsewhere that the ruling rested on a misconstruction of the nature of IP, its relationship to property and to constitutional rights.[77] Even if correct at the time, however, intervening developments in the Charter and IP jurisprudence present compelling grounds for concluding that it is no longer good law.[78] While some Canadian courts have since given greater credence to the possibility of a conflict between trademark protection and freedom of expression, there remains a distinct ambivalence around the issue, and no direct engagement with the section 1 criteria for justifying trademark limitations on free speech.[79] *Michelin* remains oft-cited and available as authority to support dismissing out of hand, as Justice Phelan did, the Charter's relevance to IP rights and their enforcement.

Of course, it simply cannot be correct that the Trademarks Act takes priority over a constitutional right. This, as Jane Bailey pithily explains, would mean putting the statutory IP horse before the constitutional cart.[80] But the characterization of trademarks as IP allows the logic of private property to prevail, distorting the nature of the rights in the balance, and suppressing the essence of trademarks *as speech*. Rather than competing speech interests, then, the court sees parody versus

has been no infringement of the *Trade-marks Act*, the principles and outcome detailed below on the infringement of the *Copyright Act*, are equally relevant to the *Trade-marks Act*."

[76] *See, e.g.*, Corporation Sun Media c. Syndicat canadien de la fonction publique, 2007 QCCS 2943, para. 32 (Can. Que.) (a Quebec Court ruled against strikers reproducing an employer newspaper's masthead on placards, reasoning that the injunction was not a limit on their free expression because use of another's property is a just limit on that freedom).

[77] Carys J Craig, *Putting the Community in Communication: Dissolving the Conflict Between Freedom of Expression and Copyright*, 56 U. OF TORONTO L. J. 75 (2006); *see also* David Fewer, *Constitutionalizing Copyright: Freedom of Expression and the Limits of Copyright in Canada*, 55 U. TOR. FAC. L. REV. 175 (1997); Jane Bailey, *Deflating the Michelin Man: Protecting Users' Rights in the Canadian Copyright Reform Process*, *in* IN THE PUBLIC INTEREST: THE FUTURE OF CANADIAN COPYRIGHT LAW 125 (Michael Geist ed., 2005); Bita Amani, *Copyright and Freedom of Expression: Fair Dealing Between Work and Play*, *in* DYNAMIC FAIR DEALING: CREATING CANADIAN CULTURE ONLINE 43 (Rosemary J. Coombe et al. eds., 2013).

[78] Graeme J. Reynolds, *Reconsidering Copyright's Constitutionality*, 53 OSGOODE HALL L. J. 898 (2016).

[79] *See* Bell ExpressVu Ltd. Partnership v. Tedmonds & Co. Inc., 2001 CanLII 28350, para. 43 (Can. Ont. Sup. Ct.) (stating, with regard to a gripe site that included the trademark in its domain name, that "the website promotes criticism of the plaintiff as a commercial enterprise. In that regard, its function could be characterized as the exercise of free speech and, consequently, may well be said to be protected by virtue of Section 2 (b) of the *Charter of Rights and Freedoms*, although that issue was not raised before me."). *But see also* United Food and Commercial Workers International Union v. Sigurdur (c.o.b. Members for Democracy), 2005 BCSC 1904, paras. 14–15 (Can.); Law Society (British Columbia) v. Canada Domain Name Exchange Corp. (2004), 243 D.L.R. (4th) 746, 753 (Can.) (finding that unmodified use of a trademark in a domain name can amount to passing off). *See generally* Scassa, *supra* note 6, at 887–89.

[80] Bailey, *supra* note 77, at 141–42.

property; rather than criticism, it sees misappropriation. And so infringement is found, and an injunction issued.

II. *United* Untied: Lessons from Cooperstock's Case

It should by now be clear that the internal limits of Canada's trademark law, described at the outset of Section I, simply failed and gave way in the *United* case. The concept of trademark "use" was stretched to capture a noncommercial activity; "services" extended to the provision of information for public benefit; "confusion" expanded to prevent an obvious parodic reference to the mark; and "dilution" was permitted to capture critical consumer commentary. Moreover, the external limits of trademark law found in the Constitution—the limited scope of federal jurisdiction and the fundamental right of free expression—also collapsed, with the latter being expressly dismissed as irrelevant. The case should therefore function as a vehicle for demonstrating the inherent weakness of relying on such implicit limits and exceptions to appropriately restrain trademark's reach. In Section II, then, my aim is to propose other routes toward adequately protecting the freedom to lawfully use a trademark as Cooperstock did: first, through the enactment of a statutory trademark fair-use provision; second, through the recognition of lawful non-infringing use as a "user's right"; and finally, through the normative shift to a communication theory of trademark law.

A. The Case for Explicit Limitations

The most obvious lesson to be learned from the *United* case is that explicit statutory exceptions and limitations upon trademark rights are essential to achieving the appropriate balance between protecting owners and users of trademarks. Conceptually, it is true that explicit exceptions are not required in order to render lawful activities that already occur outside the boundaries of the owner's claim to right. Practically and politically, however, the textual omission of such exceptions and the vagueness of these boundaries create the perfect conditions for over-claiming owners to succeed. As David Vaver notes, the failure to statutorily specify explicit exceptions means that they have to be "squeezed out of [the] Act … by a process of sophisticated, extensive, and expensive interpretation, making users look as if they are taking advantage of some loophole they have found only through the ingenuity of their lawyer."[81] (This, of course, leaves little hope for the user without a lawyer.) In contrast, the Act sets out a broad list of owners' rights, which

[81] Vaver, *supra* note 7, at 193.

tend in turn to be expansively construed. In the wake of the *United* case, it is obvious that Canada's trademark regime now needs "an appropriate limitation infrastructure that is capable of counterbalancing the broad grant of protection."[82] The CIPPIC intervenor factum in support of Cooperstock's appeal nicely captured the problem as follows:

> Unlike the Copyright Act, the Trademarks Act contains few explicit exceptions or user rights. This textual imbalance invites overreach: while the statute provides ample textual evidence of its objective, the lack of explicit acknowledgement of users offers courts few cues to constrain oppressive use of trade-mark rights.[83]

If Canada is to shore up its trademark limits, a good starting point can be found in the U.S. Lanham Act and the exclusions from dilution liability added in 2006.[84] Under these provisions, no actionable dilution can result from "any fair use, including a nominative or descriptive fair use, or facilitation of such fair use, of a famous mark" in connection with comparative advertising, "news reporting and commentary," "any non-commercial use of the mark," and—most notably for our purposes—"identifying and parodying, criticizing, or commenting upon the famous mark owner or the goods or services of the famous mark owner."[85] In the United States, these explicit exceptions have enabled courts to better mediate the tension between trademark protection and free speech, permitting parodic plays on famous marks whether in service of commercial gain[86] or biting critique.[87] Such a provision, in the Canadian context, could at least have signaled to the court that Cooperstock's use of the UNITED mark to identify, comment on, and criticize the services offered by United Airlines should be a fair and lawful permitted use.[88]

There are two important restrictions here, however, that mean Canadian policymakers ought to look beyond the U.S. example in formulating a new fair-use exception. First, the U.S. exception is available only for uses "other than as a

[82] *Cf.* Martin Senftleben, *Adapting EU Trademark Law to New Technologies: Back to Basics?*, *in* CONSTRUCTING EUROPEAN ON INTELLECTUAL PROPERTY 137, 176 (Christophe Geiger ed., 2013) (arguing that such a "limitation infrastructure" is needed in the context of EU trademark law).

[83] Memorandum of Fact and Law of Samuelson-Glushko Canadian Internet Policy and Public Interest Clinic, *supra* note 4, para. 14.

[84] *Cf.* Senftleben, *supra* note 82, at 172 (referencing Trademark Dilution Revision Act of 2006 (H.R. 683) amending the U.S. Trademark Act of 1946 (15 U.S.C. 1125)).

[85] Trademarks Act, 15 U.S.C. § 1125 (C)(3).

[86] *See, e.g.*, Malletier, S.A. v. My Other Bag, Inc., 156 F. Supp. 3d 425, 433–38 (S.D.N.Y. 2016); Louis Vuitton Malletier S.A. v. Haute Diggity Dog, LLC, 507 F.3d 252, 260 (4th Cir. 2007).

[87] *See* Radiance Foundation, Inc. v. National Association for the Advancement of Colored People, 786 F.3d 316, 330 (4th Cir. 2015) (finding that replacing "Advancement" with "Abortion" in the National Association for the Advancement of Colored People trademark "falls plainly within the fair and non-commercial use exclusions").

[88] *See* Bereskin, *supra* note 14, at 836–37 (proposing amendments to § 22 of Canada's Trademarks Act including the addition of explicit exclusions for parody, criticism, comment, and "any *bona fide* noncommercial or expressive use of a mark as a trademark or otherwise").

designation of source for the person's own goods or services."[89] As Stacy Dogan and Mark Lemley have noted in the U.S. context, this unfortunately excludes cases where critics or parodists are using the famous mark to brand their own products or services.[90] If Canada had an exception to depreciation liability crafted along similar lines, Cooperstock would have been entitled to benefit from it; however, the (mistaken) finding that he was using the mark as a trademark in association with services would have been sufficient to deprive him of those benefits. The other restriction, of course, is that the exception applies only to dilution by blurring or tarnishment, leaving open the risk of liability for confusion. While most parodies are by definition unlikely to confuse, confusion is a "fact-specific inquiry, often heavily reliant on manipulable survey evidence and subject to an ever-expanding notion of what it takes to confuse."[91] The *United* case demonstrated the confusion doctrine's expansiveness and malleability. For this reason, too, even if Canadian law had included an equivalent exception, Cooperstock would likely not have been adequately shielded from liability.

What is really required in order to appropriately protect expressive uses such as Cooperstock's is a free-standing trademark fair-use defense similar to the fair dealing defense found in Canada's Copyright Act.[92] Such a provision could, for example, explicitly state that no registration of a trademark prevents a person from making any fair use, including a nominative or descriptive fair use, of a mark for purposes of parody or satire, criticism or review, news reporting, comparative advertising, or any noncommercial use. The assessment of fairness could, borrowing from the Supreme Court's copyright jurisprudence, involve consideration of the purpose and character of the use, the nature of the mark and the goods and services in association with which it is registered, available alternatives to the use, and its effect on the value of the goodwill attaching to the mark.[93] These factors would, of course, have to be analyzed in light of the objectives of the Trademarks Act—in particular, the dual purposes of preventing consumer confusion and unfair competition—and with a view to *Charter* values including, most notably, freedom of expression. Even a small risk of consumer confusion, for example, would weigh against a finding of fairness in such an analysis, but it would not necessarily preclude fair use in cases where the countervailing speech interests are substantial.[94] Since copyright can vest in trademarks, as it did in the UNITED logos, thereby establishing a double layer of IP rights, an added benefit of enacting this kind of

89 Trademarks Act, 15 U.S.C. § 1125 (C)(3).

90 Stacey L. Dogan & Mark A. Lemley, *Parody as Brand*, 47 U. C. DAVIS L. REV. 473, 488, 503 (2013).

91 *Id.* at 487.

92 Copyright Act, R.S.C. 1985, c C-42, §§ 29, 29.1, 29.2 (Can.).

93 CCH v. Law Society of Upper Canada, 2004 SCC 13, [2004] 1 S.C.R. 339, para. 53 (Can.).

94 *See* Dogan & Lemley, *supra* note 90, at 505 (suggesting that, in the case of brand parodies, "the risk of confusion . . . might be so small, and countervailing speech interests so substantial, that courts should dispense with analysis of likelihood of confusion" (*citing* Rogers v. Grimaldi, 875 F.2d 994, 999 (2d Cir. 1989)).

parallel fair-use provision would be reducing the potential for trademark protection to undermine the carefully drawn limits of copyright control, and vice versa.

It should be emphasized that a fair-use defense, drafted along these lines, would not be adding new exceptions into the trademark system or taking bites out of existing trademark rights; rather, it would be an explicit statutory foothold for users defending lawful activities that do not interfere with the existing rights and legitimate interests of the trademark owner, properly construed—and a clear cue to courts to appropriately constrain oppressive overreaching by trademark owners. As Canada's Supreme Court recognized in *Mattel*,

> Trade-mark law rests on principles of fair dealing. It is sometimes said to hold the balance between free competition and fair competition.
>
> Fairness, of course, requires consideration of the interest of the public and other merchants and the benefits of open competition as well as the interest of the trade-mark owner in protecting its investment in the mark. *Care must be taken not to create a zone of exclusivity and protection that overshoots the purpose of trade-mark law.*[95]

B. Taking the User-Rights Route

Although explicit limits and exceptions are necessary to clearly demarcate the boundaries of the owner's zone of exclusivity, they occupy a negative space in the IP imaginary, and tend to be easily diminished or set aside in the face of positive claims of right. If owners' rights need an appropriate counterbalance in the trademark system, then "balancing owner rights against user exceptions is incongruous."[96] As Vaver has noted, it "starts off with the scales biased towards rights and against exceptions."[97] Trademark law requires not only the clear articulation of exceptions, then, but their recognition as positive user rights that form an integral part of the overall trademark system and its operation.

In the copyright context, the Supreme Court of Canada has famously effectuated this conceptual shift, consistently employing the term "user rights" since 2004 to describe any actions, including those covered by fair dealing and other exceptions, that users and the public may carry out without infringing the copyright owner's exclusive rights.[98] In the paradigm-shifting case of *CCH v. Law Society of Upper*

[95] Mattel, Inc. v. 3894207 Canada Inc., 2006 SCC 22, [2006] 1 S.C.R. 772, paras. 21–22 (Can.) (emphasis added).

[96] Vaver, *supra* note 7, at 192.

[97] David Vaver, *User Rights*, 25 INTELL. PROP. J. 105, 109 (2013).

[98] CCH v. Law Society of Upper Canada, 2004 SCC 13, [2004] 1 S.C.R. 339, para. 48 (Can.); Alberta (Education) v. Canadian Copyright Licensing Agency (Access Copyright), 2012 SCC 37, [2012] 2 S.C.R. 345, para. 22 (Can.); SOCAN v. Bell Canada, 2012 SCC 36, [2012] 2 S.C.R. 326, paras. 9–10 (Can.); Keatley Surveying Ltd. *v.* Teranet Inc., 2019 SCC 43, paras. 44–47 (Can.); York University v. Canadian Copyright Licensing Agency (Access Copyright), 2021 SCC 32, paras. 90–95 (Can.).

Canada, a unanimous Court endorsed Vaver's assertion that "User rights are not just loopholes. Both owner rights and user rights should therefore be given the fair and balanced reading that befits remedial legislation."[99] Fair dealing was thus declared an "integral part" of the copyright scheme and awarded a "large and liberal interpretation in order to ensure that users' rights are not unduly constrained."[100]

In the trademark system, there has thus far been no equivalent judicial acknowledgment of user rights as such. There is no obvious reason why not. Perhaps it is because the attendant concept of a policy "balance" has been framed, in trademark jurisprudence, as a matter of competition (free versus fair) and so cast in terms of the competing rights of traders, while the public's interest has been relegated to a mere proxy for confusion (relevant primarily for determining whether a trader's rights have been violated). The would-be rights-bearing "user," in this frame, is thereby reduced to either competitor or consumer. Perhaps (as I discuss further below) it is because the idea of the trademark has concretized into commercial property in the legal imagination, such that its significance as a vehicle of expression, information, or education has been more thoroughly obscured. Or perhaps, as Vaver suggested in 2018, there has simply not yet been, in Canadian trademark law, the same opportunity or impetus to cast user rights in such terms.

> Canadian courts have not yet had the occasion or need to employ the language of user rights to describe what people other than trademark owners can legitimately do with or to trademarks. ... The presumption in favour of applying the same [user rights] policy to the [Trademarks Act] (and for that matter to other IP rights) seems nevertheless strong ... and no apparent contrary trademark policy applies.[101]

A coherent picture of the centrality and significance of user rights within the trademark scheme—and across IP regimes more broadly—is nonetheless critical to ensuring that the proliferation of ever-expanding and overlapping rights does not interfere with the legitimate use of trademarks by competitors, traders, consumers, and the public at large. In *Théberge v. Galerie d'Art du Petit Champlain Inc.*, the pivotal case that laid the groundwork for the initial recognition of copyright user rights, the Supreme Court cautioned that "[e]xcessive control by holders of copyrights *and other forms of intellectual property* may unduly limit the ability of the public domain to incorporate and embellish creative innovation in the long-term interests of society as a whole, or create practical obstacles to proper utilization."[102]

[99] 2004 SCC 13, para. 48 (Can.).

[100] *Id.* para. 51.

[101] Vaver, *supra* note 7, at 192–93. The necessary occasion seemed finally to have arrived when Cooperstock was granted leave to appeal, which is why the non-disclosed settlement with United Airlines Inc. was so disappointing to many observers and would-be intervenors.

[102] Théberge v. Galerie d'Art du Petit Champlain Inc. [2002] 2 S.C.R. 336, 355 (Can.).

In the *United* case, excessive control by the trademark owner unduly limited Cooperstock's ability to incorporate the trademark into his consumer complaint's website in the creation of a pointed parody for the purpose of effective critique. This is the kind of obstacle to the proper utilization of IP-protected subject matter of which the Supreme Court warned, and yet the Federal Court concerned itself with the protection of only the trademark owner's rights while perceiving no countervailing user rights against which to balance them.

It is to be hoped, then, that future courts interpreting exceptions and limitations within the Trademarks Act heed Vaver's call to recognize user rights as such, and to give them a fair and balanced reading to temper the reach of owners' rights, just as Canadian copyright jurisprudence has done for over fifteen years. It should not be hard to capture a coherent conception of user rights that transcends the boundaries of IP's categories and safeguards the public interest and the public domain against IP enclosures more broadly. If copyright user rights are indeed a matter of right, then it makes little sense to permit trademark rights to simply override them. Moreover, it should be recalled, if the public domain is the default for free competition and free expression, it is not user rights that are the exception, but owner rights.

C. From Dominion to Dialogue

A final vital lesson can be pulled from the wreckage of the *United* ruling, however: even the enactment of explicit exceptions and the rhetorical embrace of user rights will be insufficient to prevent the overreach of trademark rights without a more fundamental shift in the normative and political discourse around trademark protection. The prioritization of IP protection over consumer critique and parody—over participatory consumer culture and free expression—allowed Justice Phelan to find for the plaintiff, not only in respect of the trademark claim, but also with regard to the copyright claim. This was notwithstanding that, in contrast to the Trademarks Act, Canada's Copyright Act contains an explicit fair dealing exception for parody, satire, criticism, and review that is judicially recognized as a user right. Justice Phelan acknowledged the Supreme Court's instructions that "the provision for fair dealing should not be interpreted restrictively," and that "users' rights are an essential part of furthering the public interest objectives of the *Copyright Act*,"[103] and yet he went on to hold that,

> Parody is not simply a defence to copyright infringement—it is also an aspect of free speech. However, like all free speech, it is not unrestricted. The Defendant's

[103] *United Airlines, Inc.*, 2017 FC 616, [2018] 1 F.C.R. 188, para. 107 (*citing* Society of Composers, Authors and Music Publishers of Canada v. Bell Canada, 2012 SCC 36, [2012] 2 S.C.R. 326, para. 11).

> website . . . is for the allowable purpose of parody, but it does not meet the second step of the test [i.e., fairness]. The questionable purpose of the dealing, amount of the dealing, and effect of the dealing all weigh in favour of the conclusion that this dealing is not fair.

Even in the copyright fair-dealing analysis, the court viewed Cooperstock's expressive activities through the lens of United's proprietary claim over its trademarks and the value of its goodwill: rather than a pointed parody of the "work," Justice Phelan saw an intent "to defame or punish the plaintiff";[104] and rather than seeing a critical commentary that would have no substitution effect in the market for the original work, he saw a risk of confusion that would harm customers' perception of United's services.[105] The protection of United's IP rights was therefore regarded as an appropriate restriction on the defendant's free speech rights.

I have argued elsewhere that the rhetorical embrace of user rights is not a panacea to the imbalance of the copyright system, and brings some additional risk of reifying individual rights claims rather than examining them in light of the social goals that the system is intend to serve.[106] The difficulty with the rights-balancing metaphor is that, by pitting owners against users, it is likely to produce a bald assessment of the relative importance of protecting owners' rights over users' rights rather a careful consideration of the various interests at stake and the broader implications of ruling one way or another. And where the balancing act is presented as placing the plaintiff's property rights against the defendant's speech rights, on either side of the metaphorical scale, then, as we have repeatedly seen, the former will likely be attributed greater weight in the balance. Each of these concerns was borne out in Cooperstock's case.

The better approach, I believe, is to consider the appropriate scope of rights and interests with a view to the objectives of the law, the relationships it shapes, and the social values that it is intended to foster. In the trademark context, this means looking at the relationships between traders as competitors, but also the relationship between the trademark owner, consumers, and the public at large. As Dev Gangjee has argued, a proprietary conception of the trademark owner's entitlement assumes a certain kind of relationship between a brand owner and the consumer that is inapt and anachronistic in the modern participatory economy. Gangjee criticizes a judicial approach (akin to Justice Phelan's) that regards the brand as "an object of property rights," and sees the "effort and investment by the trade mark owner to create the brand . . . as the basis for preventing the unauthorised

[104] *United Airlines, Inc.*, 2017 FC 616, para. 125.

[105] *Id.* para. 138 ("In this case, it is not the effect on the market that ought to be considered, but rather the confusion caused by the similarity between UNTIED.com and the United Website."); *See also id.* para. 140.

[106] *See* Carys J. Craig, *Globalizing User Rights-Talk: On Copyright Limits and Rhetorical Risks*, 33 Am. U. Int'l L. Rev. 1 (2017).

misappropriation of brand image."[107] This proprietary paradigm, he explains, fails to acknowledge "that brand formation is dialogic and iterative, as opposed to being the result of a one-way broadcast."[108] Brands like United's are not generated by the singular efforts of the brand owner, but "are negotiated, context-sensitive and constantly reproduced by a range of actors."[109] It is in the interaction between the corporate owner and the consumer that trademarks as brands are continually constructed and reconstructed through "social communication processes."[110]

The significance of this social construction of brands explains why United would want to limit Cooperstock's capacity to reconstruct the UNITED/UNTIED mark as something that has come undone. But it also underscores why United ought not to be permitted to invoke its brand *qua* private property in order to do so. The UNITED brand is necessarily open-ended and dynamic, not the singular static creation of United. The consumer is not reducible to a passive recipient of the brand owner's intended messaging, but is a co-creator of the brand as a contested site of meaning that is always in flux. As Rosemary Coombe has explained, our engagement, as consumers and citizens, with commercial signs involves a collective *drive-to-meaning*: "the consumption of commodified representational forms is productive activity in which people engage in meaning-making to adapt signs, texts, and images to their own agendas."[111] This is, of course, exactly what Cooperstock was doing.

When we regard the trademark in these terms, it ceases to resemble a static object of ownership. Situated in cultural context, the trademark is better understood as sign or text: a "signifier," in semiotic theory;[112] or, in dialogic theory, an "utterance."[113] As such, it is never "monologic" (single-voiced) but is necessarily a site of discursive struggle.[114] As Coombe cautioned, the protection that trademark law affords "may deprive us of the optimal cultural conditions for dialogic practice."[115]

[107] *See* Dev S. Gangjee, *Property in Brands: The Commodification of Conversation, in* CONCEPTS OF PROPERTY IN INTELLECTUAL PROPERTY LAW 29, 58 (Helena Howe & Jonathan Griffiths eds., 2013), http://papers.ssrn.com/sol3/papers.cfm?abstract_id=2249765.

[108] *Id.*

[109] *Id. See also* Florian Martin-Bariteau, *The Idea of Property in Intellectual Property*, 52(3) U. BRIT. COL. L. REV. 891, n. 20 and accompanying text (suggesting that a proprietary philosophy obscures the informational dimension of trademarks in cases like *Cooperstock*, where fundamental freedoms to access information and to express criticism are at stake).

[110] *Id.* at 57.

[111] Rosemary Coombe, *Objects of Property and Subjects of Politics: Intellectual Property Laws and Democratic Dialogue*, 69 TEX. L. REV. 1853, 1863 (1990–91).

[112] *See generally* Barton Beebe, *The Semiotic Analysis of Trade Mark Law*, 51 UCLA L. REV. 621 (2004).

[113] *See* MIKHAIL M. BAKHTIN, THE DIALOGIC IMAGINATION: FOUR ESSAYS 354 (Michael Holquist ed., Caryl Emerson & Michael Holquist trans., 1981).

[114] Notably, for Bakhtin, parody is the archetypal example of multivocal (double-voiced) utterance. *See* MIKHAIL BAKHTIN, PROBLEMS OF DOSTOEVSKY'S POETICS 194 (Caryl Emerson ed. & trans., 1984) ("[I]n all possible varieties of parodistic discourse the relationship between the author's and the other person's aspirations remains the same: these aspirations pull in different directions, in contrast to the unidirectional aspirations of [singled-voiced (monologic) discourse]).

[115] Coombe, *supra* note 111, at 1866.

Certainly, trademark law awards the owner a privileged position in the public discourse, giving it the power to prevent others from making confusing uses of the mark that might harm its capacity to function as a distinctive communicator of meaning. But trademark law should not—indeed cannot—give the owner a monopoly on meaning.

Michael Spence has also argued that that language of property is inapposite to trademark law's task, producing a presumption that the trademark owner "ought, absent good reason to the contrary, to control all its potential uses"[116]—a presumption that pervades Justice Phelan's judgment. Palpable in the Court's reasons was the desire to grant strong protection to a highly valuable mark. This desire, Spence notes, reflects "the corollary of the property *topos* that investment should be protected."[117] Spence similarly proposes a shift from what he calls the "property *topos*" to the "speech *topos*" as a way to both ground and limit trademark rights. Trademark law is "a regime concerned, at its very heart, with the regulation of speech," he argues, which has "important consequences for the interpretation of the legislative schema."[118] Trademark law prevents potentially misleading commercial speech, of course, but also protects the owner's expressive autonomy. According to Spence, the owner should not be compelled to speak through others' unauthorized use of its mark or have its meaning "recoded"; but by the same token, its claim must be limited by the expressive autonomy of others who wish to allude to the mark, "especially where it is necessary for successful criticism of the mark, its owner or her goods or services."[119] Regarded in these terms, Cooperstock's exercise of expressive autonomy established a just limit to the expressive autonomy of United, speaking as he was on his own behalf.[120]

To Spence's position I would add that expressive autonomy should be understood in relational terms: the concept of "autonomy within relations"[121] places greater import on our essential interdependence, emphasizing that the act of communication is not an isolated exercise of individual autonomy but an interdependent process of exchange that is interactive and interanimating. While a property model understands the interaction of owner and user as one of exclusion and misappropriation, the communication model perceives that interaction as dialogic. This dialogic construction of meaning demands greater space for discursive struggle and the transformation or recoding of meaning as an exercise of expressive agency by the relational, socially situated user.[122] As such, it is this conceptual

[116] Spence, *supra* note 53, at 496.

[117] *Id.* at 497.

[118] *Id.*

[119] *Id.* at 510.

[120] Spence may disagree, however, if he were to regard Cooperstock's speech as a recoding of the UNITED mark rather than a necessary allusion for comparison or cultural reference. *See id.* at 513.

[121] *See generally* JENNIFER NEDELSKY, LAW'S RELATIONS: A RELATIONAL THEORY OF SELF, AUTONOMY, AND LAW (2011).

[122] The proposed theory of trademark law centered on relations of communication rather than property draws on ideas that I have advanced elsewhere in respect of copyright law. *See, e.g.*, Carys J. Craig,

shift from dominion to dialogue that is, in my opinion, critical to redefining and appropriately delimiting trademark rights.

Recognizing the communicative function of the mark as its defining characteristic means recognizing its capacity to indicate not only the source of goods and services, but also all of the fluid meanings that emerge and evolve through our interaction with the mark, from producers' positive brand images to consumers' critical counter-narratives. As Teresa Scassa notes, it is precisely because the trademark is so "densely packed with meaning"—because of "the elliptical way in which [it] can convey complex messages"—that it is "an ideal vehicle for critical expression."[123] Outside of the trademark context, the Supreme Court of Canada has already recognized the social value of consumers' "counter-advertising activities" as a protected form of expression.

> Consumers may express their frustration or disappointment with a product or service. Their freedom of expression in this respect is not limited to private communications intended solely for the vendor or supplier of the service. Consumers may share their concerns, worries or even anger with other consumers and try to warn them against the practices of a business. Given the tremendous importance of economic activity in our society, a consumer's "counter-advertising" assists in circulating information and protecting the interests of society just as much as does advertising or certain forms of political expression. This type of communication may be of considerable social importance, even beyond the merely commercial sphere.[124]

It is only by denying the nature of a trademark as communication, in this sense, and instead treating it as a species of valuable private property to be controlled by the corporate owner, that Canadian courts have used trademark (and copyright) law to silence critical counter-messaging through the transformative use of commercial symbols. But if we expect the public to consume commodified signs, to assign value and meaning to them to the benefit of their owners, and to contribute to their construction and reconstruction, then we must respect that the public's reception and consumption of these signs will necessarily be a productive one: the very law that protects trademarks as sites of shared and shifting meaning cannot deny the public its informal discursive power to attach new meanings, use the signs in new contexts, discuss them, distort them, and critique them.

Transforming "Total Concept & Feel": Dialogic Creativity and Copyright's Substantial Similarity Doctrine, 38 Card. J. of A. & Ent. 603 (2020).

[123] Scassa, *supra* note 6, at 886.

[124] R. v. Guignard, 2002 SCC 14, [2002] 1 S.C.R. 472, para. 23 (Can.).

In the digital era, more than ever, it is the task of the trademark owner to engage effectively in this cultural conversation as a speaker in its own right, to attempt to create and maintain its desired meaning in the midst of this "heteroglossia" (the diversity of voices or clashing points of view that reside simultaneously within the mark).[125] It is not, and has never been, the task of trademark law to shield the trademark owner from this public discourse—under the pretense of preventing misappropriation—as the Federal Court sought to shield United from Cooperstock's critique.

Conclusion

The problem that pervaded the court's reasoning in *United Airlines, Inc. v. Cooperstock* was the perception of the United logos as valuable objects over which the corporate IP owner was entitled to exercise near-absolute control. The case reveals the flaw of relying on internal limits and implicit exceptions to circumscribe the scope of trademark owner's control. It underscores the need for explicit exceptions that reflect the internal and external limits of trademark rights and ensure adequate breathing space for parody, criticism, and other fair uses and free expression. The case also reveals the need for a positive conception of "user rights" in the trademark scheme parallel to that already recognized in Canada's copyright system. But if user rights are to have any real traction in the legal landscape of trademark law, Cooperstock's plight suggests that a more fundamental shift is needed in the judicial mindset. Commodification has to give way to communication as a framing idea. Trademark law requires a fuller appreciation of the communicative and social value of marks as indicators of source and incubators of meaning—but also, therefore, as public sites of dialogic engagement and discursive struggle.

[125] Bakhtin uses the term "heteroglossia" (or untranslated: *raznojazychie*) to capture the dynamic complexity and clamorousness of multivocal utterances: Mikhail Bakhtin, *Discourse in the Novel, in* THE DIALOGIC IMAGINATION: FOUR ESSAYS BY M.M. BAKHTIN 259, 271 (C. Emerson & M. Holquist eds., 1975).

5
Fame, Parody, and Policing in Trademark Law

*Mark A. Lemley**

Introduction

Trademark owners regularly overreach. They often threaten or sue people they have no business suing, including satirists, parodists, noncommercial users, and gripe sites. When they do, they often justify their aggressive legal conduct by pointing to the need to protect their trademarks by policing infringement. Courts have in fact indicated at various points that policing is, if not strictly necessary, at least a way to strengthen a mark. But courts have never held that efforts to block speech-related uses are necessary or even helpful in obtaining a strong mark. Several scholars have accordingly argued that overzealous policing is unnecessary, has harmful effects, and ought to be punished. But trademark owners continue to do it, in part because it is largely (though not completely) costless, and because if there is even a chance a failure to police will cost owners their trademark, they won't want to take the chance. So, not only does trademark law currently fail to prevent overreaching it affirmatively encourages it.

In this chapter, I suggest a way that we can align trademark-owner enforcement incentives with good public policy. The presence of unauthorized parodies, satires, and complaint sites related to a mark should be evidence of the fame of the mark and perhaps even a requirement for status as a famous mark. Taking this approach would be consistent with what we know about how society interacts with trademarks. Famous marks become part of a social conversation in a way that ordinary marks don't.[1] My approach has empirical support: The best-known brands draw more parodies and criticism sites than non-famous marks, and those parodies

* Thanks to Barton Beebe, Stacy Dogan, Eric Goldman, Leah Chan Grinvald, Rose Hagan, Mark McKenna, Lisa Larrimore Ouellette, Alexandra Roberts, Steve Ross, and Rebecca Tushnet for comments and helpful discussions and James Yoon and Andrew McCreary for excellent research assistance. This article was first published in the Michigan State Law Review.

[1] *See* Jessica Kiser, *Brandright*, 70 Ark. L. Rev. 489, 493 (2017); Giulio Ernesto Yaquinto, Note, *The Social Significance of Modern Trademarks: Authorizing the Appropriation of Marks as Source Identifiers for Expressive Works*, 95 Tex. L. Rev. 739, 740 (2017); Rochelle Cooper Dreyfuss, *Expressive Genericity: Trademarks as Language in the Pepsi Generation*, 65 Notre Dame L. Rev. 397, 397 (2014).

Mark A. Lemley, *Fame, Parody, and Policing in Trademark Law* In: *Charting Limitations on Trademark Rights*. Edited by: Haochen Sun and Barton Beebe, Oxford University Press. © Mark A. Lemley 2023.
DOI: 10.1093/oso/9780198871248.003.0006

don't interfere with the fame of the mark. And my approach would give trademark owners an affirmative reason to leave critics, satirists, and parodists alone.

In Section I, I talk about the problem. In Section II, I talk about how we might solve it and consider some objections.

I. The Trademark Police State

Trademark owners regularly make extremely broad claims for their marks, trying to control simple shapes, words, or even letters regardless of context or of whether trademark law gives any right over those things. Sometimes these claims are brought against competitors.[2] Other times they are brought against companies in very different product fields who want to use a similar mark or logo.[3]

More alarming, trademark owners regularly bring claims against social and political speech that uses their marks in ways they don't like. Trademark owners sue parodists.[4] They sue satirists.[5] They sue gripe

[2] *See, e.g.*, M.Z. Berger & Co. v. Swatch AG, 787 F.3d 1368, 1370, 1371 (Fed. Cir. 2015) (holding that the registrant of "iWatch" lacked the requisite intent for validity in a case brought by competitor Swatch); Deere & Co. v. M.T.D. Prods., Inc., 41 F.3d 39, 41 (2d Cir. 1994) (affirming the injunction of a mark's use by a competitor, even in the context of an attack ad).

[3] *See, e.g.*, Kellogg Co. v. Toucan Golf, Inc., 337 F.3d 616, 624–25 (6th Cir. 2003) (denying claims by a cereal maker with "Toucan Sam" word mark and logos against a golfing company with "Toucan Gold" word mark and logos); Kim Bhasin, *Adidas Trademark War Means Three Stripes and You're in Court*, BLOOMBERG (Mar. 15, 2017 4:00 AM), https://www.bloomberg.com/news/articles/2017-03-15/adidas-trademark-war-means-three-stripes-and-you-re-out [https://perma.cc/F5FT-XSD9] (describing Adidas contesting Tesla's Model 3 car logo registration for supposed similarity to its three stripes, leading Tesla to withdraw its application and change its logo without litigation). Parodies of course often involve unrelated products if they involve products at all. *See, e.g.*, Ringling Bros.-Barnum & Bailey Combined Shows, Inc. v. Utah Div. of Travel Dev., 955 F. Supp. 605, 608–09 (E.D. Va. 1997) (alleging that the mark "Greatest Snow on Earth" for state license plate and tourism marketing purposes diluted plaintiff's "Greatest Show on Earth" mark for a circus).

[4] *See, e.g.*, E.S.S. Entm't 2000, Inc. v. Rock Star Videos, Inc., 547 F.3d 1095, 1097, 1101 (9th Cir. 2008) (holding the "Pig Pen" club depicted in the streets of a Grand Theft Audio video game was protected parody of the "Play Pen" club); Mattel, Inc. v. Walking Mountain Prods., 353 F.3d 792, 796 (9th Cir. 2003) (affirming summary judgment for defendant artist of "Barbie Enchiladas," "Fondue a la Barbie," and other artistic parodies); Mattel, Inc. v. MCA Records, Inc., 296 F.3d 894, 908 (9th Cir. 2002) (holding "[t]he parties are advised to chill" in the case of Barbie maker against the record company behind "The Barbie Girl" song); Hormel Foods Corp. v. Jim Henson Prods., Inc., 73 F.3d 497, 500 (2d Cir. 1996) (holding Muppet character "Spa'am" did not infringe SPAM trademark); Louis Vuitton Malletier, S.A. v. My Other Bag, Inc., 156 F. Supp. 3d 425, 430 (S.D.N.Y. 2016) (holding a canvas tote that depicted a Louis Vuitton handbag with the text "My Other Bag" in a parody of "my other car" bumper stickers did not infringe Louis Vuitton's trademarks); *see also* Stacey L. Dogan & Mark A. Lemley, *Parody as Brand*, 47 U.C. DAVIS L. REV. 473, 474–77 (2013) (reviewing trademark cases involving parodies).

[5] *See, e.g.*, Dr. Seuss Enters., L.P. v. Penguin Books USA, Inc., 109 F.3d 1394, 1400–01, 1406 (9th Cir. 1997) (holding use of Dr. Seuss trademark was satiric not parodic and so unprotected); L.L. Bean, Inc. v. Drake Publishers, Inc., 811 F.2d 26, 27, 34 (1st Cir. 1987) (holding a pornographic magazine's two-page "L.L. Beam's Back-To-School-Sex-Catalog [sic]" feature was a protected parody of the L.L. Bean catalogue); Bill Donahue, *Brand Battles: HBO Aims to Depose 'Game of Thorns'*, LAW 360 (Oct. 12, 2018), https://www.law360.com/articles/1091764 [https://perma.cc/KP7J-T3X8] (reporting a challenge by the owners of the Game of Thrones trademark against an effort by a botanical garden to brand its educational programs "Game of Thorns"); Bill Donahue, *Brand Battles: NASA, Ivy League, "Lord of the Rings,"* LAW 360 (Oct. 5, 2018), https://www.law360.com/articles/1089922 [https://perma.cc/

sites.[6] They sue competitors who make fun of them[7] and other companies who make cultural references to them.[8] They sue movies and TV shows that depict their products in ways they find unflattering.[9] They sue politicians who use their marks in campaign ads and speeches.[10] They sue people who use their trademarks to talk about the plaintiff's own products.[11] They sue people who make posters, t-shirts, and plush toys that evoke their marks, even when it is beyond doubt that it is not the trademark owners who are selling those products.[12]

NBD6-D3XY] (reporting a challenge by the owners of the Lord of the Rings trademark against a confectioner who wanted to use "Lord of Meringues" as a trademark); *see also* Dogan & Lemley, *supra* note 4, at 498–500 (discussing cases and the elusive distinction between parody and satire); *cf.* Campbell v. Acuff-Rose Music, Inc., 510 U.S. 569, 580–81 (1994) (distinguishing parody in a copyright context, which pokes fun at the protected material, from satire, which uses the protected material to poke fun at something else, but noting that both can be protected).

[6] *See, e.g.*, Lamparello v. Falwell, 420 F.3d 309, 311, 321–22 (4th Cir. 2005) (holding no actionable infringement for use of Reverend Jerry Falwell's mark in www.fallwell.com, a noncommercial site critical of Falwell's views on gay people); Bosley Med. Inst. v. Kremer, 403 F.3d 672, 674 (9th Cir. 2005); TMI, Inc., v. Maxwell, 368 F.3d 433, 434, 440 (5th Cir. 2004) (holding no violation of the Lanham Act for www.trendmakerhome.com, a website critical of the company of that name); Taubman Co. v. Webfeats, 319 F.3d 770, 778 (6th Cir. 2003); Savannah Coll. of Art & Design, Inc., v. Houeix, 369 F. Supp. 2d 929, 935, 957–58 (S.D. Ohio 2004) (holding graduate student's scad.info and other websites critical of SCAD not actionable under the Lanham Act because noncommercial uses of the mark are not actionable under the Lanham Act); Bally Total Fitness v. Faber, 29 F. Supp. 2d 1161, 1168 (C.D. Cal. 1998).

[7] *See, e.g., Deere & Co.*, 41 F.3d at 41 (affirming the injunction of a competitor's attack ad with an animation of a John Deere deer fleeing a small barking dog and its own Yard-Man lawn tractor).

[8] *See, e.g.*, Louis Vuitton Malletier, S.A. v. Hyundai Motor Am., No. 10 Civ. 1611(PKC), 2012 WL 1022247, at *1 (S.D.N.Y. Mar. 22, 2012) (finding that a one-second shot in a Hyundai Super Bowl commercial of a basketball covered in interlocking LV marks infringed on and diluted Louis Vuitton's trademark); Am. Dairy Queen Corp. v. New Line Prods., Inc., 35 F. Supp. 2d 727, 728–29 (D. Minn. 1998) (enjoining a film about rural beauty contest seeking to use "Dairy Queens" as title).

[9] *See* Mark A. Lemley & Mark McKenna, *Irrelevant Confusion*, 62 STAN. L. REV. 413, 420–21& nn.31–34 (2010) (describing instances where New York University, Stanford University, the University of Utah, and Major League Baseball objected to their depictions in television shows and movies); William McGeveran, *Rethinking Trademark Fair Use*, 94 IOWA L. REV. 49 (2008).

[10] *See, e.g.*, MasterCard Int'l, Inc. v. Nader 2000 Primary Comm., Inc., No. 00 Civ.6068(GBD), 2004 WL 434404, at *1, *16 (S.D.N.Y. Mar. 8, 2004) (finding that a political ad using Mastercard's "Priceless" template to critique the presence of money in politics to be noncommercial and non-misleading). I represented Nader in this case. *See also* Hershey Co. v. Friends of Steve Hershey, 33 F. Supp. 3d 588, 595 (D. Md. 2014) (granting an injunction for candy bar maker against Senator Hershey's campaign for using Hershey Co.'s trade dress to leverage its goodwill and not "for parody, political commentary, or other communicative purposes"); Lucasfilm Ltd. v. High Frontier, 622 F. Supp. 931, 935–36 (D.D.C. 1985) (dismissing a filmmaker's complaint against political groups using "Star Wars" to describe President Reagan's Strategic Defense Initiative).

[11] *See, e.g.*, Toyota Motor Sales, U.S.A., Inc., v. Tabari, 610 F.3d 1171, 1182–83 (9th Cir. 2010) (vacating an injunction against a non-misleading use of Toyota marks by an independent auto broker); Playboy Enters., Inc. v. Welles, 279 F.3d 796, 799–800 (9th Cir. 2002) (holding a former Playboy Playmate's use of Playboy's marks to describe her career nominative); New Kids on the Block v. News Am. Publ'g, 971 F.2d 302, 308–09 (9th Cir. 1992) (holding the use of band's name in newspaper poll was nominative under a new test).

[12] *See* Bd. of Supervisors for La. State Univ. Agric. & Mech. Coll. v. Smack Apparel Co., 550 F.3d 465, 481–82 n.54 (5th Cir. 2008) (finding infringement even though parties earlier stipulated that no consumer was actually confused about the origin or licensure of knock-off university sports apparel); Louis Vuitton Malletier S.A. v. Haute Diggity Dog, L.L.C., 507 F.3d 252, 261, 263 (4th Cir. 2007) (holding that a plush "Chewy Vuitton" puppy toy was a non-infringing parody of Louis Vuitton, which succeeded by allowing consumers to "to perceive the target of the parody, while simultaneously allowing them to recognize the changes to the mark that make the parody funny or biting"); N. Face Apparel

Sometimes—too often—the trademark owners win these suits.[13] More often they lose.[14] But even claims that are unlikely to win often have the desired effect of scaring off the users. Defending a trademark case is expensive, the outcome is uncertain, and the payoff is limited—you get to keep doing what you were already doing. As a result, far too many people and companies with meritorious defenses simply drop their parody, satire, complaint, or commentary rather than face the prospect of litigation.[15] The result is that even though trademark owners tend to lose most cases against political and social speech, they still end up shutting down quite a bit of socially valuable speech that the law is not intended to target. These efforts likely deter even more protected speech from ever occurring, particularly

Corp. v. Williams Pharmacy, Inc., No. 4:09CV2029RWS, 2010 WL 546928, at *1 (E.D. Mo. Feb. 9, 2010) (discussing a case The North Face brought against the maker of "The South Butt" apparel); Smith v. Wal-Mart Stores, Inc., 537 F. Supp. 2d 1302, 1340 (N.D. Ga. 2008) (holding "WALOCAUST," "WAL-QAEDA," and similar terms used on merchandise sold by a critic of Wal-Mart to be First Amendment-protected, non-infringing uses); Coca-Cola Co. v. Gemini Rising, Inc., 346 F. Supp. 1183, 1193 (E.D.N.Y. 1972) (enjoining the sale of "Enjoy Cocaine" poster stylized like "Enjoy Coca-Cola" poster); Cat Weaver, *Blurring Luxury and Art: Nadia Plesner vs Louis Vuitton*, HyperAllergic (Mar. 25, 2011), https://hyperallergic.com/21392/nadia-plesner-vs-louis-vuitton/ [https://perma.cc/J3QF-72CA] (discussing Louis Vuitton's suit against an artist who depicted a child in a painting holding a Louis Vuitton purse).

[13] *See, e.g.*, Elvis Presley Enters., Inc. v. Capece, 141 F.3d 188, 191 (5th Cir. 1998) (enjoining "Velvet Elvis" as restaurant name); Gucci Shops, Inc. v. R.H. Macy & Co., 446 F. Supp. 838, 839, 841 (S.D.N.Y. 1977) (enjoining the sales of "Gucchi Goo" diaper bags); Motion Picture Ass'n of Am., Inc., v. Respect Sportswear, Inc., 83 U.S.P.Q.2d 1555, 1564 (T.T.A.B. 2007) (denying the registration of "RATED R SPORTSWEAR" lest consumers believe the Motion Picture Association of America also monitors apparel); *see also* Dogan & Lemley, *supra* note 4, at 478 n.27, 484–85 (citing trademark cases, many successful, enjoining parodies); Lemley & McKenna, *supra* note 11, at 417–20 (describing successful cases against defendants using trademarks in artistic, parodic, and other non-confusing ways); Xiyin Tang, *Against Fair Use: The Case for a Genericness Defense in Expressive Trademark Uses*, 101 Iowa L. Rev. 2021, 2039 (2016) (explaining that the current doctrine privileges only certain types of expressive uses, notably parodies).

[14] *See, e.g.*, William McGeveran, *The Imaginary Trademark Parody Crisis (And the Real One)*, 90 Wash. L. Rev. 713, 728–30 (2015) (explaining that after *Campbell* protected a parodic use of a copyrighted work, "courts now favor [i.e., allow] trademark parodies," too).

[15] *See, e.g.*, Glynn S. Lunney, Jr., *Two-Tiered Trademark*, 56 Hous. L. Rev. 295, 297 (2018) ("[T]he party that cannot afford the high and increasing cost of participation in the trademark system loses . . . not because justice . . . dictates that they lose[,] but because they cannot afford to participate in the system. . . [R]esolution will turn solely on which party can afford to litigate."); Leah Chan Grinvald, *Shaming Trademark Bullies*, Wis. L. Rev. 625, 628–30, 652 (2011) (explaining how the costs of rebuffing "trademark bullies" makes "ceasing to use the trademark at stake without a battle" perhaps the least expensive option); McGeveran, *supra* note 9, at 52 ("The lethal combination of uncertain standards with lengthy and costly litigation creates a classic chilling effect upon the unlicensed use of trademarks to facilitate speech, even when such uses are perfectly lawful."); Kenneth L. Port, *Trademark Extortion: The End of Trademark Law*, 65 Wash. & Lee L. Rev. 585, 588–91 (2008) (describing trademark "strike suits" that would likely lose on the merits but that, even when not litigated, accomplish the mark owner's goal of expanding the effective scope of her mark); Deven R. Desai & Sandra L. Reirson, *Confronting the Genericism Conundrum*, 28 Cardozo L. Rev. 1789, 1839 (2007) ("Typically, the threat of litigation alone (even when ever so lightly implied) by a corporate giant is sufficient to dissuade a person from making fair use of a trademark."); *cf.* James Gibson, *Risk Aversion and Rights Accretion in Intellectual Property Law*, 116 Yale L. J. 882, 913 (2007) ("[T]rademark users who could mount a decent defense against an infringement claim [often will] nevertheless choose to seek a license.").

because trademark owners are aggressively sending threatening cease-and-desist letters even when they don't file suit.[16]

When pressed as to why they bring weak trademark claims against protected speech, or even against extremely remote marks, trademark owners frequently fall back on the justification that they have an obligation to police their trademarks against potentially infringing uses.[17] If they don't aggressively enforce their marks, they worry that the value of their marks will be weakened by multiple, conflicting uses.[18] In extreme cases, they worry that they will lose their marks altogether by having courts deem them generic or abandoned or else lose the right to enforce them through laches.[19]

It is tempting to dismiss these claims as cynical efforts to justify conduct that is in fact intended to deter and suppress protected speech the trademark owner simply doesn't like. And in many cases, that is probably the explanation. There doesn't seem to be any case punishing a trademark owner for failing to police a mark against the sorts of speech with which I am concerned here. Indeed, I didn't find a single case holding a mark abandoned or otherwise lost *solely* for failure to police the mark at all. All the cases considering the issue point in the opposite direction.[20] Further, policing alone is generally insufficient to save a mark from

[16] *See, e.g.*, Leah Chan Grinvald, *Policing the Cease-and-Desist Letter*, 49 U.S.F. L. Rev. 411, 411–12 (2015) (noting that 97% of disputes never result in a lawsuit, much less a judgment, and proposing ways to regulate abusive cease-and-desist letters); Irina D. Manta, *Bearing Down on Trademark Bullies*, 22 Fordham Intell. Prop., Media & Ent. L. J. 853, 854–57 (2012); William McGeveran, *The Trademark Fair Use Reform Act*, 90 B.U. L. Rev. 2267, 2269 (2010) ("For every speaker who fights back in court, countless others cautiously back away."); Elizabeth L. Rosenblatt, *Rethinking the Parameters of Trademark Use in Entertainment*, 61 Fla. L. Rev. 1011, 1014 (2009) ("Ultimately, current law creates a doctrinally imbalanced system that chills speech, increases the transaction costs of content creation, and disproportionately harms small or independent content creators.").

[17] *See* William T. Gallagher, *Trademark and Copyright Enforcement in the Shadow of IP Law*, 28 Santa Clara Computer & High Tech. L. J. 453, 490–91 n.115 (2012) (recounting interviews with practitioners who offer this justification for threatening to sue others even when the merits of their claim are weak and describing case law); Port, *supra* note 15, at 587 (citing Wallpaper Mfrs., Ltd. v. Crown Wallcovering Corp., 680 F.2d 755, 766 (C.C.P.A. 1982)) ("Of course, trademark holders must police their trademarks or suffer the fate of a court subsequently finding that trademark holders acquiesced to infringing uses or that the mark now lacks distinctiveness.").

[18] Jeremy Sheff refers to this as fear-driven enforcement. Jeremy N. Sheff, *Fear and Loathing in Trademark Enforcement*, 22 Fordham Intell. Prop., Media, & Ent. L. J. 873, 874–77 (2012).

[19] *See* Grupo Gigante S.A. de C.V. v. Dallo & Co., 391 F.3d 1088, 1101–02 (9th Cir. 2004) (setting out the test for laches and stating that "[c]ompanies expecting judicial enforcement of their marks must conduct an effective policing effort" (emphasis omitted) (quoting Am. Int'l Grp., Inc. v. Am. Int'l Bank, 926 F.2d 829, 834 (9th Cir. 1991) (Kozinski, J., dissenting))); Desai & Rierson, *supra* note 15, at 1791, 1834–42 (discussing the perceived need to police infringement to avoid genericide).

[20] For cases rejecting abandonment claims based on failure to police, see, for example, Palm Bay Imports, Inc. v. Veuve Clicquot Ponsardin Maison Fondee En 1772, 396 F.3d 1369, 1373 (Fed. Cir. 2005) (finding no abandonment despite at least five different alcoholic beverages that use the term VEUVE); Hermes Int'l v. Lederer de Paris Fifth Avenue, Inc., 219 F.3d 104, 110 (2d Cir. 2000); Navajo Nation v. Urban Outfitters, Inc., 212 F. Supp. 3d 1098, 1105 (D.N.M. 2016) ("[T]he existence of third-party infringers does not by itself constitute abandonment of a mark where the mark owner does not consent to its use, provided that the mark does not lose all ability to identify the senior user."); and Patsy's Italian Rest., Inc. v. Banas, 508 F. Supp. 2d 194, 212 (E.D.N.Y. 2007).

becoming generic.[21] Courts have generally considered policing (or lack thereof) as just one piece of evidence when evaluating strength of the mark, likelihood of confusion, genericide, and laches. It is tempting therefore to view the whole requirement of trademark policing as a myth, rather like the received (but inaccurate) wisdom that you shouldn't let your mark be used as a verb for fear that it will be declared generic.[22]

But the reality is a bit more complicated. A failure to police *can* be a factor leading to genericide, even if it is not itself determinative.[23] Policing can influence the scope of protection. Some courts have found trademarks to be stronger because of vigorous efforts to police the mark against infringing uses.[24] On the flip side, a number of courts have found the strength of the mark decreased due to the presence of a number of other similar marks, and the mark thus entitled to only a narrow scope of protection.[25] While that is not specifically a finding that failure to police narrows the scope of a trademark owner's rights, it provides a significant

[21] *See* Anti-Monopoly, Inc. v. Gen. Mills Fun Grp., Inc., 684 F.2d 1316, 1322 (9th Cir. 1982) ("[Policing], however, is not of itself sufficient to create legally protectable rights."); Hickory Farms, Inc. v. Snackmasters, Inc., 509 F. Supp. 2d 716, 723 (N.D. Ill. 2007) ("[P]olicing is of no consequence to a resolution of whether a mark is generic.") (quoting Murphy Door Bed Co. v. Interior Sleep Systems Inc., 874 F.2d 95, 101 (2d Cir. 1989)); *see also* Pilates, Inc. v. Current Concepts, Inc., 120 F. Supp. 2d 286, 306 (S.D.N.Y. 2000).

[22] *See* Rose A. Hagan, *The Myths of Genericide*, 22 IPL Newsl. 13, 13 (2004) (finding that no trademark in history has been held generic merely because it was used as a verb). That myth was dispelled for good, I suspect, in Elliott v. Google Inc., 860 F.3d 1151, 1155 (9th Cir. 2017).

[23] *See* BellSouth Corp. v. DataNational Corp., 60 F.3d 1565, 1570 (Fed. Cir. 1995) ("While the 'Walking Fingers' logo may once have been a strong candidate for trademark protection, through common usage by virtually all classified directory publishers it can no longer be understood to represent a source of the directories."); Malaco Leaf, AB v. Promotion in Motion, Inc., 287 F. Supp. 2d 355, 363 (S.D.N.Y. 2003) ("This Court agrees that the generic design of Malaco's Swedish Fish, along with extensive third party use of the design and Malaco's failure to police infringing third-party uses, renders the Swedish Fish design generic and unprotectable.").

[24] *See* Morningside Grp. Ltd. v. Morningside Capital Grp., L.L.C., 182 F.3d 133, 139 (2d Cir. 1999) ("[T]he successful policing of a mark adds to its strength to the extent that it prevents weakening of the mark's distinctiveness in the relevant market."); Abraham v. Alpha Chi Omega, 781 F. Supp. 2d 396, 419 (N.D. Tex. 2011); Cullman Ventures, Inc. v. Columbian Art Works, Inc., 717 F. Supp. 96, 124 (S.D.N.Y. 1989).

[25] *See, e.g.*, CareFirst of Maryland, Inc. v. First Care, P.C., 434 F.3d 263, 270 (4th Cir. 2006) ("This evidence of extensive third-party use also demonstrates that CareFirst's mark lacks commercial strength in many parts of the country."); Supreme Assembly, Order of Rainbow for Girls v. J.H. Ray Jewelry Co., 676 F.2d 1079, 1083–84 (5th Cir. 1982) (treating an organization's historical lack of control over its marks as important in determining that there was no likelihood of confusion as to the source of the mark); Sun Banks of Fla., Inc. v. Sun Federal Sav. & Loan Ass'n, 651 F.2d 311, 316 (5th Cir. 1981) (indicating that in 1976, there were over 4400 businesses registered with the word "Sun" in their names); Amstar Corp. v. Domino's Pizza, Inc., 615 F.2d 252, 265 (5th Cir. 1980) (reasoning that "[a] trademark owner that strongly believed its customers were being deceived would hardly have remained idle for such an extended period of time," and so narrowing Amstar's DOMINO mark to sugar field); Armstrong Cork Co. v. World Carpets, Inc., 597 F.2d 496, 505 (5th Cir. 1979) (reasoning that the fact eighty-five firms using WORLD in carpet retailing and manufacturing "militates against the finding of likelihood of confusion"); Fuel Clothing Co. v. Nike, Inc., 7 F. Supp. 3d 594, 611–13 (D.S.C. 2014) (reasoning that the fact that over 1000 marks included "Fuel" weakened the strength of plaintiff's mark, and granting summary judgment to defendant on most claims); Trs. of Columbia Univ. v. Columbia/HCA Healthcare Corp., 964 F. Supp. 733, 744–45 (S.D.N.Y. 1997) (finding "Columbia" relatively weak as mark in healthcare industry because of substantial third-party use by hospitals, healthcare services, and institutions).

legal incentive to police because failure to do so can allow similar marks to proliferate and cabin the trademark owner's rights.

Further, while policing alone won't prevent a mark from becoming generic, some courts that have rejected claims of genericide have pointed to the absence of competing uses of the mark as a factor, and that absence sometimes results from aggressive enforcement.[26]

Policing is also relevant to laches. Courts will not enforce a trademark if the plaintiff has unreasonably delayed in filing suit and the defendant is prejudiced as a result.[27] Unreasonable delay is measured from the time of either actual or constructive knowledge of the competing use.[28] The constructive knowledge standard effectively imposes on a trademark owner the duty to be aware of potential infringers, and probably to take some action, because trademark owners that should have been aware of a use won't avoid laches because of their ignorance.[29]

The received wisdom that trademark owners must police infringement of their marks, then, is overstated but contains important kernels of truth. Owners don't *have to* police their marks. But doing so helps in various ways. Lawyers who advise trademark owners to police aren't wrong, at least not entirely. The issue is gray, not black and white.

[26] *See, e.g.*, Pfizer Inc. v. Sachs, 652 F. Supp. 2d 512, 521 (S.D.N.Y. 2009) ("Pfizer's active policing efforts also refute Defendants' claim that the Viagra Marks are generic."); Frito-Lay, Inc. v. Bachman Co., 704 F. Supp. 432, 440 (S.D.N.Y. 1989) ("[D]ue to Frito-Lay's vigorous policing efforts . . . [defendant] can offer no evidence of widespread industry use.").

[27] *See, e.g.*, Hot Wax, Inc. v. Turtle Wax, Inc., 191 F.3d 813, 824 (7th Cir. 1999) (holding laches applied because "Hot Wax sat idly by and chose not to challenge" while Turtle Wax invested in the mark for a ten- to twenty-year period); Kason Indus., Inc. v. Component Hardware Grp., Inc., 120 F.3d 1199, 1203 (11th Cir. 1997) (setting out test for doctrine of laches in trademark, including delay without excuse); Sara Lee Corp. v. Kayser-Roth Corp., 81 F.3d 455, 461 (4th Cir. 1996) ("In a trademark case, courts may apply the doctrine of estoppel by laches to deny relief to a plaintiff who, though having knowledge of an infringement, has, to the detriment of the defendant, unreasonably delayed in seeking redress.").

[28] *Kason*, 120 F.3d at 1203. *But cf.* What-A-Burger of Virginia, Inc. v. Whataburger, Inc., 357 F.3d 441, 449 (4th Cir. 2004) ("Instead of focusing on when the trademark owner first knew that another party was using its mark, the court should be trying to determine the time at which the use became infringing and the time at which the owner should have known it . . . .").

[29] *See* E-Systems, Inc., v. Monitek, Inc., 720 F.2d 604, 607 (9th Cir. 1983) ("Plaintiff ought to have discovered defendant's use sooner had it been diligently seeking to enforce its mark."); Black Diamond Sportswear, Inc. v. Black Diamond Equip., Ltd., No. 06-3508-cv, 2007 WL 2914452, at *3 (2d Cir. Oct. 5, 2007) ("A trademark owner is 'chargeable with such knowledge as he might have obtained upon [due] inquiry.'" (alteration in original) (quoting Polaroid Corp. v. Polarad Elecs. Corp., 182 F. Supp. 350, 355 (E.D.N.Y. 1960))); *accord* Cybergun, S.A. v. Jag Precision, No. 2:12-cv-00074-APG-GWF, 2014 WL 7336074, at *3 (D. Nev. Dec. 19, 2014); Brown v. Sixteen, Inc., No. 02 Civ. 4630(DAB), 2009 WL 1159161, at *5 (S.D.N.Y. Apr. 28, 2009); Saul Zaentz Co. v. Wozniak Travel, Inc., 627 F. Supp. 2d 1096, 1114 (N.D. Cal. 2008) (explaining "plaintiff is charged with constructive knowledge"); Miller v. Glenn Miller Prods., 318 F. Supp. 2d 923, 943 (C.D. Cal. 2004); *cf.* Grupo Gigante S.A. de C.V. v. Dallo & Co., 391 F.3d 1088, 1101–02 (9th Cir. 2004) (stating a rule that "[c]ompanies expecting judicial enforcement of their marks must conduct an effective policing effort," though in a case where plaintiff did not claim ignorance of defendant's uses (emphasis omitted) (quoting Am. Int'l Group, Inc. v. Am. Int'l Bank, 926 F.2d 829, 834 (9th Cir. 1991) (Kozinski, J., dissenting))).

II. Policing Parodies

The desirability of stopping obvious acts of infringement—counterfeiting or the adoption of the same mark by a direct competitor—does not mean that trademark owners must or should sue anyone who uses their mark or anything like it. And as noted above, overreaching by trademark owners who bring claims against parodists or critics rather than their commercial competitors causes harm to the world. We should discourage such overreach. The question is how.

One obvious response is for courts to make clear that policing one's mark against infringing uses doesn't require policing against non-infringing uses like parody, criticism, non-trademark use,[30] or nominative use of the mark to refer to the trademark owner's own goods.[31] This seems easy, indeed almost tautological: Trademark owners don't have to sue people for things that don't actually violate their rights. I suppose some trademark owners might (wrongly) think such uses are infringing and therefore that they have to pursue parodists and nominative fair users even if they don't want to. But the law already provides that trademark owners are not required to act against every infringing use—acting against the most damaging uses is sufficient.[32] Even if a trademark owner thought a parody was infringing, that infringement would surely not be the core sort the policing requirement is directed

[30] This is an argument I have made elsewhere. *See* Dogan & Lemley, *supra* note 4, at 477–80 & nn.26–28 (arguing for use of the mark as a brand in order to be actionable infringement and citing court opinions adopting this trademark use doctrine often by referencing the "in connection with" or the "use in commerce" language of the Lanham Act); Stacey L. Dogan & Mark A. Lemley, *Grounding Trademark Law Through Trademark Use*, 92 Iowa L. Rev. 1669, 1682 (2007) ("Strictly speaking, trademark infringement should require not only that a defendant be using the mark to promote its own products or services but also that it be using it 'as a mark'—i.e., to indicate the source or sponsorship of those products or services."). As examples of courts implicitly adopting a trademark use doctrine, see Louis Vuitton Malletier v. Burlington Coat Factory Warehouse Corp., 426 F.3d 532, 538–39 (2d Cir. 2005) ("[T]he Lanham Act requires a court to analyze the similarity of the products in light of the way in which the marks are actually displayed in their purchasing context" because the "Act seeks to eliminate the confusion that is created in the marketplace by the sale of products bearing highly similar marks."); and Interactive Prods. Corp. v. A2Z Mobile Office Sols. Inc., 326 F.3d 687, 698 (6th Cir. 2003) ("Because post-domain paths do not typically signify source, it is unlikely that the presence of another's trademark in a post-domain path of a URL would ever violate trademark law."). As an example of a court implicitly rejecting this trademark use doctrine, see Rosetta Stone Ltd. v. Google Inc., 676 F.3d 144, 151–52, 161–63 (4th Cir. 2012) (reversing summary judgment for defendant where defendant used trademark only as a keyword to identify when to place an ad for competing product and not in the ad itself).

[31] *See, e.g.*, Int'l Info. Sys. Sec. Certification Consortium, Inc. v. Security Univ., L.L.C., 823 F.3d 153 (2d Cir. 2016); Century 21 Real Estate Corp. v. Lendingtree, Inc., 425 F.3d 211, 232 (3d Cir. 2005); New Kids on the Block v. News Am. Publ'g, 971 F.2d 302, 306–07 (9th Cir. 1992) (holding use of band's name in newspaper poll was nominative under new test); *see also* Dogan & Lemley, *supra* note 4, at 505–08 (discussing nominative fair-use doctrine and cases); McGeveran, *supra* note 9, at 88–97 (arguing that the nominative fair-use doctrine fails to serve as an adequate "early screening mechanism").

[32] *See, e.g.*, Cullman Ventures, Inc. v. Columbian Art Works, Inc., 717 F. Supp. 96, 127 (S.D.N.Y. 1989) (noting approvingly that plaintiff policed the two most damaging uses of its mark by others); Elizabeth Taylor Cosmetics Co. v. Annick Goutal, S.A.R.L., 673 F. Supp. 1238, 1248 (S.D.N.Y. 1987) (explaining that "a trademark owner is not required to act against every infringing use no matter how inconsequential"); Playboy Enters., Inc. v. Chuckleberry Publ'g, Inc., 486 F. Supp. 414, 422–23 (S.D.N.Y. 1980) ("The owner of a mark is not required to police every conceivably related use . . . .").

against. Parodies, nominative uses, and the like don't pose any of the risks that motivate policing. They won't make a mark generic because they refer back to and therefore strengthen rather than weaken the connection between the mark and its owner.[33] And they won't weaken a mark by crowding the field because they aren't competitive uses. At most, deciding not to sue non-infringing parodists might raise a laches defense if a trademark owner later decides to sue non-infringing parodists. But so what? They weren't going to win that suit anyway.[34]

It can't hurt for courts to make clear that any policing obligation does not extend to efforts to stop non-infringing uses like parodies. But for the reasons just mentioned, trademark owners—at least those advised by savvy counsel—should be unlikely to think they have to sue parodists in order to protect their mark. A more likely explanation is that they want to stop the parodies, either by persuading a court to do so or by using the cost and uncertainty of litigation to drive small users out of business.[35] And if that's their goal, just telling them they don't need to do it won't stop them.

We need better reasons for trademark owners to lay off parodies and other socially beneficial uses of trademarks. Prior scholars have suggested sticks: penalties for frivolous lawsuits or for dubious threat letters, greater fee shifting, declaring the mark expressively generic, and the like.[36] Those are probably good ideas, though they may not protect the people who most need protecting—those who fold up

[33] *See, e.g.*, Louis Vuitton Malletier S.A. v. Haute Diggity Dog, L.L.C., 507 F.3d 252, 260–61 (4th Cir. 2007) (holding plush "Chewy Vuitton" puppy toys to be a non-infringing parody of bags with Louis Vuitton marks because they allow consumers "to perceive the target of the parody, while simultaneously allowing them to recognize the changes to the mark that make the parody funny or biting"); Jordache Enters. v. Hogg Wyld, Ltd., 828 F.2d 1482, 1489–90 (10th Cir. 1987) (holding "it is not likely that public identification of JORDACHE with the plaintiff will be eroded [by defendant's parody 'Lardashe']; indeed, parody tends to increase public identification of a plaintiff's mark with the plaintiff").

[34] McGeveran, *supra* note 9, at 52.

[35] *See* Chan Grinvald, *supra* note 15, at 651 (summarizing the competitive benefit to mark owners from controlling their trademark while imposing costs on other users who may be their rivals or potential rivals); Yvette Joy Liebesman & Benjamin Wilson, *The Mark of a Resold Good*, 20 GEO. MASON L. REV. 157, 163–64 (2012) (describing how small resellers of products may close rather than face litigation from those who own trademarks related to those products). Sheff refers to this as loathing-based as opposed to fear-based enforcement. *See* Sheff, *supra* note 18, at 875–77.

[36] *See, e.g.*, Chan Grinvald, *supra* note 15, at 669 (proposing consumer-supported shaming); Chan Grinvald, *supra* note 18, at 414–15 (proposing the regulation of cease-and-desist letters); Leah Chan Grinvald, *Social Media, Sharing, and Intellectual Property Law*, 64 DEPAUL L. REV. 1045, 1072–73 (2015) (suggesting better access to low-cost legal services); Leah Chan Grinvald, *Charitable Trademarks*, 50 AKRON L. REV. 817, 854, 860 (2016) (suggesting heightened pleading requirements and social shaming, particularly against overreaching nonprofits); Stacey Dogan, *Bullying and Opportunism in Trademark and Right of Publicity Law*, 96 B.U. L. REV. 1293, 1317–18 (2016); Manta, *supra* note 16, at 858–62 (proposing judicial sanctions and fee-shifting), 862–63 (proposing measures akin to anti-SLAPP (Strategic Lawsuit Against Public Participation) protections); Gallagher, *supra* note 17, at 495–96; Kiser, *supra* note 1, at 540 (arguing for a legal right for fan sites to use brands); *cf.* Paul J. Heald, *Payment Demands for Spurious Copyrights: Four Causes of Action*, 1 J. INTELL. PROP. L. 259, 262 (1994) (assessing, in the copyright context, approaches to combating wrongful copyright infringement claims through actions based in breach of warranty, unjust enrichment, fraud, and false advertising); *see also* Dreyfuss, *supra* note 1, at 399; Tang, *supra* note 13, at 2028–29.

shop in response to a scary-looking cease-and-desist letter because they don't know any better or can't afford to vindicate their rights.

My goal here is to suggest a carrot, not a stick. If we want trademark owners to be motivated not to sue parody and criticism sites, we should make the existence of those sites a good rather than a bad thing for trademark owners. I propose that the law view the existence of parody and criticism of a brand as affirmative evidence that the brand is famous and maybe even treat it as a requirement for fame.

Brands want to be famous.[37] Famous trademarks are strong marks entitled to a broader scope of protection against likely consumer confusion.[38] Further, only famous marks are entitled to extra protection against trademark dilution even in the absence of consumer confusion.[39] Once the Federal Trademark Dilution Act was passed in 1995, many companies sought and were granted famous status for marks that were not actually very famous.[40] Congress raised the standard of fame in the Trademark Dilution Reform Act (TDRA) of 2006. Under that narrowed definition, "a mark is famous if it is widely recognized by the general consuming public of the United States as a designation of source of the goods or services of the mark's owner."[41] Since 2006, local fame and fame in certain markets no longer count, and even well-known marks like those of Coach and the University of Texas Longhorns have been held not to qualify.[42]

Fame is likely to be particularly relevant in cases of parody and other forms of protected speech about trademarks. Parodies, satire, and criticism naturally target or employ well-known brands; making fun of a trademark no one has ever heard of seems a bootless enterprise, and a satire based on a meme no one understands won't be very effective.[43] Similarly, companies have a greater need to talk about famous marks in order to compare their goods to the market leader or explain why

[37] On the value of fame to trademark owners, see Leah Chan Grinvald, *Contracting Trademark Fame?*, 47 Loy. U. Chi. L. J. 1291, 1305–11 (2016).

[38] *See* Nabisco, Inc. v. P.F. Brands, Inc., 191 F.3d 208, 214–17 (2d Cir. 1999) (setting out special statutory protections accorded famous marks and explaining their intent).

[39] *See* 15 U.S.C. § 1125(c) (2012).

[40] *See, e.g.*, Times Mirror Magazines, Inc. v. Las Vegas Sports News, L.L.C., 212 F.3d 157, 169–70 (3d Cir. 2000) (affirming "The Sporting News" famous in sports context over vigorous dissent); Ringling Bros.-Barnum & Bailey Combined Shows, Inc. v. Utah Div. of Travel Dev., 955 F. Supp. 605, 605–06 (E.D. Va. 1997) (finding "Greatest Show on Earth" to be famous); Am. Exp. Co. v. CFK, Inc., 947 F. Supp 310, 312 (E.D. Mich. 1996) (finding "Don't Leave Home Without It" to be a famous mark). In Appendix A, I contrast examples like these with others found famous after Congress raised the fame standard by passing the Trademark Dilution Reform Act (TDRA) of 2006. *See infra* Appendix A.

[41] § 1125(c)(2)(A).

[42] Coach Servs., Inc., v. Triumph Learning L.L.C., 668 F.3d 1356, 1372 (Fed. Cir. 2012) (finding Coach not famous for dilution purposes); Bd. of Regents, Univ. of Texas Sys. *ex rel.* Univ. of Texas at Austin v. KST Elec., Ltd., 550 F. Supp. 2d 657, 678–79 (W.D. Tex. 2008) (finding the Texas Longhorn logo not famous). I present a full list of marks adjudicated famous and not famous under both the old and the new law in Appendix A.

[43] *See, e.g.*, Dr. Seuss Enters., L.P. v. Penguin Books USA, Inc., 109 F.3d 1394, 1400–01, 1406 (9th Cir. 1997) (satirizing the O.J. Simpson trial through a Dr. Seuss-styled book); Louis Vuitton Malletier, S.A. v. Hyundai Motor Am., No. 10 Civ. 1611(PKC), 2012 WL 1022247, at *1 (S.D.N.Y. Mar. 22, 2012) (satirizing luxury via a one-second shot of a basketball covered in Louis Vuitton marks in a Hyundai commercial); Coca-Cola Co. v. Gemini Rising, Inc., 346 F. Supp. 1183, 1193 (E.D.N.Y. 1972) (parodying "Enjoy Coca-Cola" via an "Enjoy Cocaine" poster); *cf.* Campbell v. Acuff-Rose Music,

their products are, say, compatible with Apple's iPhone. And the public as a whole may appropriate a mark for cultural conversation, but it is more likely to do so if the mark is famous and therefore well understood.[44]

Further, each of these types of uses reinforces rather than dilutes the significance of the brand in question. A parody or satire only works because people get the joke--because they simultaneously recognize the reference to the brand and understand that the parody is *not* the brand.[45] The point of nominative fair uses--comparative advertising, discussing your relationship with the branded product, and the like--is to use the trademark to refer not to your own goods but to the trademark owner's. Similarly, trademarks in expressive products are there because the author wants to talk about the trademarks. They too reinforce the semantic connection between the brand and the product it refers to.[46] So it makes sense to think that famous marks are the ones most likely to attract parodies and other speech-related uses and that those uses reinforce rather than dilute the significance of the mark as a referent for the trademark owner's goods in the minds of the public. For both reasons, the presence of parodies and other referential uses surely correlates with fame.

Notably, the most famous brands are also the most likely to sue parodists. I collected data on trademark complaints involving both marks held famous under the 2006 TDRA and marks held not famous under the same statute.[47] Owners of trademarks held famous under the higher TDRA standard filed 562 trademark suits

Inc., 510 U.S. 569, 586 (1994) (underscoring that "parodies almost invariably copy publicly known, expressive works" in a copyright context).

[44] Barbie, for instance, has been appropriated by several artists using it as a shorthand to comment on society. *See* Mattel, Inc. v. Walking Mountain Prods., 353 F.3d 792, 796 (9th Cir. 2003) (discussing "Barbie Enchiladas" visual art); Mattel, Inc. v. MCA Records, Inc., 296 F.3d 894, 902 (9th Cir. 2002) (discussing "The Barbie Girl" song). *See generally* Dreyfuss, *supra* note 1 (explaining how trademarks function as "ideograms" and examining the law's difficulty in policing and protecting such uses appropriately).

[45] Successful parodies are permitted not least because they do not confuse consumers. *See* Louis Vuitton Malletier S.A. v. Haute Diggity Dog, L.L.C., 507 F.3d 252, 260–61 (4th Cir. 2007) (reasoning "an effective parody will actually diminish the likelihood of confusion" because it enables audiences "to perceive the target of the parody, while simultaneously allowing them to recognize the changes to the mark that make the parody funny or biting"); L.L. Bean, Inc. v. Drake Publishers, Inc., 811 F.2d 26, 34 (1st Cir. 1987) ("[A] trademark parody... juxtapose[es] the irreverent representation of the trademark with the idealized image created by the mark's owner."); *cf. Campbell*, 510 U.S. at 599 (explaining that the successful parodist makes an original statement about something already popularly known). By contrast, unsuccessful parodies may infringe precisely because they confuse consumers. *See Dr. Seuss Enters.*, 109 F.3d at 1405 (making this point); *see also* Charles E. Colman, *Trademark Law and the Prickly Ambivalence of Post-Parodies*, 163 U. Pa. L. Rev. Online 11, 41–42 (2014) (indicating the same).

[46] *See* Rebecca Tushnet, *Gone in Sixty Milliseconds: Trademark Law and Cognitive Science*, 86 Tex. L. Rev. 507, 516–17, 525–27, 537 (2008) (summarizing and challenging the view that unauthorized uses tend to weaken or replace a mark's association with a product, citing research showing "exposure to near variants or uses in other contexts makes the trademark more familiar and thus more easily retrieved from memory," much as "Tiffany's-the-restaurant may make us think of Tiffany's-the-jeweler when we are at lunch thinking of gifts for Mother's Day").

[47] And by "I collected," I mean my research assistants did all the hard work.

involving those brands between 2007 and 2017. Of those cases, seventeen were brought against uses alleged to be parodies. By contrast, companies owning marks held not famous filed 561 suits involving those marks, none against parodists. But almost all of those suits were filed by one company--Coach, which brought 540 suits. Excluding Coach, other non-famous brands brought only twenty-one lawsuits, none involving parodies.[48]

I don't mean to make too much of this data. It includes only the actual marks held famous under the new law, not marks that are surely famous under both laws (e.g., Barbie, Google, and the Louis Vuitton "LV" logo). It excludes cease-and-desist letters that never made it to court and court cases that never made it to decision. And it excludes at least some suits against parodies by marks that are probably famous but whose fame was not in serious question in the case.[49] So one should not conclude from this that people only parody famous marks.

Nonetheless, three things stand out. First, famous mark owners seem to be the only ones targeting parodies. Second, only a minority of famous mark owners in my study filed any claims against parodies at all. Many famous brands, even those who do plenty of enforcement, sue only traditional infringers or counterfeiters. That hasn't prevented their marks from being declared famous. Third, even famous mark owners who do target parodies bring only a small fraction of their suits against parodies, meaning stopping parodies isn't their ordinary form of policing.

All of this suggests that encouraging famous mark owners to celebrate (or at least tolerate) parodies, satire, and other expressive uses is likely to be effective in targeting the worst cases of trademark overreach. Companies don't need to target parodies or other expressive uses to survive or to thrive.

The change I propose is simple: Courts should consider the existence, number, and prominence of unauthorized parodies, satires, or other expressive and referential uses of a mark directed at the general public as evidence tending to show that the mark is famous for both dilution and likelihood of confusion purposes, and the absence of such uses as tending to show that the mark is not famous and not as strong.[50] Considering parodies as a factor favoring fame is straightforward to do under the judicially created likelihood of confusion test, which considers the strength and renown of the mark in assessing confusion. It is also straightforward under the existing

[48] The complete list of cases we collected is available on request.

[49] *See, e.g.*, Louis Vuitton Malletier, S.A. v. My Other Bag, Inc., 674 F. App'x 16, 19 (2d Cir. 2016) (affirming summary judgment for defendant maker of "My Other Bag" referencing Louis Vuitton bag without explicitly assessing whether Louis Vuitton was, as it must be for federal dilution statute to apply, famous); Louis Vuitton Malletier, S.A. v. Hyundai Motor Am., No. 10 Civ. 1611(PKC), 2012 WL 1022247, at *1 (S.D.N.Y. Mar. 22, 2012) (finding that a one-second shot in Hyundai's Super Bowl commercial that showed a basketball covered in interlocking LV marks infringed and diluted Louis Vuitton's trademark). Louis Vuitton still had to prove fame, of course, but it was not in serious question. *See id.* at *2.

[50] This is consistent with Lisa Ouellette's suggestion that we judge trademarks in part by how people actually treat and use them in Internet searches. *See* Lisa Larrimore Ouellette, *The Google Shortcut to Trademark Law*, 102 CALIF. L. REV. 351, 372 (2014). Alexandra Roberts makes a parallel suggestion—that public talk about marks (which can include parodies and other expressive uses) is evidence of

dilution statute, which provides that "[i]n determining whether a mark possesses the requisite degree of recognition, the court may consider all relevant factors."[51] The existence of expressive and referential uses specifically seems relevant to the "extent ... of advertising and publicity of the mark ... by ... third parties," one of the elements for fame.[52] My proposal should encourage trademark lawyers to advise their clients to let such uses be. Trademark owners don't need to police expressive uses even today, and my approach would give them a reason not to.

We could go further, making the existence of parodies or expressive uses a requirement for fame. That would have some advantages, including changing the incentives of companies that are unquestionably famous. But that stronger version would require Congress to change the dilution statute.[53]

Indeed, one might worry about the opposite problem—companies trying to encourage or fake parodies or other expressive uses to meet the new requirement of fame. Courts should ensure that the uses in question are independent and

secondary meaning of those marks. *See* Alexandra J. Roberts, *Mark Talk*, https://papers.ssrn.com/sol3/papers.cfm?abstract_id=3239734 (Univ. of N.H. Sch. of Law, Working Paper 2018).

[51] 15 U.S.C. § 1125(c)(2)(A) (2012).

[52] *Id.*

[53] There is a robust debate on whether dilution law is a good idea at all. Many are skeptical. *See* Barton Beebe, Symposium Review, *The Continuing Debacle of U.S. Antidilution Law: Evidence from the First Year of Trademark Dilution Revision Act Case Law*, 24 SANTA CLARA COMPUTER & HIGH TECH. L. J. 449, 450 (2007) (reviewing a year's cases and finding the dilution cause of action used redundantly alongside infringement cause of action, suggesting its limited value); Barton Beebe et al., *Testing for Trademark Dilution in Court and in the Lab*, 86 U. CHI. L. REV. (forthcoming 2019) (casting doubt on evidence of dilution by blurring); Kenneth L. Port, *The Commodification of Trademarks: Some Final Thoughts on Trademark Dilution*, 46 HOFSTRA L. REV 669, 669 (2017) (arguing that the Federal Trademark Dilution Act "has not been the panacea for famous marks it was intended to be and has created perverse unintended consequences"); Jeremy N. Sheff, *Finding Dilution* 1 (St. John's Sch. of Law, Working Paper No. 18-002, 2018) ("[W]hen we finally cut our way through the fog we will find that dilution is simply not there. It is, at bottom, an entirely empty concept . . . ."); Tushnet, *supra* note 46, at 568 (concluding dilution is not well-supported by cognitive science and an "otherwise ... obscure concept"). Others defend dilution law. *See* Jerre B. Swann, *An Interdisciplinary Approach to Brand Strength*, 96 TRADEMARK REP. 943, 975–76 (2006); Jerre B. Swann, *An Intuitive Approach to Dilution*, 89 TRADEMARK REP. 907, 907 (1999). For an overview of dilution doctrine and the theory that underlies it—or not—see Stacey L. Dogan & Mark A. Lemley, *What the Right of Publicity Can Learn from Trademark Law*, 58 STAN. L. REV. 1161, 1197–200 (2006). There is also some question of whether it is constitutional after *Matal v. Tam*, which invalidated one of the trademark statute's restrictions on speech for being insufficiently narrow for the purposes of facilitating commerce. *See* Matal v. Tam, 137 S. Ct. 1744, 1764–65 (2017) (holding Lanham Act's requirement that the Patent and Trademark Office deny registration to disparaging marks violated First Amendment because it was not "narrowly drawn" to bar only commercially disruptive marks); *see also* Lisa P. Ramsey, *Free Speech Challenges to Trademark Law After* Matal v. Tam, 56 HOUS. L. REV. 401, 401–02 (2018).

I am sensitive to the concern that my proposal may enable companies to use the dilution statute when we might be better off not having one at all. But we have dilution law, and in this chapter I take it for granted. Further, even if we were to eliminate dilution law, fame still matters to infringement law, because famous marks are—rightly or wrongly—given broader protection than less famous marks. *Cf.* Barton Beebe & C. Scott Hemphill, *The Scope of Strong Marks: Should Trademark Law Protect the Strong More Than the Weak?*, 92 N.Y.U. L. REV. 1339, 1339 (2017) (arguing that strong marks are actually less likely to be confused with imitations). So, even without dilution traditional trademark owners will seek fame, and we can use that desire to achieve social good.

unauthorized. For my proposal to work, a company should not be able to point to expressive uses of its work if it also sues or threatens those uses. Indeed, suing expressive users should probably disqualify the company from relying on expressive uses to prove fame altogether.[54] It certainly shouldn't be able to both try to shut down a parody or nominative use and also be able to point to that use as evidence of fame. Requiring that the expressive uses be truly independent may also help avoid a related problem—the assumption that everything requires a license and that the "safe" thing to do is get one even for uses the law expressly permits.[55]

My proposal won't prevent all trademark overreach by any means. Some companies just don't like being made fun of, and they may continue to threaten suit whether the law supports them or not. So, it may make sense to combine this proposal with other efforts to punish trademark overreach[56] to make clearer that these uses are lawful.[57] But if the goal is to change trademark owner behavior, giving them an affirmative reason to tolerate parodies and other expressive uses—and giving their lawyers a reason to counsel restraint[58]—is a logical way to get there.[59]

Conclusion

Trademark owners often threaten parodists, satirists, and others who make lawful expressive uses of their marks, offering the rationale that they must police their mark against infringement or lose it. But they shouldn't. The law doesn't require policing such uses. Parody, criticism, and being part of the cultural conversation come with the territory of fame. The law should reflect that by treating the existence of those referential uses as indicating that the trademark is strong. By doing so, the law can help align the incentives of trademark owners with good public policy.

[54] Some rare suits against expressive uses might have merit, and those should not be disqualifying.

[55] *See* Gibson, *supra* note 15, at 884, 907–08, 912–27 (examining how trademark owners' "rights" snowball when others believe it is "[b]etter [to be] safe than sued"); *cf.* Lawrence Lessig, *The Creative Commons*, 65 MONT. L. REV. 1, 12 (2004) (describing "the permission culture that our law has produced" in copyright).

[56] *See supra* text accompanying note 38 (citing other scholars who suggest legal sticks, social shame, and other remedies).

[57] *See* Dogan & Lemley, *supra* note 4, at 474 (arguing for positive doctrinal reforms to increase clarity and predictability given that current confusion leaves "would-be parodists vulnerable to threats of legal action by trademark holders"); McGeveran, *supra* note 9, at 49 (making a similar point about the problem of uncertainty and recommending "simpler affirmative defenses that reduce uncertainty and allow for quick adjudication").

[58] On the role of lawyers in encouraging or restraining client impulses to attack uses they dislike, see Sheff, *supra* note18, at 882.

[59] As Glynn Lunney has observed, trademark law often moves in the wrong direction because rules that promote competition generally hurt the self-interest of repeat players in trademark cases, who want to capture rents by excluding competition. *See generally* Glynn S. Lunney, Jr., *Trademark's Judicial De-Evolution: Why Courts Get Trademark Cases Wrong Repeatedly*, 106 CALIF. L. REV. 1195 (2018). Giving trademark owners an incentive to align their behavior with good social policy might help to break that cycle.

Appendix A

Fame of Marks Adjudicated Before and After the TDRA

Famous	
1996	**2006**
AOL	Adidas three-stripe mark
Arthur the Aardvark	Audi
Audi	America's Team (Dallas Cowboys)
Barbie	Apple iPhone trade dress
Budweiser	Big Gulp
Camel	BlackBerry
Candyland	Burberry
Cartier	Chanel
Don't Leave Home Without Us	Citibank
Etch-A-Sketch	Delta
Goldfish	Just Do It
Ford	Louis Vuitton Multicolore
Greatest Show on Earth (circus)	McDonald's "Mc" prefix
Hotmail	Miss USA
Intermatic	Motown
James Bond	Newport
Jews for Jesus	NYC Triathlon
Lexington	Nike
Nailtiques	Pepsi
NASDAQ	Rolex
NBA logo	Rolls-Royce
Nike	Starbucks
Panavision	The House that Ruth Built
Porsche	The Other White Meat
Prozac	Viagra
Sporting News	Victoria's Secret
Toys 'R Us	Visa
Tylenol	
Velveeta	
Victoria's Secret	
Wawa	
Winston	

(continued)

Not Famous	
1996	**2006**
Applesee	App Store
Authority	Bio-Safe
Avery Dennison	Charlotte
Bongo	Coach
Clue	It's A
Columbia	Lingo (food market in Del.)
Dearest	Magenta color (T-Mobile)
Fun Ship	Marker's Mark trade dress
King of the Mountain Sports	Majestic
Lane Capital Management	Movie Mania
Petro	Rocky Top
Star Market	Steak-umm
Stealth	Top
Children's Place	University of Texas longhorn logo
Teton Glacier	
Tornado	
Trek	
Tycos	
We	
Weather Guard	
Washington Speakers Bureau	
We'll Pick You Up	
We'll Take Good Care of You	

6

Safeguarding Freedom of Artistic Expression in the European Union

Toward a Legal Presumption of Fair Use

Martin Senftleben

E.U. trademark law sets forth a peculiar rule for assessing whether use of trademarks in an artistic context constitutes permissible fair use. For artistic use to be deemed noninfringing, it must comply with honest practices in industrial and commercial matters (Section I). While the introduction of a fairness rule for artistic expression is a positive development (Section II), the alignment of the assessment with behavioral standards in industry and commerce poses a threat to art autonomy. The moment artists are bound to follow industrial and commercial dictates, behavioral norms of trade and commerce may erode the independence of the literary and artistic field. Replicating standard confusion and dilution criteria in the honest practices analysis, Court of Justice of the European Union (CJEU) jurisprudence enhances this risk (Section III). As the status quo is inacceptable in the light of freedom of expression and freedom of the arts (Section IV), it is advisable to introduce a bias in favor of artists: a legal presumption of fair use (Section V). Court decisions on both sides of the Atlantic offer support for this solution (Section VI) and pave the way for an honest practices test that safeguards independent, artistic expression (concluding Section VII).

I. Requirement of Honest Commercial Practices

With the 2015 reform of E.U. trademark law,[1] a specific guideline for reconciling trademark protection with freedom of artistic expression made its way into the

[1] At the end of 2015, the reform led to the trademark norms enshrined in the current versions of the EUTMR and the TMD. As to the underlying preparatory work in the area of limitations of trademark rights, *see* Ronald Knaak et al., Study on the Functioning of the European Trade Mark System, Max Planck Institute for Intellectual Property & Competition Law Research Paper No. 12-13, Munich: Max Planck Institute 2011, available at http://ec.europa.eu/internal_market/indprop/tm/index_en.htm, 117–124.

Martin Senftleben, *Safeguarding Freedom of Artistic Expression in the European Union* In: *Charting Limitations on Trademark Rights*. Edited by: Haochen Sun and Barton Beebe, Oxford University Press. © Martin Senftleben 2023.
DOI: 10.1093/oso/9780198871248.003.0007

Trade Mark Directive (TMD)[2] and the European Union Trade Mark Regulation (EUTMR).[3] Recital 21 EUTMR and Recital 27 TMD stipulate that

> [u]se of a trade mark by third parties for the purpose of artistic expression should be considered as being fair as long as it is at the same time in accordance with honest practices in industrial and commercial matters.

This fairness rule supplements the provisions on limitations of trademark rights. Article 14(1) EUTMR and Article 14(1) TMD exempt several types of use from the control of trademark proprietors, including forms of use that may become relevant in the context of artistic expression. Article 14(1)(c) EUTMR and Article 14(1)(c) TMD permit so-called referential use without prior authorization of the trademark owner (Section I.A). Article 14(1)(b) EUTMR and Article 14(1)(b) TMD prevent the trademark owner from invoking trademark rights against descriptive use (Section I.B) and non-distinctive use (Section I.C). All these limitations of trademark rights, however, only apply when the use complies with the general requirement of honest practices in industrial and commercial matters. This horizontal requirement is laid down in Article 14(2) EUTMR and Article 14(2) TMD.

A. Referential Use Defense

Artists using trademarked source material for their creative work may invoke the defense of referential use which is laid down in Article 14(1)(c) EUTMR and Article 14(1)(c) TMD. These provisions define referential use as use "for the purpose of identifying or referring to goods or services as those of the proprietor of that trade mark." A parody using a trademark to symbolize and criticize policies of the trademark proprietor may fall within the scope of this referential use concept. Prior to the 2015 trademark law reform, E.U. law only exempted the unauthorized use of trademarks to "indicate the intended purpose of a product or service."[4] The law reform broadened the referential use concept substantially.[5] As indicated, the

[2] Directive (EU) 2015/2436 of the European Parliament and of the Council of Dec. 16, 2015 to approximate the laws of the Member States relating to trade marks, Official Journal of the European Communities L 336, 1 (2015).

[3] Regulation (EU) 2017/1001 of the European Parliament and of the Council of June 14, 2017 on the European Union Trade Mark (codification), Official Journal of the European Communities L 154, 1 (2017).

[4] Directive 2008/95/EC of the European Parliament and of the Council of Oct. 22, 2008, art. 6(1)(c) to approximate the laws of the Member States relating to trade marks (codified version), Official Journal of the European Communities L 299, 25 (2008). *Cf.* CJEU, Mar. 17, 2005, Case No. C-228/03, Gillette/LA-Laboratories, para. 49.

[5] As to the considerations underlying the broadening of the referential use concept as a result of the trademark law reform, *see* ANNETTE KUR & MARTIN SENFTLEBEN, EUROPEAN TRADE MARK LAW—A COMMENTARY, paras. 6.39–6.41 (2017).

current version of the provision seems capable of offering breathing space for artistic forms of use, such as use for the purposes of parody.

The potential of the new version of the referential use defense to cover artistic use, however, has hardly ever been tested in practice. Nonetheless, it seems possible to illustrate its ambit of operation in the light of case scenarios that predate the trademark law reform. The 2005 case *Lila Postkarte* of the German Federal Supreme Court, for instance, concerned the marketing of postcards that alluded ironically to trademarks and advertising campaigns of the chocolate producer Milka. On purple background corresponding to Milka's abstract color mark, the postcard sought to ridicule the nature idyll with cows and mountains that is evoked in Milka advertising. It showed the following poem attributed to "Rainer Maria Milka":

> *Über allen Wipfeln ist Ruh,*
> *irgendwo blökt eine Kuh.*
> *Muh!*[6]

Discussing this ironic play with Milka insignia, the German Federal Supreme Court applied a broad notion of actionable use as a trademark in the light of the jurisprudence of the CJEU.[7] Following this approach, the fact that the postcard producer merely referred to Milka trademarks (without employing the Milka trademarks as indications of origin) was sufficient to meet the threshold requirement of use in relation to goods and services.[8] The German Federal Supreme Court deemed it sufficient that the postcard called to mind the well-known Milka signs.[9] Accordingly, the Court embarked on a scrutiny of the trademark parody in the light of the dilution criteria of detriment to distinctive character or repute, and the taking of unfair advantage.[10] Weighing Milka's concerns about a disparagement of the trademarks against the fundamental guarantee of freedom of the arts, however, the Court finally concluded that the freedom of art had to prevail in the light of the

6 "It is calm above the tree tops, somewhere a cow is bellowing. Moo!" The attribution to "Rainer Maria Rilke" is an allusion to the famous German writer Rainer Maria Rilke. *See* German Federal Supreme Court, Feb. 2005, 3, Case No. I ZR 159/02, Lila Postkarte, *Gewerblicher Rechtsschutz und Urheberrecht* 2005, 583. *Cf.* Christian Born, *Zur Zulässigkeit einer humorvollen Markenparodie—Anmerkungen zum Urteil des BGH "Lila Postkarte,"* 192 GEWERBLICHER RECHTSSCHUTZ UND URHEBERRECHT [G. R. U. R.] 192 (2006).

7 *See* the reference to CJEU, Oct. 23, 2003, Case No. C-408/01, Adidas/Fitnessworld, para. 39, in the decision "Lila Postkarte" of the German Federal Supreme Court, *id.* 584. With regard to the qualification of decorative use as relevant trademark use, *see also* Annette Kur, *Confusion over Use?—Die Benutzung "als Marke" im Lichte der EuGH-Rechtsprechung* 1 G. R. U. R. 5–6 (2008)).

8 For this general prerequisite of trademark infringement actions in the European Union, *see* art. 9(2) EUTMR and art. 10(2) TMD. *Cf.* KUR & SENFTLEBEN, *supra* note 5, paras. 5.49–5.56.

9 German Federal Supreme Court, *id.* 584.

10 Art. 10(2)(c) TMD; art. 9(2)(c) TMD.

ironic statement made with the postcard.[11] The use of Milka trademarks was found to have taken place with "due cause" in the sense of Article 10(2)(c) TMD.[12] At the time of the decision, the inherent limitation of dilution claims in the European Union to use "without due cause"[13] constituted the only defense argument for artistic users. Arguably, the case scenario underlying the *Lila Postkarte* lawsuit, nowadays, would also allow the successful invocation of the referential use defense following from Article 14(1)(c) TMD and Article 14(1)(c) EUTMR.[14]

B. Descriptive Use Defense

A further example of a defense argument that can support artistic expression is the defense of descriptive use. In line with Article 17 TRIPS which explicitly refers to "fair use of descriptive terms," Article 14(1)(b) EUTMR and Article 14(1)(b) TMD permit the unauthorized use of "signs or indications which [. . .] concern the kind, quality, quantity, intended purpose, value, geographical origin, the time of production of goods or of rendering of the service, or other characteristics of the goods or services." This limitation of trademark rights can play an important role when work titles or other signs with cultural significance are registered as trademarks. In the decision *Marlene Dietrich*—concerning an attempt to register a portrait photograph of the famous actress as a trademark—the German Federal Supreme Court held that a photograph of Marlene Dietrich constituted a descriptive indication of product characteristics in respect of books, magazines, photographs, posters, CDs, DVDs, musical performances, and film productions.[15] On the basis of the descriptive use defense, use of the portrait photograph as an indication of film, book, or poster characteristics thus remains permissible even if trademark rights are acquired through use in trade.[16]

[11] German Federal Supreme Court, *id.* at 584–85. For a further case in which freedom of speech prevailed over trademark protection, *see* German Federal Supreme Court, Mar. 11, 2008, Case No. VI ZR 7/07, "Gen-Milch," *Neue Juristische Wochenschrift* 2008, 2110.

[12] German Federal Supreme Court, Feb. 3, 2005, Case No. I ZR 159/02, *Gewerblicher Rechtsschutz und Urheberrecht* 2005, 583 (585). As to the defence of due cause, *see* CJEU, Sept. 22, 2011, Case No. C-323/09, Interflora/Marks & Spencer, para. 91; CJEU, Feb. 6, 2014, Case No. C-65/12, Leidseplein Beheer/Red Bull, paras. 54–58.

Cf. Vinciane Vanovermeire, *Inschrijving als merk van een in het publiek domain gevallen werk*, *in* Le Cumul des Droits Intellectuels 177, 187–88 (Alexander Cruquenaire & Séverine Dusollier eds., 2009).

[13] Art. 10(2)(c) TMD; art. 9(2)(c) EUTMR. *Cf.* Kur & Senftleben, *supra* note 5, paras. 5.265–5.268 and 6.59–6.63; Vincenzo Di Cataldo, *The Trade Mark with a Reputation in EU Law—Some Remarks on the Negative Condition "Without Due Cause,"* 42 I. I. C. 833, 833 (2011).

[14] For a more detailed discussion of the scope of the referential use defence in current E.U. trademark law, *see* Martin Senftleben, The Copyright/Trademark Interface—How the Expansion of Trademark Protection Is Stifling Cultural Creativity 507–09 (2020).

[15] German Federal Supreme Court, Apr. 24, 2008, Case No. I ZB 21/06, Marlene-Dietrich-Bildnis, paras. 12–15.

[16] In *Marlene Dietrich*, the German Federal Supreme Court denied trademark protection in respect of the mentioned goods and services because of a lack of distinctive character. *See* German Federal

However, the concept of descriptive use has its limits. Use of a trademarked Marlene Dietrich portrait in a parody or in appropriation art, for instance, is unlikely to constitute permissible descriptive use. It incorporates the trademark itself—in this case a portrait of the actress—in the product. In contrast to a label that is merely attached to the product (and may indicate certain product features), the portrait becomes a central element of the very contents of the product. Decorative use of this nature is unlikely to fall within the scope of the descriptive use concept.[17] As the CJEU concluded in *Adidas/Marca*, the purely decorative use of a two-stripe motif on sports clothing "is not intended to give an indication concerning one of the characteristics of those goods."[18] Constituting design features, the stripes were not intended to indicate the characteristics of the sports and leisure garments.[19] Similarly, the Court denied descriptive use in *Opel/Autec* on the ground that the faithful reproduction of the Opel logo on a scale model car could not be regarded as an indication of product characteristics. Instead, the logo became part of the product itself.

> However, the affixing of a sign which is identical to a trade mark registered, inter alia, in respect of motor vehicles to scale models of that make of vehicle in order to reproduce those vehicles faithfully is not intended to provide an indication as to a characteristic of those scale models, but is merely an element in the faithful reproduction of the original vehicles.[20]

C. Non-Distinctive Use Defense

Besides the descriptive use defense, Article 14(1)(b) EUTMR and Article 14(1)(b) TMD also stipulate that the grant of trademark rights shall not entitle the proprietor to prohibit a third party from using "signs or indications which are not distinctive." Evidently, this exemption of non-distinctive use constitutes an important additional defense argument. Annette Kur draws the following line between descriptive use and non-distinctive use:

> Similar to descriptive signs which, even when they are registered after having acquired distinctiveness, still contain residues of their original descriptive character

Supreme Court, *id.* paras. 12–15. As to CJEU case law addressing the descriptive use defence, *see* CJEU, Jan. 7, 2004, Case No. C-100/02, Gerolsteiner/Putsch, paras. 25–26.

[17] Kur & Senftleben, *supra* note 5, paras. 6.23–6.27; Lionel Bently et al., Intellectual Property Law 1068 (5th ed., 2018); Karl-Heinz Fezer, Markenrecht 1602–1603 (4th ed., 2009).

[18] CJEU, Apr. 10, 2008, Case No. C-102/07, Adidas/Marca, para. 48.

[19] *Id.* para. 48.

[20] CJEU, Jan. 25, 2007, Case No. C-48/05, Adam Opel/Autec, para. 44.

> that others are free to make use of, inherently indistinctive signs as well will never become the "sole property" of the trademark holder, but must leave room for use by others that only relates to the sign in its original, non-distinctive capacity.[21]

This explanation sheds light on the important function which the exemption of non-distinctive use may fulfill when trademark protection is acquired with regard to literary and artistic works. In its primary state, a cultural icon, such as the *Mona Lisa* or *The Night Watch* (*De Nachtwacht*), lacks the inherent distinctive character necessary to serve as an identifier of commercial source—at least in respect of literary and artistic productions.[22] The trademark owner must actively transform the sign into a badge of origin. Regardless of the acquisition of distinctive character through use, however, a non-distinctive "residue" in the sense of Kur's explanation, namely the sign's original cultural meaning, always remains. As other types of non-distinctive and descriptive signs,[23] a cultural sign never becomes the sole property of the trademark owner. The sign's literary and artistic character—the residue stemming from the sign's evolution in the cultural domain—is beyond reach for the trademark owner.[24] As this cultural residue is non-distinctive in the context of literary and artistic productions, it falls outside the scope of trademark rights which, by definition, should only cover the secondary, source-identifying meaning added by the trademark owner. Exempting use of non-distinctive signs or indications, Article 14(1)(b) EUTMR and Article 14(1)(b) TMD thus offer room for artistic use that only relates to a sign in its original cultural (and non-distinctive) capacity.[25] As use of a sign with cultural significance to indicate a specific artistic position is use of the sign as a non-distinctive artistic reference point, the non-distinctive use defense can be deemed applicable. Rightly understood, Article 14(1)(b) EUTMR and Article 14(1)(b) TMD therefore cover use of a trademarked cultural sign in an

[21] Annette Kur, *Yellow Dictionaries, Red Banking Services, Some Candies, and a Sitting Bunny: Protection of Color and Shape Marks from a German and European Perspective*, *in* The Protection of Non-Traditional Trademarks—Critical Perspectives 89 (Irene Calboli & Martin Senftleben eds., 2018).

[22] *Cf.* German Federal Patent Court, Nov. 25, 1997, Case No. 24 W (pat) 188/96, Mona Lisa, *Gewerblicher Rechtsschutz und Urheberrecht* 1998, 1021 and 1023; Court of Appeals of The Hague, Aug. 29, 2017, Case No. 200.205.771/01, ECLI:NL:GHDHA:2017:2446, Chiever/Benelux-Organisatie voor de Intellectuele Eigendom ("Nachtwacht"), para. 12.

[23] Kur, *supra* note 21, at 103, gives the example of a shape which, as such, is non-distinctive but may acquire distinctive character through use. Notwithstanding the acquisition of distinctive character, the non-distinctive use defence may allow use of a similar product shape in packages clearly indicating the defendant's own word mark. Arguably, this use only relates to the non-distinctive properties of the shape and the function of indicating commercial source is left to the defendant's own word mark on the packages.

[24] For an aesthetic functionality concept reflecting these residues of "widely shared cognitive, psychological, or aesthetic propensities," *see* Justin Hughes, *Cognitive and Aesthetic Functionality in Trademark Law* 36 Cardozo L. Rev. 1227, 1231 (2015).

[25] *Cf.* Ansgar Ohly, *Schutz von Kulturgütern durch das Markenrecht?*, *in* Festschrift für Paul Ströbele: zum 75 325 (337–38) (Franz Hacker & Frederik Thiering eds., 2019), who also sees room for the cultivation of this defence argument in cases of remix in the artistic domain.

artistic way—as an indication of a cultural meaning that does not concern the sign's trademark function of indicating commercial source.[26]

D. Horizontal Requirement of Honest Practices

All limitations listed in Article 14(1) EUTMR and Article 14(1) TMD are subject to the general proviso of "honest practices" set forth in Article 14(2) EUTMR and Article 14(2) TMD. In line with this overarching requirement, the limitation of trademark rights in favor of referential, descriptive, and non-distinctive use "shall only apply where the use made by the third party is in accordance with honest practices in industrial or commercial matters."

Against this background, the meaning of the new fairness rule in Recital 21 EUTMR and Recital 27 TMD comes to light which, as explained above, entered the picture with the 2015 trademark law reform. With regard to artistic expression, Recital 21 EUTMR and Recital 27 TMD confirm that the honest practices test is fully applicable. The fact that artistic expression is at stake does not exempt the artist from the obligation to ensure compliance with "honest practices in industrial and commercial matters."

II. Increasing Need for a Fair-Use Rule

In principle, the evolution of a fairness rule for artistic expression is a positive development. Iconic trademarks offer a rich spectrum of expressive meanings that are often indispensable for the artistic discourse.[27] As Rochelle Dreyfuss already observed thirty years ago, trademarks

> have become products in their own right, valued as indicators of the status, preferences, and aspirations of those who use them. Some trademarks have worked their way into the English language; others provide bases for vibrant, evocative metaphors. In a sense, trademarks are the emerging lingua franca: with a sufficient command of these terms, one can make oneself understood the world over, and in the process, enjoy the comforts of home.[28]

[26] For a more detailed discussion of this field of application of the non-distinctive use defence, *see* SENFTLEBEN, *supra* note 14, at 509–12.

[27] Keith Aoki, *How the World Dreams Itself to be American: Reflections on the Relationship Between the Expanding Scope of Trademark Protection and Free Speech Norms*, 17 LOY. L.A. ENT. L.J. 523, 542–45 (1996–97).

[28] Rochelle Cooper Dreyfuss, *Expressive Genericity: Trademarks as Language in the Pepsi Generation*, 65 NOTRE DAME L. REV. 397, 397–98 (1989–90).

Trademarks have thus become focal points of communication: densely packed information units "infused with sets of denotations and associated connotations."[29] From the perspective of artistic expression, trademarks can be deemed "rhetorically unique" because of the specific mix of core denotations and additional connotations which these signs obtain as a result of lifestyle messages stemming from advertising of the trademark proprietor and comments and nuances added by consumers.[30] Arguably, use in an artistic setting constitutes a specific form of using trademarks in a metaphorical sense: not as identifiers of commercial source but as symbols of personal or societal conditions.[31] Considering the density and richness of lifestyle messages which trademarks evoke, an artist seeking to criticize current societal conditions and personal attitudes should be able to play freely with trademarks in her creative work.

The need to offer room for artistic expression in trademark law has also increased because more and more cultural symbols become targets of commercial branding efforts. As a result, they attract not only copyright but also trademark protection. An artist using a branded cultural symbol in a derivative work will thus have to rebut not only copyright infringement arguments but also allegations of trademark infringement.[32] With the commercial success of character merchandising, the combination of copyright and trademark claims has become a standard protection strategy in the field of contemporary cultural symbols that evolve from literary and artistic mainstream productions.[33] In the case of Mickey Mouse, for

[29] *Id.* at 415.

[30] *Id.* at 413 and 418. As to the influence of consumers on the development of the meaning of trademarks, *see* Jessica Litman, *Breakfast with Batman: The Public Interest in the Advertising Age*, 108 YALE L.J. 1717, 1731–32 (1999); Dev Saif Gangjee, *Property in Brands: the Commodification of Conversation*, *in* CONCEPTS OF PROPERTY IN INTELLECTUAL PROPERTY LAW 29 (51–56) , (Helena R. Howe & Jonathan Griffiths eds., 2013); David Tan, *The Semiotics of Alpha Brands: Encoding/Decoding/Recoding/Transcoding of Louis Vuitton and Implications for Trademark Laws*, 32 CARDOZO ARTS & ENT. L.J. 225 (2013–14); Deborah R. Gerhardt, *Consumer Investment in Trademarks*, 88 N.C.L. REV. 427 (2009–10); Steven Wilf, *Who Authors Trademarks?*, 17 CARDOZO ARTS & ENT. L.J. 1, 4–5 (1999).

[31] *Cf.* Dreyfuss, *supra* note 28, at 418; Stacey L. Dogan & Mark A. Lemley, *The Trademark Use Requirement in Dilution Cases*, 24 SANTA CLARA COMPUTER & HIGH TECH. L.J. 541, 542 (2007–08). For an example of case law recognizing this metaphorical play as a central feature of the use of trade symbols in an artistic setting, *see* German Federal Supreme Court, Feb. 3, 2005, Case No. I ZR 159/02, LILA POSTKARTE, GEWERBLICHER RECHTSSCHUTZ UND URBERRECHT, 584–85 (2005).

[32] For instance, *see* Court of Appeals of Amsterdam, Sept. 13, 2011, Case No. ECLI:NL:GHAMS:2011:BS7825, Mercis and Bruna/Punt, AMI 2012, at 28, para. 4.1 and 4.19, which concerned a combined copyright and trademark infringement claim against a biting parody of "Miffy" (*Nijntje*) showing the Dutch fictional character known from children's books, among other things, as a 9/11 terrorist. For a discussion of the case and cumulative copyright and trademark protection, *see* SENFTLEBEN, *supra* note 14, at 171–74.

[33] *Cf.* Rebecca Schoff Curtin, *Zombie Cinderella and the Undead Public Domain*, 85 TENN. L. REV. 961, 971 (2017–18); Jane C. Ginsburg, *Licensing Commercial Value: from Copyright to Trademarks and Back*, *in* THE LAW AND PRACTICE OF TRADEMARK TRANSACTIONS—A GLOBAL AND LOCAL OUTLOOK 53 (53–54) (Irene Calboli & Jacques de Werra eds., 2016); Irene Calboli, *Overlapping Trademark and Copyright Protection: A Call for Concern and Action*, 2014 U. ILL. L. REV. ONLINE 25, 29–30 (2014); Joseph P. Liu, *The New Public Domain*, 2013 U. ILL. L. REV. 1395, 1433–38 (2013).

example, not only the name[34] but also several drawings are registered as trademarks in respect of a wide variety of goods and services.[35] The registrations are not confined to goods and services that are unrelated to the primary information products. They encompass audiovisual recordings and players, including CDs and DVDs, printed publications, including books and comic strips, and the production, presentation, distribution, and rental of films.[36] Mickey Mouse, however, is not a singular case. The broad spectrum of names and drawings of fictional characters that have been registered as trademarks includes further Disney characters, Marvel superheroes, Harry Potter protagonists, the Peanuts, Lucky Luke and the Daltons, Asterix and Obelix, Suske and Wiske, Tintin and Snowy, etc. etc.[37] As in the case of Mickey Mouse, trademark registrations often cover not only merchandising articles but also goods and services that are directly related to the underlying primary literary and artistic productions.

The cumulation of copyright and trademark protection in the area of fictional characters, however, is only one side of the coin. In principle, it is also possible to acquire trademark rights to cultural heritage symbols that are in the public domain.[38] Edvard Munch's *Scream* (*Skrik*) has been registered as a trademark at the international level with legal effect in the European Union, Japan, and the United States.[39] In France, Vermeer's famous *Milkmaid* (*Het Melkmeisje*) has been used for the marketing of dairy products to such an extent that it seems safe to assume that the registered cultural icon has become a well-known mark.[40] In Germany, the State of Saxony-Anhalt managed to acquire E.U. trademark rights in the ancient Nebra Sky Disk that was found on its territory.[41] Despite a finding of lack of

[34] IR No. 983421, MICKEY; EUTMs No. 002827426 and 005240668, MICKEY MOUSE. *See also* Disney's registration of the word mark MICKEY in France, No. 1567169 and 1128324, and Germany, No. 39716409. For the particulars of the registrations, *see* www.tmdn.org/tmview/.

[35] IR No. 135377 and 296478; EUTMs No. 003335981 and 003332913.

[36] IR No. 296478; EUTMs No. 003335981 and 003332913.

[37] For an overview of registrations and EUTM registration numbers, *see* SENFTLEBEN, *supra* note 14, at 2–4 and 121–22.

[38] Vanovermeire, *supra* note 12, at 182. For examples ranging from Raphael Putti to Michelangelo's "Creation of Adam" and a Rembrandt self-portrait, *see* Volker Bugdahl, *Marken und Kunst—Kunst und Marken*, MARKENRECHT 369 (372–73) (2010); Ansgar Ohly, *Von einem Indianerhäuptling, einer Himmelsscheibe, einer Jeans und dem Lächeln der Mona Lisa—Überlegungen zum Verhältnis zwischen Urheber- und Kennzeichenrecht, in* GRUNDLAGEN UND GRUNDFRAGEN DES GEISTIGEN EIGENTUMS, Festgabe für Diethelm Klippel zum 65. Geburtstag 203, 205, 208–10 (Louis Pahlow & Jens Eisfeld eds., 2008).

[39] IR No. 1179290 concerning beers, mineral waters and other alcoholic and nonalcoholic beverages.

[40] EUTM No. 002998334 concerning, among other goods, dietetic foodstuffs and baby food; vegetables, fruits, meat, poultry, game, fish, and seafood; milk products; coffee, tea, cocoa, and chocolate products; bakery products, snack foods, breakfast cereals, and ice cream. *Cf.* Frédéric Bianchi, *La Laitière: comment un tableau de Vermeer a fini sur un pot de yaourt*, BFM BUSINESS (Feb. 20, 2017), available at: https://bfmbusiness.bfmtv.com/entreprise/la-laitiere-comment-un-tableau-de-vermeer-a-fini-sur-un-pot-de-yaourt-1106560.html (last visited on Jan. 18, 2021).

[41] EUTM No. 009763475. As to the previous controversy about the grant of the trademark right in Germany, *see* Regional Court of Magdeburg, Oct. 16, 2003, Case No. 7 O 847/03, "Himmelsscheibe von Nebra," *Gewerblicher Rechtsschutz und Urheberrecht* 2004, 672. *Cf.* Malte Stieper, *Geistiges Eigentum an Kulturgütern—Möglichkeiten und Grenzen der Remonopolisierung gemeinfreier Werke*, 114 G. R. U. R. 1083, 1090–91 (2012); Ohly, *supra* note 38, at 209–11.

distinctive character at Benelux level,[42] the European Union Intellectual Property Office (EUIPO) also registered the original Dutch titles of Anne Frank's famous books—*Het achterhuis* (*The Secret Annex*) and *Het dagboek van Anne Frank* (*The Diary of Anne Frank*)—in respect of books, films, theater productions, and guided tours.[43] Similarly, the verdict of insufficient distinctive character in the Benelux[44] could not prevent the EUIPO from granting E.U.-wide trademark rights to Rembrandt's *The Night Watch*.[45]

The described enhanced impact of trademarks and trademark protection on artistic creativity can thus be traced back to parallel developments that reinforce the need to create breathing space for artistic expression in trademark law:

- the increasing necessity for artists to use trademarks as reflections of societal conditions and personal attitudes, and the expansion of trademark protection that allows trademark proprietors to threaten artists with infringement claims;[46] and
- the increasing tendency to grant trademark rights in contemporary cultural symbols and cultural heritage material which exposes artists to trademark infringement claims that may have a deterrent effect on artistic expression.[47]

[42] Court of Appeals of Brussels, Oct. 3, 2013, Case Nos. 2013/7132 and 2013/7133, Anne Frank Foundation/Benelux Office for Intellectual Property, para. 8. As the CJEU, Sept. 6, 2018, Case No. C-488/16P, Bundesverband Souvenir—Geschenke—Ehrenpreise ("Neuschwanstein"), para. 72, pointed out, the E.U. trademark system is "an autonomous system with its own set of objectives and rules peculiar to it; it applies independently of any national system." Hence, the EUIPO was not bound to follow the decision on distinctiveness taken by the Court of Appeals of Brussels on the basis of the harmonized Benelux trademark system.

[43] *See* EUTM No. 012451787 (HET ACHTERHUIS) and EUTM No. 012452281 (HET DAGBOEK VAN ANNE FRANK) which cover various goods and services in classes 9, 16, and 41.

[44] Court of Appeals of The Hague, Aug. 29, 2017, Case No. 200.205.771/01, ECLI:NL:GHDHA:2017:2446, Chiever/Benelux-Organisatie voor de Intellectuele Eigendom ("Nachtwacht"), para. 12.

[45] EUTM No. 016613903 concerning the chemical element strontium.

[46] *Cf.* Łukasz Żelechowski, *Invoking Freedom of Expression and Freedom of Competition in Trade Mark Infringement Disputes: Legal Mechanisms for Striking a Balance*, 19 E.R.A. Forum 115, 115–35 (2018); Sabine Jacques, *A Parody Exception: Why Trade Mark Owners Should Get the Joke*, 38 E.I.P.R. 471, 479 (2016); Martin Senftleben, *Free Signs and Free Use—How to Offer Room for Freedom of Expression within the Trademark System*, *in* Research Handbook on Human Rights and Intellectual Property 354 (Christipher Geiger ed., 2015); Lisa P. Ramsey & Jens Schovsbo, *Mechanisms for Limiting Trade Mark Rights to Further Competition and Free Speech*, 44 I.I.C. 671 (2013); Ilanah Simon Fhima, *Trade Marks and Free Speech*, 44 I.I.C. 293 (2013); Wolfgang Sakulin, Trademark Protection and Freedom of Expression—An Inquiry into the Conflict between Trademark Rights and Freedom of Expression under European Law 247–82 (2010); Christophe Geiger, *Trade Marks and Freedom of Expression—the Proportionality of Criticism*, 38 I.I.C. 317 (2007).

[47] *Cf.* Senftleben, *supra* note 14, at 202–05; Lisa P. Ramsey, *Free Speech Challenges to Trademark Law after Matal v. Tam*, 56 Hous. L. Rev. 401, 427 (2018–19); Jens Schovsbo, *"Mark My Words"—Trademarks and Fundamental Rights in the EU*, 8 U.C. Irvine L. Rev. 555, 562 (2018); Amy Adler, *Fair Use and the Future of Art*, 91 N.Y.U. L. Rev. 559, 566 (2016); Mark A. Lemley & Mark McKenna, *Irrelevant Confusion*, 62 Stan. L. Rev. 413, 418–22 and 443 (2009–10); Arpan Banerjee, *Non-Origin Infringement—Has Trade Mark Law Gone Too Far?*, 43 I.I.C. 555, 564 (2012); William McGeveran, *Four Free Speech Goals for Trademark Law*, 18 Fordham Intell. Prop. Media & Ent. L.J. 1205, 1206–07 and 1224–25 (2007–08); Jesse A. Hofrichter, *Tool of the Trademark: Brand Criticism and Free Speech Problems with the Federal Dilution Revision Act of 2006*, 28 Cardozo L. Rev. 1923, 1926 (2006–07).

Given these parallel trends, the adoption of a fairness rule in Recital 21 EUTMR and Recital 27 TMD that specifically deals with artistic expression is an important and welcome step in the right direction.

III. Inappropriate Assessment Scheme

The alignment of the fairness rule with behavioral standards in industry and commerce, however, is problematic. As already explained above, Recital 21 EUTMR and Recital 27 TMD allow a finding of fair use for the purpose of artistic expression only "as long as it is at the same time in accordance with honest practices in industrial and commercial matters." Immediately, this legislative guideline raises the question whether this standard of honesty can ever be an appropriate yardstick for the assessment of unauthorized use in an artistic context. The fair use analysis may be doomed to fail because industrial and commercial considerations are inapt to clarify the legitimacy of use in the cultural domain. Practical (Section III.A), socio-cultural (Section III.B), and legal-doctrinal (Section III.C) considerations militate against reliance on industrial and commercial standards when artistic expression is at stake.

A. Practical Concerns

From a practical point of view, an artist can hardly be expected to be aware of behavioral standards in industry and commerce. The proviso of honest practices in industrial and commercial matters is impractical and disadvantageous for artists because they do not have the knowledge necessary to ensure compliance with these standards. The information deficit weakens the strategic position of artists in infringement proceedings. Even if the burden of establishing dishonest practices is placed on the trademark proprietor,[48] the artist must ascertain which behavioral norms are applicable to successfully rebut dishonesty arguments. As a trader, the trademark owner can be expected to be well acquainted with standards of honesty in industrial and commercial matters. The artist, by contrast, must first explore applicable behavioral norms. The use of industrial and commercial standards as a yardstick for the assessment of artistic use thus causes an information imbalance that gives the trademark proprietor an advantage. In contrast to artists, trademark owners can remain in their own sector and play a home game.

[48] For arguments in favour of this distribution of the burden of proof, *see* KUR & SENFTLEBEN, *supra* note 5, paras. 6.78–6.79.

B. Theoretical Concerns

Recital 21 EUTMR and Recital 27 TMD, however, also give rise to a more fundamental issue. They raise the question whether artists and artistic productions ought to be subject to industrial and commercial behavioral norms *at all*. The subordination of artistic expression to an industrial and commercial assessment standard is highly undesirable. It obliges artists to align their cultural work with commercial standards of fairness and honesty that are inappropriate from the outset. Cultural sociology sheds light on the serious risk of eroding art autonomy that arises from the current configuration of the fairness test for artistic expression in E.U. trademark law. The sociological analysis of the field of literary and artistic production conducted by Pierre Bourdieu leaves no doubt that a thriving literary and artistic sector—capable of unmasking deficiencies in society and providing impulses for the improvement of social and political conditions[49]—requires independence of artists from economic and political powers.

Refining Niklas Luhmann's concept of relatively closed social systems with a distinct identity and a boundary between them and their environment,[50] Pierre Bourdieu developed the concept of "fields" in society. Although constituting an autonomous social space with individual rules, dominance structures, and an established set of opinions, a field is not isolated from other social spaces and processes surrounding it. According to Bourdieu, the structure of a field results from constant internal fights of competing players for predominance and leadership.[51] A field's degree of autonomy, then, depends on the extent to which external players can influence these internal fights.[52] For the assessment of the autonomy of a given field, it is thus necessary to examine its relationship with the social environment in which it is embedded at a given point in time.[53]

Applying this theoretical model to the field of literary and artistic production, Bourdieu assumes that the field's autonomy rests on the rejection of the capitalism of the bourgeoisie. The specific "nomos" of the literary and artistic field lies in the independence from economic and political powers.[54] Instead of aligning their work with commercial or political considerations, autonomous artists aim at internal recognition within the field. The artists emancipate themselves from the

[49] For a more detailed discussion of these societal functions of art, *see* Senftleben, *supra* note 14, at 54–66.

[50] Niklas Luhmann, Soziale Systeme: Grundriss einer allgemeinen Theorie 31, 35–70 (1984).

[51] Pierre Bourdieu, *Die Logik der Felder*, *in* Reflexive Anthropologie 124,134–35 (Pierre Bourdieu & Loic J.D. Wacquant eds., 2009); Pierre Bourdieu, Die Regeln der Kunst. Genese und Struktur des literarischen Feldes (1999) (French original: Pierre. Bourdieu, Les règles de l'art. Genèse et structure du champ littéraire 253–55, 368 (1992).

[52] Pierre Bourdieu et al., *Dialog über die Kulturgeschichte*, 26 Freibeuter—Vierteljahreszeitschrift für Kultur und Politik 22, 28 (1985).

[53] Bourdieu, *supra* note 51, at 134; Joseph Jurt, Bourdieu 91–92 (2008).

[54] Bourdieu, *supra* note 51, at 103–05.

focus on commercial necessities and rewards.[55] As a result, the consecration mechanisms in the literary and artistic field—the power to set quality standards and dominate the internal discourse—become self-referential: *l'art pour l'art*. The field of literature and art becomes a universe countering the profit logic that impregnates the economic and political discourse in society.[56] The break with commercial and political powers constitutes the basis of an artist's independent, autonomous existence.[57] It allows artworks to critically reflect on societal conditions and pave the way for necessary reforms.[58]

It follows from this configuration of the field of literary and artistic production that an artist must not be obliged to align his or her work with behavioral standards that stem from another field of society. From this perspective, it is intolerable that Recital 21 EUTMR and Recital 27 TMD put pressure on artists to observe standards of honesty in industrial and commercial matters. Recital 21 EUTMR and Recital 27 TMD appear as an institutionalized subordination of cultural productions to the predominant commercial orientation of modern capitalist societies.[59]

The potential corrosive effect of this legislative decision must not be underestimated. On the basis of his analysis of the power relations in the literary and artistic field, Bourdieu already painted an alarming picture of the field's degree of autonomy thirty years ago. In the light of reduced state subsidies for cultural productions and the rise of culture sponsoring by enterprises, Bourdieu warned of an increasing mutual penetration of the world of art and the world of money: he saw more and more literary and artistic productions becoming subject to entrepreneurial marketing strategies and commercial pressures.[60] Therefore, he predicted the loss of autonomous literary and artistic productions.[61] Considering the growing influence of commercial players and profit rationales, he feared that commercial influences would finally suppress the critical thinking that is necessary for independent avant-garde works.[62]

Considering these insights from cultural sociology it is evident that the reference point chosen in Recital 21 EUTMR and Recital 27 TMD is fundamentally wrong. The requirement of use in accordance with behavioral norms in the industrial and

[55] *Id.* at 344.

[56] *Cf.* Alexander Peukert, *Fictitious Commodities: A Theory of Intellectual Property Inspired by Karl Polanyi's Great Transformation*, 29 FORDHAM INTELL. PROP. MEDIA & ENT. L.J. 1151, 1178–79 (2018–19).

[57] Bourdieu, *supra* note 51, at 105.

[58] *Id.* at 342.

[59] *See* Jeanne C. Fromer, *A Psychology of Intellectual Property*, 104 NW. U. L. REV. 1441, 1479–80 (2010), with regard to consumers' preference for limited newness in the area of literary and artistic works; Christopher Buccafusco et al., *The Nature of Sequential Innovation*, 59 WM. & MARY L. REV. 1, 41–43 (2017–18), for a discussion of consumers' preference for established, known forms of literary and artistic expression, and the impact of this preference on innovation in the cultural domain.

[60] Bourdieu, *supra* note 51, at 530.

[61] *Id.* at 533.

[62] *Id.* at 531.

commercial sector cements the supremacy of trade and commerce over the field of art and culture: even if use appears fair and legitimate in the light of artistic standards, it may still amount to trademark infringement when established industrial and commercial practices point in the opposite direction. The legislator allows the logic of commerce and trade to prevail over the *l'art pour l'art* logic of culture and art—an alarming decision that encourages the erosion of the autonomy of literary and artistic productions.

C. Legal-Doctrinal Concerns

The problem becomes even bigger when legal-doctrinal developments are factored into the equation. The CJEU tends to determine compliance with honesty in industrial and commercial matters on the basis of the same criteria that inform the analysis of *prima facie* infringement in trademark confusion and dilution cases.[63] This jurisprudence strengthens concerns that, examining artistic use in the light of the honest practices proviso, industrial and commercial standards will prevail and finally erode art autonomy. As currently applied, the inquiry into honest commercial practices is far from including values from other societal domains, such as the field of literary and artistic production. Instead, the CJEU simply replicates infringement criteria that belong to the canon of standard behavioral norms in the sector of industry and commerce. In *Gillette*, the Court held that use would fail to comply with honest practices in industrial and commercial matters if, for example:

- it is done in such a manner as to give the impression that there is a commercial connection between the third party and the trade mark owner;
- it affects the value of the trade mark by taking unfair advantage of its distinctive character or repute;
- it entails the discrediting or denigration of that mark;
- or where the third party presents its product as an imitation or replica of the product bearing the trade mark of which it is not the owner.[64]

[63] CJEU, July 8, 2010, C-558/08, Portakabin, para. 69; CJEU, Mar. 17, 2005, Case No. C-228/03, Gillette/LA-Laboratories, para. 49. *Cf.* KUR & SENFTLEBEN, *supra* note 5, para. 6.73; Martin Senftleben et al., *The Recommendation on Measures to Safeguard Freedom of Expression and Undistorted Competition: Guiding Principles for the Further Development of EU Trade Mark Law*, 37 E.I.P.R. 337, 339 (2015); Martin Senftleben, *Adapting EU Trademark Law to New Technologies—Back to Basics?*, *in* CONSTRUCTING EUROPEAN INTELLECTUAL PROPERTY 137, 168–69 (Christopher Geiger ed., 2013); Ilanah Simon Fhima & Sir Robin Jacob, *Unfair Advantage Law in the European Union*, *in* INTERNATIONAL TRADEMARK DILUTION 251, 274 (Daniel R. Bereskin ed., 2014); Ilanah Simon Fhima, *The Role of Legitimacy in Trade Mark Law*, 65 C.L.P. 489, 501–02 (2012).

[64] CJEU, Mar. 17, 2005, Case No. C-228/03, Gillette/LA-Laboratories, para. 49.

While some of these assessment factors can be traced back to E.U. legislation in the field of comparative advertising,[65] the prohibition of use that gives the impression of a commercial connection with the trademark owner, and the ban on use that damages or takes unfair advantage of the mark's distinctive character or repute, correspond to infringement criteria in the field of trademark protection against confusion and dilution.[66] The risk of circularity is obvious: by copying almost literally the criteria for establishing *prima facie* infringement, the CJEU subjects defenses to additional scrutiny in the light of the same criteria that enabled the trademark owner to bring the infringement claim in the first place. This circular line of reasoning may render defense arguments, such as referential, non-distinctive, and descriptive use, moot in practice.[67] In the keyword advertising case *Portakabin*, for instance, the Court did not find it contradictory to conclude that

> the circumstances under which a trade mark proprietor is, pursuant to Article 5(1) of Directive 89/104 [nowadays Article 10(2)(a) TMD], entitled to prevent an advertiser from using a sign identical with, or similar to, that trade mark as a keyword may [. . .] easily correspond to a situation in which the advertiser cannot claim that it is acting in accordance with honest practices in industrial or commercial matters, and cannot therefore validly rely on the exception[68]

The corrosive effect of this circular approach on defense arguments that could support artistic expression is evident. Following the current CJEU approach, the same behavioral norms—stemming from the sector of industry and commerce—that have led to a finding of prima facie infringement, support a finding of dishonest practices. In consequence, the requirement of use in accordance with honest practices in industrial and commercial matters degenerates into a torpedo which the trademark proprietor can employ to neutralize limitations of trademark rights that provide defense arguments for artists. The symmetry of criteria for assessing prima facie infringement and determining honesty in industrial and commercial matters can easily lead to a situation where a finding of a likelihood of confusion or dilution already foreshadows the denial of compliance with honest commercial practices.

IV. Way Out of the Dilemma

Hence, the question arises whether, despite the approach chosen by the CJEU, it is possible to alleviate the problems arising from a fairness rule for artistic expression

[65] Art. 4(d), (f), (g), and (h) MCAD. *Cf.* Kur & Senftleben, *supra* note 5, para. 6.72.
[66] Art. 9(2)(b) and (c) EUTMR; art. 10(2)(b) and (c) TMD.
[67] *Cf.* Kur & Senftleben, *supra* note 5, para. 6.73; Senftleben et al., *supra* note 63, at 339; *id.* at 168–69; Fhima & Jacob, *supra* note 63, 274; Fhima, *supra* note 63, at 501–02.
[68] CJEU, July 8, 2010, C-558/08, Portakabin, para. 69.

that is aligned with behavioral standards in the industrial and commercial domain. A first signpost for potential solutions came to light during the debate on the amendment of E.U. trademark law. Seeking to provide guidance for the 2015 reform, the "Recommendation on Measures to Safeguard Freedom of Expression and Undistorted Competition in EU Trade Mark Law"[69] proposed to solve the problem of circularity in the honest practices jurisprudence as follows:

> The only way to make sense of the wording would be to clarify that although the basic concepts (likelihood of confusion, abuse of reputation) informing the evaluation of honest business practices are the same as those governing infringement, their application is different in that the leeway for using a basically conflicting mark is much broader where applications or limitations apply, thereby confining the proprietor's right to oppose such use to cases of disproportionate harm.[70]

In the debate, Annette Kur added the following, more detailed explanation:

> It is therefore important to emphasize that instead of applying those factors in the same way as when infringement is prima facie established, the interpretation must proceed in a more fine-grained fashion, taking account of the countervailing interests safeguarded by the limitations. This means that the concrete manner and dimensions of the use made must be appraised for their appropriateness and proportionality in view of all circumstances. Furthermore, the principle should be established that insofar as the limitations apply, use of the mark can only be qualified, but not entirely prohibited.[71]

The argument thus runs as follows: even if the assessment of honesty in industrial and commercial matters rests on the same criteria that have previously been used to establish prima facie infringement, the outcome can still be different when the criteria are applied in a more flexible way. The required flexibility can be derived from the values underlying the adoption of limitations in E.U. trademark law, such as the defenses for referential, non-distinctive, and descriptive use. Weighing the interests of the trademark owner against the interests of the defendant, trademark judges can attach particular importance to the values that support the position of the defendant and avoid the verdict of infringement. In the balancing process, the principle of proportionality plays a central role. The scope of the trademark owner's exclusive rights should be confined to cases of disproportionate harm.

[69] Senftleben et al., *supra* note 63, at 341–43. *Cf.* Kur, *supra* note 21, at 105; KUR & SENFTLEBEN, *supra* note 5, para. 6.74.
[70] Senftleben et al., *supra* note 63, at 339.
[71] Kur, *supra* note 21, at 105. *Cf. also* KUR & SENFTLEBEN, *supra* note 5, para. 6.74; Senftleben et al., *supra* note 63, at 339.

When a trademark is used for the purpose of artistic expression, these guidelines allow the artist to prevail for at least two reasons: the need to reconcile trademark protection with freedom of expression and freedom of the arts (Section IV.A), and the disproportionality of enforcing trademark rights even though artistic use is unlikely to imperil the essential origin function of trademarks (Section IV.B).

A. Fundamental Rights

Artistic expression enjoys protection on the basis of the constitutional guarantee of freedom of expression and freedom of the arts in Articles 11 and 13 of the E.U. Charter of Fundamental Rights (CFR).[72] The artist and the trademark proprietor thus meet at eye level. While the trademark owner can invoke the recognition of intellectual property in Article 17(2) CFR,[73] the artist can rely on Articles 11 and 13 CFR. The legal position of the artist is not a priori weaker than the status which the trademark owner enjoys. In copyright law, the CJEU already gave parody and quotation rules that serve freedom of expression and freedom of the arts,[74] the elevated status of "user rights."[75] In *Funke Medien* and *Spiegel Online*, the Court explicitly confirmed the status of user rights by pointing out that,

> although Article 5 [of the Information Society Directive[76]] is expressly entitled "Exceptions and limitations", it should be noted that those exceptions or

[72] Charter of Fundamental Rights of the European Union, Official Journal of the European Communities C 364, 1 (2000).

[73] *Cf.* Daniel Jongsma, Creating EU Copyright Law—Striking a Fair Balance (Ph.D. dissertation), Helsinki: Hanken School of Economics 2019 (163–68); Jonathan Griffiths, *Fundamental Rights and European IP Law—the Case of Art 17(2) of the EU Charter*, *in* Constructing European Intellectual Property Achievements and New Perspectives 75, 75–93 (Christopher Geiger ed., 2013); Christophe Geiger, *Intellectual Property Shall be Protected!? Article 17(2) of the Charter of Fundamental Rights of the European Union: A Mysterious Provision with an Unclear Scope*, 31 E.I.P.R. 113, 113–17 (2009).

[74] Art. 5(3)(d) and (k) ISD. *Cf.* CJEU, Dec. 1, 2011, Case No. C-145/10, Painer, para. 132–34; CJEU, Sept. 3, 2014, Case No. C-201/13, Deckmyn, paras. 25–27. *Cf.* Jongsma, *supra* note 73, at 126–35. For a decision devoting specific attention to freedom of the arts, *see* CJEU, July 29, 2019, Case No. C-476/17, Pelham and Others, paras. 31–35. *Cf.* Christophe Geiger & Elena Izyumenko, *The Constitutionalization of Intellectual Property Law in the EU and the Funke Medien, Pelham and Spiegel Online Decisions of the CJEU: Progress, but Still Some Way to Go!*, 51 I.I.C. 282, 293–94 (2020).

[75] As to the influence of freedom of expression on copyright protection, *cf.* Geiger & Izyumenko, *supra* note 74, at 292–98; Jongsma, *supra* note 73, at 195–222; P. Bernt Hugenholtz, *Flexible Copyright, Can EU Author's Right Accommodate Fair Use?*, *in* Copyright Law in an Age of Limitations and Exceptions 242 (Ruth L. Okediji ed., 2016); Christophe Geiger & Elena Izyumenko, *Copyright on the Human Rights' Trial: Redefining the Boundaries of Exclusivity Through Freedom of Expression*, 45 I.I.C. 316, 316 (2014); Neil Weinstock Netanel, *Copyright and a Democratic Civil Society*, 106 Yale L.J. 283, 283 (1996).

[76] Directive 2001/29/EC of the European Parliament and of the Council of May 22, 2001 on the Harmonisation of Certain Aspects of Copyright and Related Rights in the Information Society, Official Journal of the European Communities L 167, 10 (2001).

limitations do themselves confer rights on the users of works or of other subject matter.[77]

Taken this development in E.U. copyright law as a reference point, it seems only a small step to draw a parallel in trademark law and recognize that, granting freedom of referential, non-distinctive, and descriptive use, Article 14(1)(b) and (c) EUTMR and Article 14(1)(b) and (c) TMD bestow user rights upon artists.[78]

B. Proportionality

In addition, use of trademarks in an artistic setting, as already pointed out above, constitutes a specific form of use. It is use in a metaphorical, non-branding[79] sense: the trademark is not employed as an identifier of commercial source but as a symbol of personal or societal conditions. Use of trademarks in art concerns a metaphorical play with the associations evoked by a trademark in the minds of consumers and the societal conditions which a trademark reflects.[80] This insight has a deep impact on the balancing exercise to be conducted in the light of the principle of proportionality. As the artist does not use the trademark as a badge of origin, the detriment to the trademark proprietor, by definition, is reduced.

Artistic use may still do harm by mocking and criticizing the trademark owner, or using the trademark for a critique of societal conditions which the trademark owner finds irreconcilable with the favorable brand image they wish to maintain.[81] Nonetheless, the fact remains that artistic use does not encroach upon the essential function of the trademark: the function of guaranteeing the commercial origin of

[77] CJEU, July 29, 2019, Case No. C-516/17, Spiegel Online, para. 54; CJEU, July 29, 2019, Case No. C-469/17, Funke Medien NRW, para. 70. For a more detailed discussion of this point, *see* Tanya Aplin & Lionel Bently, Global Mandatory Fair Use: The Nature and Scope of the Right to Quote Copyright Works 75–84 (2020); Geiger & Izyumenko, *supra* note 74, at 292–98.

[78] For a decision relying on freedom of the arts as a factor that weighs against the grant of trademark rights, see EFTA Court, Apr. 6, 2017, Case No. E-5/16, Municipality of Oslo ("Vigeland"), para. 65. For a general confirmation of the need to observe freedom of expression in E.U. trademark law, *see* CJEU, Feb. 27, 2020, Case No. C-240/18P, Constantin Film/EUIPO ('Fack Ju Göhte'), para. 56. *Cf.* Senftleben, *supra* note 14, at 342.

[79] Dogan & Lemley, *supra* note 31, at 542.

[80] *Cf.* Dreyfuss, *supra* note 28, at 418; Dogan & Lemley, *supra* note 31, at 542. For an example of case law recognizing this metaphorical play as a central feature of the use of trade symbols in an artistic setting, *see* German Federal Supreme Court, Feb. 3, 2005, Case No. I ZR 159/02, Lila Postkarte, *Gewerblicher Rechtsschutz und Urheberrecht* 2005, 584–85.

[81] For an example of case law discussing this type of artistic expression, *see* District Court of The Hague, May 4, 2011, Case No. LJN BQ3525, Nadia Plesner/Louis Vuitton, paras. 2.1–2.8. *Cf.* Alexander Peukert, *Vom Warenzeichen zum Markeneigentum. Ein polanyischer Erklärungsversuch*, *in* Marktkommunikation zwischen Geistigem Eigentum und Verbraucherschutz. Festschrift für Karl-Heinz Fezer zum 70, 405, 424 (Wolfgang Büscher et al. eds., 2016); Dirk Visser, *Darfurnica: modellenrecht versus kunstvrijheid*, Nederlands Juristenblad [N. J. B.] 740, 740–42 (2011).

goods or services.[82] From this perspective, the detriment to the trademark owner is limited from the outset.

V. Legal Presumption of Compliance with Honest Practices

Taking the described insights together—the anchorage of artistic expression in constitutional freedoms and the proportionality of harm flowing from a metaphorical play with trademarks—it becomes possible to weave a general bias in favor of artistic expression into the fabric of the honest practices test: a legal bias in the sense of a legal presumption of fair use that allows use of a trademark for the purpose of artistic expression to routinely survive scrutiny in the light of the honest practices proviso. Following this maxim, use of trademarks should be deemed fair in artistic contexts unless the trademark proprietor manages to overcome the legal presumption by presenting individualized facts[83] that provide proof of unusually grave trademark harm. More specifically, the trademark owner should be obliged to demonstrate that, despite the artistic setting, the use *explicitly* misleads consumers as to the commercial origin of the artwork. In the case of a trademark with a reputation that enjoys protection against dilution,[84] the trademark owner should be obliged to show that the use *deliberately* blurs, tarnishes, or exploits in an unfair manner the distinctiveness or repute of the trademark with a reputation.[85] As the words "explicitly" and "deliberately" indicate, the threshold for a finding of dishonest practices should thus be higher than in the regular confusion or dilution analysis. This approach is in line with the above-described strategy for remedying the circularity in CJEU jurisprudence. Although assessment criteria are used that have already supported a finding of prima facie infringement, the outcome of the honest practices analysis can be different because the criteria are applied in a

[82] CJEU, Dec. 3, 1981, Case No. C-1/81, Pfizer vs. Eurim-Pharm, para. 8; CJEU, Nov. 12, 2002, Case No. C-206/01, Arsenal/Reed, para. 48. *Cf.* Ilanah Simon Fhima, *How Does 'Essential Function' Doctrine Drive European Trade Mark Law?*, 36 I.I.C. 401 (2005).

[83] Benkler, *supra* note 75, at 362–63.

[84] CJEU, Sept. 14, 1999, Case No. C-375/97, General Motors/Yplon ("Chevy"), paras. 24–28; CJEU, Oct. 6, 2009, Case No. C-301/07, Pago/Tirolmilch, paras. 29–30; CJEU, Sept. 3, 2015, Case No. C-125/14, Iron & Smith/Unilever, paras. 28–30. *Cf.* KUR & SENFTLEBEN, *supra* note 5, paras. 5.201–5.204; Jerre B. Swann, *The Evolution of Dilution in the United States from 1927 to 2013*, 103 TRADEMARK REP. 721, 721 (2013); Michael Handler, *Trade Mark Dilution in Australia?*, 29 E.I.P.R. 307, 307 (2007); Martin Senftleben, *The Trademark Tower of Babel—Dilution Concepts in International, US and EC Trademark Law*, 40 I.I.C. 45, 50–55 (2009); Barton Beebe, *A Defense of the New Federal Trademark Antidilution Law*, 16 FORDHAM INTELL. PROP. MEDIA & ENT. L.J. 1143, 1157 (2005–06); J. Thomas McCarthy, *Dilution of a Trademark: European and United States Law Compared*, 94 TRADEMARK REP. 1163, 1163 (2004).

[85] As to the use of these criteria in the dilution analysis in EU trademark law, *see* art. 10(2)(c) TMD; art. 9(2)(c) EUTMR; and the distinction between three different anti-dilution actions in CJEU, June 18, 2009, Case No. C-487/07, L'Oréal/Bellure, paras. 39–41. *Cf.* KUR & SENFTLEBEN, *supra* note 5, paras. 5.182–5.192; Senftleben, *supra* note 63, at 152.

modified way—in a way that lends sufficient weight to freedom of expression and freedom of the arts.

Interestingly, this modification of the honest practices test in cases of artistic expression finds support in Recital 21 EUTMR and Recital 27 TMD themselves. As discussed, these Recitals are problematic because they endanger art autonomy by stipulating that use for the purpose of artistic expression could only be deemed fair as long as it is in accordance with honest practices in industrial and commercial matters. In addition, however, Recital 21 EUTMR and Recital 27 recall the necessity to safeguard freedom of expression:

> Furthermore, this Regulation [this Directive] should be applied in a way that ensures full respect for fundamental rights and freedoms, and in particular the freedom of expression.

As Jens Schovsbo explains, this additional reference to freedom of expression impacts the application of all individual norms of E.U. trademark law, including the honest practices proviso itself.

> The first part of the Recital provides for limitations but only to the extent that the use by third parties is fair and in accordance with honest practices in industrial and commercial matters. The application of fundamental rights and freedoms is not, however, made subject to the "fair and honest practices" test. Instead, this part constitutes a freestanding test (cf. the use of the word "furthermore"). This is also the effect of the use of the opening word—"furthermore"—and by the adjective "*full* respect." It thus follows from the wording of the Recital itself that these interests should be taken into account when applying any rule or principle of trademark law [. . .] including the definition of which uses are "fair" and in conformity with "honest practices."[86] (emphasis in the original text)

Therefore, it is important to recognize that the honest practices proviso itself is subject to more thorough scrutiny in the light of freedom of expression. In cases where trademarks appear in a literary and artistic context, the second part of Recital 21 EUTMR and Recital 27 TMD (the sentence starting with "furthermore") makes it necessary to give the honest practices proviso a meaning which "fully" respects freedom of expression. To achieve this goal, it is consistent to weave the described bias in favor of users in the artistic domain into the honest practices test. Instead of the standard confusion or dilution analysis, a higher threshold for demonstrating dishonest use must be applied.

[86] Schovsbo, *supra* note 47, at 568.

The proposed higher bar of *explicitly* misleading or *deliberately* diluting use implements this approach. Only if use in the artistic domain is evidently disproportionate and harmful, the trademark owner should be able to demonstrate unusual circumstances that attest to dishonest practices and neutralize an artist's invocation of referential, non-distinctive, or descriptive use arguments. Only then, it is justified to allow behavioral standards of industry and commerce to inform the analysis because the literary and artistic context proves to be a mere disguise for obvious trademark infringement. As this configuration of the honest practices test in cases of artistic use follows from the second "furthermore" part of Recital 21 EUTMR and Recital 27 TMD, the proposed solution based on a legal presumption of fair use is fully in line with E.U. trademark law. It is even a legal obligation that follows directly from the explicit confirmation of the need to safeguard freedom of expression in Recital 21 EUTMR and Recital 27 TMD.[87]

Moreover, the proposed distribution of the burden of proof is no outlier in E.U. trademark law. Article 9(3)(f) EUTMR and Article 10(3)(f) TMD already provide for a similar solution with regard to comparative advertising. Stipulating that unauthorized use in comparative advertising is only actionable if it is contrary to the rules laid down in the Directive on Misleading and Comparative Advertising (MCAD),[88] Article 9(3)(f) EUTMR and Article 10(3)(f) TMD impose the burden of proving noncompliance with one of the advertising requirements on the trademark proprietor.[89] This can be seen as a corollary of the freedom of lawful comparative advertising which the CJEU recognized in *O2/Hutchison* and *L'Oréal/Bellure*.[90] In line with these decisions, use in comparative advertising that fulfills the MCAD requirements is exempted from the control of the trademark proprietor. If, however, E.U. trademark law achieves this result by reversing the burden of proof in respect of freedom of commercial expression, there is substantial reason to take the same step with regard to freedom of artistic expression. In the human rights analysis following from the jurisprudence of the European Court of Human Rights (ECtHR),[91] freedom of commercial expression carries less weight than freedom of artistic or political expression.[92] Therefore, measures to safeguard

[87] Schovsbo, *supra* note 47, at 568, rightly refers to a "freestanding" obligation to provide sufficient room for freedom of expression. For a confirmation of the impact of freedom of expression on the application of trademark norms, *see* CJEU, Feb. 27, 2020, Case No. C-240/18P, Constantin Film/EUIPO ("Fack Ju Göhte"), para. 56.

[88] Directive 2006/114/EC of the European Parliament and of the Council of Dec. 12, 2006 Concerning Misleading and Comparative Advertising (codified version), Official Journal of the European Communities L 376, 21 (2006).

[89] KUR & SENFTLEBEN, *supra* note 5, paras. 5.308–5.309.

[90] CJEU, June12, 2008, Case No. C-533/06, O2/Hutchison, para. 45; CJEU, June 18, 2009, Case No. C-487/07, L'Oréal/Bellure, para. 54. *Cf.* KUR & SENFTLEBEN, *supra* note 5, para. 5.308.

[91] For an overview of criteria and the interplay between CJEU and ECtHR jurisprudence, *see* Geiger & Izyumenko, *supra* note 74, at 292–302.

[92] As to the recognition of the fundamental freedom of expression with regard to commercial speech, *see* ECtHR, May 22, 1990, App. No. 12726/87, Autronic/Switzerland, para. 47. With regard to the wider margin of appreciation in cases concerning commercial freedom of expression, *see* ECtHR, Nov.

artistic expression should be at least as effective as those adopted to offer room for commercial freedom of speech.[93] As the burden of proof rests on the trademark owner in the case of comparative advertising, it is consistent to take the same approach to use of trademarks in artistic contexts.

The proposed interpretation of the honest practices test in cases of artistic expression—leading to a legal presumption of fair use—also alleviates the problem of a circular line of reasoning in CJEU jurisprudence. Providing qualified confusion and dilution criteria for the honest practices inquiry, this interpretation obliges the trademark owner to demonstrate a higher degree of harm. The artistic use of a trademark can be deemed to comply with honest practices in industrial and commercial matters as long as it does not *explicitly* mislead consumers as to the commercial source of the literary and artistic work, and as long as it does not *deliberately* damage or derive unfair advantage from the distinctiveness or repute of the trademark at issue. Introducing the higher threshold of explicitly confusing or deliberately diluting use, the leeway for users in the artistic domain becomes broader and the rights of the trademark owner remain limited to cases of disproportionate harm.[94]

To some extent, the qualified confusion and dilution criteria for the honest practices test also takes care of the concern that behavioral standards in the sector of industry and commerce may prevail over art autonomy and govern creative processes in the artistic domain. Instead of allowing trademark categories of infringement to dominate the analysis, the question of an artistic context enters the picture and raises the bar for a finding of dishonest practices. In cases where a trademark is artistically relevant to the cultural production at issue, the trademark proprietor can only succeed if the allegedly infringing use explicitly misleads the public or deliberately dilutes the mark. As a result, an assessment criterion from the artistic domain—the artistic setting of the use—reduces the impact of trademark rights. Instead of allowing any form of confusion or dilution to tip the scales against the user in the artistic domain, only forms of use are actionable that are clearly harmful from a trademark perspective. The supremacy of behavioral standards known from the field of industry and commerce is confined to cases of evidently disproportionate harm which the trademark owner can hardly be expected to tolerate.

20, 1989, App. No. 10572/83, Markt Intern Verlag GmbH and Klaus Beermann/Germany, paras. 26 and 32–38.

[93] As to the elevated status of freedom of artistic expression, *see* Geiger & Izyumenko, *supra* note 74, at 293–94. *Cf.* ECtHR, May 24, 1988, App. No. 10737/84, Müller and Others/Switzerland, para. 27; ECtHR, July 8, 1999, App. No. 23168/94, Karataş/Turkey, paras. 49–52; CJEU, July 29, 2019, Case No. C-476/17, Pelham and Others, para. 34.

[94] *Cf.* the above-cited recommendation by Senftleben et al., *supra* note 53, at 339. *Cf.* the analysis by Schovsbo, *supra* note 47, at 578–79, who raises the question whether "the courts should begin their analysis from the perspective of the artist or from the perspective of what is fair as seen from a commercial point of view," and recommends an interpretation that supports artistic freedom of expression.

In sum, a circular repetition of standard confusion or dilution criteria in the honest practices analysis—and an erosion of art autonomy—can be prevented by aligning the honest practices proviso with the test of explicitly confusing or deliberately diluting use. This qualified test of confusion or dilution should constitute the threshold for rebutting the legal presumption of non-actionable use in an artistic context. When the higher threshold of explicitly misleading or deliberately diluting use is applied to identify dishonest practices in connection with the use of trademarks in an artistic setting, the honest practices test no longer deprives limitations of trademark rights of their function to offer room for freedom of expression and freedom of the arts. Instead, the honest practices inquiry starts with a bias in favor of the artist—the presumption of fair use—and raises the question whether the trademark owner can rebut this legal presumption by providing proof of evidently disproportionate harm that unmasks the artistic use argument as mere pretense to conceal blatant trademark infringement.

VI. Case Law Precedents

Case law developments on both sides of the Atlantic offer additional support for this solution of the honest practices dilemma. With regard to protection against confusion, the evolution of the so-called "Rogers" test in the United States is of particular importance (Section VI.A). As to dilution claims, the decision of the Benelux Court of Justice in *Moët Hennessy/Cedric Art* offers a blueprint for the implementation of the described bias in favor of artistic use (Section VI.B).

A. Higher Threshold for Protection Against Confusion

The development of the "Rogers" test in the United States began with the decision of the U.S. Court of Appeals for the Second Circuit in *Rogers/Grimaldi*. In this case, the Court was called upon to decide on an infringement claim brought by the actress Ginger Rogers against the use of her name in the title of Federico Fellini's film *Ginger and Fred*. The film told the story of two fictional Italian cabaret performers—Pippo and Amelia—who imitated Ginger Rogers and Fred Astaire and became known in Italy as "Ginger and Fred." Seeking to make a satiric comment on television variety shows, the film focused on a televised reunion of Pippo and Amelia many years after their retirement. Ginger Rogers based her infringement claim on the argument that the film's title created the false impression that she was associated with the film production.[95]

[95] U.S. Court of Appeals for the Second Circuit, May 5, 1989, Rogers/Grimaldi, 875 F.2d 994 (2nd Cir. 1989), 997.

Dealing with this claim, the Court of Appeals emphasized the expressive dimension of film titles. Judge Newman explained that filmmakers frequently relied on "word-play, ambiguity, irony, and allusion in titling their works."[96] The Court also lent weight to the interest of the audience in sufficient breathing space for free expression. The subtleties of a title could enrich the understanding of the work. Consumers of artistic works had a dual interest against this background: on the one hand, the interest in not being misled; on the other hand, the interest in enjoying the results of the filmmaker's freedom of expression. For all these reasons, the Court concluded that the expressive element of titles of literary and artistic works required more protection than the labeling of ordinary commercial products.

> We believe that in general the [Lanham] Act should be construed to apply to artistic works only where the public interest in avoiding consumer confusion outweighs the public interest in free expression.[97]

From the outset, the Court thus established a bias in favor of users in the artistic domain. Instead of allowing concerns about regular confusion harm to occupy center stage, the Court was willing to let the interest in free expression prevail. This approach corresponds with the strategy recommended above: To avoid an erosion of art autonomy and offer sufficient room for freedom of expression and freedom of the arts, it is necessary to depart from the standard trademark infringement analysis and factor an element into the honest practices analysis that permits the expressive nature of the use to tip the scales in favor of the artistic user. In *Rogers*, this approach culminated in the creation of an assessment framework which later became known as the "Rogers" test.[98]

> In the context of allegedly misleading titles using a celebrity's name, that balance will normally not support application of the [Lanham] Act unless the title has no artistic relevance to the underlying work whatsoever, or, if it has some artistic relevance, unless the title explicitly misleads as to the source or the content of the work.[99]

Hence, permitted use in an artistic context is the rule; infringing use is the exception. Only if the unauthorized use *explicitly* misleads the public can an infringement claim have success.[100] Following this approach, the Second Circuit focused

[96] *Id.* 998.
[97] *Id.* 999.
[98] *Cf.* Graeme Dinwoodie, Rogers *and the Structure of Trademark Defenses*, *in* CHARTING LIMITATIONS ON TRADEMARK RIGHTS (Beebe & Haochen Sun eds., forthcoming 2022); Irenel Calboli, *Overlapping Rights: The Negative Effects of Trademarking Creative Works*, *in* THE EVOLUTION AND EQUILIBRIUM OF COPYRIGHT IN THE DIGITAL AGE 52, 72–76 (Susy Frankel & Daniel Gervais eds., 2014).
[99] U.S. Court of Appeals for the Second Circuit, *supra* note 95, at 999.
[100] Dinwoodie, *supra* note 98, at 2–3.

on the question of whether there were clear indications that the name "Ginger" had been included in the film title for the very purpose of giving the false impression that Ginger Rogers endorsed and supported the film production. As there was no evidence that the film title was explicitly misleading in this sense, the Court found no infringement.

> The survey evidence, even if its validity is assumed, indicates at most that some members of the public would draw the incorrect inference that Rogers had some involvement with the film. But that risk of misunderstanding, not engendered by any overt claim in the title, is so outweighed by the interests in artistic expression as to preclude application of the Lanham Act.[101]

The Court thus suppressed standard infringement arguments and, instead, lent weight to the expressive nature of the allegedly infringing use. Ginger Rogers could only have rebutted the presumption of noninfringement by demonstrating explicitly misleading use under the guise of literary and artistic expression. This approach—allowing artistic relevance to pose a substantial obstacle to standard trademark infringement arguments—is fully in line with the configuration of the honest practices proviso that has been proposed above.

Subsequent developments in U.S. case law confirm that the "Rogers" test can provide a useful template for trademark cases. *Rogers* concerned the allegedly misleading use of a celebrity's name in a film title.[102] The Second Circuit, however, did not hesitate to broaden the test's ambit of operation several months later in *Cliffs Notes/Bantham Doubleday*—a case that concerned book parodies in study guide format which imitated distinctive elements of the covers of Cliffs Notes' study guides for short stories, plays and books.[103] Dealing with the satiric play with the format and style of Cliffs Notes' books, the Second Circuit pointed out that the case did not raise the question of whether a title was false advertising but whether the appearance of a work's cover was confusingly similar to the elements of an earlier cover enjoying trademark protection. The Court also recognized that in *Cliffs Notes*, the element of parody entered the picture which had not been present in *Rogers*. These differences, however, did not inhibit the Second Circuit from relying on the "Rogers" test. To the contrary, the Court emphasized that it was appropriate to weigh the public interest in free expression against the public interest in avoiding consumer confusion in any case where an expressive work was alleged to infringe a trademark right under the U.S. Lanham Act.

[101] U.S. Court of Appeals for the Second Circuit, *supra* note 95, at 1001.

[102] *Id.*999.

[103] U.S. Court of Appeals for the Second Circuit, 5 Sept. 1989, Cliffs Notes/Bantham Doubleday Dell Publishing Group, 886 F.2d 490 (2nd Cir. 1989), 492. *Cf.* Dinwoodie, *supra* note 98, at 2–3.

> Thus, we hold that the Rogers balancing approach is generally applicable to Lanham Act claims against works of artistic expression, a category that includes parody.[104]

Applying the "Rogers" test, the Court then dismissed the infringement claim as a matter of law even though the district judge had found a strong likelihood of confusion. The Second Circuit recalled that trademark owners had to tolerate more and surmount a higher hurdle when artistic expression was involved.[105]

B. Higher Threshold for Protection Against Dilution

In the field of protection against dilution, a similar tendency of immunizing artistic use against trademark infringement claims comes to the fore in the decision of the Benelux Court of Justice in *Moët Hennessy/Cedric Art*. The case concerned the open-ended defense of "due cause" which, under Article 9(2)(c) EUTMR and Article 10(2)(c) TMD, makes it possible to escape dilution claims based on blurring, tarnishment, or free-riding arguments.[106] In Benelux trademark law, the "due cause" defense is also available under Article 2.20(2)(d) of the Benelux Convention on Intellectual Property (BCIP) which offers trademark owners the possibility of bringing infringement claims even if use does not serve the purpose of distinguishing goods or services in the course of trade.[107] Prior to the decision of the Benelux Court of Justice, the due cause defense already prevented the condemnation of biting "Miffy" (*Nijntje*) parodies that had depicted the trademarked children's book character as a 9/11 terrorist.[108] In *Moët Hennessy*, the Benelux Court of Justice went a step further. Reaching beyond parody cases, it developed an *exceptio artis* on the basis of the due cause defense. The case concerned the use of the trademarked Dom Pérignon bottle[109] in stylized form and neon colors in

[104] U.S. Court of Appeals for the Second Circuit, *supra* note 103, at 495–96.

[105] *Id.* at 498.

[106] As to these three anti-dilution actions, *see* CJEU, June 18, 2009, Case No. C-487/07, L'Oréal/Bellure, paras. 39–41. *Cf.* Kur & Senftleben, *supra* note 5, paras. 5.182–5.192; Senftleben, *supra* note 63, at 152. As to the defence of due cause, *see* CJEU, Sept. 22, 2011, Case No. C-323/09, Interflora/Marks & Spencer, para. 91; CJEU, Feb. 6, 2014, Case No. C-65/12, Leidseplein Beheer/Red Bull, paras. 54–58. *Cf.* Kur & Senftleben, *supra* note 5, paras. 5.265–5.268 and 6.59–6.63; Di Cataldo, *supra* note 13, at 833.

[107] *Cf.* Vanovermeire, *supra* note 12, at 187–88.

[108] Court of Appeals of Amsterdam, Sept. 13, 2011, Case No. ECLI:NL:GHAMS:2011:BS7825, Mercis and Bruna/Punt, *Tijdschrift voor auteurs-, media- en informatierecht* 2012, 28, para. 4.19. For a further example of the successful invocation of the due cause defence in an artistic context, *see* German Federal Supreme Court, Feb. 3, 2005, Case No. I ZR 159/02, Lila Postkarte, *Gewerblicher Rechtsschutz und Urheberrecht* 2005, 583 (585). *Cf.* Martin Senftleben, *The Perfect Match—Civil Law Judges and Open-Ended Fair Use Provisions*, 33 Am. U. Int'l L. Rev. 231, 256–65 (2018).

[109] IR No. 323543.

paintings which, according to the artist Cédric Peers, played with pointillism and pop art.[110]

Assessing this unauthorized use of Hennessy's trademark, the Benelux Court of Justice stated that artistic freedom—as an aspect of the artist's right to freedom of expression—could constitute a due cause when "there is an artistic expression that is the original result of a creative shaping process."[111] The Court added, however, that the artistic expression must not specifically aim at harming the trademark or the proprietor of the trademark.[112] The Court thus brought the question into focus whether the artist aims at causing damage. Accordingly, it required evidence of an intention to harm the trademark or the trademark owner. As the "Rogers" test in the United States, the decision in *Moët Hennessy* points in the direction of a legal presumption of noninfringement that can only be rebutted when exceptional circumstances arise. Interestingly, the Benelux Court of Justice explicitly relied on Article 10(1) of the European Convention on Human Rights (ECHR) to undergird the artist's right to include trademarks in artistic expression without prior authorization. Instead of referring to trademark norms, such as the honest practices proviso, the Court based the prohibition of use that specifically aims at bringing harm on Article 10(2) ECHR which allows limitations of freedom of expression that are "necessary in a democratic society [...] for the protection of the reputation or rights of others."[113] Hence, the Court viewed the trademark infringement claim through the prism of fundamental rights and refrained from presuming any superiority of trademark protection that could have led to an assessment on the basis of regular confusion or dilution standards. Instead of scrutinizing the artistic use in the light of trademark infringement categories, such as blurring, tarnishment, and unfair free-riding, the Court aligned its ruling with the guarantee of freedom of expression in the ECHR and required use that specifically aims at causing damage.

C. Lessons to Learn

Admittedly, neither the U.S. nor the Benelux decision directly addressed the honest practices proviso laid down in Article 14(2) EUTMR and Article 14(2) TMD. Nonetheless, the two rulings are of particular importance because both of them establish a bias in favor of the artist (instead of the trademark owner) that raises the bar for a successful confusion or dilution claim. The U.S. Court of Appeals for the Second Circuit required *explicitly* misleading use in *Rogers*.[114] The Benelux

[110] *See* https://www.cedricgallery.com/ for examples.
[111] Benelux Court of Justice, Oct. 14, 2019, Case No. A2018/1/8, Moët Hennessy/Cedric Art, para. 9.
[112] *Id.* para. 9.
[113] *Id.* para. 9.
[114] U.S. Court of Appeals for the Second Circuit, 5 May 1989, Rogers/Grimaldi, 875 F.2d 994 (2nd Cir. 1989), 999.

Court of Justice insisted on use that *aims at* harming the trademark or the proprietor of the trademark.[115] Applying this approach *mutatis mutandis* to the proviso of honest practices in industrial and commercial matters, it becomes possible to arrive at the legal presumption of fair use that has been discussed above. Imposing an obligation on the trademark owner to demonstrate *explicitly* confusing or *deliberately* diluting use to overcome the legal presumption of permissible artistic expression, the proposed bias in favor of artistic use can make its way into the honest practices test and prevent the erosion of art autonomy that could follow from a focus on behavioral norms in the industrial and commercial sector.

Conclusion

In E.U. trademark law, artists can invoke defenses for referential, descriptive, and noninfringing use to justify the use of trademarks in their creative work. The requirement of use in compliance with honest practices, however, subordinates artistic creativity to behavioral standards in the field of industry and commerce, and poses a threat to art autonomy. The CJEU enhances this risk by replicating standard confusion and dilution criteria in the honest practices analysis. To offer sufficient room for freedom of expression and freedom of the arts, it is indispensable to change this configuration of the E.U. limitation infrastructure for artistic use. As a way out of the dilemma, it is advisable to introduce a legal presumption of fair use which the trademark owner can only overcome by showing that the artistic use explicitly causes confusion or deliberately blurs, tarnishes, or takes unfair advantage of the distinctive character or repute of a trademark with a reputation.

[115] Benelux Court of Justice, *supra* note 111, para. 9.

PART III
SCOPE OF LIMITATIONS

7

Limitations on Pharmaceutical Trade Marks in Britain in the Twentieth Century

Lionel Bently[1]

Although the nature of production and distribution of pharmaceuticals, as well as the character of pharmaceuticals themselves, were subjects of massive transformation over the twentieth century,[2] one feature that remained constant was skepticism about the use of trademarks in relation to so-called "ethical drugs."[3] The basis for this skepticism was that while pharmaceutical trademarks have frequently been associated with higher drug prices, and add complexity for those operating in the medical field (by creating nomenclatural distinctions without therapeutic differences), it was not clear whether, and if so to what extent, the use of such marks brought benefits of reduced search costs that are normally used to justify protecting trademarks. In other words, it was unclear that the social benefits deriving from such marks outweighed the social costs associated with their use. The skepticism was evidenced in laws, proposals, and practices that conditioned and limited, and even proposed the abolition of, trademarks for pharmaceuticals.

The historical analysis focuses on three expressions of this skepticism. First, the passage of the Trade Marks Act 1919, imposing limitations and conditions applicable to pharmaceutical marks. Second, the recommendation of the Sainsbury Committee, appointed to consider the relationship between the pharmaceutical industry and the National Health Service (NHS), in its 1967 report, that such marks were abolished. Third, proposals to compel pharmacists to substitute generic drugs for those prescribed by way of trademarks, in both the Greenfield Report of 1982 and a 1994 recommendation of the House of Commons Health Committee. While each reflects persistent unease with the operation of pharmaceutical trademarks they also point to different "ways of regulating" such names.[4] With the Trade Marks

[1] Many people have now read and commented on different versions of this essay. In addition to the editors of this volume, I am especially indebted to Alan Durant, Phill Johnson, John Liddicoat, David Simon, Brad Sherman, and Kara Swanson. I benefited from research assistance of Alec Thompson.

[2] Graham Dutfield, That High Design of Purest Gold: A Critical History of the Pharmaceutical Industry 1880–2020 (2020).

[3] "Ethical drugs," in contrast to quack remedies, are drugs developed on the basis of research; not, in general, advertised directly to the public; and available primarily through prescription.

[4] Ways of Regulating Drugs in the 19th and 20th Centuries (Jean-Paul Gaudillière & Volker Hess eds., 2013) (describing five ways of regulating drugs in the twentieth century—"professional," "administrative," "industrial," "public," and "juridical.")

Lionel Bently, *Limitations on Pharmaceutical Trade Marks in Britain in the Twentieth Century* In: *Charting Limitations on Trademark Rights*. Edited by: Haochen Sun and Barton Beebe, Oxford University Press. © Lionel Bently 2023.
DOI: 10.1093/oso/9780198871248.003.0008

Act, intellectual property mechanisms were used to induce trademark proprietors to provide alternative, non-proprietary, terms—effectively to help provide doctors and pharmacists with a common language for drugs. The 1967 proposal to abolish trade markswould have involved a radical, public law response to bring an end to the practice of general practitioners in prescribing by way of trademarks (a practice that persisted despite the availability of an official regime of non-proprietary designations). The substitution proposals would have marked a reluctant acceptance that general practitioners could not be induced to prescribe by reference to the non-proprietary names, requiring pharmacists instead to determine equivalence between drugs. Ultimately, none of the initiatives survived or succeeded, private trademarks have been left intact, but indirect mechanisms have been used, with perhaps surprising effectiveness, to educate doctors from utilizing trade names. Through a combination of information-provision, professional norm-setting, and auditing, the significance of trademarks has been marginalized and their retention made tolerable.

I. The Start of the Twentieth Century: The Emergence of Problems with Trademarks for Pharmaceuticals

By the beginning of the twentieth century, legal protection of trademarks and trade names was well established. Such protection was premised on the use by a third party of insignia (in principle, unlimited in kind) associated with a claimant trader that would lead consumers to be deceived into believing the third party's goods or services had been produced or provided by the claimant. This system, now commonly referred to as the law of "passing off," was the legal structure on to which a system of trademark registration had been attached by way of the Trade Mark (Registration) Act 1875. Initially limited in coverage, there had been successive expansions in the scope of registrability in 1883, 1889, and 1905. In 1905, registered trademarks were placed on a more comprehensive statutory basis, the Act then defining infringement (at least in outline) and specifying limitations to the rights of trade mark proprietors.[5]

The laws of passing off and registered trademarks applied to marks used on pharmaceuticals as much as to any other goods.[6] Moreover, commercial practice in relation to pharmaceutical marks echoed that in other sectors in two important respects. First, there was a growing use of invented or arbitrary words as marks. If the case law from before 1870 is a good indication, most trademarks were the names of the business—DAY AND MARTIN'S blacking, HOLLOWAY'S pills, the SINGER

[5] Trade Marks Act, 1905 §§ 36, 43, 44.

[6] Paris Convention for the Protection of Industrial Property, art. 7, Mar. 20, 1883, 21 U.S.T. 1583, 828 U.N.T.S. 305.

MANUFACTURING CO.'s sewing machine, etc. From the 1870s onwards, it had become increasingly common for traders to designate their goods using arbitrary names (rather than explicitly referring to the manufacturer)—for example, designating tobacco products as WOODBINES (rather than, say, D & G WILLS's 1d cigarettes); or SUNLIGHT for soap (rather than LEVER BROS' fine white soap). As a result, it had become common for the public to refer to these names as the very name of the products, asking, for example, for a packet of WOODBINES or a bar of SUNLIGHT. The clear distinction between the trade source and the generic product designation was elided. The same practice had been adopted by German manufacturers for names of medicinal products: ASPIRIN was Bayer's name for the painkiller made from "acetyl-salycilic acid"; HEROIN was the same firm's name for "Acetomorphine."

Secondly, by the start of the twentieth century a broad range of traders were spending very considerable sums advertising goods. Indeed, increases in use of advertising were associated with embryonic signs of professionalization of advertising, attempts to offer scientific accounts of the way advertising worked and its reconceptualization as an important business investment, often necessary for commercial success. A guide issued by Thomas Brookes Browne is illustrative.[7] Established in 1872, T.B. Browne served as an advertising agency (offering "World-Wide Advertising") and a trademark agency.[8] In the second edition of its "epitome of useful information," published in 1915, it stated that a trader "cannot do better" that adopting an invented or non-descriptive word.[9]

> The word selected should be one which can be easily remembered. The adoption of an ill-sounding, ugly, long or awkward word is not to be commended. The well-proved experience of commerce is that a word Trade Mark, chosen for the sake of euphony and ease of repetition, is the best for its purpose.[10]

As with regular trademarks, similar catchy names were utilized by manufacturers of medical products. Although in the case of ethical pharmaceuticals, rather than "quack remedies," that advertising would not have been in the mainstream press (except perhaps in the colonies),[11] billboards, or buses, but in the trade

[7] T.B. Browne Ltd., An Epitome of Useful Information Relating to Trade Marks, Letters Patents, Designs Copyright and the Use of the Royal Arms Compiled for the Use of Manufacturers, Inventors, Business and Others (1915). My thanks to Jose Bellido for supplying a copy of this volume.

[8] Stefan Schwarzkopf, *Turning Trademarks into Brands: How Advertising Agencies Practiced and Conceptualized Branding, 1890–1930*, *in* Trademarks, Brands, and Competitiveness 165, 170 (Teresa da Silva Lopes & Paul Duguid eds., 2010).

[9] T.B. Browne Ltd., *supra* note 7, at 5.

[10] *Id.*

[11] For example, during the first decade of the twentieth century, Bayer advertised its products by trademark (and with no reference to the chemical or common names) in the *Civil and Military Gazette*, a paper published in Lahore: *see, e.g.*, Civil and Military Gazette, Mar. 1, 1901 at 15 (advertising SOMATOSE, TANNIGEN, ASPIRIN).

press—journals such as *The British Medical Journal*,[12] *Chemist and Druggist*, *The Lancet*, and *The Pharmaceutical Journal*—or directly to doctors via leaflets and salesmen. German manufacturers had proved particularly adept at soliciting articles about their drugs to feature in journals.[13] All this will have reinforced familiarity of physicians with the trademarked names rather than the chemical ones. As one commentator explained, Bayer pushes ASPIRIN "with the most diligence and intelligence possible."[14]

By the time of the First World War, two problems with pharmaceutical trademarks—which would remain for the rest of the century—were starting to appear. The first related to the capacity of pharmaceutical trademarks quickly to become the dominant way of referring to medicine itself and thus to confer a significant competitive advantage that was not attributable to indicating origin. Indicative of this was clear evidence that the adoption and use of marks could affect prices of medicines that were assumed, by many if not all, to be equivalent. Indeed, in 1917, *Chemist and Druggist*, published a list comparing the prices of drugs that were no longer under patent protection, but were sold under the trademark of the originator, compared with the prices of competitors.[15] This list indicated startling disparities that seem to suggest that the trademarks conferred very considerable commercial advantages on the originator, often more than double the price, sometimes as much as six times. For example, the antiseptic thymol iodide, which had been patented by Bayer (but entered the public domain in 1903), sold for six times more under the name ARISTOL than the price when sold by competitors; and diethylbarbituric acid, a treatment for insomnia, which had been patented by Merck (the patent had expired in 1911), sold for five times the price under Merck's mark VERONAL as that charged by competitors. In 1917, the Medical Research Committee, the precursor to the Medical Research Council, and already involved in testing the efficacy and safety of drugs, stated:[16] "It is notorious... that trademarks, under the existing law as interpreted by the Courts, can be and are habitually used not merely to indicate a particular brand of substance, but to secure an effective monopoly in the substance itself."

The second problem raised by trademarks for pharmaceuticals was virtually the opposite. This had been articulated by the Select Committee on Proprietary Medicines in its report in August 1914,[17] which found that "any number of

[12] Peter Bartrip, Mirror of Medicine: A History of the British Medical Journal 174–80, 198–202 (1990).

[13] Axel C. Hüntelmann, *A Different Mode of Marketing? The Importance of Scientific Articles in the Marketing Process of Salvarsan*, 29 Hist. & Tech. 116 (2013).

[14] *British Pharmacopoeia. A New Group of Drugs*, The Scotsman, Jan. 22, 1915, at 4 (referring also to names being "drummed in" by "persistent advertising and canvassing").

[15] Woolley to Martin, Patent Office (Nov. 27, 1917) in BT 209/506.

[16] Memorandum by the Medical Research Committee upon the use of Registered Trade Marks for Therapeutic Substances (Aug. 1, 1917), BT 209/502.

[17] House of Commons Select Committee on Patent Medicines, *Report of the Select Committee on Patent Medicines*, 1914, HC 414.

different names may be secured as trademarks for the same drug," noting that acetyl-salicylic acid was sold as "ASPIRIN, SALETIN, SALACETIN, XAXA etc," each at a different price.[18] If doctors prescribed such drugs by trademark, pharmacists were obliged to supply the same. Substitution was not permitted.[19] Given that a single drug could be marketed by multiple manufacturers under a plethora of trademarks, a pharmacist would need to stock all of these, just in case a physician prescribed one of them.

Both problems were related, in part, to the absence of a common language for medicines. The problem of the market power that was conferred on the originator of drugs who generated the name of the drug and then protected it as a trademark lay in the fact that there was no alternative way for others to communicate that they were offering or asking for the same drug. Exclusivity over the name would amount to a monopoly over the product. With a common language, in contrast, doctors would be able to prescribe the drug by the common language term and pharmacists could supply any of the version of the drug once it could be manufactured by different suppliers. The problem of the proliferation of trade names for substantially equivalent versions of the same medicine lay in the fact that in prescribing, doctors necessarily resorted to trade names. If a common language existed, and physicians were indifferent as between equivalent medicines, they could simply choose to prescribe using the common name—a practice that would later come to be termed "generic prescribing."[20]

Such a language had long been desired to assist communications between physicians and also between physicians and pharmacist. The most high-profile attempt to solve the problem that individual doctors might not necessarily be referring to the same substances was by way of so-called pharmacopoeias, encyclopedias of medicines. These had been published by the various national colleges of physicians from as early as 1699,[21] but in 1858 the task of producing a British pharmacopoeia was statutorily assigned to the British Medical Association.[22] The first edition came out in 1864, and by 1914 the volume was in its fifth edition (1867, 1885, 1898, 1914).[23] However, the *British Pharmacopoeia* was a poor mechanism to solve the

[18] *See also Trade-Marks of Alien Enemies*, CHEMIST & DRUGGIST, Sept. 26, 1914, at 444, 448; *Synthetic Medicinal Chemicals*, 1(2821) BRIT. MED. J. 168 (1915).

[19] House of Commons Select Committee on Patent Medicines, *supra* note 17, at xxxii, [16]; THE BRITISH PHARMACEUTICAL CODEX: AN IMPERIAL DISPENSATORY FOR THE USE OF MEDICAL PRACTITIONERS AND PHARMACISTS, at viii (1907) (hereinafter THE PHARMACEUTICAL CODEX); *Trade Names*, BRIT. & COLONIAL DRUGGIST, June 4, 1915, at 322 (1915); *British Pharmacopoeia. A New Group of Drugs*, *supra* note 14. For the legal basis, *see* JOHN CUTLER, PASSING OFF 71 (1904); LEWIS BOYD SEBASTIAN, THE LAW OF TRADE MARKS 296–97 (1911).

[20] *Synthetic Medicinal Chemicals*, *supra* note 18 (recommending use of "the ordinary chemical name" if it is short enough for common use"); THE PHARMACEUTICAL CODEX, *supra* note 19, at viii (prescribers prefer "to encourage the use of names which everyone is free to use").

[21] The Edinburgh, Dublin, and London pharmacopoeias date respectively to 1699, 1807, and 1618, with the latest versions in 1841, 1850, and 1851.

[22] Medical Act, 1858 § 54 (repealed by the Medical Act, 1950 § 23).

[23] For accounts of the development of the *British Pharmacopoeia*, *see* HAROLD DAVIS, BENTLEY'S TEXTBOOK OF PHARMACEUTICS ch. 1 (6th ed., 1954).

two problems. In particular, the terms used in the *British Pharmacopoeia* were not close to being as readily pronounceable,[24] nor memorable, as the trademark names that had been adopted (and come to be widely used). In one arresting example, an expert sought to explain the popularity of German-manufactured "acetomorphine" as attributable to the adoption of a trademark—HEROIN.[25] Whatever the merits of that particular claim, there were abundant comments that trademarks were much easier to remember and use than the names in the *British Pharmacopoeia*.[26] The divergence was said to be especially pronounced in relation to the products of the German manufacturers who had created simple, usable names whereas the chemical name would be "too long and cumbrous for common use."[27]

There were other problems with the *British Pharmacopoeia* as a workable lexicon and reference work for the newer remedies. The pharmacopoeias were published relatively infrequently, and from the late nineteenth century had been slow to feature the "newer remedies" developed after the emergence of synthetic chemistry.[28] Moreover, the volumes did not mention trademarks at all, so could not possibly work as a reference tool which physicians could use to substitute familiar trademarks with general descriptive designations. In that respect, *The Pharmaceutical Codex*, first published in 1907 by the Pharmaceutical Society of Great Britain,[29] offered more promise, in particular in that it referenced some trademarks: for example, "ACETYSAL, ALETODIN, ASPIRIN, SALETIN, XAXA, etc" for Acidum Salaceticum;[30] or ADNEPHRIN, ADRENALIN, ADRIN, EPIRENAN, HAEMOSTASIN, HEMISINE, PARANEPHRIN, RENAGLANDIN, RENOSTYPTICIN, SUPRARENIN, SUPRARENALIN, and VASOCONSTRICTINE" for Adrenina.[31] Indeed, some of those who gave evidence to the 1914 Select Committee thought the *Codex* would go a long way toward solving the difficulties presented by a multiplicity of trade names for essentially the same active ingredient.[32] But the Committee was not persuaded, and instead recommended limiting the duration of protection of medical trademarks.[33]

[24] *The Status of Aspirin*, BRIT. & COLONIAL DRUGGIST 133 (1915) (praising "the euphony and elegance" of ASPIRIN); *Salvarsan the Slayer*, THE DISS EXPRESS Aug. 15, 1913, at 6; *Board of Guardians and District Councils*, LONDONDERRY SENTINEL, Mar. 11, 1918, at 7 (hilarity expressed at the chemical name of UROTROPINE).

[25] F.A. Hocking, *The War and Our Supply of Drugs*, 65 J. ROYAL SOC'Y ARTS 275, 282 (1917).

[26] *Id.* at 283 (comment by chairman); *British Pharmacopoeia. A New Group of Drugs*, *supra* note 14.

[27] *Synthetic Medicinal Chemicals*, *supra* note 18.

[28] VIRGIL COBLENTZ, THE NEWER REMEDIES (3d ed., 1899) (identifying 2000 new products between 1882 and 1899).

[29] THE PHARMACEUTICAL CODEX, *supra* note 19. *The Codex* had been prepared by the authority of the council of the Pharmaceutical Society of Great Britain.

[30] *Id.* at 46.

[31] *Id.* at 62.

[32] House of Commons Select Committee on Patent Medicines, *supra* note 17, at 66, QQ. 2867–72 (Edward Harrison, a pharmaceutical chemist); Thomas Stephenson, *British Pharmacopoeia and the New Remedies*, THE SCOTSMAN, Jan. 23, 1915, at 12 (letter).

[33] House of Commons Select Committee on Patent Medicines, *supra* note 17, at xlvii (recommendation [57], (6)–(7)).

The problems with pharmaceutical trademarks became more pressing with the outbreak of the First World War. At that point, trade with Germany ceased, and with it the supply of synthetic chemicals which German manufacturers had pioneered. These included the so-called "newer remedies." In August 1914, the British government allowed the production of such chemicals in the United Kingdom, waiving the operation of any relevant patents. The government also recognized that the law of registered trademarks might also significantly impair the marketing of such remedies. This was because German manufacturers had obtained trademarks for those names,[34] and the products had often become known by the trademarks (rather than the chemical names). To remedy such problems, the government proposed a mechanism to invalidate or suspend enemy-owned trademarks.[35] Over the next few years, trademark registrations were suspended in thirty-one cases and invalidated in eighteen.[36] These included ASPIRIN, SALVARSAN, UROTROPINE, LYSOL, GLYCIN, METOL, and PEROLIN. The case of UROTROPINE is particularly instructive. Initially the trademark of the German firm, Schering, the drug appeared in both the *British Pharmacopoeia*, where it was designated "hexamine," and in *The Codex*, where it was designated "formamina."[37] Moreover, *The Codex* cited ten other brand names: AMINOFORM, AMMONIO-FOMALDEHYDE, AMMONALDEHYDE, CYSTAMIN, CYSTOGEN, FORMIN, METRAMINE, URISOL, URITONE, and VESALVINE for formamina.[38] Nevertheless, the Comptroller General of Patents and Trade Marks heard evidence on behalf of Burroughs Wellcome that doctors would prescribe UROTROPINE and it was therefore necessary that Burroughs be permitted to call its version UROTROPINE.[39] Evidently, the Comptroller was persuaded that UROTROPINE was the "name or only practicable name" for the drug, and in due course, the Board of Trade invalidated the mark under the Wartime legislation.[40]

[34] Francis H. Carr, *Synthetic Organic Drugs*, CHEMIST & DRUGGIST, July 29, 1916, at 778–79.

[35] Patents, Designs and Trade Marks (Temporary) Rules 1914, Stat. R & O 1914/1255; Trade Marks (Temporary) Rules 1914, Stat. R & O 1914/1256. The Rules included power for the Board "at any time, in their absolute discretion, revoke any avoidance or suspension of any registration of a Trade Mark ordered by them." Background to the Act and the Rules can be found in BT 209/115.

[36] Twenty-one were suspended in 1914, two in 1916, eight in 1917. There were twelve cancellations in 1914, three in 1916, three in 1917. Examples of applications that were refused included the LYSOL device mark and the word mark ODOL.

[37] THE PHARMACEUTICAL CODEX, *supra* note 19, at 445 (formamina); BRITISH PHARMACOPOEIA 171 (1914) (hexamina). For background, *see* CHRISTOPHER KOBRAK, NATIONAL CULTURES AND INTERNATIONAL COMPETITION: THE EXPERIENCE OF SCHERING AG 1851–1950 117, n.28 (2002).

[38] THE PHARMACEUTICAL CODEX, *supra* note 19, at 446.

[39] *Trade-Marks of Alien Enemies*, *supra* note 18, at 444–45; *German Patents and Trade Marks. Application Respecting "Urotropine,"* 94 PHARMACEUTICAL J. & PHARMACIST 339 (1915).

[40] *Miscellaneous and General. The Trade Mark "Urotropine,"* 94 PHARMACEUTICAL J. & PHARMACIST 646 (1915).

II. The 1919 Trade Marks Act: Special Rules for Pharmaceutical Marks

In 1916, the Comptroller-General of Patents and Trade Marks, Temple-Franks, was asked for suggestions on appropriate reforms of Trade Mark law that would be useful after the War. Among his responses was the following clause:

> The name of any patented article or any article manufactured under an expired patent or secret process or *any word that is used or proposed to be used as the name of a known drug or of any chemical or medicinal preparation where the process of manufacture of ingredients are known to the trade or public* shall not be deemed to be a distinctive mark for the purpose of registration.[41]

Importantly the focus here was on *use as the name of the product*, a characteristic that linked both of the concerns that had emerged in the pre-War era: *use as the name* was the mechanism by which marks such as ASPIRIN gained their market power and was the cause of the difficulties with the multiplication of names. The proposal was considered by a committee established by the Board of Trade under the chairmanship of Lord Parker of Waddington.[42] The members differed in their reactions to the proposed rule on chemical and medical names. For Arthur J. Walter K.C., the leader of the patent bar, it was inappropriate to have a special regime for a particular class of substance.[43] He objected to "applying to one class of substances [a] different rule to the rules applying to Word Marks." He explained that he was unable to see why KODAK for cameras should be treated differently from ASPIRIN for acetyl-salicylic acid. In contrast, Henry Cooke, a partner for the solicitors Bristows, Cooke and Carpmael, was willing to recognize as appropriate the use of different rules to different types of articles: "it is obvious" he wrote "that different considerations apply to the different classes of articles above mentioned."

In the end, the Committee decided it would be better to replace the Comptroller's clause with one that extended well beyond drugs, chemical, or medical preparations. As the root cause of the difficulty was the *use* of the trademark as if it were a name, the limitation should extend beyond the medical field. In due course a Trade Marks Bill 1917 giving effect to the Committee's recommendations was introduced into the House of Commons.[44] Clause 7 allowed the removal of a word mark from the register of marks where the proprietor

[41] Memorandum on Amendments to Patent, Design and Trade Mark Law, BT draft proposal (Mar. 1916) (TNA: BT 209/485) (W. Temple Franks), at 11–12. The form of exclusion—deeming words inherently non-distinctive—was likely modelled on the Trade Marks Act 1905, § 64(10).

[42] Draft Report, at 6–7, in BT 209/485.

[43] Memorandum from Arthur Walter on Proposed Alterations in Patents Act 12–13, BT 209/485 (1916).

[44] Trade Marks Bill 1917, HC Bill [105], pt. B.

> by advertisement or otherwise so acts as to lead to the general use by the public of the word so registered as the name or general description of any article or type of article, and not denoting or connoting an article or type of article made, sold, certified, dealt with or offered for sale by himself.

Applying this, Bayer's mark ASPIRIN would not be impugned if Bayer had consistently marketed it as "ASPIRIN brand acetyl-salicylic acid," but might be if Bayer were to market its painkiller just as ASPIRIN. As the memorandum accompanying the Bill explained

> The evils resulting from the possession of any monopoly in the name of article, have been most conspicuous in the case of drugs, and, in particular, of drugs which were originally protected by a patent . . . A very good example of this abuse is the word "ASPIRIN"[45]

Unfortunately, because of the general applicability of the proposed clause, it threatened the trademark interests of a wide range of traders whose trademarks were used as the names of products to which they were applied.[46] Speaking on behalf of a deputation to the Board of Trade from the Trade Mark Owners Association,[47] the solicitor Theodore McKenna acknowledged that the Board might want a reform targeted at the "misnaming of simple substance drugs,"[48] but argued it was wrongheaded to attempt to change the law applicable to all trademarks to fix that particular problem.[49] Not surprisingly, the 1917 Bill attracted almost universal criticism of the manufacturing trade such that the Board of Trade quickly accepted that the clause would have to be dropped.

Once the 1917 Bill had been withdrawn, the Board of Trade sought to solve the problem in a different way.[50] First, it narrowed its field of application by refocusing on word marks for "*chemical substances*."[51] Second, rather than address the language problem by keeping trademarks out of the zone of product names, it sought instead to link the validity of marks to the existence of a common descriptive

[45] BT209/503 (memorandum accompanying bill) published as *The Trade Marks Bill. Its Proposals and Purpose*, 100 Board of Trade J & Com. Gazette 60 (1918).

[46] Saxone Shoe Co Ltd to A Shaw, M.P., Dec. 6, 1917 in BT 209/506.

[47] Trade Marks Bill. Deputation from the Trade Mark Association Limited to the Board of Trade, at 3 (Mar. 15, 1918) in BT209/508.

[48] *Id.* at 12.

[49] *Id.* at 13.

[50] Another informal departmental committee, comprising Temple Franks, Theodore McKenna, Duncan Kerly, Henry Cooke, and William Tennant, met on May 7 and 13, 1918: Trade Marks Bill. Lord Parkers Committee after introduction of the bill BT 209/504 (containing invitations and responses in Apr./May 1918).

[51] Note on Suggested Amendments to Trade Marks Bill, at 2, BT 209/504 (no date, but around May 1918) (noting criticism of original bill was that it "would hit almost every kind of trade mark"). Various handwritten drafts of the newer version limiting the operation of the clause to single chemical substances appear in the file (Apr.–June 1918).

language. As with the 1917 Bill, the mark might be expunged where it had been used as the name or only practicable designation of any single chemical substance, but not if it had been used only to denote a "brand or make" and "in association with a suitable and practicable name open to public use." Requiring such designation would reinforce both the importance of *The British Pharmacopoeia* and *The Codex*, in so far as they already supplied a suitable common term, but also help remedy the gaps that arose from the accelerating speed in the production of new remedies (with which these periodic publications could not keep pace). This was because the private interests of the trademark owner in avoiding expungement would become the engine for the production of a workable common language. The condition for the validity of a trademark for a drug—and its use as the name thereof—would be the continued availability of a common term and the use of that term alongside the trademark. As Temple Franks noted:

> Although not going so far as I would have liked, it will, I think, deal with the mischief which has been so apparent in the past, with regard to German drugs and chemicals.[52]

Although it passed through the Commons, Clause 6(2) of the 1919 Bill was further modified in the House of Lords in the face of objections from the Chambers of Commerce.[53] Three components of the clause were amended. First, the term "a chemical substance" was changed to "a single chemical element or single chemical compound, as distinguished from a mixture." This excluded the possibility that the name given to a soap, for example LUX,[54] might be vulnerable as a "chemical substance": soap not being a single element or compound. Second, rather than making revocation conditional on the proprietor having used the word as the name, the amended condition required that the name had become "the only practicable name or description" of the relevant entity (the proprietor's use being relevant only to the proviso). Third, the circumstances in which the rule operated were narrowed from where the word was either "the name or only practicable name" for a chemical substance, to the single requirement that the word had become "the only practicable name or description." The resulting clause was as follows:

> No word which is the only practicable name or description of any single chemical element or single chemical compound, as distinguished from a mixture, shall be registered as a trade mark, and any such word now or hereafter on the register

[52] W. Temple Franks, Trade Marks Bill. Amendment Proposed in Lord Parker's Committee (June 4, 1918) BT209/505 (front cover).

[53] Association of British Chambers of Commerce to W. Temple Franks, Oct. 20, 1919; Association of British Chambers of Commerce, Trade Marks Bill (Note of meeting on Oct. 15, 1919); Charles Musgrave to W. Temple Franks, Nov. 8, 1919, all in BT209/511.

[54] *Property in Trade Mark Names. German Monopoly Attacked*, TIMES, Aug. 8, 1919.

> may, notwithstanding section forty-one of the principal Act, be removed by the court from the register on the application of any person aggrieved[55]

The proviso remained untouched. The Act received Royal Assent on December 28, 1919.[56]

The 1919 Act thus sought to use the *threat* of invalidation to achieve the goal of generating and maintaining usable public names alongside private trademarks. The goal was that the trademarks should operate only as indications of manufacturing source and be protectable only so long as there was a functioning public descriptive name. This effect can be seen clearly in the advice that the patent and trademark agents Haseltine, Lake & Co. now offered its clients:

> the best way for the owner of a word Trade Mark to escape the prejudicial effect of the new provisions . . . is to use the word Trade Mark always in close association with a name for the commodity in such a manner as to indicate the Trade Mark and put into the mouth of the public the name of the article. This might, we think, be done in the manner indicated below by examples:-
>
> In the case . . . of a chemical substance, etc:
> BLEACHING POWDER
> "ABCD" BRAND
> (TRADE MARK).
>
> Where the commodity was or is a novel one in constitution at the time the Mark was or is first used in connection with it, and the generic names or descriptions broadly applicable to it, are too wide to be of any use to the public to identify the commodity by known name, then the proprietor should evolve some suitably appropriate or descriptive name or phrase for it to use as a name in conjunction with the Trade Mark.[57]

In this example, the trademark is subordinated to the public name, which is clearly distinguished from the trademark by the addition of the word "brand" and indication that it is a trademark. The publicly usable description is bleaching powder, rather than calcium hypochlorite, presumably because the latter was assumed not to be practicable.

The 1919 Act was an important experiment, because it left the generation of the alternative, non-proprietary terms to private parties. The threat to render a trademark invalid was invoked to induce the use of private marks together with designations that would be available for use by others. The idea was to use private

[55] Hansard (HL) (Dec. 8, 1919) (37) cols. 725–35.
[56] Hansard (HC) (Dec. 28, 1919) (123) cols. 1300–02.
[57] Haseltine, Lake & Co., Information and Notes on Some of the Provisions of "The Patents and Designs Act, 1919", and "The Trade Marks Act, 1919" 45–46 (1920).

incentives to generate "generic terms," to disseminate those terms, educate relevant public, and thus to enable competitors, though using those terms, to present their offerings as equivalent.[58] As Sir Frank Hartley later explained: "before any official machinery was created to assist in the matter, manufacturers themselves had to coin non-proprietary names and secure publicity for them."[59] The regulatory provision supplemented the statutory codification of the patent expiry doctrine, thus regulating the behavior of a patentee of a medicine during, not just at or after, the lapse of the patent; as well as being applicable in cases where the medical product had not been patented at all. In principle, it would apply to any manufacturer of a chemical product, even a competitor to the originator, whose success threatened to transform a mark into the only practicable name for the goods: they, like an original patentee, would also need to take care to ensure that a generally available term accompanied the use of their mark and that the mark was not allowed to slip into uses other than to designate a particular brand.

The amendments the Trade Marks Bill underwent in the House of Lords may well have stifled the ability of the law to solve the problem of the multiplication of names, as had been hoped by the Board of Trade and Parker Committee. The amendments meant that a manufacturer need only use a second name where the trade-marked name was or had become the "only practicable name or description" of the chemical (an objective limitation) rather than, as had been proposed, whenever a mark was used as the name of the product (a behavioral criterion). Quite how many fewer marks were caught depended on when a name was "practicable." The mere existence of a chemical or technical name was not regarded by the contemporaneous textbooks as "practicable",[60] but they failed to make clear whether they meant the true (*i.e.* standard) chemical name,[61] the *British Pharmacopoeia* or *Codex* term, or all of these.

[58] There are interesting parallels with, and differences from, the UPOV regime, which requires the provision of a non-proprietary designation for a new plant variety: *see* JAY SANDERSON, PLANTS, PEOPLE AND PRACTICES: THE NATURE AND HISTORY OF THE UPOV CONVENTION 139–61 (2017).

[59] Frank Hartley, The Nomenclature of Drugs, 168 PHARM. J. (1952) 23, 24.

[60] D.M. KERLY AND F.G. UNDERHAY, THE TRADE MARKS ACT, 1919 21 (1920), for example, said that "practicable" was understood in terms of use for sale or ordinary use by the public and technical names of chemicals were given as an example of a name that was not "practicable." LEWIS BOYD SEBASTIAN ET AL., THE LAW OF TRADE MARK REGISTRATION 112 (2d ed., 1922) (a difficult scientific description would not be regarded as practicable).

[61] Efforts to develop an internationally agreed system of chemical nomenclature were growing in intensity and ultimately would lead to the International Union for Pure and Applied Chemistry's system of nomenclature (agreed at Liège in 1930). These names sought to reflect the structure of the chemicals and were often very lengthy—and certainly would not have been "practicable." For background, *see* B. Bensaude-Vincent, *Languages in Chemistry*, *in* THE CAMBRIDGE HISTORY OF SCIENCE, VOL. 5: THE MODERN PHYSICAL AND MATHEMATICAL SCIENCES 174–90 (Mary Jo Nye ed., 2003); MAURICE P. CROSLAND, HISTORICAL STUDIES IN THE LANGUAGE OF CHEMISTRY (1962); Evan Hepler Smith, *"Just as the Structural Formula Does": Names, Diagrams, and the Structure of Organic Chemistry at the 1892 Geneva Nomenclature Congress* 62 AMBIX 1–28 (2015); Evan Hepler-Smith, *Systematic Flexibility and the History of the IUPAC Nomenclature of Organic Chemistry* 37(2) CHEMISTRY INTERNATIONAL 10–14 (2015).

It is not possible to conclude much about how effective the 1919 reform proved to be in inducing the development of a set of common descriptive terms for chemicals in general, and medicines more specifically. We have already noted what was advised by trademark practitioners such as Haseltine, Lake & Co., which is suggestive of some likely positive impact. Moreover, Director of Research at British Drugs Houses Sir Frank Hartley described an equivalent rule, which had been re-enacted in the 1938 Trade Marks Act,[62] as "an important provision."[63] However, the picture was soon muddied by the addition of legal obligations to label drugs sold under proprietary names with their "scientific" or "proper name."[64] This requirement appeared first in 1927 in the regulation of "biologics" and associated drugs that could not adequately be tested by "direct chemical means".[65] A similar obligation was imposed more generally by the Poisons Rules 1935 (adopted in accordance with powers in the Pharmacy and Poisons Act 1933).[66] The effect of these regimes was that "self-coined" non-proprietary names, developed to comply with the 1919 Act, became inadequate—and manufacturers were required to use "official" names, so far as these existed.[67]

[62] Trade Marks Act, 1938, § 15(3). The minor amendments related to the threshold at which the proprietor must comply with the condition (or face invalidation), and the character of the nonproprietary term that must be developed or used to comply with the proviso: as to the former, the threshold that the mark be the "only practicable name" was replaced with the requirement that it be the "commonly used and accepted name," and the proviso provided that this would not be liable to invalidation if the word was used to denote the proprietor's brand as "in association with a suitable name or description open to the public use" (as opposed to a "suitable and practicable" name). The preceding committee, chaired by Lord Goschen, had recommended these amendments, in part to make the provision "more logical": *Report of the Departmental Committee on the Law and Practice Relating to Trade Marks*, 1934, Cm. 4568, [291]–[292]. The minutes of the meetings of the Committee indicate that the amendments were suggested by Mr. J.E. James: BT304/1, Minute 141 (Feb. 21, 1934).

[63] Hartley, *supra* note 59, 24 (1952) (referring to Trade Marks Act 1938, § 15(3)). The editors of the *Pharmaceutical Journal* also claimed that the 1938 Act went part way towards meeting demand for "one drug, one name": *Proprietary or Non-Proprietary Names*, 168 PHARM. J. 18 (1952).

[64] That is, its accepted scientific name or some name descriptive of its true nature and origin: *The Therapeutic Substances Act*, 2(3376) BRIT. MED. J. Supp 105-6 (1925); *The Therapeutic Substances Regulations*, 209 THE LANCET 1302 (1927); H. Treves Brown, *United Kingdom Drug Law*, 6 FOOD DRUG COSM. L. J. 655, 660 (1951). The nonproprietary names was required to feature as prominently as the proprietary one.

[65] Despite its broadly worded title, the Therapeutic Substances Act 1925 applied to biological products (such as vaccines, serums, toxins, antitoxins, and antigens); synthetic substances comprising "salvarsan" and its analogues; and insulin and preparations of the pituitary gland. For these substances, manufacturers needed to be licensed and inspected.

[66] Poisons Rules 1935, r. 17(1) ("all traders selling poisons, including manufacturers' are by law required to label the container of a poison with its name as given in the Poisons List, or, where the term used in the Poisons List describes a group of poisons and not the poison specifically, with its name as given in the *British Pharmacopoeia* or *British Pharmaceutical Codex*. When there is no specific name for the poison in the Poisons List, the *Pharmacopoeia*, or the *Codex*, the label must give the accepted scientific name or name descriptive of the true nature and origin of the poison.").

[67] Hartley, *supra* note 59.

III. Official Names and Calls for Abolition of Trade Marks

Commentators continued to refer to problems with multiplication of names, particularly following the so-called "therapeutic revolution" that began with the introduction of the sulfonamides in the late 1930s. Writing in *The Lancet* in 1941, Dennis Ardley observed the following:

> Most of the sulphonamides in common use have three kinds of name-a chemical name often occupying a line of print, a scientific synonym or pet-name, being the chemical name in a shortened form, and a various number of trade names. The synonym is the one intended for use in scientific articles, but unfortunately not all the compounds have one, and in some cases the trade name is at present unavoidable.[68]

If prescribers were finding that they had to use the trade name, then the 1919 Act was not working in the way that had been hoped. In 1942, one commentator noted that procaine, the *British Pharmacopoeia* term for an anesthetic alkaloid, was sold under trademarks including ALLOCAINE, AETHOCAINE, KEROCAIN, NEOCAIN, NOVOCAIN, PLANOCAINE, SEVIVAINE, and SYNCAINE, and that the confusion this had engendered had led to cases of doctors wrongly prescribing PERCAINE, also an anesthetic but with a different pharmacology, in place of procaine.[69] In the light of this, *The Lancet* later observed that it would be "a blessing to both prescribers and dispensers to use just an approved name and the manufacturer's name"—i.e., to abandon the trademarks.[70] Further concerns appeared in relation to the new sulfanilamides, the first antibacterials that worked inside the body (and over which patent protection had lapsed long before this use was appreciated in the 1930s).[71] Perhaps because of its public domain status, the drug had come to be marketed under a huge number of names. Reporting that there were fifty-four such names, *The Lancet* asked:

> Has not the time come for manufacturers to sacrifice their trade names for this compound (and perhaps for some others) and content themselves with the label "Sulphanilamide Robinson" or "Sulphanilamide Jones"?[72]

[68] Dennis G. Ardley, *The Common Sulphonamides Nomenclature, Structure and Uses*, 238 The Lancet 625 (1941).

[69] *Procaine and Percaine*, 240 The Lancet 221; *Nupercaine and Procaine*, 240 The Lancet 340 (referring to Raymond Greene, *Babel in Endocrinology* (letter), 240 The Lancet 231; 625. PERCAINE was the registered mark of Clayton Aniline Co Ltd, and used for a derivative of quinine.

[70] *Nupercaine and Procaine*, *supra* note 69, at 340.

[71] *Drugs and the Doctor*, 2(4372) Brit. Med. J. 535 (1944).

[72] *Trade Names of Sulphonamides and Sulphones*, 241 The Lancet 821 (1943).

The matter resurfaced both at the start and the end of the 1950s,[73] but really reached a crunch point in the 1960s.

A further initiative to tackle the problem of the multiplication of names was the adoption of so-called "approved names." In 1939,[74] the General Medical Council (GMC) decided to extend the role of the British Pharmacopoeia Commission (in cooperation with the Medical Research Council and Association of British Chemical Manufacturers) to the publication of "approved names" for pure compounds (not mixtures)—an initiative that commenced in 1939. As with the 1919 Act, the impetus again came from the German control of the names of medicinal products, and the new system offered approved public designations for foreign proprietary terms. However, the project was soon recognized as being of longer-term value. As the GMC explained, the hope was that by publishing promptly approved names would "lead to their general adoption,"[75] and thereby "avoid the difficulties which arise from the multiplication of names for the same medicinal substance."[76] Conscious of the limitations of the *British Pharmacopoeia* itself (and the characteristics of the proprietary marks which were being adopted), the Commission developed some "principles of nomenclature," that recognized, to some extent, "usability": the name should not be more than four syllables, be "distinctive in sound and spelling" and not be difficult to pronounce or remember.[77] At the same time, the rules also recommended that "the accurate chemical name should be used if suitable" and "when it is unsuitable an attempt should first be made to form a name by the combination of significant syllables from the scientific chemical name, and to include an indication of the potent element or constituent of a compound."

The system of approved names was, after the War, supplemented by an equivalent international initiative under the aegis of the World Health Organization (WHO): the system of international non-proprietary names (so-called INNs), and formulated on very similar principles to the approved names.[78] The British responded to the WHO initiative by giving preferential consideration to the adoption

[73] *Proprietary and Approved Names*, 259 The Lancet 251 (1952); G.F. Walker, *Multiplication of Trade Names*, 2(5147) Brit. Med. J. 305 (1959).

[74] As early as 1915, *The British Medical Journal* had suggested, there was a need for a system of non-proprietary names be agreed on and published to supplement those in the *British Pharmacopoeia* and *Codex*; *Synthetic Medicinal Chemicals*, *supra* note 18.

[75] *British Pharmacopoeia. British Equivalents for Proprietary Drugs*, 2(4216) Brit. Med. J. 590 (1941).

[76] *Approved Names for Drugs. The Pharmacopoeia Commission's Policy*, 2(4270) Brit. Med. J. 555; *British Pharmacopoeia Commission: Approved Names*, 2(4624) Brit. Med. J. 435 (1949).

[77] *Approved Names for Drugs*, *supra* note 76, at 555.

[78] WHO, WHA Res. 3.11, *Non-Proprietary Names for Drugs* (May 19, 1950), https://apps.who.int/iris/bitstream/handle/10665/86211/WHA3.11_eng.pdf; *International Non-Proprietary Names*, 1(4962) Brit. Med. J. 1381 (1955). "General Principles for Guidance in Devising International Non-proprietary Names for Pharmaceutical Substances" stated that the names "should be distinctive in sound and spelling. They should not be inconveniently long and should not be liable to confusion with names in common use." Group relationships in INNs are indicated by the use of common stems, as suffixes or prefixes. WHO, *INN System and Protection of INN*, INN Working Doc. 08.228 (2008), https://www.wipo.int/edocs/mdocs/sct/en/sct_19/sct_19_4.doc.

of INNs as British Approved Names (BANs) (though differences persisted well into the late 1990s).[79]

Some recognized the value of the BAN and INN systems in facilitating communication,[80] and particularly in informing "prescribers and pharmacists that the same drug is being described under more than one trade name."[81] Nevertheless, both were also subject to considerable criticism.[82] Rather like the criticisms of *The British Pharmacopoeia* before the First World War, it was repeatedly said that the names approved under the BAN system are simply not as usable or memorable as the names developed for use as trademarks. For example, it was said that methaminodiazepoxide (now, chlordiazepoxide) is not as memorable or usable as Librium, the trade name adopted by the Swiss pharmaceutical firm Hoffman La Roche.[83]

Contemporaries offered three reasons why trade names out-competed approved names. First, because pharmaceutical firms devoted considerable time and effort to developing such names: indeed, in 1958, *The Lancet* reported that "at least one firm has called in cybernetics to prepare many mellifluous names."[84] In contrast, BANs and INNs were produced by a committee, often in response to a proposed name that was suggested by the original manufacturer (and thus clearly not as favored as its chosen trademark).[85] Second, the formulation of suitable BANs and INNs was constrained both by the principle that the name should provide some medically useful information and not conflict with existing trademarks.[86] Third, trade names were reinforced through systematic, insistent, and effective advertising.[87]

The multiplication of trade names for pharmaceuticals became a matter of greater concern following the establishment of the NHS in 1948, a service which aimed to offer comprehensive health care to all and without cost to the patient. This revolutionary shift in the structure of health care linked the practice of pharmaceutical prescription to governmental expenditure.[88] Spending on

[79] Fernando A. Navarro et al., *Naming of Drugs*, 313(7058) BRIT. MED. J. 688 (1996).

[80] Peter J. Banfield, *Approved Names*, 278 THE LANCET 313 (1961).

[81] Derrick M. Dunlop & Tom C. Denston, *Naming of Drugs: B.P. Commission Replies to Criticisms*, 2(5095) BRIT. MED. J. 561 (1958).

[82] *The Drugs Bill*, 262 THE LANCET 815 (1953); R.G. Miller, *Names of Drugs*, 275 THE LANCET 1348 (1960).

[83] Toine Pieters, *The Antidepressant Era Revisited, in* THE ROUTLEDGE HISTORY OF MADNESS AND MENTAL HEALTH 379, 383 (Greg Eghigian ed., 2017).

[84] *Economy in Prescribing*, 271 THE LANCET 1376 (1958); BRIAN INGLIS, DRUGS, DOCTORS AND DISEASE (1965) 192. The claim that one firm was using robots to coin new trade names appeared in *The Battle of the Drugs is on—And You Might be a Casualty*, DAILY HERALD, Feb. 23, 1957.

[85] Dinesh K. Mehta & Jeffrey K. Aronson, *Give a Drug a Good Name*, 369 THE LANCET 1326 (2007).

[86] Dunlop & Denston, *supra* note 81.

[87] Herbert Herxheimer et al., *Prescribing and Propaganda*, 263 THE LANCET 42 (1954); Dunlop & Denston, *supra* note 81.

[88] Since 2009, these values have been embodied in an "NHS Constitution": though this includes a commitment to providing "the most effective, fair and sustainable use of finite resources." Some of the problems the NHS faced had already been recognized under the National Health Insurance Scheme inaugurated in 1912: *see* Ministry of Health, *Final Report of the Committee on Cost of Prescribing* [22] (1959) (hereafter, 'Hinchcliffe Report')..

pharmaceuticals—the "drugs bill"—rose from £16 million in 1948 to £45 million in 1952 and £100 million by 1960.[89] Although some such expenditure related to a significant increase in prescriptions, and to the introduction of new patented drugs,[90] some of it seemed to be attributable to prescribing more expensive proprietary versions of drugs that could have been dispensed more cheaply under their official or approved names.[91] This was particularly the case in relation to drugs prescribed by "general practitioners" where pharmacists were not permitted to substitute cheaper generic versions.[92] As *The Lancet* observed "the service cannot afford to waste money on names."[93]

A Committee was established in 1949—the Joint Committee on Prescribing, chaired by Sir Henry Cohen—to consider "whether it is desirable and practicable to restrict or discourage the prescribing by practitioners ... of unnecessarily expensive brands of standard drugs."[94] The Committee immediately recommended that a letter was sent from the Chief Medical Officer to all GPs suggesting that significant savings could be made if many proprietary brands were prescribed as their standard (generic) alternatives.[95] The message was often to be repeated. After its second interim report in 1950, which affirmed the freedom of doctors to prescribe whatever they regarded as necessary for the treatment of their patients,[96] Sir John Charles, Chief Medical Officer of the Ministry of Health, asked that "save in any exceptional case where there is an overriding medical consideration, doctors will seriously consider, before ordering one of these proprietary preparations, whether the alternative standard drug could not be ordered without detriment to the patient's condition."[97] However, the Committee did commence that task of classifying around 5000 existing products into six categories as a guide to prescribers.[98] Around 650 were regarded as of dubious value. In 1953, the Minister for Health,

[89] Judy Slinn, *Price Controls or Control through Prices? Regulating the Cost and Consumption of Prescription Pharmaceuticals in the UK, 1948–67*, 47 Bus. Hist. 352, 355 (2005).

[90] Hinchcliffe Final Report, *supra* note 88, [12](iii), [75] (referring to tetracyclines and corticosteroids).

[91] Prior to the NHS, E.W. Godding found that prescribing by reference to the official name was prevalent in relation to patients protected under the National Health Insurance Act, whereas proprietary medicines were more frequently prescribed to private patients: EdmundW. Godding, *Proprietary Medicines under the National Health Insurance Act*, 252 The Lancet 465 (1948).

[92] In hospitals, substitution was common (and later would be the norm, and was thought to raise no legal or ethical problems as there was no pharmacist intermediary): Hinchcliffe Final Report, *supra* note 88, [325] (1959).

[93] *Expensive Prescriptions*, 256 The Lancet 59 (1950).

[94] Ministry of Health, *Report of the Joint Committee on Prescribing* [1] (1954) [hereafter, Cohen Report].

[95] *Id.* [3] (this interim recommendation was not published); Sir Wilson Jameson, Chief Medical Officer, Dear Doctor letter (Jan. 20, 1950), in TNA: MH 133/82; John Charles, Chief Medical Officer, Letter, Dear Doctor (July 4, 1950), in TNA: MH 133/82. Darrin Baines, *The Prescription Charge and the Hinchcliffe Committee: Prescribing History*, 24 Prescriber 40 (2013).

[96] *Id.* [4]. Excluding preparations advertised directly to the public.

[97] *Economy in Prescribing: Committee's Interim Report*, 256 The Lancet 66 (1950).

[98] It did not feel it was competent to advise on the question of cost: Cohen Report, *supra* note 91, [4](f).

Iain Macleod asked doctors not to prescribe these drugs of doubtful therapeutic value and "suggested to doctors that they should not prescribe other proprietary preparations without first comparing the cost with that of equivalent or similar standard preparations."[99]

However, exhortation was not sufficient to keep the drugs bill in check.[100] The Cohen Committee had recommended that some classes of drugs only be prescribed if the government had agreed a fair pricing scheme with the manufacturer.[101] This led the Ministry of Health to try to tackle costs of drugs through direct arrangement with pharmaceutical producers.[102] In 1957, an arrangement known as the Voluntary Price Regulation Scheme, was entered into between the Association of the British Pharmaceutical Industry (ABPI) and the Department of Health.[103] Redubbed the Pharmaceutical Price Regulation Scheme (PPRS) in 1978 (and now the Voluntary Scheme on Branded Medicine: Pricing and Access (VPAS) in 2019), the scheme did not (and even today does not) differentiate between drugs that were protected by patents and those for which no patent had been granted or any patent expired. Although the operation of the scheme altered many times over the sixty-five years of its operation, it has allowed companies to set initial prices and tended then to regulate changes in prices and, later, profits. According to a recent review by Marc Rodwin, unfortunately, these "policies did not effectively control spending and had limited effects on purchase prices."[104]

Just as the voluntary price regulation scheme was being concluded, a further committee was established in June 1957 under Sir Harry Hinchcliffe "to investigate the factors contributing to this cost [of prescriptions] and to make recommendations." After eleven meetings, it issued an interim report,[105] the Committee finding there to be no evidence of serious irresponsibility on the part of doctors but that "some economy is possible without sacrifice of efficiency."[106] The Committee recognized the pressures doctors faced, and were very understanding of their tendency to prescribe branded drugs.[107] However, it recommended that doctors be given " more adequate information to assist" them in their "difficult

[99] HC Deb (July 23, 1953) (518) col. 54W.

[100] Hinchcliffe Final Report, *supra* note 88, [8] ("we asked ourselves at the outset whether further letters of exhortation were likely to produce any tangible effect.").

[101] Cohen Report, *supra* note 91, [4](f).

[102] For details, *see* Slinn, *supra* note 89, at 357; Hinchcliffe Final Report, *supra* note 88, [221]–[223]; *Report of the Committee of Enquiry into the Relationship of the Pharmaceutical Industry with the National Health Service*, 1967, Cm. 3410, 27 ff, [84] ff (hereinafter *Sainsbury Report*).

[103] The ABPI appeared in 1948, replacing the Wholesale Drugs Trade Association.

[104] Marc A. Rodwin, *How the United Kingdom Controls Pharmaceutical Prices & Spending: Learning from Its Experience*, 51 INT'L J. HEALTH SERV. 229 (2021). Adrian Towse, *If It Ain't Broke, Don't Price Fix It: The OFT and the PPRS*, 16 HEALTH ECON. 653 (2007).

[105] Ministry of Health, *Interim Report of the Committee on Cost of Prescribing* (1958) (hereafter, 'Hinchcliffe Interim Report').

[106] *Id.* [4].

[107] *Id.* [9].

task,"—including, importantly, information as to cost.[108] One vehicle for doing so was the British National Formulary (BNF), a standard prescriber's formulary, produced by the British Medical Association (BMA) and Pharmaceutical Society of Great Britain (PSGB) and first published in 1949,[109] and thereafter every two and a half years.[110] Although doctors were not required to restrict prescription to the drugs in the Formulary, Hinchcliffe recommended that the BNF be supplied to all clinical students as well as to hospital doctors, the idea being to try and get them to look first the formulary and to prescribe using approved names.[111] The Interim Report also proposed the creation of a comprehensive prescribing handbook with prices of drugs, as well as a legal obligation on advertisers of drugs to indicate the retail price.[112]

The committee also reported that "one of the greatest difficulties facing the general practitioner in deciding what he should prescribe for a patient lies in the number of different names by which new drugs may be known."[113] It attributed this in part to the time taken to evolve and publicize "simple approved names for new products."

> At present a year or two may elapse before an approved name is formulated for a new drug. During this period doctors get into the habit of prescribing the new preparations by their trade names, which are coined immediately in the case of larger drug firms by staff employed specifically for the purpose and are deliberately designed to be easily written and memorised. As a result of high pressure salesmanship these branded names become household words in the general practitioner's vocabulary very soon after the preparations are placed on the market.[114]

The Interim Report therefore proposed that the Pharmacopoeia Commission should be asked to review the principles on which the selection of approved names is based so as to make them "as simple as possible,"[115] and to authorize approved names more promptly. The Interim Report also sought to encourage manufacturers

[108] *Id.* [10]. At [26] it stated that "it is imprudent that doctors should continue to prescribe drugs in ignorance of their cost."

[109] As the seventh edition of Bentley on Pharmaceutics explained, the formulary "lists important preparations which are only obtainable in proprietary form; for these drugs the Approved Names are used in the titles": HAROLD DAVIS, BENTLEY'S TEXTBOOK OF PHARMACEUTICS 23 (7th ed., 1961).; "appendices gave a list of proprietary preparations and standard equivalents").

[110] Hinchcliffe Interim Report, *supra* note 105, [12].

[111] *Id.* [14]–[15]. *See also* Hinchliffe Final Report, *supra* note 88, [49] (reporting that Minister had sent BNF to all clinical students, GPs and hospital doctors), [133]–[135].

[112] Hinchcliffe Interim Report, *supra* note 105,[18], [27]. In the Final Report *supra* note 88, [207], it noted that "increasing numbers of drug manufacturers are co-operating by giving prices in their literature."

[113] Hinchcliffe Interim Report, *supra* note 105, [41].

[114] *Id.* [43].

[115] *Id.* [42]. The Interim Report doubted the informational value involved in deriving the approved name from the drug's chemical constitution.

to ask the Commission to confer an approved name before marketing the drug and that the Ministry work with the ABPI to ensure that the approved name "should appear on labels and advertising literature for proprietary preparations as prominently as the trade one."[116]

In its Final Report,[117] the Committee was rather defensive of branded pharmaceuticals, noting that it was "an oversimplification" to assume that proprietary products have "much cheaper standard equivalents,"[118] observing that differences in formulation between different brands might matter,[119] and acknowledging that trademarks safeguard against firms that "do no worthwhile research."[120] Although skeptical about the role of pharmaceutical advertising, which it said was often "carried out to extravagant lengths,"[121] the Final Report reaffirmed to doctors right to prescribe,[122] including by reference to brand names,[123] again emphasizing the importance of education and information, as opposed to advertising, "as the key to good prescribing."[124] It recommended the publication of a new journal, *The Prescribers' Journal*, for circulation to all doctors and senior students in the health service.[125]

Proliferation of names continued, despite the introduction of the "approved name" regime in 1939, the BNF and INNs. Indeed, pharmaceutical firms sometimes used different names in different countries,[126] and even different names for different dosages and indications of the same drug.[127] Periodically, criticisms would appear in the medical journals. Commentators referred to the "babel" in the drug trade and "the present chaos of drug names."[128] *The Lancet* described the proliferation of brand names as "a source of boundless baffledom and confusion."[129] *The British Medical Journal* acknowledged "the pharmaceutical Tower of Babel which complicates medical teaching, publication, and practice."[130] Similar criticisms were simultaneously being made in the United States, in the Senate hearings that were to culminate in the Kefauver-Harris Amendments (of the U.S. Medicines

[116] *Id.* [46].
[117] Hinchcliffe Final Report, *supra* note 88; Baines, *supra* note 95.
[118] Hinchcliffe Final Report, *supra* note 88, [211].
[119] *Id.* [213].
[120] *Id.* [212].
[121] *Id.* [207].
[122] *Id.* [189]–[200].
[123] *Id.* [213].
[124] *Id.* [160]. When prescribing by brand name, the prescriber should be convinced of the superiority of a brand "by private experience or published evidence and not by unsubstantiated claims by manufacturers' representatives or in their advertising literature."
[125] *Id.* [163].
[126] O.L. Wade, *Proprietary Names of Drugs*, 277 The Lancet 170 (1961).
[127] Alastair MacGregor, *Proprietary Names of Drugs*, 277 The Lancet 399 (1961).
[128] Herxheimer et al., *supra* note 87; MacGregor, *supra* note 127 (referring to "the chaos that is developing in this field, to the increasing confusion of the medical and pharmaceutical professions").
[129] *After Sainsbury*, 290 The Lancet 759 (1967).
[130] *Brand Names*, 1(5595) Brit. Med. J. 781 (1968).

Regulation) in 1962.[131] While these did not abolish trade names,[132] much of the evidence provided in the committee hearings supported such a move.[133] For example, Dr. Solomon Garb of Albany Medical School, speculated as to how the market for baked beans would operate if their manufacturers used the same marketing and branding techniques as pharmaceutical manufacturers.

> They would all stop using the word "beans", and each would give the product a new, coined name. Some might use anagrams of beans, like "Sneabs" or "Nabes", and others might call them "Lo Cals" or "Hi Pros". Picture the confusion in the grocery store if beans were no longer named "beans", but if each maker gave a completely new name to his product. Further, try to imagine what would happen if there were 300 to 500 additional new names of this type in the grocery store every year.[134]

Recognizing the problem, Dr. Harry Dowling, University of Illinois proposed that only a single trademark be permitted for a particular substance, and that competitors who sought to compete with the originator were instead required either to gain permission to use the name or to use the approved name and designate their version of the drug only with the corporate name.[135] This was an idea that was already circulating, and had been mentioned by the *New England Journal of Medicine*'s Committee on Advertising in an editorial in 1960.[136]

The discussions in the United States were echoed in medical publications in Britain. In the 1960 edition of his classic textbook *Clinical Pharmacology*, Professor Desmond Laurence of University College Hospital referred back with approval to suggestions in *The Lancet* in the 1940s that manufacturers stop using marks (which had led to fatal cases of confusion) and instead indicate the name of the manufacturer after the official or approved name of the drug.[137] Shortly afterwards, *The Lancet* published an article by "a correspondent" under the title "The Industry It Deserves," taking issue both with Dowling's arguments before the U.S. Senate Committee, and Laurence's views; in particular contesting their claims that use of

[131] Daniel C. Morgan & Samuel E. Allison, *The Kefauver Drug Hearings in Perspective*, 45 Sw. Soc. Sci. Q. 59 (1964).

[132] William W. Goodrich, *FDA's Regulation under the Kefauver-Harris Drug Amendments of 1962*, 18 Food Drug Cosm. L. J. 561, 562–63 (1963); William W. Goodrich, *A Look into the Nooks and Corners of the Kefauver-Harris Drug Amendments of 1962*, 19 Bus. L. 187, 188 (1963).

[133] The Reports can be found in U.S. Congress, Senate, Subcommittee on Antitrust and Monopoly of the Committee on the Judiciary, Report, Administered Prices, Drugs, Report No. 448, 87th Cong., 1st Sess., 1961.

[134] *Hearings*, 1959, pt. 18, at 10481, cited in Andrew Pressey, *The Man Who Managed Your Marketing?*, 7 J. Hist. Res. Mark. 429, 443 (2015).

[135] Harry F. Dowling, *The Pharmaceutical Industry and the Sector*, 264 New Eng. J. Med. 75 (1961).

[136] *Drug Terminology and the Urgent Need for Reform*, 263 New Eng. J. Med. 21 (1960).

[137] Desmond Roger Laurence & Richard Moulton, Clinical Pharmacology 454–55 (1960).

the manufacturers' names would provide prescribers and dispensers with the information they needed.[138] According to the anonymous author,

> Dowling, and also Laurence, think that drugs should be promoted not under trade names but as Drug X (Smith) or Drug X (Jones), according to the manufacturer concerned. But this is like asking car manufacturers to advertise their cars with no more embellishment than Motor Car (Birmingham) or Motor Car (Coventry). Unless the consumer could be persuaded that the air at Coventry was better than that of Birmingham, having a mysterious property which gave cars some highly desirable unique advantage, the idea must be a failure. When tried by one manufacturer in this country it only resulted in loss of business.

This article, in turn, generated correspondence canvassing the advantages and disadvantages of trade names for drugs.[139] Of course, Laurence defended his initial idea, observing that the correspondent "dismisses the suggestion as impracticable but, . . . fails to give a convincing reason why, or to offer a constructive alternative." Others defended the status quo: some asserted doctors needed brand names, either during periods when approved names were unavailable[140] or to differentiate between versions of the same active ingredient that were regarded by the prescriber as having different effects.[141] One respondent, from the American pharmaceutical firm Parke, Davis and Co., asserted that the fact that doctors continued to use trade names for prescription itself was conclusive evidence that they found such names useful: to limit manufacturers to use of their own corporate names would be to "put the clock back at least a generation to the 1920s and 1930s when this and similar systems of nomenclature were common."[142]

As a result, the ground was laid for more formal consideration of the desirability of trademarks for medical products, and the opportunity arose when in 1965 a committee was appointed to examine the relationship between the pharmaceutical industry and the NHS. Chaired by Lord (Alan) Sainsbury, the eleven-person committee included the health economist Brian Abel-Smith, economist of the patent system, Edith Penrose, trademark law expert R.G. Lloyd, and pharmacologist Professor G.V.R. Born from the Royal College of Surgeons. Established in 1965, the Committee was tasked with reviewing the entire relationship between the pharmaceutical industry and "making recommendations."[143] Reporting in 1967,

138 Correspondent, *The Industry it Deserves*, THE LANCET 278 (1961).

139 D.R. Laurence, *The Industry It Deserves?*, 278 THE LANCET 1041 (1961); G.A. Schmeidler, *The Industry It Deserves?*, 278 THE LANCET 1093 (1961); A.P. Launchbury, *The Industry It Deserves?*, 278 THE LANCET 1202 (1961); B. Herbert, *The Industry It Deserves?*, 278 THE LANCET 1151 (1961); J.A.L. Gorringe, *The Industry It Deserves?*, 278 THE LANCET 1255 (1961).

140 Schmeidler, *supra* note 139; *Contra* Launchbury, *supra* note 139.

141 Herbert, *supra* note 139.

142 Gorringe, *supra* note 139.

143 *Sainsbury Report*, *supra* note 102.

after fifty full days and twenty part days of meetings, as well as eleven days visiting factories,[144] the Committee made various recommendations. Most relevant to us, after "lengthy and careful consideration,"[145] the Report boldly recommended that there should be no brand names for new pharmaceutical products licensed on the advice of a proposed new regulator (the Medicines Commission) and that the Trade Marks Act should be appropriately amended.[146] All such products, whether the subject of patents or not, should be marketed only under a name approved by the Commission (which, notably, was expected to develop more usable names than were hitherto accepted by the Pharmacopoeia Commission as approved names).[147] The Report explained the advantages with its proposed approach.[148] First, it stated that there would be cost-savings if each medicine had only one name for purposes of medical practice.[149] It was impracticable to get doctors to prescribe by approved names while brand names were being heavily advertised.[150] Second, the change would reduce the possibility for confusion. It reported that many representatives of the medical profession had given evidence to the committee condemning the proliferation of the names of pharmaceutical products and the confusion caused by the practice of prescribing by brand names. The Report referred to section 15 of the Trade Marks Act 1938, describing it as "complicated" and in need of revision.[151]

This part of the Sainsbury Report was controversial.[152] *The Lancet* approved of the proposal, concluding that the committee's arguments were "fair and convincing" and urging the government not to be deflected from taking action by the industry's inevitable canvassing.[153] The industry response was, unsurprisingly, negative.[154] On the day of its release, President of the Association of British Pharmaceutical Manufacturers Stanley Fenwick had called the proposal to abolish brands one of "the more unacceptable" of the Committee's recommendations, and one that illustrated its "insularity and inability to appreciate long-term effects."[155] Others involved in medicine and pharmacy saw merit in the proposal,[156] but also

[144] *Id.* [152] ff (findings on brand names).

[145] *Id.* [272]. The idea emerged from a paper written by Dutton, the secretary, requiring use of "NHS names": TNA: MH 104/40. Professor Edith Penrose's analysis can be found in a note "on the advantages and disadvantages of the abolition of brand names" in TNA: MH 104/62.

[146] *Id.* [274].

[147] *Id.* [279].

[148] *Id.* [266]–[282].

[149] *Id.* [268].

[150] *Id.* [270].

[151] *Id.* [273].

[152] *Approved Names*, 295 The Lancet 228 (1970). For a review, *see* William Breckon, The Drug Makers 110–14 (1972).

[153] *After Sainsbury*, *supra* note 129.

[154] The ABPI even published its own assessment: Ass'n Brit. Pharm. Indus., The Pharmaceutical Industry and the Nation's Health (1967); Phillip Colebrook, *Pharmaceuticals an Industry Facing Danger?*, Times, Sept. 28, 1967.

[155] Ann Shearer, *Industry Fear Drug Research Will Stop*, The Guardian, Sept. 29, 1967.

[156] *See, e.g.*, *Sainsbury Report*, 4(5570) Brit. Med. J. 1 (1967); A.C. Dornhurst and D.R. Laurence, *Sainsbury Report*, Times, Oct. 24, 1967, at 11; *Pharmacists and the Sainsbury Report*, 4 4(5581) Brit. Med. J. 739 (1967) (JA Baker (Westminster Hospital)).

certain problems.[157] Importantly, although recognizing the difficulties with the existing arrangements as to naming, *The British Medical Journal* came out against the Sainsbury proposal,[158] and with that, any interest the government of the day had in this particular proposal dissipated.[159] In June 1968, the Minister for Health in the Labour government declared it would not be pursuing the idea.[160] The matter was quietly abandoned.[161]

Three main arguments appeared against abolishing trademarks for medical products.[162] The first, and probably most important, was that brand names might provide important therapeutic information. The second was that brand names were an important aspect of U.K. success in exporting pharmaceuticals. The third was that the proposal raised difficult questions of legality.

The most important argument against abolishing brand names for medical products lay in the claim (as noted, accepted already in part in the Hinchcliffe Report) that not all versions of medical products could be adequately described by reference to the approved name (or INN).[163] This was because all an approved name told a doctor was the active ingredient.[164] However, it had become apparent that differences existed between various formulations which might have therapeutic significance, particularly because different versions might make the ingredient available within the patient's body at different rates. As Sir Frank Hartley, the then Dean of the School of Pharmacy, University of London, explained, a drug's formulation—that is, presentation of drugs so far as particle size—could have a profound effect on the biological availability of a drug. In the jargon, chemical equivalence (designated by the approved name) is not "bioequivalence" and thus,

[157] School of Pharmacy at the University of London also held a conference to discuss the Sainsbury proposals on Nov. 10, 1967. The arguments were summarized in *Pharmacists and the Sainsbury Report*, *supra* note 156.

[158] *Brand Names*, *supra* note 130.

[159] As early as Dec. 1967, the Ministry of Health had said it would take a "non-committal line" preferring to use the recommendation as a bargaining chip in price negotiations with the ABPI: G.G. Hulme to William Wallace (Board of Trade) (Dec. 7, 1967) in MH 104/97.

[160] Hansard (HC) (June 4, 1968) (767) cols. 45–46 (Kenneth Robinson).

[161] *Approved Names*, *supra* note 152 ("quietly dropped.").

[162] Other arguments were made. For example David Moreau of Syntex Pharmaceuticals argued there were already examples of unbranded pharmaceuticals circulating that turned out to be of substandard quality. *Damaging to Exports and Research*, TIMES, Sept. 29, 1967.

[163] *Id.* ("There is a mistaken belief that the active constituent, to which the official name only refers, constitutes the sole basis for a drug's effectiveness. This is by no means always the case, since the physiological response to a drug may also be a function of its pharmaceutical form ... The prescription of a well-known firm's branded product ensures that the medicine has a quality on which the manufacturer is staking his reputation.").

[164] Practical discussions over the equivalence of branded and generic drugs occurred during the processes of classification of drugs by the Standing Joint Committee on Classification of Proprietary Preparations, and in particular the preparation of a letter from the Chief Medical Officer, G.E. Godber, dated May 20, 1963 to general practitioners identifying fifty-three frequently prescribed branded preparations for which there were cheaper generic versions that could be prescribed to produce the same therapeutic effect, and thus save the NHS up to £1million: TNA: MH 133/114 (containing the letter and the background discussions, including objections by members of the ABPI to the branded drugs being described as equivalent).

importantly, is not "therapeutic equivalence."[165] And if approved names did not signal equivalence, all that doctors could rely on to do so were trademarks.[166]

A second argument, probably influential with some in government, was that abolishing such trademarks would negatively affect trade. Nigel Fisher, Director of Bayer and Winthrop, was reported to have said that the proposal on brand names would hobble British firms when exporting and provide incentives to foreign firms to utilize brands to access the U.K. market.[167] Sir Michael Perrin, Chairman of the Wellcome Foundation, wrote to *The Times*,[168] arguing that busy doctors would not remember to put the manufacturer's name, and that abandoning trademarks would be bad for pharmaceutical exports because the reputation of a company name might be yet to be established. There was evidence, at least, that pharmaceutical exports were doing well. By 1967, exports stood at £75 million pa, imports at £15 million, giving a substantial trade surplus.[169] One issue with exports was that foreign countries might not offer any patent protection, or perhaps only process patents, which were easily invented around. As Dr. Charles Stevens explained, while brand names might seem unnecessary in Britain, because of this aspect of patent law, protection of trademarks was essential for a drug firm's overseas sales.[170] Whatever the merits of these arguments, the government was not prepared to take such a risk. Sir Kenneth Robinson, the Minister for Health, stated that the government believed "that the abolition of brand names by Britain in isolation could well have more serious economic consequences than the Committee envisaged, and would in fact be likely to put British-based firms at a disadvantage in export markets."[171]

The third argument—perhaps of most interest to scholars of international intellectual property law—was that any such move might be unlawful. As *The British Medical Journal* noted, the Sainsbury Committee appreciated that some revision of the Trade Marks Act would be necessary were brand names abolished, "but it is questionable if the committee realized how complicated this would be." The

[165] As the Ministry of Health would later recognize, the point was a good one in relation to some drugs and not others, and trademarks might not themselves guarantee bio-availability: W. Scott Moncrieff (Department of Health and Social Security) to Haines (Mathys Committee) (Mar. 12, 1973), in BT 209/1412.

[166] The Sainsbury Committee in fact was keen to preserve the power of a doctor to prescribe a drug by way of its manufacturer, but argued that this was most clearly done by reference to the manufacturer rather than a trademark.

[167] *Damaging to Exports and Research*, *supra* note 162. In fact, the Sainsbury Report would have required importers to designate drugs only by manufacturer and the "common name": [276]. *See also* ICI to Ministry of Health (Dec. 23, 1967) in MH104/97.

[168] M. Perrin, *Implication of Drugs Report*, TIMES, Oct. 4, 1967, at 11.

[169] F.H. Happold, *The Risks of a Cheap Drugs Policy*, TIMES, May 2, 1967, at 25 (noting that this was in large part because foreign firms operated here, without whom exports would be a mere £35 million); *British Drug Exports Reach Record £75 million*, TIMES, June 9, 1967.

[170] *Pharmacists and The Sainsbury Report*, *supra* note 156. The same argument was recognized by the Hinchcliffe Final Report (1959), *supra* note 88, [210] (trademarks safeguard "against those firms who do no worthwhile research but who take advantage of anomalies in patent laws to copy the originator's products. This is especially so in certain important export markets").

[171] Hansard (HC) (June 4, 1968) (767) cols. 45–46.

government minister, likewise, explained the decision not to pursue the proposal by reference to the facts that "any amendment of the trademark law also needs to take account of our international obligations."[172] What was he thinking of? Background documents indicate that this is a reference to Article 7 of the Paris Convention which by then stated that "The nature of the goods to which a trademark is to be applied shall in no case form an obstacle to the registration of the mark."[173] Insofar as the Sainsbury Committee's recommendation was that registration of marks for medicinal products *ipso facto* be prohibited and existing registrations be invalidated, the proposal would clearly have placed the United Kingdom in breach.[174] Indeed, the Board of Trade had doubts as to whether it would accord with the spirit of the Convention to prohibit the use of such marks, given that the indirect effect would be that a person could not register because they would not be able to claim a bona fide intention to use the mark.[175]

IV. The Era of Medicines Regulation and Demands for Substitution

Trademarks for medical products may have survived the threat posed by the Sainsbury Report,[176] but they soon came to be subject to the new system of

[172] William Wallace (Board to Trade) to G.G. Hulme, Ministry of Health (Dec. 21, 1967), MH 104/97 (proposal "almost certainly contrary" to obligations under Paris Convention, citing art. 6 quinquies and "more importantly" art. 7); Memorandum by the ABPI on the Denial of Brand Names for New Pharmaceutical Products (Jan. 1968), in MH 104/97, f. 6.

[173] The original wording had been amended as a result of the Hague revisions in 1925, and is discussed by Sam Ricketson, *The Trade Mark Provisions of the Paris Convention, in* CAMBRIDGE HANDBOOK ON INTERNATIONAL AND COMPARATIVE TRADE MARK LAW (Irene Calboli & Jane C. Ginsburg eds., 2020). A proposal to extend the nondiscrimination rule further, to cover both renewal and use, at the Lisbon revision in 1958 was rejected. The provision was replicated and extended to services in the Trade-Related Aspects of Intellectual Property Rights (TRIPS) Agreement, art. 15(4).

[174] Wallace to Hulme, *supra* note 172.

[175] More recently, Daniel Gervais had argued that a prohibition on registration of tobacco products would be contrary to art. 7 of Paris, and a prohibition on use for certain products might be contrary to its "spirit": DANIEL GERVAIS, ANALYSIS OF THE COMPATIBILITY OF CERTAIN TOBACCO PRODUCT PACKAGING RULES WITH THE TRIPS AGREEMENT AND THE PARIS CONVENTION [21], [57], [59] (2010), https://www.jti.com/sites/default/files/key-regulatory-submissions-documents/expert-reports/intellectual-property/1-gervais.pdf. However, the WTO Panel adopted a narrow understanding of art. 7 as limited to the process of registration in Panel Report, *Australia—Certain Measures Concerning Trademarks, Geographical Indications and Other Plain Packaging Requirements Applicable to Tobacco Products and Packaging*, [7.1776]–[7.1913], esp. [7.1908], WTO Docs. WT/DS435/R, WT/DS441/R, WT/DS458/R, WT/DS467/R (adopted June 28, 2018). Moreover, it seems clear that the regulation of the use of marks on certain potentially harmful products is permitted, particularly in the interests of public health: Appellate Body Report, *Australia—Certain Measures Concerning Trademarks, Geographical Indications and Other Plain Packaging Requirements Applicable to Tobacco Products and Packaging*, [6.649], WTO Doc. WT/DS435/AB/R (adopted June 9, 2020).

[176] Similar proposals to abolish trademarks for drugs continued to circulate in the United States: Henry Gewirtz & Saxon Graham, *Pharmaceuticals: Valley of the Lies*, 7 TRANS-ACTIONS 5, 10 (1970).

regulation of medicines, which in its modern form began with the Medicines Act 1968.[177] Passed in the aftermath of the thalidomide tragedy,[178] since the Act came into operation in 1971 drug manufacturers have been obliged to submit new drug applications for approval by a regulator prior to their marketing.[179] The process requires the applicant to establish both the safety of the drug and its effectiveness. Although already developed with an eye on the United Kingdom joining the European Community, the 1968 regime was transformed as a result of harmonization in the European Union, most notably by Directive 2001/83/EC of the European Parliament and of the Council on the Community code relating to medicinal products for human use.[180]

Today, regulation of medicines is a field of its own.[181] One small part concerns the regulation of names used on the label and packaging of medical products.[182] Although the naming requirements have altered over the fifty-year operation of the system, it has been a constant requirement that any invented name be accompanied by a common name or the international non-proprietary name.[183] Initially, under the Medicines (Labelling) Regulations, issued under section 85 of the Medicines Act 1968, containers and packages were required to indicate, inter alia, "the name" of the medicinal product being either the appropriate non-proprietary name or a proprietary designation as well as the INN.[184] Similar rules were adopted in E.U. law in 1992,[185] requiring that the outer packaging of medicinal products specify "the name of the medicinal product followed by the common name where the product contains only one active ingredient and if its name is an invented name." Today, the Human Medicines Regulations 2012 require that any private marks or names used as the designation of a medical product must always appear alongside a public name,[186] i.e., one that any producer can use to designate a product with the

[177] Reviewed by Harvey Teff, *Regulation under the Medicines Act 1968: A Continuing Prescription for Health*, 47 MOD. L. REV. 30 (1984).

[178] Kenneth Robinson, Minister of Health, HC Deb (15 Feb. 1968) (758) col. 1600 ff. (Second Reading). Government White Paper, *Forthcoming Legislation on the Safety, Quality and Design of Drugs and Medicines*, 1967, Cmnd. 2295.

[179] Initially this was to the Committee on Safety of Medicines (CSM); and, as part of the European Union, the European Medicines Agency. Today it is the Commission and Medical and Heathcare Products Regulatory Agency (MHRA).

[180] Regulation (EC) No. 726/2004 of the European Parliament and of the Council of Mar. 31, 2004 Laying Down Community Procedures for the Authorisation and Supervision of Medicinal Products for Human and Veterinary Use and Establishing a European Medicines, 2004 O.J. (L 136) 1.

[181] EMILY JACKSON, LAW AND THE REGULATION OF MEDICINES (2012).

[182] Where the product contains up to three active substances.

[183] Failure to comply with the labelling requirements created under the Medicines Act 1968, § 85(1) was a criminal offence, punishable by fine and imprisonment: Medicines Act 1985, §§ 85(3), 91.

[184] Medicines (Labelling) Regulations 1976, SI 1976/1726, sch. 1.

[185] Council Directive 92/27/EEC of Mar. 31, 1992 on the Labelling of Medicinal Products for Human Use and on Package Leaflets, art. 2(1), 1992 O.J. (L 113) 8, 9.

[186] Human Medicines Regulations 2012, SI 2012/1916, reg. 257, sch. 24, pt. 1. These reflect the requirements of Directive 2001/83/EC of the European Parliament and of the Council of Nov. 6, 2001 on the Community code relating to medicinal products for human use, art. 54, (itself amended on this point by Directive 2004/27/EC of the European Parliament and of the Council of Mar. 31, 2004). Since Jan. 1, 2021, this is retained E.U. law.

same key ingredients.[187] In general, the public name that must be used is the INN" designated by the WHO, though if no such name exists, the "usual common name" must be used.[188] Breach of the Regulations would amount to a criminal offense.[189] The effect is that if a drug is labeled with a private mark, such as LIPITOR, it must always appear alongside a public name, such as the INN, atorvastatin.

By 1968, trademark law no longer played a primary role in generating the public names (even if their use remains advisable to avoid problems of genericism). As already observed, the 1919 provision had been re-enacted, with minor amendments, in section 15(3) of the 1938 Act. However, by 1974 when the Mathys Committee conducted its review of trademark law, there was no longer any interest in using the trademark regime to regulate the names of medicines.[190] The most obvious reason is that the regulation of such names was now done—and importantly, done better—within the emerging labyrinth of regulations governing the approval and marketing of medicines. Allied to that, however, there was a growing sense that trademark law should concern itself with its own issues, rather than incorporate other regulatory tasks. In effect, trademark law became increasingly normatively closed.[191] As the Mathys report explained:

> We believe attempts to solve problems specific to one part of industry... by putting limits on the use of specific groups of trade marks should be resisted and where it has been done the generally accepted freedom of use should be restored.[192]

The role of the trademark system had, by gradual shifts in medical naming and bigger shifts in medical regulation, become irrelevant as a regulatory tool. As harmonization of trademark law of the European Community came under serious consideration during the 1970s and 1980s, no-one pushed for section 6 of the 1919 Act, or its successor (section 15 of the 1938 Act) to be replicated.

[187] The regulations are in fact slightly more complicated in structure, differentiating between invented names, common names, scientific names, and INNs, and presenting, in effect, six possible configurations: invented name plus INN; common name plus INN; scientific name plus INN; or, if there is no INN, invented name plus common name; common name alone; or scientific name plus common name.

[188] For example, a BAN. AMANTADINE is not an INN but a BAN and DCF.

[189] Medicines Act, 1968, § 85.

[190] Departmental Committee on British Trade Mark Law and Practice, Department of Health and Social Security. *Notes of Oral Evidence Given by Mr G. Carter, Mr R.F. Tyas and Mr R.N. Williams on 31 July 1973*, in BT 209/1412 (DHSS had no intention of reviving issues relating to use of brand names raised in Sainsbury Report).

[191] Mathys himself referred to the "emotional approach," of which he did not approve, preferring the position that trademark law should apply equally "across the board": Mathys to D. Falconer QC (Oct. 4, 1973), in BT 209/1412.

[192] Department of Trade and Industry, *Report of the Committee to Examine British Trade Mark Law and Practice*, 1974, Cm. 5601, [161].

Rules against substitution, long the domain of passing off and trademark law, were absorbed into the regulatory labyrinth.[193] The Medicines Act 1968 provided that no person shall, to the prejudice to the person (if any) for whom the product was prescribed by the practitioner, supply any medicinal product which is not of the nature or quality specified in the prescription.[194] So, if a doctor prescribes using a trademark, a pharmacist must supply the same—at least where not doing so would "cause prejudice." Moreover, under Human Medicines Regulations 2012,[195] a pharmacist is prohibited from supplying a prescription-only medicine except "*in accordance* with a prescription given by an appropriate practitioner"; and is under a duty to provide the drugs "so ordered," i.e., as specified in a prescription.[196]

To say that the issue of regulating the use and presentation of medical names was relocated from trademark law to the law of medicines is not to say that there were no further discussions about problems with trademarks for medical products; just that they tended to be raised in a different regulatory environment. Most of these discussions related to the persistent problem of the NHS budget, which continued to rise during the 1980s. Although some reductions were achieved by designating some drugs as "over the counter" (and thus paid for by the end user rather than the state),[197] the focus has largely been on two strategies: first, whether pharmacists should be offered more freedom to substitute cheaper brands (or unbranded drugs) where a doctor prescribed a specific brand; and second, by trying to influence general practitioners to prescribe more cost-effectively, in particular, by prescribing using a generic name rather than a trade name.[198]

The possibility of permitting substitution by pharmacists has been raised repeatedly (and is frequently the subject of international debate).[199] It was rejected by Hinchcliffe in 1958 and again by Sainsbury in 1967.[200] However, substitution

[193] Substitution is the norm in hospitals, because the prescriber is indistinguishable legally from the supplier: E.C. Huskisson, *Trade Names or Proper Names? A Problem for the Prescriber*, 4(5886) BRIT. MED. J. 225 (1973) (in NHS hospitals pharmacists often substitute); House of Commons Health Committee, *Second Report: Priority Setting in the NHS: the NHS Drugs Budget* (1994), Vol. 1, [193]; Howard Stokoe & Phil Deady, *Purchasing Medicines*, *in* HOSPITAL PHARMACY 28 (Martin Stephens ed., 2011) (substitution the norm in hospitals).

[194] Medicines Act, 1968, § 64(1), (5) (formerly § 64(1), and (6), as enacted); R (ex p. Association of Pharmaceutical Importers) v. Secretary of State for Health [2001] EWCA Civ 1896, [6].

[195] Human Medicines Regulations 2012, SI 2012/1916, reg. 214.

[196] National Health Service (Pharmaceutical and Local Pharmaceutical Services) Regulations 2013, SI 2013/349, sch. 4, para 5.

[197] In 1985, the Conservative government introduced a "limited list" of drugs that could not be prescribed: *see* House of Commons Health Committee, *supra* note 193, [94] ff. By 2003, £1.8 billion was spent on over-the-counter medicines: House of Commons Health Committee, *The Influence of the Pharmaceutical Industry*, 2004–05, HC 42-I.

[198] The fact that neither the doctor nor patient is directly concerned by price had long been seen as a driver of increased expenditure: *Sainsbury Report*, *supra* note 102, [2], [41].

[199] In 1982, *The Lancet* referred to substitution as "an issue which just refuses to go away": *Drug Substitution, Savings, and Safety*, 320 THE LANCET 640 (1982). On the emergence of such laws in the United States, *see* Jillena A. Warner, *Consumer Protection and Prescription Drugs: The Generic Drug Substitution Laws*, 67 KENTUCKY L. J. 384 (1978).

[200] Hinchcliffe Final Report, *supra* note 88, [332]–[335] (not a practical or desirable method of securing economies in the drug bill.)

was approved by a committee of fourteen "purely medical men" in the Greenfield Report of 1983,[201] though the committee acknowledged that it was not qualified to consider the commercial and economic consequences.[202] Some bills to give effect to the recommendation were tabled in parliament,[203] but the recommendation was not taken up by a Conservative administration that was keen not to do anything to harm investment in the pharmaceutical industry,[204] which was regarded as an important asset in terms both of exports and employment.[205] Substitution (by way of a tick in scheme) was recommended by the House of Commons Health Committee in July 1994,[206] but rejected by the government that autumn as not necessary.[207] Finally, substitution was raised in 2008 in the context of the revision of the PPRS, when—perhaps surprisingly (given the stand it had always taken)—the pharmaceutical industry preferred such a policy to a proposal to cap of prices on branded (but not patented) drugs.[208] However, after consultation, the government again decided against introducing substitution.[209]

Three features of the debates over substitution are worth noting. The first is that they have largely been conducted in terms of the divergent expertise of pharmacists and general practitioners and each of these groups appropriate professional roles. In general, it is accepted that the issue of prescribing is one for the general practitioner, and thus it is disputed whether the task of selecting particular versions of a

[201] Informal Working Group on Effective Prescribing, *Report of the Informal Working Group on Effective Prescribing* [24] (1983) (hereinafter *Greenfield Report*) (doctors would have to specify they want the brand name drug dispensed). The Report and background can be viewed at TNA: MH 149/2495.

[202] *Id.* [23].

[203] Generic Dispensing Bill 1983, Bill No. 68; Generic Substitution (National Health Services) Bill 1983, Bill No. 137 (Apr.); Generic Substitution (National Health Services) Bill, Bill No. 34, HC 1R, July 22, 1983; Generic Substitution (National Health Services) Bill 1984, Bill No. 139 (all introduced by Lauri Pavitt MP). (These bills all gave a discretion to pharmacists unless the GP indicated "no substitute.") For a proposal allowing doctors to opt-in to substitution, *see* N. Timmins, *Doctors Accuse Government of Capitulating to Drug Industry*, TIMES, June 22, 1984. The debate is summarized in P.B., *In 48 hours the Flood of Drugs Sent to One Doctor's Surgery*, TIMES, Nov. 1, 1984 (with reference to a survey as to the reasons doctors prescribed brand names rather than INNs—familiarity through advertising, memorability and length).

[204] Ken Clarke, Minister for Health, Hansard (HC) (Dec. 8, 1983) (50) col. 474 (explaining that the general practitioners were divided over its desirability and that it raised difficult question of allocation of responsibility between practitioners and pharmacists and preferring encouragement of generic prescribing); Rodney Deitch, *Effective Prescribing and Promotional Cost*, 321 THE LANCET 368 (1983).

[205] By then, net exports were worth about £570 million, and the industry was said to employ 70,000 people. Norman Fowler, Hansard (HC) (Jan. 18, 1983) (35) col. 156.

[206] House of Commons Health Committee, *supra* note 193, [195]–[200].

[207] *Government Response to the Second Report from the Health Committee Session 1993–1994*, 1994, Cm. 2683, [54]; Audit Commission, *A Prescription for Improvement* (1994).

[208] Andrew Jack, *Generic Substitution of Drugs to Be Introduced in 2010*, 337 BRIT. MED. J. a2699 (2008).

[209] Zosia Kmietowicz, *Government Drops Plans for Generic Substitution Amid Safety Concerns*, 341 BRIT. MED. J. c5780 (2010). A critical discussion of the Government's decision is provided in MARTIN DUERDEN ET AL., THE QUALITY OF GP PRESCRIBING 76–79 (2011), https://www.kingsfund.org.uk/sites/default/files/field/field_document/quality-gp-prescribing-gp-inquiry-research-paper-mar11.pdf.

drug is one for which pharmacists should be made responsible.[210] Second, and related, while the pharmaceutical industry has fiercely opposed substitution,[211] the debates rarely seemed to have discussed the rights of trademark holders, or indeed their investments (other than at the general level of highlighting that substitution will reduce industry profits and investment).[212] Nothing seems to be said about harm to the investments that have been made in promotion. This is surprising given the longstanding characterization of substitution as an "evil," an existential threat to trademark proprietors.[213] Third, at lease in more recent times, the gains that could be made from introducing substitution have always been seen as marginal, given the success of efforts to incentivize general practitioners to prescribe by approved name.

In 1973, only 26% of prescriptions were written generically, and in 1982, it was reported to have fallen to 20%;[214] however, by 1987, this number had grown to 36%; in 1994, 50%;[215] in 1997, 60%; in 1999, 70%;[216] in 2003, 77.8%;[217] and by 2007, 83% (around which it has continued to hover until 2017—the last year for which statistics are available).[218] This remarkable shift builds on efforts to inform and educate doctors about the relationship between branded drugs and generics; and to build confidence in the quality of generics (through the regulatory processes first brought into law by the 1968 Act). However, the informational and educational strategies were supplemented through various techniques to improve "cost consciousness" among general practitioners, who continue to be the source of most prescriptions. These have included reorganization of the funding of GP practices,[219] so that they benefit from reduced levels of spending; creating lists of drugs of recognized cost-effectiveness, in particular through the vehicle of the National

[210] Ken Clarke, *supra* note 204 (explaining that the general practitioners were divided over its desirability and that it raised difficult question of allocation of responsibility between practitioners and pharmacists); Lord Glenarthur, Hansard (HL) (Feb. 6, 1985) (459) cols. 1194–99.

[211] House of Commons Health Committee, *supra* note 193, [197].

[212] *Id.* [198].

[213] A U.S. journal published by New York drug wholesalers and manufacturers Lehn and Fink, entitled "Notes on New Remedies," referred to substitution as a "dreaded offence": (1895–97) 8(1) *Notes on New Remedies* 12 (discussing "FERROPYRIN") (Sept. 1895). An article by a doctor in Brooklyn, New York, published in *Medical News*, described such substitution as an "atrocious crime" akin to the work of an assassin. William J. Cruikshank, *The Substitution of Drugs in the Dispensing of the Physician's Prescription*, MEDICAL NEWS, Nov. 25, 1905, at 1023.

[214] Huskisson, *supra* note 193; *Greenfield Report*, *supra* note 201, [17].

[215] House of Commons Health Committee, *supra* note 193, [192].

[216] Hanchard to Knapton (Sept. 20 1999), in TNA: JA 614/153.

[217] House of Commons Health Committee, *supra* note 193, [27].

[218] House of Commons Committee on Public Accounts, *Department of Health: Prescribing Costs in Primary Care*, 2007–08, HC 173, [7]. Between 2007 and 2017, between 82.6% and 84.1% were prescribed generically, while the number prescribed generically but dispensed in proprietary form fell to 6.1% in 2017. Statistics from 1994 can be found on *Prescriptions Dispensed in the Community*, NHS DIGITAL, https://digital.nhs.uk/data-and-information/publications/statistical/prescriptions-dispensed-in-the-community (last visited June 9, 2022).

[219] White Paper, *Working for Patients*, 1989, Cm. 555, ch. 6 (proposals on GP budgets), ch. 7 (on prescribing budgets); House of Commons Health Committee, *supra* note 193, [146]–[150]; Darrin Baines, *Working for Patients: NHS Reform and Drug Budgets*, 25 PRESCRIBER 20 (2014) (reviewing White Paper).

Institute for Clinical Excellence, established in April 1999 (and now known as the National Institute for Health and Care Excellence).[220]

The effect has been to make it standard practice to designate more drugs by their approved names/INNs rather than brand names.[221] Not all such drugs will be dispensed generically—those that are still under patent or only available in branded form will inevitably be dispensed as such. But the practical impact on the role and significance of trademarks for pharmaceuticals is profound. Long regarded with skepticism, the role of trademarks is marginalized because the standard practice is now to ignore such marks.

Conclusion

The different approaches taken to the regulation of medical names over the twentieth century are suggestive of a deep-seated unease with trademark protection for medicines. It is clear that branded medicines often cost more, and that the proliferation of such names has frequently led to confusion among medical practitioners. As such, they have been seen as the source of substantial social costs. On the other hand, it has not been evident to medical practitioners nor policymakers what the public benefits of such brands are. Since at least the time of the Pharmacy Act 1868, the seller's identity has been required to appear on medicines,[222] which makes it clear that a trademark is not needed as an indicator of origin (a trademark usually provides less information about origin than the manufacturer's name). In the post-thalidomide-tragedy era, with rigorous systems of quality control, including requirements of "pharmacokinetic bioequivalence," in most cases brands do not operate as indicators of therapeutic quality. Of course, there may be different shapes, colors, films, and so on, but in most instances none of these have a bearing on what matters to prescribers and patients, namely, therapeutic effectiveness. It is clear, on the other hand, that brands are associated with other recognized functions of trademarks. First, they are linked to investment in marketing and promotion,[223] but, while pharmaceutical promotion has often served to educate

[220] Established by the National Institute for Clinical Excellence (Establishment and Constitution) Order 1999, SI 1999/220, NICE's tasks were quickly amended by SI 1999/2219 to relate in part to "the effective use of available resources in the health service." In practice, "NICE guidance has a vital role in determining the availability of treatments within the NHS": R (ex p Eisai Ltd) v. National Institute for Health and Clinical Excellence [2008] EWCA Civ 438, [7].

[221] NHS Executive, Quality and Performance in the NHS: High Level Performance Indicators 44 (1999).

[222] Pharmacy Act 1868, § 17 (as amended); Poison and Pharmacy Act 1908, § 5.

[223] For historical overviews of such advertising, *see* A. Richard Green et al., *Marketing Medicine: Charting the Rise of Modern Therapeutics through a Systematic Review of Adverts in UK Medical Journals (1950–1980)*, 84 Brit. J. Clinical Pharmacology 1668 (2018); A. Richard Green et al., *Examining the "Psychopharmacology Revolution" (1950–1980) Through the Advertising of Psychoactive Drugs in the British Medical Journal*, 32 J. Psychopharmacology 1056 (2018).

prescribers,[224] the historical record suggests that, despite direct and indirect regulation (e.g., under the calculation of prices via the PPRS),[225] promotion has often been regarded by contemporaries as excessive.[226] Second, of course, trademarks have often been better communicators—they are shorter, more memorable, and more euphonious—than approved names and INNs; but these communicative advantages of brand names have frequently been regarded as a problem, rather than a benefit. The presence of trademarks, as a matter of practice, for much of the twentieth century, impeded more universal use of the official, approved, non-proprietary terminology.

And yet, trademarks for medical products survived. Two arguments seem repeatedly to have saved them from threats of abolition or mandatory generic substitution.

The first is that the legitimacy of branded medicines is somehow linked to incentives for research. Though perhaps counter-intuitive to intellectual property scholars, who draw categorical distinctions between patents which are thought of in terms of incentives to, and rewards for, research and innovation, and trademarks which are thought of in informational terms, the argument has been repeatedly made that trademarks, typically associated with originators of drugs, offer an additional mechanism for appropriating the benefits of research investment. This idea was expressed as early as the 1914 Select Committee Report, and frequently repeated through the century,[227] not least in the opposition to the Sainsbury Committee's proposal to abolish brand names for pharmaceuticals.[228] The argument featured in the 1980s as a reason offered against permitting substitution.[229] The argument that trademarks were required to incentivize research have often

[224] Hartley, *supra* note 59 (trade names essential as a means of getting a product known) (Hartley was at this time Director of Research at British Drug Houses—later bought by E. Merck of Germany).

[225] House of Commons Health Committee, *supra* note 193, [57] (describing limits of costs that are deductible under PPRS). The Prescription Medicines Code of Practice Authority seeks ensure that manufacturers follow the code of practice on the promotion of drugs published by the ABPI.

[226] Hinchcliffe Final Report (1959), *supra* note 88, [207] ("sales propaganda of some of the drug firms is carried to extravagant lengths"); House of Commons Health Committee, *supra* note 193, [176]–[182] (evidence of excessive promotion); House of Commons Health, *supra* note 193, [76]–[85], [192]–[234] (on promotion of drugs to doctors); Zosia *Kmietowicz, NHS Criticised for Lax Control Over Drugs Industry*, 330 BRIT. MED. J. 805 (2005).

[227] *Proprietary and Approved Names*, *supra* note 72 ("Enterprise in research deserves its reward"); Herxheimer et al., *supra* note 87; Hinchcliffe Final Report, *supra* note 88, [210] (trademarks safeguard "against those firms who do no worthwhile research") and [254] ("proprietary names are worth more to them than patent rights").

[228] ABPI, *supra* note 172, f. 6, (emphasizing the importance of trademarks to protect research that could not be patented, e.g., new medical uses of known substances, such as the analgesic action of paracetamol).

[229] Ken Clarke (Minister for Health), Hansard (HC) 18 June 1985 (81) col. 154 (generic substitution "would have a ruinous effect on a wide range of the pharmaceutical industry and, in the end, could cost the country the introduction of valuable new drugs of genuine therapeutic value"); R. Venning to Long, 'Generic Substitution – Statement', 7 October 1983 in TNA: MH149/495 (and the documents in the file more generally); Andrew Veitch, *Fowler's Blood Money*, THE GUARDIAN, May 14, 1983.

been grounded in limitations on domestic and/or foreign patent laws which no longer exist.[230]

The second, and more effective of the arguments, has been that brands operate as indicators of quality in those areas where contemporary science has been unable to give certainty about equivalence.[231] The perception of two brands as the same or equivalent involves a judgment which is requires consensus from those involved—most obviously prescribing doctors—both about what outcomes matter and how particular drugs work.[232] During the First World War, it was argued that trademarks were valuable because drugs with the same active ingredient did not necessarily operate in the same way;[233] and the problems with assessing the quality of British versions of the anti-syphilitic SALVARSAN (dioxydiamido-arseno-benzol) were such that each batch had to be tested by the Medical Research Council.[234] The problem of equivalence resurfaced in the 1960s and 1970s,[235] when it was found that chemical equivalence did not provide information about bio-availability.[236] Even with rigorous clinical trials preceding marketing, and requirements of "pharmacokinetic bioequivalence," the difficulty with guaranteeing therapeutic equivalence has remained a reason raised to oppose proposals for substitution.[237] Where there are doubts or uncertainties, and despite the fact that in law a trademark is no guarantee at all,[238] trademarks have frequently been seen as the only available guarantor of quality.[239]

[230] For example, thevulnerability of pharmaceutical patents to compulsory licensing was limited in the Patents Act 1977, and further restrictions on compulsory licensing were added to implement TRIPS. The limitation in many foreign countries of patents on pharmaceuticals to processes (as opposed to products) was also curtailed as a result of TRIPS. In addition, new medical uses were made patentable under the European Patent Convention 1973 and extended, initially through case law, to second and further medical uses, a move codified in the EPC 2000.

[231] For a recent examination of differences between branded and generic drugs, *see* Yang Yu & Marc Maliepaard, *Interchangeability of Generics-Experiences and Outlook Toward Pharmacokinetics Variability and Generic-Generic Substitution*, 105 Clinical Pharmacology & Therapeutics 292 (2019).

[232] *See* Jeremy Greene, Generic: The Unbranding of Modern Medicine (2016).

[233] *Der Selvftmord der Englisglischen Handelsmarke* (The Suicide of the British Trademark), *Frankfurter-Zeitung*, Jan. 5, 1915, in BT209/115 (Sicker, Pollak, & Derriman, Patent Agents, trans.), enclosed in a letter to Temple-Franks dated Jan 16., 1915.

[234] National Health Insurance, Medical Research Committee, *Interim Report on Work in Connection with the War*, 1915, Cm. 7922, 6;Jonathan Liebenau, *Business: The Formation of the Pharmaceutical Industry in Britain, Germany, and the United States before 1914*, 30 Bus. Hist. 117, 124–25 (1988); K.J. Williams, British Pharmaceutical Industry, Synthetic Drug Manufacture and the Clinical Testing of Novel Drugs 1895–1939, at 163–67 (2005) (Ph.D. thesis, University of Manchester).

[235] A seminal study was Gerhard Levy & Eino Nelson, *Pharmaceutical Formulation and Therapeutic Efficacy*, 177 J. Am. Med. Ass'n. 68 (1961). *See* Greene, *supra* note 232, 93–109 (2014).

[236] Herbert, *supra* note 139 (highlighting the problem of equating therapeutic efficacy with pharmaceutical formulation, suggesting that trade names in fact could be useful additions to, e.g., generic names); Huskisson, *supra* note 193.

[237] House of Commons Health Committee, *supra* note 193, [186].

[238] Greene, *supra* note 232, at 107 (quoting Edward Feldman of the U.S. National Formulary).

[239] Huskisson, *supra* note 193. *Cf.* Scott-Moncrieff to Haines, Mar. 12, 1973, [9.2] in TNA: BT209/1412.

The argument that brand names are indicators of quality has gained wide acceptance in relation to "biological products," that is, a group of medications (such as vaccines, tissues, and recombinant proteins) that are generated not by chemical synthesis but "whose active substance is made by a living organism." The category includes monoclonal antibodies. While it is acknowledged that competitors can produce products that are sufficiently therapeutically similar to be prescribed for the same conditions as an originator's "biologic" (and are thus dubbed "biosimilars"),[240] These specific differences mean that doctors are advised to prescribe by brand name and it is recommended that patients are not switched from one brand to another.[241]

The story of the treatment of pharmaceutical trademarks in twentieth-century Britain highlights that not all trademarks function in the same way; the linguistic, cultural, scientific, and commercial context may matter. The specific context may enhance the costs of trademarks and limit their social benefits; or, as with biosimilars, it might reinforce their value (at least until the scientific community agrees which, if any, are interchangeable). And, of course, those costs and benefits may change over time. While international law governing trademarks may require that the goods or services are not to be an obstacle to registration as trademarks, some of the social disadvantages in the way trademarks operate in different contexts can be accommodated through limitations, for example, conditions on the use of such marks (such as requiring that the use of the trademark be accompanied by use of non-proprietary terms). The story also highlights that limitations on the practical impact of the legal protection of trademarks may be found outside, as well as within, trademark laws—indeed, outside, as well as within law. The emasculation of pharmaceutical trademarks was achieved piece by piece, through the construction of a system of generic nomenclature, the establishment of governmental controls over product quality, through education and incentivization of doctors, and it has been driven by a persistent government interest in minimizing the cost of health care.

[240] Jeffrey K. Aronson & Robin E. Ferner, *How Similar are Biosimilars?*, 353 Brit. Med. J. i2721 (2016); Jeffrey K. Aronson et al., *Prescribing Biosimilars*, 362 Brit. Med. J. k3141 (2018).

[241] *See Guidance on Prescribing*, National Institute for Health and Care Excellence, https://bnf.nice.org.uk/medicines-guidance/guidance-on-prescribing (last visited June 3, 2022) ("Biological medicines must be prescribed by brand name and the brand name specified on the prescription should be dispensed in order to avoid inadvertent switching. Automatic substitution of brands at the point of dispensing is not appropriate for biological medicines.").

8
The Exceptional Nature of the Right to Control Use in Advertising

Robert G. Burrell

Introduction

The attempt to identify and develop new limiting doctrines has become a significant theme in trademark scholarship.[1] The central concern has been to explore whether exceptions and limitations could ameliorate the problems caused by the expansion of trademark rights. Some commentators—including the present author—have expressed caution about this turn, worried that exceptions may not live up to their promise and may distract us from the more important project of resisting and rolling back the extension of trademark protection.[2] This chapter explores the relationship between trademark rights and trademark exceptions by looking at the right of trademark owners to control use in advertising. Use in advertising is a productive vehicle for exploring the relationship between rights and exceptions because it is an area that has long attracted both judicial activism and legislative intervention, at least in the British Commonwealth. The central argument is that bringing a right to control use of a sign in advertising within the architecture of a registration-based trademark system is much more problematic than has generally been acknowledged. However, radically recasting the advertising right (or removing it altogether) would be conceptually difficult as well as politically inconceivable. This is therefore an area where exceptions must inevitably play a central role in ensuring that trademark rights are kept within appropriate bounds. But advertising also offers a case study in the dangerous slippage that can occur when we shift our focus from rights to exceptions. If we are going to lean more heavily

[1] Important early contributions to this debate include William McGeveran, *Rethinking Trademark Fair Use*, 94 Iowa L. Rev. 115 (2008)>; Graeme Dinwoodie, *Developing Defenses in Trademark Law*, 13 Lewis & Clark L. Rev. 99 (2009). For a recent contribution, *see, e.g.*, Jennifer Davis, *Limitations to Trademark Protection as Defences to Infringement*, *in* The Cambridge Handbook of International and Comparative Trademark Law (Irene Calboli & Jane C. Ginsburg eds., 2020).

[2] *See, e.g.*, Michael Grynberg, *Things are Worse than We Think: Trademark Defenses in a "Formalist" Age*, 24 Berkeley Tech. L. J. 897 (2009) (arguing that "narrow carveouts and safe harbors will do little to counter future expansions of trademark liability" and "urging continued resistance of trademark's expansion"); Robert Burrell & Dev Gangjee, *Trade Marks and Freedom of Expression: A Call for Caution*, 41 Int'l Rev. Intell. Prop. & Competition L. 544 (2010) (arguing, for example, that defenses to allow trademark parodies are likely to both undershoot and overshoot their target).

Robert G. Burrell, *The Exceptional Nature of the Right to Control Use in Advertising* In: *Charting Limitations on Trademark Rights*. Edited by: Haochen Sun and Barton Beebe, Oxford University Press. © Robert G. Burrell 2023.
DOI: 10.1093/oso/9780198871248.003.0009

on exceptions to curtail the expansion of trademarks, we must become better at guarding against the sort of slippage described below.

This chapter starts by problematizing the advertising right as it operates within registration-based systems. Having concluded that exceptions must play a role in dealing with unauthorized use of a mark in advertising, it then uses three case studies to explore the form that such exceptions might take. It argues that problems with the nature of the advertising right have never been confronted head on, and that current doctrines that permit some forms of unauthorized use in advertising leave trademark owners with unjustifiably broad rights. Nevertheless, there are also indications of how exceptions might be crafted to permit the sort of fact-sensitive inquiry that use in advertising demands.

Before plunging into the above, it is necessary to provide a brief explanation of the terminology employed in this chapter. Specifically, the key organizing rubrics of "advertising right" and "trademark exceptions" are both being used as short hands. In most legal systems, including those discussed below, there is no separate "advertising right" per se. The ability of trademark owners to control use in advertising is instead an offshoot of a more general right to control commercial uses of trademarks "in relation" to goods, as where marks are used in business papers, catalogues, or letterheads. In practice though, it is use in advertising that has proved controversial and around which significant bodies of case law have developed. Consequently, when we are thinking about designing trademark exceptions, we can usefully treat advertising as a separate category and hence owners as enjoying an analytically separate right. This is not, however, to suggest that exceptions should be narrowly tailored to curtail the scope of this "advertising right." The point is merely to concentrate the analysis on the area of most concern.

As regards the language of exceptions, this is being used broadly to refer to a range of policy driven doctrines that allow defendants to escape liability. Consequently, as used in this chapter, the term "exceptions" is broad enough to encompass the British Commonwealth requirement of "use as a trademark." As will be seen, this requirement was a key mechanism for limiting the scope of trademark rights under old British trademark law, and it retains this role in countries like Australia and New Zealand. In theory it is for the trademark owner to prove that the use was "use as a trademark," but in practice the defendant has to plead and will bear much of the burden of establishing that its use was other than use as a trademark and, as such, it functions much like a defense. In addition, the language of "exceptions" as used here includes narrowly tailored carve outs from the scope of rights as, for example, when oral use of a sign is excluded from the scope of liability in order to allow salespersons to make comparisons between products, an example that will be discussed in detail toward the end of this chapter.[3]

[3] This chapter does not therefore engage in the academic debate as to whether the language of "exceptions," "limitations," "defenses," or "user's rights" is to be preferred. This is not to denigrate the importance of this debate; it is simply not the focus of the analysis.

I. Use in Advertising and the Logics of Registration

Imagine a newly established public body charged with improving the health of the nation. One of its earliest campaigns targets smoking, but it wants to find a new way of presenting the antismoking message and it therefore consults with an external advertising agency. The idea emerges to build the campaign around an imaginary brand of cigarettes called CONQUEST. The campaign centers on the free distribution of high-quality imitation packets of cigarettes marked with the CONQUEST name. Inside the packets are rolled up pieces of paper, made to look like a row of cigarettes, that give advice on how to quit smoking. Associated newspaper adverts feature images of a CONQUEST packet together with slogans designed to carry a subtle antismoking message, such as "The ultimate choice of smokers" and "Switch to Conquest for longer lasting satisfaction." Prior to launching the campaign, the public body searches the trademark register, but only thinks to search in class 16 (which covers packaging, paper, and cardboard goods) and thereby fails to note that CONQUEST is registered in class 34 for tobacco products. The owner of the CONQUEST mark sues for trademark infringement and claims damages, arguing that its mark has been irretrievably damaged through its association with a public health campaign.

The above scenario formed the background to the 1982 decision of the High Court of Ireland in *Gallaher (Dublin) Ltd v. The Health Education Bureau*.[4] The Court held that the mark had been used in relation to cigarettes (and not merely in relation to a health campaign) and found for the plaintiff.

It should be acknowledged that *Gallaher* has never been entirely free from controversy in Commonwealth trademark circles.[5] Moreover, in an age where cigarette manufacturers are required in many jurisdictions to sell their products in "plain packaging," deliberately designed by the state to be as unattractive as possible, it is tempting to dismiss this case as being a product of a different time. In fact, however, in a registration-based system, *Gallaher* represents the natural consequence of bringing rights over advertising within the trademark owner's exclusive domain. For readers more familiar with the U.S. use-based system, this may seem like a surprising assertion, since there was no danger of consumer confusion. The defendant's health promotion packet was not for sale and no rival product was being touted. The defendant in this case was not intending to refer to the plaintiff's goods and the plaintiff was not required to lead evidence to demonstrate that consumers who saw the defendant's packet had the plaintiff's product brought to mind. Nor was the plaintiff required to demonstrate harm to its reputation or the value of

[4] [1982] F. S. R. 464 (H.C.) (Ir.).

[5] *See* D.R. Shanahan, Australian Law of Trade Marks and Passing Off 337 (2d ed. 1990); Robert Burrell & Michael Handler, Australian Trade Mark Law 375 (2d ed. 2016) (discussing in particular the Court's conclusions as to whether "use of a mark" has to be "use in the course of trade").

its brand and, in any event, it should be noted that protection against dilution did not form part of old Irish law (i.e., prior to European harmonization). What we see in this case therefore is the trademark owner being given a strong form of control over the use of its mark in advertising. But this feature of the case is not anomalous. Rather, it is the product of the normal mechanics of registration.

To understand why *Gallaher* is unremarkable, it is useful to review how infringement is dealt with in a registration-based trademark system. Such systems invariably provide trademark owners with strong rights to prevent use of identical marks in relation to the goods or services for which the mark is registered (as was found to have occurred in *Gallaher*). In some jurisdictions, including the European Union, New Zealand, and the United Kingdom, this is conceptualized as "double identity" infringement and attracts a form of strict liability, subject to the defendant being able to bring itself within an exception.[6] Moreover, even in jurisdictions that do not formally separate out double identity, such as Australia, infringement analysis tends to end up in much the same place: if the defendant has used an identical mark for identical goods the burden will fall on the defendant to bring itself within some form of exception. At the international level, this approach receives strong support from the TRIPS Agreement, which in Article 16(1) provides:

> The owner of a registered trademark shall have the exclusive right to prevent all third parties not having the owner's consent from using in the course of trade identical or similar signs for goods or services which are identical or similar to those in respect of which the trademark is registered where such use would result in a likelihood of confusion. *In case of the use of an identical sign for identical goods or services, a likelihood of confusion shall be presumed* . . .[7]

The justification for making special provision for double identity cases is almost invariably framed by reference to the branding of goods. The argument is that the placement of an identical mark on identical products must give rise to at least a presumption of confusion. It therefore follows that the defendant should only be able to escape liability by demonstrating that it falls within an exception. There is something in this argument, although it is worth noting that it does not hold entirely, even for branding of goods cases. This is because the process of registration

[6] In the European Union and the United Kingdom, double identity infringement provisions have been interpreted to require that the use has adversely affected one of the "functions" of the mark. This requirement functions as a *de facto* defense, although technically it is a precondition for the establishment of liability. For discussion, *see, e.g.*, Luis Porangaba, *A Contextual Account of the Trade Mark Functions Theory*, INTELL. PROP. Q. 230 (2018) (arguing that the functions enquiry serves to bring contextual considerations into the infringement analysis, much like the Commonwealth "use as a trademark" doctrine). The role of a functions analysis is discussed in more detail, below.

[7] Agreement on Trade-Related Aspects of Intellectual Property Rights, art. 16(1), Apr. 15, 1994, Marrakesh Agreement Establishing the World Trade Organization, Annex 1C, 1869 U.N.T.S. 299, 33 I.L.M. 1197 (1994) (emphasis added).

produces a bureaucratized species of property right that sits some way removed from the signs encountered by consumers in the marketplace. Under a registration-based system, the plaintiff's trademark will be the sign that appears on the register. If the plaintiff has registered a word mark, the plaintiff's monopoly will extend to that word written in any script and reproduced in any color. The fact that the brand name that appears on the goods is rendered in a pink cursive font will not limit the scope of the plaintiff's protection. The use of the same word but rendered in a different font and different color will therefore still constitute use of an identical mark. The plaintiff's trademark will then be compared with the sign used by the defendant. However, this sign will have to be isolated from a mass of other material. Extraneous matter, such as differences in the color or shape of goods or differences in the type of packaging or general labeling employed, will be excluded from the analysis. Moreover, even when it comes to comparing the words themselves, it is possible that minor variations in orthography will be overlooked—identity may not mean absolute identity, even once the analysis has been confined to a textual comparison.[8]

Similar points can be made about the goods and services enquiry. When asking whether the defendant's goods and services are identical to those provided by the trademark owner, we are primarily concerned with the scope of the registration. The question is whether the goods and services provided by the defendant fall within the specification set out on the register. Consequently, provided the trademark owner has been careful to specify its products using broad terminology, its monopoly will extend beyond the goods or services it actually offers. Again, this is part of the ordinary mechanics of registration. It has always been accepted that it is possible to push out the boundaries of protection through the way the specification is drafted.[9] Admittedly, there is growing concern in many jurisdictions over the

[8] In the European Union and the United Kingdom it is clear that slight variations will not necessarily preclude a finding of identity. Case No. C-291/00, LTJ Diffusion S.A. v. Sadas Vertbaudet S.A., [2003] E. C. R. I-2799, [54] ("A sign is identical with the trade mark where it reproduces, without any modification or addition, all the elements constituting the trade mark or where, viewed as a whole, it contains differences so insignificant that they may go unnoticed by the average consumer"). The U.K. cases have, however, been far from consistent in how this test has been applied. *Compare* United Airlines Inc v. United Airways Ltd [2011] E. W. H. C. 2411 (Ch.), [41] (UNITED AIRLINES and UNITED AIRWAYS held identical on an application for summary judgment) *with* Bayer Cropscience SA v. Agropharm [2004] E. W. H. C. 1661 (Ch.), [34] (serious issue to be tried as to whether PATRIOT C and PATRIOT P are identical to PATRIOT). *See also* Belinda Isaac & Rajiv Joshi, *What Does Identical Mean*? 27 Eur. Intell. Prop. Rev. 184 (2005). In New Zealand, the Office has indicated that it is guided by *LTJ Diffusion: Trade Marks Practice Guidelines Relative Grounds—Identical or Similar Trade Marks*, Intellectual Property Office of New Zealand, https://www.iponz.govt.nz/about-ip/trade-marks/practice-guidelines (last visited June 15, 2021). New Zealand courts have also been content to cite *LTJ Diffusion*, but have tended towards a restrictive interpretation of the sorts of differences that can be discounted. *See, e.g.*, Australasian Conference Association Ltd v. A Little Bit of Britain Ltd [2018] N. Z. H. C. 2501 (WEETABIX not identical to WEET-BIX).

[9] *See, e.g.*, Report of Committee Appointed during 1938 by the Then Attorney-General to Consider What Alterations Are Desirable in the Trade Marks Law of the Commonwealth [33] (1954) (noting that toothpaste manufacturers could legitimately broaden their sphere of protection by describing their goods as "dentifrices" rather than "toothpastes" and implicitly accepting that in so doing they would not open themselves up to a challenge on the grounds of non-use). More recently,

use of very broad terminology in specifications.[10] This may eventually lead to prohibitions on claims for terms such as "computer software" or "clothing" that cover a huge array of goods and that stretch across markets that are segmented in terms of price point, trade channels and the characteristics of the average consumer. But even if the use of certain broad terms comes to be prohibited, the overall point about the nature of registration remains—it will always be possible to draft a claim that goes beyond the scope of the use. Even if a claim for "clothing" comes to be regarded as impermissibly broad, there is no suggestion that a claim for "leather garments" would not be regarded as acceptable at the point of registration. Moreover, it seems likely to remain the case that use in relation to, say, leather jackets would preserve such a registration in its entirety.[11]

Registration therefore creates a sphere of exclusivity around a mark that cannot be justified solely by reference to the need to prevent consumer confusion. From the owner's perspective, this creates a degree of exclusive space for its brand. From a public policy perspective, however, this additional degree of protection requires some other justification. The most plausible justification lies in some combination of: (i) ensuring that traders have an incentive to register their marks because of the informational benefits that flow from having a widely used, publicly accessible register; and (ii) enforcement costs—strict liability in double identity cases lowers the costs of enforcing rights and, on balance, it makes sense to apply a presumption in favor of the trademark owner in cases where consumers are most likely to suffer harm, even if at the margins this results in liability going beyond what a confusion-based analysis would warrant.[12] When these considerations are taken into account, a double identity rule is largely unobjectionable insofar as we are dealing with the branding of goods.

In contrast, when one turns to the right to prevent use of a trademark in advertising, it is far less clear that a double identity rule can be justified. The difficulty is that advertisements can carry a whole host of non-confusing messages. An unauthorized third party may need to include a trademark in an advertisement in order to indicate that it sells, repairs, or provides reviews of the trademarked goods.

something of this idea can be seen in Sky Plc v. Skykick UK Ltd [2020] E. W. H. C. 990 (Ch.), [28] ("[A]s the non-use cases show, even in that context proprietors also have a legitimate interest in seeking a modest penumbra of protection extending beyond the specific goods and services in relation to which use had been proved.").

[10] In the United Kingdom these concerns have been brought into sharp relief by the Sky/Skykick litigation which showed up gaps in the European legislative framework. Case No. C-371/18, Sky Plc v. Skykick UK Ltd, ECLI:EU:C:2020:45 (Jan. 29, 2020); *Sky Plc*, *supra* note 9.

[11] *Cf.* Turok v. Deluxe Holding AG [2012] A.T.M.O. 105 (Austl.). For discussion, *see* Robert Burrell & Michael Handler, *(Re)Claiming Trade Mark Protection*, *in* RESEARCH HANDBOOK ON TRADEMARK LAW REFORM (Graeme B. Dinwoodie & Mark D. Janis eds., 2021).

[12] For a more developed version of this argument, *see* Robert Burrell, *Rethinking the Relationship between Registered and Unregistered Trade Marks*, *in* ACROSS INTELLECTUAL PROPERTY: ESSAYS IN HONOUR OF SAM RICKETSON (Graeme W. Austin et al. eds., 2020). On enforcement costs more generally, *see* Robert Bone, *Enforcement Costs and Trademark Puzzles*, 90 VIRGINIA L. REV. 2099 (2004).

There are also strong pro-competition reasons for allowing comparative advertising, that is, to allow traders to indicate that they sell products that are an alternative to or a replacement for the trademarked goods. These are merely illustrations. There are many other types of use in advertising that will not give rise to confusion. This is a lesson that ought to have been learned, if it had not been learned before, from keyword advertising cases and other cases involving use of marks in the online environment. Take, for example, the Australian case of *Veda Advantage Ltd v. Malouf Group Enterprises Pty Ltd*,[13] a Federal Court decision from 2016. In that case the plaintiff was a data analytics company that provided credit reports to lending institutions and was the registered owner of VEDA for financial services. It brought infringement proceedings against a party that had purchased Google AdWords containing the term "veda," which were used to generate advertisements for its credit repair services, which promised potential users a way to "Fix Your Veda File Now" and "Fix Your Veda History." Cases like this do not fall comfortably within established categories of when nominative use ought to be permissible—it is not a case involving repair, retail, or comparative advertising—and yet is exactly the sort of case where unauthorized use benefits consumers. This raises questions about the best way to deal with these sorts of uses. One possibility is a broad and flexible nominative use exception, but another is for the advertising right to be recast and, at a minimum, taken outside the scope of the double identity rule.

The suggestion that use in advertising might need to be treated differently from use on goods is not without historical precedent. Most notably, in *Singer Manufacturing Company v. Wilson*,[14] Jessel M.R. indicated that a distinction should be drawn between two categories of case that are "of a totally different character" from one another. The first category of cases involves the branding of goods. In this type of case,

> it is quite immaterial that the maker of the goods to which, what I will call for the sake of shortness, the trade-mark, is affixed, did not know that it was a trade-mark, and had not the slightest intention of defrauding anybody . . . and he would be restrained by injunction though he thought he himself had invented the trade-mark and *bona fide* intended it to designate goods of his own manufacture.[15]

In contrast, in cases other than those involving the branding of goods, "as in every other case of fraud—for it must be fraud—the case must be proved."[16] Jessel M.R. drew this distinction in a case where the defendant had used the word "Singer" as a generic description of the type of sewing machine he manufactured

[13] [2016] F.C.A. 255 (Austl.).
[14] (1876) 2 Ch. D 434 (C.A.) (Eng.).
[15] *Id.* at 441–42.
[16] *Id.* at 444.

in advertisements and price lists, but had invariably included a statement making it clear that he was the manufacturer of the goods.[17] Significantly, moreover, his Lordship justified this distinction by reference to the need to permit comparative-type advertising.[18]

The Court of Appeal affirmed summary judgment[19] in favor of the defendant and was, with one qualification discussed below, supportive of the idea that "trademark cases" and "advertising cases" needed to be distinguished. The distinction did not, however, survive. On appeal to the House of Lords,[20] Lord Cairns rejected the suggestion that there was a categorical difference between use on goods and use in advertising. His Lordship took a very a different approach to the possibility that the defendant's advertisements might cause confusion, noting that they might be read by "common workmen and workwomen having very few and very limited ideas, and a very imperfect knowledge upon the subject of [sewing] machines."[21] Putting to one side the unflattering description of the cognitive ability of working class consumers, this statement revealed a fear that consumers might only know that they wanted a "singer sewing machine" and would not realize that the defendant was not the original manufacturer of such machines.

For the modern reader concerned about the progressive expansion of trademark law, Lord Cairns' speech is problematic not only for its elitist overtones. There is force in the argument that situations of this type might equally be characterized as involving consumers who are content with a "singer-style" machine and are indifferent to the identity of the manufacturer. Indeed, this case could be said to illustrate one of the drivers of trademark expansion: the failure to be clear as to when misconception or uncertainty on the part of consumers causes genuine harm of a type that the law should intervene to prevent.[22]

Nevertheless, in rejecting the idea that advertising cases should be governed by separate principles, Lord Cairns was motivated by concerns that need to be taken seriously. Whereas Jessel M.R. focused on the "obvious" desirability of allowing comparative-type advertising, Lord Cairns posited the example of a false "representation made by advertisements that the articles sold at a particular shop are articles manufactured by A. B." It was not long, moreover, before courts were

[17] *Id.* at 438.
[18] *See id.* at 447 (discussing a hypothetical producer of "German champagne" wishing to use the names of famous French champagne houses as a reference point to explain the qualities of its products).
[19] This is an anachronism. To be precise, Jessel M.R. issued a decree in favour of the defendant, having concluded that it was unnecessary to hear the defendant's evidence. This was a procedural innovation and one that was heavily criticized by the House of Lords on further appeal. This complicates the interpretation of the case and a close reading suggests that a majority of their Lordships (Lords Blackburn and Gordon) were open to the idea that advertising cases should be treated differently. This is not, however, the path that the law took, and the point being made here is that there are good reasons for not rushing to embrace the use on goods/use in advertising distinction.
[20] (1877) L.R. 3 H.L. 376, 390.
[21] *Id.* at 390.
[22] Mark Lemley & Mark McKenna, *Irrelevant Confusion*, 62 STANFORD L. REV. 413 (2010).

confronted with advertising cases in which it was impossible to have sympathy for the defendant. For instance, in the 1888 case of *Jay v. Ladler*, an injunction was granted to prevent the defendant's use of a device consisting of a "lady and a bear" in circulars advertising its business as a furrier, this being similar to the device used by the plaintiff and registered in relation to a limited range of furrier's goods.[23] This result seems uncontroversial, and it is important to remember that there are advertising-type uses that unquestionably cause consumer confusion. To take a hypothetical example, consider a beer tent set up at a street festival that has a sign outside which states, falsely, "All of our beers come from the METROPOLIS microbrewery." A consumer going into the tent will assume that all of the beers that he or she sees have been brewed by Metropolis. Moreover, even if the consumer is familiar with some Metropolis products, he or she may be unsurprised and untroubled to be confronted with a series of beers with unfamiliar names, since microbreweries tend to innovate regularly with their product lines. There is no reasonable argument that this sort of misleading use ought to be allowed within our existing trademark paradigm. Indeed, even if trademark protection were to be cut back drastically to a right to prevent counterfeiting, there would still be a strong argument that this type of use should be prohibited.

The above illustrations do not take us quite so far as being able to conclude that use in advertising should attract double identity protection. It might be argued that all that has been demonstrated is that trademarks can be used in advertisements in a range of different ways, pointing to the need for a fact-intensive enquiry of precisely the type that the double identity rule seeks to sidestep. However, it must also be acknowledged that although it is useful for analytical purposes to refer to "use in advertising," this is not a fixed or stable concept. This means there would be real difficulties in using this idea as the basis of a coherent legal category, for instance that sits outside of double identity provisions. In the case of service marks, in particular, there would be profound difficulties in drawing a line between advertising use and use in immediate relation to the services, as where the mark is used on a shop front, on sandwich boards placed in close proximity to the premises, and so forth. Some indication of the difficulty of demarcating a separate category of use in advertising can even be seen in *Singer v. Wilson*, which was decided long before the protection of service marks began to be discussed. In the Court of Appeal, Mellish L.J. qualified his acceptance of the idea that use on goods and use in advertising could be distinguished, noting that if the defendant "had put up a label in his shop stating 'The Singer Machine sold here,' or something like that, unqualified in any way, I should have had great doubt whether that was not a wrongful act."[24] But if there is no bright line distinction between use on the goods and use on an advertisement in a shop in immediate proximity to the goods, it is difficult to see how

[23] (1888) 40 Ch. D 649 (Ch) (Eng.).
[24] (1876) 2 Ch. D 434, 460 (C.A.) (Eng.).

such a distinction could be drawn between use in an advertisement in the shop and use in advertisement immediately outside the shop, and so forth.

Ultimately, therefore, there is a compelling argument that the most conceptually coherent way of dealing with advertising-type uses in a registration-based system is to accept that double identity liability attaches, but to ensure that defendants have the benefit of a robust exception. In other words, this is one of the areas of trademark law where problems of overexpansion cannot be avoided by demanding robust evidence of confusion or a dilution-based harm.[25] It is this feature that makes use in advertising such a valuable vehicle for thinking about trademark exceptions generally.

II. Designing a Workable Exception

If we are going to rely on exceptions to facilitate forms of advertising that are unlikely to cause confusion/are likely be welfare enhancing, close attention needs to be paid to questions of legislative drafting. There is now a significant body of literature that can inform our thinking on these questions. In the copyright context in particular, considerable attention has been given to the design of exceptions, with theoretical literature supported by a growing body of empirical evidence.[26] This literature offers important insights, including on the critical question of the relationship between legislative design and judicial interpretation. Drawing on the insights from this literature, this section uses three case studies to illustrate some of the issues that have arisen in relation to existing exceptions for advertising use, and some of the traps that need to be avoided.

A. Nominative Use in the European Union

The first case study is the harmonized European trademark system. It will be argued that there are numerous flaws in the European legislative framework, as the exceptions relating to nominative use are both limited and fragmented. This was particularly true under the original legislative framework, but even under the revised 2015 legislation significant problems remain.

Under the original framework, the most general nominative use provision permitted unauthorized use of a sign where "necessary to indicate the intended purpose of a product or service, in particular as accessories or spare parts," provided the use was "in accordance with honest practices in industrial or commercial

[25] *Cf.* Burrell & Gangjee, *supra* note 2.

[26] For a particularly important recent contribution, *see* Emily Hudson, Drafting Copyright Exceptions: From the Law in Books to the Law in Action (2020).

matters."[27] Case law interpreting this provision was, admittedly, not uniformly restrictive. For example, the Court of Justice of the European Union ("CJEU") indicated that independent traders offering maintenance and repair services might be able to avail themselves of the exception when using a mark to indicate the nature of their services.[28] In a subsequent decision, however, the CJEU clarified that in order for the use of a mark to be "necessary" there must be no other way of conveying the same information,[29] such that use would not be justifiable in circumstances where the defendant might instead have referenced "technical standards or norms generally used for the type of product marketed by the third party and known to the public for which that type of product is intended."[30] Even more importantly, the operation of the exception was always cabined by the requirement that the defendant establish that its use was for the purpose of indicating "the intended purpose" of a product or service. This left a huge range of referential uses outside the scope of the exception, including parodies, other critical forms of reference, and, most relevantly for present purposes, a host of non-confusing forms of advertisement, including many uses of trademarks as keywords.

The restricted nature of the "intended purpose" exception was such that even the advertisement of onsold and secondhand goods was not normally covered. The objective of this exception was limited to the sale and advertisement of "goods or services which are supplementary to the goods or services offered by a trade mark proprietor."[31] The advertising and sale of onsold and secondhand goods therefore largely fell to be dealt with under the "exhaustion provision." It was clear from an early stage that the exhaustion or first sale doctrine developed by the Court of Justice (largely in the period before trademark law was harmonized) must allow for some unauthorized use of a mark in marketing and advertising material. However, in developing the exhaustion doctrine, the Court also always envisaged that the sale and marketing of a product in an altered condition might take a defendant outside the scope of the exhaustion exception.[32] This body of case law was codified under the harmonized regime, with the Directive establishing a statutory exhaustion exception, but one that did "not apply where there exist legitimate reasons for the proprietor to oppose further commercialisation of the goods, especially where the condition of the goods is changed or impaired after they have been put on the market."[33] In decisions interpreting the harmonized regime, the Court of Justice

[27] Directive 2008/95/EC, of the European Parliament and of the Council of Oct. 22, 2008 to Approximate the Laws of the Member States Relating to Trade Marks, 2001 O.J. (L 299), art. 6(1)(c).

[28] Case No. C-63/97, BMW v. Deenik, [1999] ECR I-905, [61].

[29] Case No. C-228/03, The Gillette Company v. LA-Laboratories, [2005] E. C. R. I-2337, [39].

[30] *Id.* at [36].

[31] *BMW*, *supra* note 28, at [61]; Case No. C-558/08, Portakabin Ltd v. Primakabin BV [2010] E. C. R. I-6963, [67].

[32] Case No. C-102/77 Hoffmann-La Roche & Co. AG v. Centrafarm, [1978] E. C. R. 1139 (dealing with the repackaging of pharmaceuticals).

[33] *See originally* First Council Directive 89/104/EEC, of Dec. 21, 1988 to approximate the laws of the Member States relating to trade marks, 1989 O.J. (L 40), art. 7; and, thereafter, Directive 2008/95/EC,

confirmed and refined its earlier approach: the exhaustion doctrine can permit use in advertising, but subject to some significant limitations. Most importantly, in *Christian Dior v. Evora* it was held that when dealing with "prestigious, luxury goods" resellers are under an obligation not to "act unfairly in relation to the legitimate interests of the trade mark owner." Resellers must endeavor to prevent their advertising from "affecting the value of the trade mark by detracting from the allure and prestigious image of the goods in question and from their aura of luxury."[34] In a subsequent cases dealing with more mundane goods, the Court of Justice held that resellers must avoid "damaging the image" of the mark.[35]

The need to preserve reputation and brand image was even more apparent in cases dealing with comparative advertising, which was and is dealt with separately from the categories set out above. The CJEU held, after a period of uncertainty, that comparative advertising was only permissible where the defendant satisfied the requirements of Article 4 of the Misleading and Comparative Advertising Directive,[36] a separate legal instrument that seeks to delineate between permissible and impermissible forms of comparative advertising generally. The consequence of aligning trademark law with this Directive was to exclude *inter alia* advertisements that did not "objectively compare material, relevant, verifiable and representative features" of goods and services; that "discredit or denigrate the trade marks … goods, services, activities or circumstances of a competitor"; that "take unfair advantage of the reputation of a trade mark"; or that "present goods or services as imitations or replicas of goods or services bearing a protected trade mark." The combined effect of these limitations is dramatic and serves to push comparative advertisements toward being dull, direct, unimaginative, and humorless.

The original E.U. framework governing nominative use therefore suffered from a range of defects. The provisions failed to deliver flexibility. But they also failed to deliver certainty, as numerous elements served to make their operation unpredictable: the requirements of "necessity" and use "in accordance with honest practices" for the general exception; the limitation that an owner might have "legitimate reasons" for opposing the further commercialization of the goods in the exhaustion exception; and the malleable and unpredictable restrictions on the scope of the comparative advertising defense. These problems are reminiscent of those that plagued copyright law in the United Kingdom prior to 2014, when U.K. copyright exceptions were liberalized.[37] As Justice Laddie famously put it:

of the European Parliament and of the Council of Oct. 22, 2008 to approximate the laws of the Member States relating to trade marks, 2008 O.J. (L 299), art. 7.

[34] Case No. C-337/95, Parfums Christian Dior SA v. Evora BV, [1997] E. C. R. I-6013, [45].

[35] *Portakabin, supra* note 31, at [91].

[36] *See* Directive 2006/114/EC, of the European Parliament and of the Council of Dec. 12, 2006 Concerning Misleading and Comparative Advertising, 2006 O.J. (L 376) 21.

[37] The 2014 reforms were the most significant reform of U.K. copyright exceptions in more than a century. A number of new exceptions were introduced and many of the existing provisions were

> It is as if every tiny exception to the grasp of the copyright monopoly has had to be fought hard for, prised out of the unwilling hand of the legislature and, once conceded, defined precisely and confined within high and immutable walls. This approach also assumes that Parliament can foresee, and therefore legislate for, all possible circumstances in which allowing copyright to be enforced would be unjustified.[38]

Once issues of judicial interpretation were added (which at times involved copyright exceptions being construed in far narrower terms than their language required), the only real certainty was that a whole raft of socially desirable re-uses of copyright material were prohibited.

Under the revised European framework governing trademarks, the general nominative use provision has been expanded with the express intention of allowing a broader range of referential uses. Some additional degree of flexibility has therefore been introduced into the system. Recital 27 of the 2015 Trade Marks Directive refers both to the need to allow "third parties to draw the consumer's attention to the resale of genuine goods" and to the "use of a trade mark by third parties for the purpose of artistic expression." This more permissive approach is reflected in Article 14 of the new Directive, which refers to allowing a trademark to be used "for the purpose of identifying or referring to goods or services as those of the proprietor of that trade mark, in particular, where the use of the trade mark is necessary to indicate the intended purpose of a product or service, in particular as accessories or spare parts." The shift to a more liberal approach is unquestionably welcome and, for the purposes of this chapter, is particularly important for advertisers of secondhand and onsold goods. Significant problems nevertheless remain. These problems flow in particular from the open-ended criteria that defendants must satisfy and from the fragmented and overlapping nature of the exceptions.

The general nominative use exception remains subject to the proviso that the use be "in accordance with honest practices in industrial or commercial matters." At first glance this is unobjectionable—after all, it would be unusual to suggest that defendants should be allowed to engage in *dishonest* commercial practices. However, the honest practices bar does not merely serve to exclude deliberately misleading or fraudulent conduct on the part of defendants.[39] Rather, the CJEU has interpreted this requirement as imposing a duty on the defendant to "act fairly

reformed. Together these changes have the capacity to have a significant liberalizing effect, but as yet the cases have not provided courts with the opportunity to confirm that the law is now on a different track.

[38] Hugh Laddie, *Copyright: Over-Strength, Over-Regulated, Over-Rated?*, 18 Eur. Intell. Prop. Rev. 253, 258 (1996).

[39] In fairness, it might be noted that this language has its origins in art. 10bis of the Paris Convention for the Protection of Industrial Property and in this context it serves to demarcate acts of unfair competition against which Member States are required to afford "effective protection." This suggests that "honest practices" should be given a broad reading.

in relation to the legitimate interests of the trade mark proprietor."[40] Again, this is not necessarily objectionable. Our experience with copyright exceptions suggests that an open-ended standard limited by a general test of fairness may well be the best option available to us. The problem lies in the way the test of "fairness" has been developed.

The CJEU has indicated that when assessing whether the defendant's use was fair, tribunals are to look at all the circumstances, including the defendant's knowledge, the efforts made to minimize harm to the trademark owner, the precise nature of the use made by the defendant, whether the use was liable to create the impression that there is a commercial connection between the defendant and the plaintiff, and whether the use adversely affects the value of the mark.[41] These criteria are to be welcomed insofar as they focus attention on whether the trademark owner has suffered a type of legally cognizable harm, which in the E.U. context includes various forms of dilution. This approach is not tautologous and does not make the exceptions redundant, since it must be remembered that the nominative use provisions, in the advertising context in particular, serve to modify the impact of the double identity rule. The problem with the fairness criteria used to assess whether the defendant's use was in accordance with honest practices is not therefore that these criteria focus on the question of harm. Rather, it is that they place weight on other extraneous considerations, such as the defendant's knowledge. The most troubling feature, however, is the thread running through cases like *Christian Dior* and *Portakabin* that defendants must strive to preserve brand image and hence brand value. This requirement adds a level of unpredictability to the nominative use exception and has the potential to introduce additional costs for traders whose business models may depend on thin margins (a particular issue for those advertising and selling secondhand and onsold goods). Furthermore, at least in conceptual terms, this factor seems to create an obligation that goes beyond the reach of blurring and tarnishing, there being nothing in the cases to suggest that a defendant can discharge its obligation to preserve brand value simply by showing that its actions were unlikely to cause either form of harm.

The obligation to preserve brand value is also relevant to the way in which the expanded nominative use and exhaustion exceptions are likely to intersect. As has been seen, the 2015 amendments have brought the advertising and selling of secondhand and onsold goods within the ambit of the general nominative use defense. But an essentially unaltered exhaustion provision continues to apply.[42] As a general matter, the existence of overlapping exceptions is not necessarily the boon

[40] This is now firmly established. *See, e.g., BMW, supra* note 28, at [36], [61].

[41] *See* Case No. C-228/03, The Gillette Company v. LA-Laboratories, [2005] E. C. R. I-2337, [42]–[46]; *Portakabin, supra* note 31, at [67]; Case No. C-245/02, Anheuser-Busch Inc. v. Budějovický Budvar, národní podnik, [2004] E. C. R. I-10989, [56].

[42] See Directive 2015/2436, of The European Parliament and of The Council of Dec. 16, 2015 to Approximate the Laws of the Member States Relating to Trade Marks, 2015 O.J. (L 336), art. 15.

to defendants that it might first appear, a point that will be explored in more detail in the second case study. The immediate concern, however, lies in the continued limitation that the exhaustion defense shall not apply in cases where the trademark proprietor has legitimate reasons for opposing further commercialization of the goods, in particular where the condition of the goods is changed or impaired. It seems likely that this limitation will be read across from the exhaustion provision to the reformulated nominative use exception. The proposition that trademark proprietors have a right to object to the resale of changed or impaired products is such a longstanding feature of E.U. trademark law it seems inevitable that the honest practices proviso will be applied in ways that produce coterminous outcomes. The effect is, once again, to extend the rights of the trademark owner beyond their usual boundaries: the notion of a "changed" product in particular is potentially extremely broad. It might mean, for example, that a car manufacturer would have grounds for objecting to the advertisement and commercial sale[43] of a family car that had been significantly altered by the addition of a larger engine, spoiler, and sports body parts. Admittedly, it might be possible to make the case that the resale of a car in such an altered condition would be permissible under the guidance developed by the CJEU. In an important article, Annette Kur has developed the argument that E.U. law can generally be interpreted in such a way as to permit the sale of repaired or refurbished goods, a result that can be justified *inter alia* by environmental goals.[44] However, in discussing the sale of secondhand cars, Kur does not go as far as to conclude that the advertisement and sale of a "souped-up" or "hot-rodded" car would be permissible.[45] She also refrains from concluding that the Munich District court erred in finding for the plaintiff in a case involving the advertisement and sale of reconditioned WLAN router boxes. More generally, Kur notes that the permissibility of the use will depend on a close analysis of the nature of the market, the attitude of consumers and the specifics of the use, all of which create uncertainty for potential defendants and hence a significant potential chilling effect.

It can therefore be concluded that the E.U. exceptions relevant to advertising remain unsatisfactory. The provisions governing nominative use and exhaustion still have the tendency to extend the rights of the trademark owner beyond their usual bounds. The way in which the provisions might apply is also highly unpredictable. They cannot therefore even be defended on the basis that although they are under-inclusive, they at least offer certainty. The circumstances in which comparative

[43] A purely private sale would not engage the rights of the trademark owner since the use would not be "use in the course of trade." *See* Case No. C-206/01, Arsenal Football Club plc v. Reed, [2002] E. C. R. I-10273, [40].

[44] Annette Kur, *"As Good as New"—Sale of Repaired or Refurbished Goods: Commendable Practice or Trade Mark Infringement?*, 70 GRUR INT'L 228 (2021).

[45] *Id.* at 230 (noting that sale of a car might be permissible with "small scratches or indents in the body parts" or following the exchange of a "motor or brakes").

advertising is permissible also remain narrow. Overall therefore, it is clear that the E.U. provisions governing use in advertising leave much to be desired.

However, before moving on to the second case study, it is important to acknowledge that no consideration has yet been given to the role that a "functions analysis" might play. A defender of the E.U. regime might stress the potential importance of this additional safety valve developed by the CJEU. In brief outline, the CJEU has modified the strict nature the double identity rule by holding that there will be no double identity infringement where the defendant's use does not affect any of the functions of the mark. These functions go beyond the "essential function" of indicating origin and include quality guarantee, investment, communication, and advertising functions. Importantly, the CJEU has used a functions analysis to create additional breathing space for advertisers. Most notably, in *Google France*[46] the CJEU employed a functions analysis in such a way as to facilitate keyword advertising. There are, however, at least two reasons why it seems unlikely that a functions analysis will solve the problems identified here. The first is that *Google France* was handed down before the liberalization of the nominative use provisions, and there is little reason to believe that the CJEU would seek to employ the functions doctrine in a way that goes beyond the new legislative settlement. The second is that *Google France* may in any event reflect certain narrow concerns of the CJEU to protect the "ordinary" operation of the internet, a concern that can also be seen for example in copyright cases dealing with hyperlinking and framing.[47] It therefore seems unlikely that a functions analysis would have much additional work to do in many of the types of case considered here, a conclusion that Kur also reaches.[48]

In short, the European Union has not got use in advertising right, but the problems with its provisions are instructive as regards how a better advertising-related exception might be drafted. In addition, the E.U. experience alerts us to a further lesson: in the examples of nominative use developed above, advertising and sale were frequently treated together. This is because cases involving the resale of goods will generally involve two potential acts of infringement: the use of the mark in advertising and marketing material, and the sale of goods under the sign. This is by no means true of all use in advertising cases: comparative advertisements, many types of keyword advertising and use on complementary goods or services will generally turn solely on use of the sign in advertisements and/or marketing material. Nevertheless, the resale cases should remind us that right to control use in advertising cannot always be viewed in isolation. There are other types of case where we will have to rely on exceptions (broadly conceived) to modify the impact

[46] Joined Cases Nos. C-236/08 to 238/08, Google France SARL v. Louis Vuitton Malletier SA, [2010] E. C. R. I-2417.

[47] *Cf.* Case No. C-160/15 GS Media BV v. Sanoma Media Netherlands BV (2016) ECLI:EU:C:2016:644; Case No. C-392/19 VG Bild-Kunst v. Stiftung PreuBishcher Kulturbesitz (2021) ECLI:EU:C:2021:181.

[48] Kur, *supra* note 44, at 229.

of the double identity rule. This helps suggest that to be effective any exception needs to be framed in broad rather than narrow terms.

B. Use as a Trademark in Australia

If the E.U. exceptions dealing with nominative use remain unsatisfactory, even under the revised legislative framework, then Australia might seem to offer a more promising model for how to implement a robust exception to permit use in advertising. Under Australian law there is a general requirement that, to be infringing, the defendant's use must be "use as a mark." This means that it is only use of a sign as a badge of origin that will infringe. Other types of use, including descriptive use, decorative use, and, most importantly for present purposes, nominative use, will not infringe. The use as a trademark doctrine has proven itself to be a flexible and valuable tool in keeping trademark rights within appropriate bounds. This doctrine meant that Australian courts had little difficulty in crafting a sensible set of rules to deal with keyword advertising, as evidenced by the Federal Court finding for the defendant in the *Veda Advantage* case, the facts of which are set out above.[49] The trademark use doctrine also means that comparative advertising will generally not infringe. In this respect the law remains much as laid down by the House of Lords in the 1934 case, *Irving's Yeast-Vite Ltd v. Horsenail.*[50]

Moreover, it is interesting to note that the leading Australian authority on use as a trademark, the decision of the High Court in *Shell Co of Australia Ltd v. Esso Standard Oil (Australia) Ltd*, involved use in advertising.[51] That case concerned a dispute over an anthropomorphic character made to resemble a drop of oil that had been featured in a television advertisement. The plaintiff argued that the advertisement infringed its trademark for a similar character, but this was rejected on the basis that the defendant had not used its character as a trademark. Similar results can be seen in more recent cases handed down by lower-level courts. For example, in *Hoser v. Sportsbet Pty Ltd*,[52] Robertson J in the Federal Court of Australia held that the use in a television advertisement of the phrase "Oi, snake man" to attract the attention of a fictional character dressed as a snake charmer did not involve use of the words "snake man" as a trademark. Similarly, in *Metricon Homes Pty Ltd v. Zac Homes Pty Ltd*,[53] a 2021 decision of the Federal Circuit Court, it was held that the use of the phrases "love where you live" and "you love where you live"

[49] *See generally* Robert Burrell & Michael Handler, *Keyword Advertising and Actionable Consumer Confusion*, in RESEARCH HANDBOOK ON INTELLECTUAL PROPERTY AND DIGITAL TECHNOLOGIES 426 (Tanya Aplin ed., 2020).

[50] (1934) 51 R.P.C. 110 (HL). This doctrine began to emerge in the 1920s. *See in particular* Edward Young & Co Ltd v. Grierson, Oldham & Co Ltd (1924) 41 R.P.C. 548 (CA) 577.

[51] (1963) 109 C.L.R. 407 (Austl.).

[52] [2018] F.C.A. 1557 (Austl.).

[53] [2021] F.C.C.A. 394 (Austl.).

in radio and online advertisements for "knock down and rebuild" building services did not constitute use as a mark.

Beyond cases solely involving use in advertising, we find instances of the trademark use doctrine being deployed to facilitate both the act of sale and accompanying advertising and promotional activities. For instance, in *Christodoulou v. Disney Enterprises Inc*, the plaintiff, who was involved in theater productions, had registered THE HUNCHBACK OF NOTRE DAME for entertainment services. He brought an action against Disney in respect of its animated films *The Hunchback of Notre Dame* and *The Hunchback of Notre Dame II*. The plaintiff's action was, however, unsuccessful—it was held that Disney's use of these words as film titles, on related goods, and in various advertisements (for example, those shown in movie theaters advertising the forthcoming release of the films) did not constitute use as a trademark. The *Christodoulou* case is also interesting insofar as it shows that the trademark use doctrine can help resolve the difficult questions around the use of the titles of public domain works as trademarks.[54] More generally, the trademark use doctrine has served as a flexible tool in Commonwealth trademark law for almost a century. It is a tool that is capable of being adapted to allow for a wide range of competition-enhancing nominative and descriptive uses, and has also proven itself useful in securing other policy objectives, including by acting as a safeguard of expressive freedom.[55]

It should come as no surprise that a defensive doctrine built around a flexible standard should be capable of successfully reconciling intellectual property protection with a range of other rights and interests. This is exactly what the fair-use doctrine in U.S. copyright law has achieved, while also helping to underpin a dynamic set of cultural industries. This is not to suggest that there might not be other ways of achieving much the same outcomes,[56] but copyright fair use unquestionably offers one template for a sensible and workable approach to designing copyright exceptions. Trademark use has much the same character, and there is some irony that it forms such an important part of trademark law in a jurisdiction where proposals to introduce fair use have proven so controversial. Moreover, again much as with copyright fair use, the uncertainty generated by reliance on a standard must

[54] *See also* Musidor BV v. Tansing (1994) 52 F.C.R. 363 (Austl.) (use of the words ROLLING STONES on copies of public domain recordings of live performances by The Rolling Stones was not use as a mark).

[55] *See, e.g.*, Mothercare UK Ltd v. Penguin Books Ltd [1988] R.P.C. 113 (C.A.) (Eng.). In deciding that use of the phrase "Mother Care/Other Care" as the title of a book did not amount to trademark use of the term MOTHERCARE, the court framed its judgment in a way that suggested concern for free speech interests, noting that the book was "a serious sociological study of the problems facing working mothers" and that Mothercare's action had been motivated by discomfort with the book's central thesis. *Id.* at 115. For discussion, *see* Patricia Loughlan, *Protecting Culturally Significant Uses of Trade Marks (Without a First Amendment)*, Eur. Intell. Prop. Rev. 328 (2000).

[56] *See* Michael Handler & Emily Hudson, *Fair Use as an Advance on Fair Dealing? Depolarising the Debate*, *in* Cambridge Handbook of Copyright Limitations and Exceptions 140 (Shyamkrishna Balganesh et al. eds., 2021).

not be overstated. Judicial decisions and industry practice can serve to crystalize sub-rules with tolerably clear boundaries that sit under the overarching standard.[57] This has occurred in the United States in relation to copyright fair use, and can also be seen in Australian case law on trademark use in relation to comparative advertising and, increasingly, keyword advertising.

Nevertheless, for all of the strengths of the trademark use doctrine, the cases do contain some troubling nooks and crannies. When problems have emerged, they have often resulted from the seemingly innocuous premise that trademark owners are entitled to the benefit of the doubt in cases where there is uncertainty as to whether consumers would respond to the sign as a badge of origin. This approach predates the definitive establishment of the trademark use doctrine by the House of Lords in *Yeast-Vite* and can be seen, for example, in *JB Stone & Co Ltd v. Steelace Manufacturing Co Ltd*, a 1929 decision of the Court of Appeal of England and Wales. In that case, the plaintiff complained of an advertisement placed by the defendant in a trade journal offering for sale "Steelace Belting (Alligator Pattern)." In the face of conflicting evidence as to whether the trade would understand "Alligator Pattern" descriptively, it was held that the defendant had made infringing use of the word ALLIGATOR, the plaintiff being entitled to the benefit of the doubt.[58]

The impulse to err on the side of protecting the interests of trademark owners was carried over and continues to be seen in the Australian case law. For example, *Caterpillar Loader Hire (Holdings) Pty Ltd v. Caterpillar Tractor Co* dealt with the question of whether there had been trademark use of the word mark CATERPILLAR in the context of a business that was carried out under the name "Willoughby's Caterpillar Loader Hire Service." The defendant had used this phrase *inter alia* in adverts in the Yellow Pages telephone directory. The Full Federal Court accepted that there was force in the argument that "Caterpillar" merely referred to the nature of the vehicles hired out by the defendant. Ultimately, however, the Full Federal Court upheld the finding at first instance that there had been use of "Caterpillar" as a mark. At first instance one reason for this finding was the defendant's determination to incorporate Caterpillar into its name despite the fact "that at all material times, he has known of the plaintiff's objection to the inclusion of the word 'Caterpillar' in the company's business name." For Walters J, knowledge of the plaintiff's objection was sufficient to create a hint of bad faith that tipped the scales in favor of the plaintiff.[59] This suspicion of the defendant's motives was also apparent in the appeal decision, where it was said, "One may ask why the appellants should have such a fixed determination to continue to use the word 'Caterpillar' in such a prominent way."[60] It is also worth pointing out that in the course of reaching

[57] *See* HUDSON, *supra* note 26.
[58] (1929) 46 R.P.C. 402 (C.A.) (Eng.). *See in particular id.* at 420 (Slesser L.J.).
[59] (1982) 31 S.A.S.R. 80 (Austl.).
[60] (1983) 1 I.P.R. 265, 279 (Austl.).

his conclusion, the first instance judge drew on the *Steelace* decision, noting, "In my opinion, the defendants' use of the word 'Caterpillar' is closely comparable to the use of the word 'Alligator' in *JB Stone & Co Ltd v. Steelace Manufacturing Co Ltd*."[61]

A more recent example of trademark owners being given the benefit of the doubt is found in *Mantra Group Pty Ltd v. Tailly Pty Ltd (No 2)*.[62] The plaintiff had managed to secure trademark registration for CIRCLE ON CAVILL, this being the name of a block of residential apartments. The plaintiff acted as the exclusive on-site letting agency for apartments in this block, many of which were available for short-term and holiday leases. However, owners of the apartments were under no obligation to use the plaintiff's services and a sizable group of owners chose to employ the defendant's offsite letting service instead. The defendant, inevitably, chose to use the words "Circle on Cavill" in its internet advertising and marketing. Confronted with a claim for registered trademark infringement, the defendant argued that it was not using these words as a trademark, but merely as a way of describing the location and name of the apartments it managed. Worryingly, the defendant's argument was rejected on the basis that it had given undue prominence to these words, without a satisfactory explanation of why mere prominence would cause consumers to understand these words as denoting the trade origin of letting agency services, rather than the place to which such services related.[63]

Trademark use has been described as a question on which "different minds may sometimes reach different conclusions."[64] Nevertheless, there is a danger that plaintiff-preferring heuristics might at times upend the normal infringement standard under Australian law. Specifically, Australian law is normally concerned with whether the junior user's conduct is "likely to deceive or cause confusion," as judged from the perspective of the hypothetical ordinary purchaser of the goods or services in question.[65] But in trademark use cases in which the court has erred on the side of protecting trademark owners, one can see this standard being watered down. The mere possibility that there might be confusion forms the basis for

[61] (1982) 31 S.A.S.R. 80, at 91 (Austl.). This statement was made in the context of a discussion of whether the defendant could rely on an express statutory defense allowing for the use in good faith "of a description of the character or quality" of goods or services, but the hint of bad faith tainted the entirety of the judgment, a point that is developed in more detail below.

[62] [2010] F.C.A. 291 (Austl.).

[63] To elaborate, Reeves J stated "the size, positioning and format of the banner heading use of those words" was such that "a member of the public, taking an objective view of the matter, would conclude that the primary, or most significant use of those words is as a badge or emblem to indicate that Tailly is the origin of the accommodation letting services at Circle on Cavill." *Id.* at [57]. However, this conclusion is problematic. It seems unlikely that consumers would afford these words trademark significance when first encountered online. It is only at the point that consumers came to make a booking that they would have cause to engage with the question of *who* was providing the services as opposed to *where* the services were being provided. It is not clear, at least from the report of the case, that there was any danger of confusion at this crucial later stage.

[64] R v. Johnstone [2003] U.K.H.L. 28, [37].

[65] Trade Marks Act 1995 (Cth), §§ 10, 44, 60, 61, 120 (Austl.).

intervention. Moreover, in each of the cases considered above, the court was influenced by the fact that the defendant could have advertised its products in some alternative way that would, in the court's opinion, have served to reduce the risk of confusion. We therefore find judges making observations that are likely to make a marketing executive's blood run cold, for instance that the defendants might have chosen to advertise their business as "This is Willoughby's Hire Service, we hire Caterpillar Loaders," or used a smaller font when trying to sell holiday accommodation in a well-known "destination" complex, or used the word "type" rather than "pattern" to describe their belting. The overall effect of giving trademark owners the benefit of the doubt is to place defendants under a special obligation to protect the rights of trademark owners. Conceptually this has much in common with the approach adopted by the CJEU in cases like *Christian Dior* and *Portakabin*, albeit in a jurisdiction that does not recognize antidilution protection.

There is another element of the arrangements in Australia that gives rise to concern, this being the way in which the trademark use doctrine intersects with the statutory exceptions in section 122 of the Trade Marks Act 1995 (Cth). Section 122 provides eight defenses to an action for infringement, including for descriptive use, nominative use and comparative advertising.[66] Section 122 therefore covers much similar ground to trademark use. The most serious concern is that armed with an express defense, courts may choose to narrow the scope of trademark use and treat the express defenses as the *only* safe harbor for some types of defendants. This would be highly undesirable because the express exceptions are hedged with qualifications, less flexible, and hence less well-suited for dealing with novel fact patterns.

The displacement of trademark use is not a purely hypothetical concern. Parallel importation used to be permissible in Australia on the basis that importing legitimate goods bearing a sign did not constitute use of that sign as a trademark.[67] Unfortunately, this view was eventually rejected, meaning that parallel importation was only permissible if the defendant could bring itself within a statutory defense. The relevant defense was so narrow and poorly designed that parallel importation became difficult, costly, and fraught with risk. As Michael Handler outlines elsewhere in this volume,[68] this necessitated a drawn out and contested law reform process that resulted in the introduction of a new exception to restore the *status quo ante*.

Thankfully the retreat from trademark use has thus far been confined to parallel importation. If this position persists then there might even be reason to suggest that the express defenses are capable of providing a secondary safety net for

[66] *See id.* § 122(1)(b)–(d).
[67] Robert Burrell & Michael Handler, *A Requiem for Champagne Heidsieck: Trade Mark Use and Parallel Importation*, 29 Austl. Intel. Prop. J. 110 (2016).
[68] See Chapter 9.

defendants and to this extent are not entirely superfluous. It has been argued elsewhere that the statutory exceptions turn on the defendant's subjective intentions. For example, the nominative use defense applies where "the person uses the trade mark in good faith to indicate the intended purpose of the goods."[69] One way of approaching this provision is to conclude that the enquiry should focus entirely on what the defendant was seeking to achieve: the defense applies when the *person uses* the sign for the approved purpose. In contrast, the question of trademark use is to be judged objectively by reference to likely consumer reaction. The express defenses might therefore have separate work to do in a case where, for example, consumers have come to attach trademark significance to what was genuinely and honestly intended to be a nominative use.[70]

Approached as a secondary safety net that turns on subjective intent, the express defenses could be a useful, or at least not dangerous, addition to the trademark use doctrine. In practice, however, the presence of the express defenses has almost certainly done more harm than good. Confronted with a claim for infringement, defendants naturally seek to rely on both the trademark use doctrine *and* the express defenses. However, many of the defenses, including the descriptive and nominative use defenses, are conditioned by the requirement that the defendant act in good faith. The subsequent inquiry into the defendant's motivations has provided an avenue for trademark owners to cast aspersions on the defendant's conduct in ways that have fed back into, and at times overwhelmed, the enquiry into whether there was use as a mark. This comes across particularly clearly in *Mantra Group v. Tailly*, where the court was much taken by two submissions made on behalf of the trademark owner. The first was that defendant had engaged in "typosquatting," which the court approached as if it were an obviously undesirable commercial practice, analogous to cybersquatting. But an alternative way of understanding the defendant's conduct was that it had done no more than look for ways to compete for customers who might not know how to spell "Circle on Cavill" in circumstances where the plaintiff controlled all the most desirable domains. The second was that the defendant, when engaged in a bitter and long-running dispute with the plaintiff, had registered the domain name "mantra.au.com." This was unwise and unquestionably done in bad faith, but ultimately had no bearing on whether consumers were likely to respond to the defendant's use of the sign "Circle on Cavill" as a trademark.[71] Something similar can be seen in the *Caterpillar* case, where the finding at first instance regarding the defendant's determination to incorporate the word Caterpillar into its name was made in the context of a discussion of the

[69] Trade Marks Act 1995 (Cth), § 122(1)(c).

[70] For further discussion, *see* BURRELL & HANDLER, *supra* note 5, at 426–28.

[71] In fairness, it should be acknowledged that Reeves J. was at pain to emphasize that he reached his conclusion on bad faith primarily by reference to other matters. *Mantra Group Pty Ltd v. Tailly Pty Ltd (No 2)* [2010] F.C.A. 291, [93] (Austl.).

application of an express defense, but on appeal was treated as going to the question of trademark use.

In sum, Australia has come closer than the European Union to finding a robust and principled way to deal with use in advertising through a defensive doctrine. Its experiences also illustrate some of the benefits of using a well-drafted standard to deal with variable fact patterns, rather than a complex web of narrow rules. Nevertheless, problems remain; and those problems help tell us something important. Before turning to draw the various threads of the analysis together it is worth turning to a third case study, being one that offers slightly different lessons.

C. Comparative Advertising in the United Kingdom Revisited

The final case study takes us back to the seminal decision of the House of Lords in *Irving's Yeast-Vite Ltd v. Horsenail* in 1934. As has already been mentioned, this decision established the trademark use doctrine and thereby, among other things, made comparative advertisements generally permissible, a position that continues in Australia to this day. In the United Kingdom, however, the permissive approach to comparative advertising and nominative use more generally did not survive. This case study tells the story of the U.K. experience.

By the time the United Kingdom came to implement the harmonized European trademark regime, it was generally understood that under the Trade Marks Act 1938, "comparative advertising was trade mark infringement."[72] This result flowed from the principal infringement provision in the 1938 Act, which provided that a trademark would be infringed *either* where the use was such that it was likely to be taken "as being use as a trade mark" *or* where it was likely to be taken as "importing a reference" to the trademark owner.[73] The drafting of this section left much to be desired and for many years there was doubt as to its operation and effect, but it was, nevertheless, generally understood to have been intended to overturn *Yeast-Vite*.[74]

The path to *Yeast-Vite* being overturned was not, however, straightforward. Following *Yeast-Vite* there was a period of uncertainty as to whether *any* use of a sign in advertising could infringe. This seems strange to modern eyes, but was a product of the way the cases on use in advertising had developed to that point. To explain, by the time *Yeast-Vite* came to be decided, a consensus had emerged that use in advertising could constitute an infringement. This was the view taken in *Jay v. Ladler*, the 1888 case involving a dispute between furriers mentioned Section I. It was a conclusion that also received strong support from the decision of Farwell

[72] Helen Norman, Intellectual Property Law Directions 423 (2014); *see* Ruth Annand & Helen Norman, Blackstone's Guide to the Trade Marks Act 1994, at 159 (1994).

[73] Trade Marks Act 1938, 1 & 2 Geo. 6., c. 22, § 4(1) (U.K.).

[74] *See, e.g.*, T.A. Blanco White, Kerly's Law of Trade Marks and Trade Names 276 (9th ed. 1966).

J. in *Bourne v. Swan & Edgar Ltd* in 1903,[75] a case that played a pivotal but now forgotten role in how the law developed. That case involved a dispute over the use by the defendant of an image of two swans facing one another in an advertisement for women's clothing. Farwell J. accepted that use in advertising could infringe and cited *Jay v. Ladler*. However, his Lordship approached this question on the basis that use in advertising did not and could not constitute use as a trademark. For Farwell J. the way of squaring the circle was to conclude that "I do not think that it can be really necessary that the mark should be used by the defendants as a trade-mark."[76] It was therefore necessary to explore whether there was a likelihood of consumers being deceived, despite the fact that the image of the two swans "did not suggest a trade-mark in any sort of way," instead being "mere embellishments, decorative additions to a pretty picture."[77] The nature of the defendant's use was merely one factor to be considered, although in the end it was determined that no reasonable person would be led to conclude that the advertisement suggested a connection with the plaintiffs.

Swan & Edgar took on new importance after the decision in *Yeast-Vite*. If trademark use was a precondition for a finding of infringement, and *Swan & Edgar* had proceeded on the basis that use in an advertisement was never use as a mark, there was room for doubt as to whether use in advertising was ever actionable. Moreover, the 1931 decision of the Court of Appeal in *In Re Nicholson and Sons' Application*, although dealing with an unusual fact pattern concerning a mark alleged to have been used continuously since before 1875, could be read as supporting the view that use in advertising could never infringe.[78] Consequently, when legislative reform was being debated in the 1930s, the question of whether comparative advertising should be permitted had become bound up with whether trademark owners should have any degree of control over use in advertising.[79]

A comprehensive revision of trademark law came with the Trade Marks Act 1938, but use in advertising had by then been addressed through the passage of the Trade Marks (Amendment) Act 1937. This was unquestionably designed to allow trademark owners to bring infringement proceedings in relation to some types of advertisement. Equally, however, parliament was keen to ensure that some forms of comparison made in the course of trade should remain permissible. Specifically, it was agreed that there could be no question of "a salesman, by saying that X goods are better than Y goods, bringing himself within the ambit of the Bill."[80] However

[75] [1903] 1 Ch. 211 (Eng.).

[76] *Id.* at 229.

[77] *Id.* at 228.

[78] [1931] 2 Ch. 1 (Eng.). *See in particular id.* at 39 (Lawrence, L.J.) ("Advertisement of a trade mark in the press or on billheads, invoices and price lists is not a user of that mark. The only way in which a trade mark can be used is upon or in connection with goods."). The subsequent decision of the House of Lords in *Bass, Ratcliff and Gretton Ltd v. Nicholson and Sons Ltd* [1932] A.C. 130 left this point unresolved.

[79] *See, e.g.*, MINUTES OF EVIDENCE TAKEN BEFORE THE DEPARTMENTAL COMMITTEE ON THE LAW AND PRACTICE RELATING TO TRADE MARKS 65–66 (1934).

[80] 325 Parl Deb H.C. (5th ser.) (1937) col. 1204 (U.K.).

the resulting legislation left much to be desired. As regards the scope of the right to control use in advertising, it is unclear whether parliament intended to provide a general right to control such use (subject to one narrow exception) or whether parliament imagined that courts would engage in a case-by-case analysis of the likelihood of consumer confusion.[81] The "salesperson exception" similarly left much to be desired. It was enacted by taking oral use outside the ambit of infringing conduct.[82] At the time this did not seem particularly radical, since it appears that by this point there had only been one case in which it had been held that oral use by a trader in the course of selling goods could constitute an infringement and, on appeal, that case had been partially reversed on other grounds.[83] The result of the 1937 reforms, however, was to create a number of strange tensions.

One problem with the form of the salesperson exception was that there was nothing in the text of the legislation to signal the thinking behind the exclusion of oral use from the scope of the expanded infringement provision. The consequence was that the rationale was soon forgotten, and the exclusion of oral use came to be understood as a quirk or historical accident, rather than a deliberate policy choice. This problem was exacerbated by the passage of the Trade Marks Act 1938, which retained the exclusion of oral use, but with no explanation or revisiting of why such use had been excluded. Consequently, anyone who delved back into the legislative history of the 1938 Act would also be left with the impression that the exclusion of oral use was an accident of history or an unintended product of the way the provision had been drafted. But even without the interposition of the 1938 Act, there is a strong likelihood that the reasons for the exclusion would have been forgotten. Yet another lesson that we can learn from copyright exceptions is that form matters. One of the strengths of the U.S. copyright fair-use exception is that it has an intuitive appeal—users report being comfortable with the language and aims of fair use.[84] An exception that does not have the same intuitive appeal must, as a

[81] The parliamentary debate focused on questions of "fraud" and "abuse" in advertising, such that it is difficult to know what was intended. It is perhaps also worth emphasizing that little additional guidance can be gained from the 1934 Goschen Committee's recommendations. The Committee had recommended overturning *Yeast-Vite*, but also that an expanded infringement provision "should be made to allow the *bona fide* use of a mark by third parties for the purpose of describing such things as refills, accessories or spare parts specially adapted for use in or with goods of the registered proprietor." The Report of the Departmental Committee on the Law and Practice Relating to Trade Marks, Cmd. 4568, at 49–50 (1934). Since parliament did not choose to implement the *bona fide* use defense in 1937, but instead focused on a salesperson exception that the Goschen Committee had not recommended, considerable caution needs to be exercised in drawing too heavily on the Committee's recommendations.

[82] This limitation was enacted in § 15(1)(b) of the Trade Marks (Amendment) Act 1937, 1 Edw. 8 & 1 Gto. 6, c. 49, which required "use upon the goods or in physical relation thereto or in an advertising circular, or other advertisement, issued to the public." The original draft legislation merely referred to "importing a reference" to the trademark without qualification as to the nature of the use.

[83] Montgomerie & Co. Ltd. v. Young Brothers (1903) 20 R.P.C. 781 (Court of Session) (Scot.) (oral misdescription of bread by shop assistants); (1904) 21 R.P.C. 204 (Court of Session) (Scot.) (interdict should not have been granted in a case where defendants had taken all reasonable steps to prevent sales staff from selling goods under the mark). *See also* Blanco White, *supra* note 74, at 283.

[84] *See* Hudson, *supra* note 26.

minimum, be anchored in a legislative form that at least signals to informed actors something of the underlying policy rationale.

The other element of the salesperson exception to which it is worth drawing attention is the way in which it was grounded in a particular set of trade practices. A salesperson exception, even if it had been understood as such, would have diminished in importance as self-service shopping became the norm in a greater number of sectors. In this respect the story is one of technological redundancy. This is yet another familiar problem from copyright law, particularly in British Commonwealth countries, where until recently rights were framed in broad, technology neutral terms, whereas exceptions were often tied to particular technologies of reproduction and dissemination. Somewhat ironically, however, the salesperson exception could have taken a different turn. Although not entirely free from doubt, it was at least arguable that any oral use, including in advertisements, was outside the scope of the expanded infringement provision.[85] It might therefore have been possible for radio and television advertisements to include non-visual references to the trademarks of competitors, but it seems that even when well-advised traders were made aware of this possibility few if any availed themselves of it.[86]

Conclusion

This chapter started from the premise that we should not be rushing to embrace a turn to exceptions or limitations as a way of keeping trademarks rights in check. In the majority of cases, the best way of bringing trademark law back within appropriate bounds is to focus on the question of harm and to demand robust evidence of confusion or a dilution-based injury. Reconfiguring trademark law in this way would not by itself, however, deal with problems of overreach caused by the double identity rule, and these problems are both most acute and most immediately visible in the case of trademarks used in unauthorized advertising. Here there is no choice but to rely on exceptions (broadly conceived). It might, of course, be argued that the double identity rule is part of the problem and that if trademark law is to be reconfigured this rule ought to be jettisoned. This may not, however, be the best approach. There is a good case that the justifications for having a registration system

[85] To explain, trademark use of a sign would probably still have been caught by § 4(1)(a) of the Trade Marks Act 1938, which provided, without qualification, that uses "that were likely to be taken as being use as a trade mark" would infringe. However, as has been seen, the expanded "importing a reference" head of infringement in § 4(1)(b) required "use upon the goods or in physical relation thereto or in an advertising circular *or other advertisement* issued to the public" (my emphasis). Read in context there is an argument that the italicized words should also have been read as also requiring a visual representation of the sign, but this point does not appear to have been litigated.

[86] My thanks go to Robin Jacob for making this observation at the conference "Limitations on Trademark Rights from Comparative and Interdisciplinary Perspectives" held at the University of Hong Kong in Jan. 2019.

point toward registered marks providing a strong but narrow form of protection, with double identity protection being preserved, but with other types case being left to a heavily fact-dependent enquiry, more reminiscent of passing off.[87] There is therefore good reason why even those who would like trademark law to be radically reconceptualized ought to engage with how to design exceptions.

Still more importantly, there is no prospect of trademark law being fundamentally recast any time soon, and the direction of travel is such that we have to think seriously about the optimal design of exceptions. As was noted in the introduction, use in advertising is a promising lens through which to explore questions of legislative design because it is an area that has already attracted both judicial activism and legislative intervention. If there is a single message to be taken from the cases studies presented here, it is that a flexible, technology neutral, and readily intelligible standard like trademark use is the most promising candidate for enabling courts to craft appropriate outcomes when confronted with novel fact patterns. This doctrine is superior to the limited and at times incoherent framework of exceptions in E.U. law, and the former U.K. approach in which *Yeast-Vite* was replaced by statutory provisions whose effects were uncertain and, for the salesman exception, at risk of rapid redundancy. However, account must still be taken of the risks that can arise once exceptions are expected to take on a more prominent role. As seen in Australia and the European Union, if one starts from the position that trademark owners have a right to prevent use in advertising and defendants must bring themselves within an exception, it is all too easy to accept that trademark owners should, at the very least, be given the benefit of the doubt; or indeed that defendants have some "duty" of good faith in relation to the trademark owner's mark or brand.

This is tied to a broader phenomenon: that once attention shifts to exceptions it seems unremarkable to suggest that such exceptions should be subject to "reasonable" limits. If we are going to lean heavily on exceptions in this and other areas, we need not merely to draw on the lessons that copyright offers (as this chapter has suggested), we also need to reorient ourselves. We must, for example, remember that there are many types of use in advertising that should never in principle be actionable. If we nevertheless choose to give trademark owners broad control over use in advertising this is for reasons of regulatory convenience. Seemingly benign ideas, like ensuring that there are "reasonable" limits to the "exceptions" that make some use in advertising permissible, must in fact be treated with great care. If we do come to place more reliance on trademark exceptions we should still keep fixed in our minds that the ultimate question should always be whether any particular use really is likely to cause the trademark owner harm.

[87] *See* Robert Burrell, Rethinking the Relationship between Registered and Unregistered Trade Marks, *in* Across Intellectual Property—Essays in Honour of Sam Ricketson (Graeme W. Austin et al. eds., 2021).

9

Reimagining Trademark Exhaustion

Does Australia's New Defense Offer a Way Forward?

Michael Handler[*]

I. The Global Convergence Toward Restrictive Trademark Exhaustion Rules

Around the world, trademark exhaustion has long been recognized to be a highly controversial issue. It is, however, an issue that is rarely considered from a comparative legal perspective. There are a number of likely reasons for this. Most obviously, there is a lack of international harmonization of trademark exhaustion rules. The most that can be said is that members of the World Trade Organization (WTO) have agreed to ensure that the scope of their domestic trademark laws are limited, so as not to allow owners to prevent all acts of importation and/or resale of goods bearing their marks, to ensure that those domestic laws do not operate as disguised restrictions on international trade.[1] Beyond this, international and bilateral agreements are silent on the form that such limitations on trademark owners' rights must take.[2] Therefore, it falls to WTO members to make decisions as to the nature and scope of their trademark exhaustion rules at a local level. These decisions will involve specific choices as to what rules will provide the optimal balance between competing economic policy considerations for that member. In short, this will involve balancing the desirability of shielding trademark owners from competition,

[1] This is the effect of two articles of the General Agreement on Tariffs and Trade 1994, Apr. 15, 1994, Marrakesh Agreement Establishing the World Trade Organization, Annex 1A, 1867 U.N.T.S. 187, 33 I.L.M. 1153 (1994) (hereinafter GATT 1994). Article XI(1) of GATT 1994 bars contracting parties from setting up prohibitions or restrictions other than duties, taxes or other charges on the importation of products from another territory. Article XX(d), however, provides that nothing in GATT 1994 "shall be construed to prevent the adoption or enforcement by any contracting party of measures necessary to ... secure compliance with laws which are not inconsistent with the provisions of this Agreement, including those relating to ... the protection of ... trade marks." This is itself subject to the requirement, also contained in article XX(d), that such measures not be "applied in a manner which would constitute a means of arbitrary or unjustifiable discrimination between countries where the same conditions prevail, or a disguised restriction on international trade." *See generally* LAZAROS G. GRIGORIADIS, TRADE MARKS AND FREE TRADE: A GLOBAL ANALYSIS 103–21 (2014).

[2] *See, e.g.*, Agreement on Trade-Related Aspects of Intellectual Property Rights art 6, Apr. 15, 1994, Marrakesh Agreement Establishing the World Trade Organization, Annex 1C, 1867 U.N.T.S. 299, 33 I.L.M. 1197 ("nothing in this Agreement shall be used to address the issue of the exhaustion of intellectual property rights").

Michael Handler, *Reimagining Trademark Exhaustion* In: *Charting Limitations on Trademark Rights*. Edited by: Haochen Sun and Barton Beebe, Oxford University Press. © Michael Handler 2023. DOI: 10.1093/oso/9780198871248.003.0010

preserving authorized distribution networks, and limiting certain forms of "free riding," on the one hand, with the desirability of enhancing competition in markets and promoting net consumer welfare by discouraging unfair price discrimination, on the other hand.[3]

At the broadest level, this means that WTO members are free to determine, in accordance with their local economic interests, whether they will adopt a system of international exhaustion, national exhaustion, or, in the case of trading blocs like the European Union, regional exhaustion.[4] Members are also free to make specific choices as to the form and scope of their local rules permitting the parallel importation and/or resale of legitimate branded goods. Three examples show the array of options that are available. First, there is the threshold question of how to define the "legitimacy" of the trademarked goods that can be imported/resold. This might involve making determinations as to when goods can be said to be first put on the market, and dealing with situations where the ownership of the same mark is divided across multiple jurisdictions. Second, members need to make decisions as to how the importation/resale of legitimate goods is to be addressed where such acts might generate a degree of consumer confusion. Specifically, how might a member deal with situations where the legitimately branded goods are sold in a degraded condition, or have been altered (for example, to comply with local regulatory requirements)? How might a member deal with repackaged or relabeled goods? What is the relevance, if any, of the fact that the owner has sold goods under the same mark in different jurisdictions, where there are material quality differences ("MQDs") between such goods? Third, members will need to make choices as to whether the importation and/or resale of legitimate goods ought to be restrained where such acts, even if they do not generate consumer confusion, might harm the reputation of the trademark owner (for example, where the owner wishes to maintain a reputation for prestige by ensuring that its goods are advertised and sold in a particular manner). Further, this range of issues might be managed through various legal techniques: for example, through limitations contained in registered trademark laws, through the development of case law fleshing out the scope of those limitations, through the development of "unfair competition" type principles that apply whether or not the mark in question is registered, or a combination of all of the above.

Given the policy choices and legal options available to WTO members, it is not surprising that local laws on trademark exhaustion differ from each other substantially in their scope and technical details. Nor is it surprising that most critical

[3] This balancing exercise has been well canvassed in the literature. *See, e.g.*, Carsten Fink, *Entering the Jungle of Intellectual Property Rights: Exhaustion and Parallel Importation*, *in* Intellectual Property and Development: Lessons from Recent Economic Research (Carsten Fink & Keith E. Maskus eds., 2005).

[4] *See generally* Shubha Ghosh & Irene Calboli, Exhausting Intellectual Property Rights: A Comparative Law and Policy Analysis 65–85 (2018).

commentary on exhaustion has tended to focus on the rules of particular jurisdictions in isolation, with relatively little regard for the approaches taken elsewhere. Over recent years, however, a body of comparative legal scholarship on trademark exhaustion has started to emerge.[5] Drawing on this scholarship, it is possible to identify a number of points of convergence among the exhaustion laws of key jurisdictions. Most notably, it is readily apparent that parallel importation and the sale of secondhand goods have come to be treated with a high degree of skepticism, in both legislatures and courts, around the world.

To explain, although a strong case has been made by legal scholars[6] and in economist-led government inquiries[7] over recent years for WTO members to embrace a liberal, competition-enhancing approach to exhaustion rules, the issue has come to be addressed by legislatures and courts in a restrictive manner. In multiple jurisdictions, rules ostensibly designed to permit parallel importation are consistently made subject to substantial qualifications and restraints. For example, legislatures and courts have taken a narrow approach to what constitutes "legitimate" goods in cases involving branded samples and testers,[8] and in cases of

[5] Notable recent examples from the last five years include *id.*; GRIGORIADIS, *supra* note 1; RESEARCH HANDBOOK ON INTELLECTUAL PROPERTY EXHAUSTION AND PARALLEL IMPORTS (Irene Calboli & Edward Lee eds., 2016); Andrea Zappalaglio, *International Exhaustion of Trade Marks and Parallel Imports in the U.S. and the EU: How to Achieve Symmetry?*, 5 QUEEN MARY J. INTELL. PROP. 68 (2015). For older interventions, *see* WARWICK A. ROTHNIE, PARALLEL IMPORTS ch. 2 (1993); Kaoru Takamatsu, *Parallel Importation of Trademarked Goods: A Comparative Analysis*, 57 WASH. L. REV. 433 (1982).

[6] *See, e.g.*, Irene Calboli, *Market Integration and (the Limits of) the First Sale Rule in North American and European Trademark Law*, 51 SANTA CLARA L. REV. 1241 (2011); Enrico Bonadio, *Parallel Imports in a Global Market: Should a Generalised International Exhaustion Be the Next Step?*, 33 EUR. INTELL. PROP. REV. 153 (2011); Frederick M. Abbott, *Second Report (Final) to the Committee on International Trade Law of the International Law Association on the Subject of the Exhaustion of Intellectual Property Rights and Parallel Importation*, *in* 69TH CONFERENCE OF THE INTERNATIONAL LAW ASSOCIATION (2000), https://papers.ssrn.com/sol3/papers.cfm?abstract_id=1921856. Others have put forward a more cautious view of the benefits of adopting more liberal exhaustion regimes (noting the limited empirical evidence in this field). *See, e.g.*, Keith E. Maskus, *Economic Perspectives on Exhaustion and Parallel Imports*, *in* RESEARCH HANDBOOK ON INTELLECTUAL PROPERTY EXHAUSTION AND PARALLEL IMPORTS (Irene Calboli & Edward Lee eds., 2016).

[7] Australia provides the clearest example over the past twenty years. *See* PRODUCTIVITY COMMISSION, INTELLECTUAL PROPERTY ARRANGEMENTS 393–97 (2016), https://www.pc.gov.au/inquiries/completed/intellectual-property/report/intellectual-property.pdf; COMPETITION POLICY REVIEW: FINAL REPORT 165–67, 174–77 (2015), https://treasury.gov.au/sites/default/files/2019-03/Competition-policy-review-report_online.pdf (hereinafter, HARPER REVIEW); HOUSE OF REPRESENTATIVES STANDING COMMITTEE ON INFRASTRUCTURE AND COMMUNICATIONS, AT WHAT COST?: IT PRICING AND THE AUSTRALIA TAX 76 (2013), www.aph.gov.au/parliamentary_business/committees/house_of_representatives_committees?url=ic/itpricing/report.html; INTELLECTUAL PROPERTY AND COMPETITION REVIEW COMMITTEE, REVIEW OF INTELLECTUAL PROPERTY LEGISLATION UNDER THE COMPETITION PRINCIPLES AGREEMENT 188–91 (2000), https://www.ipaustralia.gov.au/sites/default/files/ergas_report_september_2000.pdf.

[8] This can be seen in restrictive decisions of the Court of Justice of the European Union. *See, e.g.*, Case No. C-324/09, L'Oréal SA v. eBay Int'l AG, 2011 E.C.R. I-6011 (testers and samples of perfume are not "put on the market" if supplied only for promotional purposes); Case No. C-127/09, Coty Prestige Lancaster Group GmbH v. Simex Trading AG, 2010 E.C.R. I-4965, para. 48 (no exhaustion of rights in relation to tester bottles of perfume supplied to retailers since the owner had not consented to the placement of the goods on the market). *See also* Samsonite IP Holdings Sarl v. An Sheng Trading Pte Ltd., [2017] S.G.H.C. 18, para. 100 (Sing. High Ct.) (samples only "put on the market" if an "independent third party has acquired the right of disposal of the goods bearing the trade mark").

divided ownership across jurisdictions.[9] When dealing with cases involving undeniably legitimate branded goods, legislatures and courts have shown themselves to be highly protective of brand owner interests by imposing strict limits on importation and resale. For instance, when considering dealings with foreign-made goods with MQDs to those sold in local markets, courts have gravitated toward a low threshold of "materiality," often relying on attenuated forms of consumer confusion as between the local and foreign branded goods, in order to enjoin defendants from importing and reselling the foreign goods.[10] Courts, particularly in the European Union, have shown a degree of hostility toward the repackaging and relabeling of legitimate products, setting up onerous and vaguely expressed requirements with which an importer must comply so as not to infringe.[11] Such courts have also shown a willingness to intervene to prevent parallel importation if this might be thought to harm the reputation of the brand owner (e.g., in its luxury goods), both in the absence of consumer confusion or any empirical evidence that the conduct in question would cause reputational damage.[12] More generally, it is striking that many jurisdictions have structured their exhaustion rules in such a way to place the burden of proof as to certain matters on the defendant, where only the plaintiff would have access to the relevant evidence, thus making it difficult for importers and resellers to have any confidence in advance as to whether or not their conduct is non-infringing.[13]

While the reasons for legislatures' and courts' skepticism toward parallel importation are certainly worth exploring in greater detail,[14] the focus of this chapter

[9] *See, e.g.*, K Mart Corp. v. Cartier, Inc., 486 U.S. 281, 292–93 (1988) (considering regulations interpreting the scope of the Tariff Act of 1930 § 526(a), 19 U.S.C.A. § 1526, and holding that parallel importation is possible only where the owners of the local and foreign marks are subject to common control, and not where the U.S. owner has licensed the foreign manufacturer to use the mark). *See also* J. THOMAS MCCARTHY, 5 MCCARTHY ON TRADEMARKS AND UNFAIR COMPETITION § 29:49 (5th ed. 2018).

[10] It is possible to point to a number of far-reaching U.S. examples, where the importation and sale of legitimate goods was held to constitute infringement on the basis of only slight MQDs. *See, e.g.*, Zino Davidoff SA v. CVS Corp., 571 F.3d 238 (2d Cir. 2009); Martin's Herend Imports, Inc. v. Diamond & Gem Trading USA Co., 112 F.3d 1296 (5th Cir. 1997); Lever Bros. Co. v. United States, 981 F.2d 1330 (D.C. Cir. 1993); Societe Des Produits Nestle SA v. Casa Helvetia, Inc., 982 F.2d 633 (1st Cir. 1992); Ferrero USA, Inc. v. Ozak Trading, Inc., 935 F.2d. 1281 (3d Cir. 1991). *See also* Colgate-Palmolive Ltd. v. Markwell Finance Ltd., [1989] R.P.C. 497 (C.A.) (Eng.).

[11] *See* LIONEL BENTLY ET AL., INTELLECTUAL PROPERTY LAW 1171–78 (6th ed. 2022).

[12] *See* Case No. C-337/95, Parfums Christian Dior SA v. Evora BV, 1997 E.C.R. I-6013. *See also* Case No. C-59/08, Copad SA v. Christian Dior Couture SA, 2009 E.C.R. I-3241, para. 37 (restriction on distributors from selling lingerie to discount stores legitimate if the sales would impact on the quality of the goods, which included their aura of luxury).

[13] *See, e.g.*, Case No. C-244/00, Van Doren + Q GmbH v. Lifestyle sports + sportswear Handelsgesellschaft mbH, 2003 E.C.R. I-3051 (onus is on the parallel importer to prove consent to the goods being put on the market). *See also Copad*, 2009 E.C.R. at para. 51 (no consent to goods being put on the market if goods distributed by licensee outside the scope of the license agreement in particular circumstances, but where the details of some of these circumstances could not be known by the importer).

[14] In addition to the familiar arguments put forward in favor of restrictive exhaustion rules (discussed *supra* note 3), it might be argued that courts and legislatures have gravitated to this position because of concerns that parallel importation potentially involves "unfairness" or "free riding" (a point

is on a more forward-looking issue. Given how restrictive most jurisdictions' laws on exhaustion have become, it is important to consider whether there are other ways WTO members could approach exhaustion and, if so, what a model for reform might look like.[15] In this regard, it is highly instructive to look at recent developments in Australia. With the introduction of a new defense to the infringement of a registered trademark contained in section 122A of the Trade Marks Act of 1995, which came into effect on August 25, 2018,[16] Australia now has one of the most liberal trademark exhaustion regimes in the world. In summary, the new defense to infringement applies if the parallel importer or reseller *reasonably believed* that the mark was originally applied to the goods by or with the consent of the owner, or a range of other parties, with "consent" being defined in exceptionally broad terms. In a reversal of the typical onus of proof, if an importer/reseller forms such a reasonable belief it will not be liable for infringement unless it persists in its conduct after information as to the *lack* of consent to application of the mark is brought to its attention. And, crucially, the defense does not in any way turn on whether the imported/resold goods have been altered, repackaged or relabeled, or if there are MQDs between the imported/resold goods and those supplied locally by or under the license of the mark owner.[17]

Section II provides context for the new Australian exhaustion laws, showing that Australia, over the course of the twentieth century, had recognized the benefits of facilitating the parallel importation of legitimate goods, but that since the mid-1990s an overly restrictive approach had come to be taken by the legislature and courts. Section III then offers a detailed examination of the liberal new section 122A defense, analyzing its scope by reference to the more restrictive pre-2018

noted in ANNETTE KUR & MARTIN SENFTLEBEN, EUROPEAN TRADE MARK LAW: A COMMENTARY para. 6.101 (2017)). Other reasons might be that courts and legislatures do not wish to be seen to be condoning the distribution of goods that have been sourced in breach of upstream license agreements, or receptive to the argument that exhaustion rules should offer a degree of "overprotection" to brand owners to prevent or discourage the importation and sale of counterfeit goods.

[15] The U.K. government recently ran a consultation as to the form its rules on the exhaustion of intellectual property rights should take, following its departure from the European Union (and, more specifically, whether its current provisions, which have been shaped by E.U. law, "best serve the U.K.'s interests"). While it concluded that there was "not enough data available to understand the economic impact of any of the alternatives to the current ... regime", it indicated that it "remains committed to exploring the opportunities which might come from a change to the regime." *See* INTELLECTUAL PROPERTY OFFICE, UK'S FUTURE EXHAUSTION OF INTELLECTUAL PROPERTY RIGHTS REGIME (June 7, 2021, updated Jan. 18, 2022), https://www.gov.uk/government/consultations/uks-future-exhaustion-of-intellectual-property-rights-regime.

[16] Trade Marks Act 1995 (Cth) § 122A (Austl.) (introduced by the Intellectual Property Laws Amendment (Productivity Commission Response Part 1 and Other Measures) Act 2018 (Cth) sch. 1, item 2 (Austl.)).

[17] Issues of consumer confusion will be relevant if an action is brought against the importer/reseller in passing off or under the Australian statutory consumer protection regime. However, even in this context, courts are likely to take countervailing pro-competition policy considerations into account. *See generally* ROBERT BURRELL & MICHAEL HANDLER, AUSTRALIAN TRADE MARK LAW ch. 13 (2d ed. 2016).

case law, and showing how it operates more favorably to importers and retailers than any other set of exhaustion rules in the world. Section IV then uses the recent Australian reforms as a springboard for a broader reconsideration of whether trademark exhaustion rules in other jurisdictions should be liberalized, showing that the Australian approach is underpinned by different ways of thinking about exhaustion—namely, as to the proper scope of registered owners' rights, as to what sort of conduct by importers and owners we want to incentivize, and as to how risk should be allocated between such parties.

II. How Did Australia Arrive at Its Current Position?

Australia has long had a clear policy position in favor of allowing the parallel importation of legitimate goods, recognizing the harm to local consumers caused by excessive restrictions on such trade.[18] This position was reflected in domestic trademark laws as they developed over the course of the twentieth century. However, problems with the initial drafting of the current statute, the Trade Marks Act of 1995, and a series of subsequent Federal Court decisions interpreting that statute, started to undermine this policy position. Understanding this background is necessary to appreciate the problems the new section 122A defense was intended to overcome, and why the new defense is so broad in its scope.[19]

Before 1995, Australian legislation did not contain provisions dealing with the exhaustion of a registered trademark owner's rights. Rather, exhaustion was an issue left to the judiciary. In 1929, in the English case of *Champagne Heidsieck et Cie Monopole Société Anonyme v. Buxton*,[20] it was held that the importation into, and subsequent sale in, the United Kingdom of genuine French champagne bearing a registered U.K. trademark that had been applied to the goods in France by the registered owner constituted neither an infringement of the registered trademark nor passing off (notwithstanding the fact that the owner had sold similarly marked champagne, but of a different quality, to its U.K. consumers). The court was particularly scathing of the idea that dealing with legitimate goods could ever constitute trademark infringement.[21] In time, *Champagne Heidsieck* came to be recognized in Australia as turning on the absence of any trademark use by the defendant—use "as a trade mark" having being held by Australian courts to

[18] *See* Mark Davison, *Parallel Importing in Australia: What Is the Objective and Is It Being Achieved?*, 38 MONASH U. L. REV. 173, 175–76 (2012) (hereinafter Davison, *What Is the Objective*). On the domestic economic factors supporting this position, *see supra* note 7.

[19] *See generally* Robert Burrell & Michael Handler, *A Requiem for Champagne Heidsieck: Trade Mark Use and Parallel Importation*, 26 AUSTL. INTELL. PROP. J. 110 (2016) (hereinafter Burrell & Handler, *A Requiem*).

[20] [1930] 1 Ch. 330 (Ch.) (Eng.)

[21] *Id.* at 338, 341.

be an essential requirement for infringement.[22] Reading *Champagne Heidsieck* in this manner thus resulted in the establishment of an international exhaustion rule in Australia. It was a rule that was comfortably applied by lower courts in cases involving similar facts to *Champagne Heidsieck*[23] and was noted by commentators as being sufficiently flexible to deal with new fact scenarios involving parallel importation and the resale of secondhand goods.[24] Having said this, it is possible to point to one case in this period in which the Federal Court was unwilling to apply *Champagne Heidsieck* to permit the importation of genuine goods that had been purchased in the United States where the Australian registered mark was owned by an authorized local distributor of the U.S. manufacturer's goods,[25] although this decision was rightly criticized as having turned on the irrelevant point that the Australian distributor had generated independent goodwill.[26] As a related matter, Australian courts had come to recognize that parallel importers could separately be liable for passing off if they made misrepresentations about the goods they were selling (e.g., that the goods were covered by warranties, or about the goods' compatibility with local technical standards).[27] However, such courts did not have the opportunity to consider whether, notwithstanding the authority of *Champagne Heidsieck*, the existence of MQDs between the imported and local goods could give rise to passing off, as U.S. and U.K. courts had come to find.[28]

In the early 1990s, a Working Party set up by the government to review Australia's trademark laws recommended that exhaustion should be addressed specifically by way of a new statutory defense to infringement. Seemingly guided by the more restrictive approach to parallel importation that had come to be taken in other

[22] *See* Shell Co. of Austl. Ltd. v. Esso Standard Oil (Austl.) Ltd., 109 C.L.R. 407, 422–23 (Austl.) (1963) (Kitto J., with whom Dixon C.J., Taylor J. and Owen J. agreed). Although both the United Kingdom and New Zealand had, by this time, amended their laws to ensure that the sort of conduct in issue in *Champagne Heidsieck* amounted to prima facie infringement, Australia had consciously decided not to go down this path. *See* Report of Committee Appointed to Consider What Alterations Are Desirable in the Trade Marks Law of the Commonwealth paras. 26–27 (1954). As a result, *Champagne Heidsieck* remained good authority as to the scope of the Australian infringement provision.

[23] *See* Delphic Wholesalers Pty Ltd. v. Elco Food Co. Pty Ltd., 8 I.P.R. 545 (Vict. Sup. Ct.) (Austl.) (1987); R. & A. Bailey & Co. Ltd. v. Boccaccio Pty Ltd., 4 N.S.W.L.R. 701 (N.S.W. Sup. Ct.) (Austl.) (1986); Atari Inc. v. Fairstar Elecs. Pty Ltd., 50 A.L.R. 274 (Fed. Ct.) (Austl.) (1982). *See also* Wingate Mktg. Pty Ltd. v. Levi Strauss & Co., 49 F.C.R. 89, 111 (Full Fed. Ct.) (Austl.) (1994) (considering the sale of secondhand goods).

[24] *See* Sam Ricketson, *The Licensing of Trade Marks and the Operation of Section 103 of the Trade Marks Act 1955 (Cth): Some Aspects of the Pioneer Case*, 14 U. W. Austl. L. Rev. 30, 67–69 (1979). *See also* D. R. Shanahan, Australian Law of Trade Marks and Passing Off 515–19 (2d ed. 1990).

[25] Fender Austl. Pty Ltd. v. Bevk, 25 F.C.R. 161 (Austl.) (1989).

[26] *See* Mark Davison, *Parallel Importing of Trade Marked Goods—An Answer to the Unasked Question*, 10 Austl. Intell. Prop. J. 146, 151–52 (1999).

[27] *See, e.g.*, Star Micronics Pty Ltd. v. Five Star Computers Pty Ltd., 18 I.P.R. 225 (Fed. Ct.) (Austl.) (1990) (false representations as to warranty coverage and compatibility of goods with local power source).

[28] *See supra* note 10 (on U.S. case law); Rothnie, *supra* note 5, at 40–44 (on passing off cases from British Commonwealth countries).

countries, as well as submissions supporting such an approach,[29] the Working Party recommended that the new defense permitting parallel importation of legitimate goods apply only if the following three conditions were met:

> (i) the mark has been applied to the goods by or with the consent of the trade mark proprietor;
> (ii) in the case of new goods the condition of the goods has not been changed or impaired; and
> (iii) where the goods are also being supplied by or with the consent of the registered proprietor, the goods the subject of the importation are not materially different from the first-mentioned goods.[30]

The government did not implement this recommendation. Rather, the Trade Marks Act of 1995, as enacted, specified that infringing use needed to be use "as a trade mark" (section 120) and provided a defense to infringement for the use of a trademark on goods "if the trade mark ha[d] been applied to, or in relation to, the goods by, or with the consent of, the registered owner of the trade mark" (section 123(1))—significantly, with no further qualifications.

It might have been thought that the new statutory requirement that infringing use be use "as a trade mark" would have entrenched the *Champagne Heidsieck* line of authority. However, by the time of the 1995 Act, a different line of High Court cases considering trademark use outside of the context of infringement had emerged, which cast doubt on the idea that an importer or reseller of legitimate branded goods was not engaging in trademark use.[31] This line of cases, as well as academic criticism of the judicial interpretation of *Champagne Heidsieck* as turning on the absence of trademark use,[32] helped bring about a substantial change under the 1995 Act. Over a series of decisions between 1999 and 2016, the Full Court of the Federal Court interpreted use "as a trade mark" in section 120 to *include* the importation and resale of legitimate goods, overturning *Champagne Heidsieck* in the process.[33] For reasons explored elsewhere, these decisions are regrettable. Not

[29] *See, e.g.*, LAW COUNCIL OF AUSTRALIA, INTELLECTUAL PROPERTY COMMITTEE, RESPONSE TO WORKING PARTY PAPER 11–12 (1992).

[30] WORKING PARTY TO REVIEW THE TRADE MARKS LEGISLATION, RECOMMENDED CHANGES TO THE AUSTRALIAN TRADE MARKS LEGISLATION 75, 78 (Recommendation 22D(4)) (1992) (hereinafter WORKING PARTY REPORT). The Working Party made a separate recommendation that use on secondhand goods should be permitted, "provided that the mark has been applied to the goods by or with the consent of the registered proprietor at the time the mark was applied to the goods." *Id.* at 78 (Recommendation 22D(5)).

[31] *See, e.g.*, Pioneer Kabushiki Kaisha v. Registrar of Trade Marks, 137 C.L.R. 670 (Austl.) (1977); W.D. & H.O. Wills (Austl.) Ltd. v. Rothmans Ltd., 94 C.L.R. 182 (Austl.) (1956).

[32] *See* Mark Davison, *Parallel Importation: Unlawful Use of Trade Marks*, 19 FED. L. REV. 420 (1990).

[33] *See* Scandinavian Tobacco Group Eersel BV v. Trojan Trading Co. Pty Ltd., 243 F.C.R. 152 (Austl.) (2016); Paul's Retail Pty Ltd. v. Lonsdale Austl. Ltd., 294 A.L.R. 72 (Austl.) (2012). These decisions confirmed obiter dicta in Paul's Retail Pty Ltd. v. Sporte Leisure Pty Ltd., 202 F.C.R. 286 (Austl.) (2012), E. & J. Gallo Winery v. Lion Nathan Austl. Pty Ltd., 175 F.C.R. 386 (Austl.) (2009), and Transp. Tyre Sales Pty Ltd. V. Mont. Tyres Rims & Tubes Pty Ltd., 93 F.C.R. 421 (Austl.) (1999).

only are they based on a misunderstanding of *Champagne Heidsieck* and the evolution of the trademark use inquiry over the course of twentieth-century Australian law, but they also eviscerated a key doctrine of Australian law that could have been used in a flexible manner to give effect to the desired policy goal of facilitating the parallel importation and resale of legitimate goods.[34] In doctrinal terms, the main consequence of these decisions was to make the section 123(1) defense to infringement the only provision relevant to determining when a registered owner's rights were exhausted.

In many respects, section 123(1), which turned solely on whether the mark had been applied to the goods by or with the owner's consent, had an expansive sphere of operation. For example, in its 2016 decision in *Scandinavian Tobacco Group Eersel BV v. Trojan Trading Co. Pty Ltd.* the Full Court of the Federal Court held that the section 123(1) defense was made out where the registered owner had applied its marks to the packaging of its cigars outside Australia, and the importer had subsequently repackaged these goods, re-applying the marks in a form that complied with Australian "tobacco plain packaging" requirements.[35] This decision was consistent with understandings that had been expressed in case law and scholarship that section 123(1) was also broad enough to apply in cases where the mark had been applied with the owner's consent to goods that had been repaired or reconditioned before import or resale,[36] and to goods with MQDs to goods supplied to the Australian market by the mark owner.[37] Further, there can be little doubt that section 123 would have been established where the registered owner applied its mark to samples or testers, even if these had never been put on the market,[38] or where the importer or reseller had marketed the owner's legitimate goods in a manner that might have affected the "prestige" of the mark.[39] It is also worth emphasizing that, in this period, Australian courts were not prepared to apply expansive notions of "misrepresentation" to find parallel importers liable for passing off or contravention of statutory prohibitions on engaging in misleading or deceptive conduct.[40] For example, in *Scandinavian Tobacco* the Full Court gave short shrift to

[34] *See* Burrell & Handler, *A Requiem*, *supra* note 19, at 117–20.

[35] *Scandinavian Tobacco*, 243 F.C.R. at 167–71.

[36] *Cf.* Wingate Mktg. Pty Ltd. v. Levi Strauss & Co., 49 F.C.R. 89 (Full Fed. Ct.) (Austl.) (1994) (sale of reconditioned Levi's jeans held not to constitute trade mark infringement). Although *Wingate* was decided under former legislation, it was held at trial in Scandinavian Tobacco Group Eersel BV v. Trojan Trading Co. Pty Ltd., 330 A.L.R. 678 (Fed. Ct.) (Austl.) (2015) that section 123 "vindicate[s] th[e] very idea found in *Wingate*." *Id.* at 696.

[37] *See* Burrell & Handler, *A Requiem*, *supra* note 19, at 121–24.

[38] *Cf.* Parfums Christian Dior (Austl.) Pty Ltd. v. Dimmeys Stores Pty Ltd., 39 I.P.R. 349 (Fed. Ct.) (Austl.) (1997) (finding a serious issue to be tried as to infringement under section 120, but not considering the potential application of the section 123 defense).

[39] This is because Australian law does not provide a cause of action for the dilution of a well-known mark, or the taking of unfair advantage of the reputation of a mark, in the absence of confusion as to origin. *See generally* Michael Handler, *Trade Mark Dilution in Australia?*, 29 EUR. INTELL. PROP. REV. 307 (2007).

[40] Since Jan. 1, 2011, the key statutory prohibition has been contained in the Competition and Consumer Act 2010 (Cth) sch. 2, § 18 (Austl.).

the argument that Australian consumers would expect that any repackaging must have been done under the authority of the mark owner, saying that such arguments did "not rise above mere conjecture."[41]

However, section 123(1) had a number of serious deficiencies that substantially narrowed its scope—these are more likely to have been the result of drafting oversights than parliament's intention to restrict the circumstances in which parallel importation was permissible. Most obviously, section 123(1) required the necessary "consent" to the application of the mark to be that of the "registered owner," a term defined as "the person in whose name the trade mark *is* registered."[42] This meant that if the mark had been applied to goods by a foreign parent company, but the Australian registration was owned by an Australian subsidiary or distributor, the defense did not apply, given the absence of any consent by the Australian registered owner.[43] More worryingly from an antitrust perspective was that, because "registered owner" was defined in the present tense, a foreign manufacturer and registered owner of the Australian mark could block the parallel importation of those goods into Australia by assigning the mark to an Australian distributor or shell company *after* the application of the mark but before the act of parallel importation (at which point in time the foreign manufacturer was no longer the "registered owner" for the purposes of establishing consent under section 123(1)).

An equally significant problem was that the defense turned on the question of the "consent" to application of the mark, rather than the legitimacy of the goods sought to be imported or resold. As confirmed by the Federal Court, this meant that where the registered owner had granted a license to the application of the mark on certain conditions—for example, that the goods were to be sold in a particular country,[44] or that only a limited number of goods could be manufactured—any conduct in breach of such conditions vitiated the owner's consent to the initial application,

[41] Scandinavian Tobacco Group Eersel BV v. Trojan Trading Co. Pty Ltd., 243 F.C.R. 152, 172 (Austl.) (2016). *See also* Pioneer Elecs. (Austl.) Pty Ltd. v. Woodlands Res. (Austl.) Pty Ltd., 49 I.P.R. 299 (Fed. Ct.) (Austl.) (2000) (interlocutory injunction not granted to restrain the sale in Australia of genuine DVD players imported from China on the basis of thin evidence of alleged misrepresentations as to safety and warranties). *Cf.* Pioneer Elecs. Austl. Pty Ltd. v. Lee, 108 F.C.R. 216 (Fed. Ct.) (Austl.) (2000) (injunction to restrain passing off granted where the importer falsely represented that the imported goods had been approved by an authorized distributor, and where the goods were not safe for sale in Australia). *See generally* Arlen Duke, *The Empire Will Strike Back: The Overlooked Dimension to the Parallel Import Debate*, 37 Melb. U. L. Rev. 585, 594–96 (2014).

[42] Trade Marks Act 1995 (Cth) § 6 (Austl.) (emphasis added).

[43] *See, e.g.*, Lonsdale Austl. Ltd. v. Paul's Retail Pty Ltd., [2012] F.C.A. 584, para. 47 (Fed. Ct.) (Austl.).

[44] *See, e.g.*, Paul's Retail Pty Ltd. v. Lonsdale Austl. Ltd., 294 A.L.R. 72 (Full Fed. Ct.) (Austl.) (2012) (no "consent" to application of the mark where the head license agreement allowed the licensee to apply the mark to goods manufactured in China for sale in Europe, and where the licensee arranged for branded goods to be manufactured in China, but where the licensee subsequently sold those goods in China to a Cypriot party for further sale in Europe (the fact that the transfer of property in the goods took place in China meant that the licensee was in breach of the agreement); Paul's Retail Pty Ltd. v. Sporte Leisure Pty Ltd., 202 F.C.R. 286 (Full Fed. Ct.) (Austl.) (2012) (no "consent" to application where the licensee was permitted to apply the mark to goods in India for sale in India, but where the licensee was approached by a Pakistani company to make branded goods for it and to sell those goods to it in Pakistan, which the licensee did, thus breaching the license agreement).

making the importation of such goods into Australia infringing. The problem here was that the goods produced in such circumstances would often be indistinguishable from those produced in accordance with the terms of the license agreement,[45] and a parallel importer would often have no way of knowing whether the goods it had purchased (likely from a downstream intermediary) had been made in breach of an upstream agreement. For example, imagine a situation where a license agreement restricted the licensee to the manufacture of 1000 goods bearing the Australian registered trademark and prohibited the sale of overruns, and the licensee was approached by two parties, A and B, to sell them 100 goods each. The licensee sold goods 901–1000 to A and goods 1001–1100 to B (this latter sale being in breach of the license agreement). Subsequently, A and B sold their goods to C, who then sold them to D for importation into Australia. To D, the 200 goods would appear to be identical and genuine. However, only those acquired through A could legally be imported into and sold in Australia. The problem was compounded by section 123(1) being structured so as to place the onus on the defendant to prove the mark had, in fact, been applied with the requisite consent—knowledge that would, in most cases, be outside the scope of any information reasonably available to either the importer or any intermediary selling the goods.

The problems with section 123(1) were noted not only by commentators[46] but also in a number of economist-led government inquiries into Australia's competition and intellectual property laws in 2015–16.[47] In particular the Productivity Commission, the Australian government's independent advisory and review body on economic matters, expressed its concern that the restrictive wording of section 123(1) and the outcomes of recent Federal Court decisions were in tension with Australia's preferred policy position of facilitating parallel importation and consumer access to genuine goods.[48] The Australian government agreed, accepting in 2017 that section 123 was "not effectively implementing the policy intention of allowing for the parallel importation of legitimate goods and has led to some uncertainty and confusion," and stating that it would seek to amend the Trade Marks Act accordingly.[49] What is remarkable, though, is the form that Australia's new parallel importation regime came to take in giving effect to this general policy intention.

[45] They might also be indistinguishable from goods to which the mark had been applied with consent, but had been subsequently distributed in breach of the license agreement. *See* Facton Ltd. v. Toast Sales Group Pty Ltd., 205 F.C.R. 378 (Fed. Ct.) (Austl.) (2012).

[46] *See* Burrell & Handler, *A Requiem*, *supra* note 19, at 124–30; Arlen Duke & Matthew E. Taylor, *Parallel Import Restrictions: Core Intellectual Property Rights or Unjustified Restraints on Trade?*, 22 Competition & Consumer L. J. 254 (2015); Warwick Rothnie, *Trade Marks and Parallel Imports*, 22 Competition & Consumer L.J. 39, 44, 47 (2014); Davison, *What Is the Objective*, *supra* note 18, at 183–86.

[47] Productivity Commission, *supra* note 7; Harper Review, *supra* note 7.

[48] Productivity Commission, *supra* note 7, at 393–94, 396–97.

[49] Australian Government, Response to the Productivity Commission Inquiry into Intellectual Property Arrangements 14 (2017), https://www.pc.gov.au/inquiries/completed/intellectual-property/intellectual-property-government-response.pdf.

As will be explained in detail in Section III, in repealing section 123(1) and introducing a new, far-reaching defense to infringement in section 122A in 2018, the Australian government has established one of the most liberal approaches toward parallel importation and the resale of secondhand goods of any major jurisdiction.[50] It is an approach that explicitly seeks to prioritize competition among sellers of branded goods and the enhancement of consumer welfare over the interests of trademark owners in preserving their authorized distribution networks and maintaining price discrimination.

III. Australia's Liberal New Exhaustion Regime

Section 122A of the Trade Marks Act of 1995 relevantly provides as follows:

> (1) In spite of section 120, a person who uses a registered trade mark in relation to goods does not infringe the trade mark if:
> (a) the goods are similar[51] to goods in respect of which the trade mark is registered; and
> (b) before the time of use, the person had made reasonable inquiries in relation to the trade mark; and
> (c) at the time of use, a reasonable person, after making those inquiries, would have concluded that the trade mark had been applied to, or in relation to, the goods by, or with the consent of, a person (a *relevant person*) who was, at the time of the application or consent (as the case may be):
> (i) the registered owner of the trade mark; or

[50] The reform agenda was largely controlled by IP Australia, the government agency that administers the Trade Marks Office. IP Australia first released an Exposure Draft of the Intellectual Property Laws Amendment (Productivity Commission Response Part 1 and Other Measures) Bill 2017 (Cth) (proposing the repeal of section 123(1) and containing a draft section 122A defense). It received submissions on the Exposure Draft (*available at* http://ipaustralia.libguides.com/c.php?g=404687&p=4450363%20-%20s-lg-box-wrapper-20498311), to which it publicly responded, indicating that changes to the proposed section 122A would be made. *See* IP Australia, IP Australia Response to Public Consultation on Exposure Draft of Intellectual Property Laws Amendment (Productivity Commission Response Part 1 and Other Matters) Bill and Regulations 2017, at 1–6 (2018). These changes were reflected in the Intellectual Property Laws Amendment (Productivity Commission Response Part 1 and Other Measures) Bill 2018 (Cth) sch. 1, item 2 (Austl.) that was introduced into parliament. The Bill was referred to the Senate Economics Legislation Committee on May 10, 2018. The Committee received submissions (*available at* https://www.aph.gov.au/Parliamentary_Business/Committees/Senate/Economics/IntellectualProperty2018/Submissions) and ultimately recommended that the Bill be passed by the Senate, without amendment. *See* Senate Economics Legislation Committee, Intellectual Property Laws Amendment (Productivity Commission Response Part 1 and Other Measures) Bill 2018 [Provisions] 21–22 (2018), https://www.aph.gov.au/Parliamentary_Business/Committees/Senate/Economics/IntellectualProperty2018/Report.

[51] "Similar" goods are defined to include goods that are "the same." Trade Marks Act 1995 (Cth) § 14(1)(a) (Austl.).

(ii) an authorised user of the trade mark[52]; or
(iii) a person permitted to use the trade mark by the registered owner; or
(iv) a person permitted to use the trade mark by an authorised user[53] ...; or
(v) a person with significant influence over the use of the trade mark by the registered owner or an authorised user; or
(vi) an associated entity[54] ... of a relevant person mentioned in subparagraph (i), (ii), (iii), (iv) or (v).

(2) A reference in paragraph (1)(c) to consent to the application of a trade mark to, or in relation to, goods includes, without limitation, a reference to:
(a) consent subject to a condition (for example, a condition that the goods are to be sold only in a foreign country); and
(b) consent that can be reasonably inferred from the conduct of a relevant person.

Like the former section 123(1), the new section 122A defense focuses on whether there was consent to the application of the mark to the goods the defendant wishes to import and/or resell. The Australian government did not consider it appropriate to add a requirement, such as exists in E.U., New Zealand, and Singaporean law, that the owner's goods must have first been "put on the market" by or with the owner's consent.[55] The effect of the Full Court of the Federal Court's importer-friendly *Scandinavian Tobacco* decision has been retained, with section 122A not imposing any new conditions on the repackaging or relabeling of legitimate goods, or the selling of goods in an otherwise altered state. In addition, the Australian government, like the Productivity Commission before it, was not persuaded by arguments that the new defense should apply only where the goods sought to be imported and/or resold did not have MQDs to those supplied by the owner or its

[52] An "authorised user" is a particular type of licensee. *Id.* § 8(1). *See generally* BURRELL & HANDLER, *supra* note 17, at 568–71, 582–88.

[53] See Trade Marks Act 1995 (Cth) § 26(1)(f) (Austl.) (on the powers of an "authorised user").

[54] *See* Corporations Act 2001 (Cth) § 50AAA (Austl.) (on when an associate will be an "associated entity" of a principal).

[55] Notably, the version of section 122A(1)(b) in the Exposure Draft of the Intellectual Property Laws Amendment (Productivity Commission Response Part 1 and Other Measures) Bill 2017 (Cth) contained this requirement. In its response to submissions on the Exposure Draft, IP Australia indicated that it had reconsidered its position, stating that the requirement was unnecessary and that other remedies (e.g., for conversion, or breach of contract) would be available for affected owners, leading to the removal of the draft clause. *See* IP AUSTRALIA, *supra* note 50, at 2. In doing so, IP Australia implicitly rejected INTA's submission that the draft section 122A(1)(b) needed to be retained and even strengthened to ensure that the importation and resale of samples and testers did not enliven the defense. *See* INTERNATIONAL TRADEMARK ASSOCIATION, SUBMISSION TO IP AUSTRALIA ON THE DRAFT LEGISLATION: INTELLECTUAL PROPERTY LAWS AMENDMENT (PRODUCTIVITY COMMISSION RESPONSE PART 1 AND OTHER MEASURES) BILL AND REGULATIONS 2017, at 3 (2017), http://ipaustralia.libguides.com/ld.php?content_id=38408694.

licensee to the Australian market.[56] In other words, all of the liberal features of the former defense to infringement have been retained.[57] What is striking is how much further the new section 122A goes—not just compared with the former defense but also compared with the exhaustion rules of all other major jurisdictions. This can be seen in three key ways.

First, section 122A(1)(c) provides that a large number of parties other than the registered owner can now apply the mark, or consent to the application of the mark, to the goods in question in order to enliven the operation of the defense. Most notably, in addition to various licensees and sub-licensees, and members of the same corporate group as the mark owner,[58] it is now the case that "a person with *significant influence* over the use of the trade mark by the registered owner or an authorised user"[59] can apply the mark or consent to its application. This concept, which owes its origins to New Zealand's exhaustion laws,[60] is remarkably broad. As the Australian government has explained, "significant influence:"

> is intended to capture any significant contractual or commercial relationship where one party influences the registered owner or authorised user or vice versa. It is intended to cover contractual arrangements, non-contractual legal arrangements (e.g., deeds or equitable interests), and a wide variety of informal understandings (e.g., where the influence is exercised through the promise of future business or the threat of withdrawing future business; or where the influence is bought through an understanding that a benefit will be provided to a third party).[61]

The key effect of this provision is that it will ensure that the operation of the parallel importation defense cannot be circumvented by a foreign manufacturer

[56] *Cf.* INTERNATIONAL TRADEMARK ASSOCIATION, *supra* note 55, at 1. The Productivity Commission had earlier considered that in cases of imported goods with MQDs to those supplied locally, sufficient information would be available to Australian consumers (e.g., as to country of origin, and price differentials) to assist them. *See* PRODUCTIVITY COMMISSION, *supra* note 7, at 395–96.

[57] Admittedly, not all of the problems with the former section 123 have been fixed. *See* ROBERT BURRELL & MICHAEL HANDLER, SUBMISSION 5 TO THE SENATE ECONOMICS SELECT COMMITTEE, INTELLECTUAL PROPERTY LAWS AMENDMENT (PRODUCTIVITY COMMISSION RESPONSE PART 1 AND OTHER MEASURES) BILL 2018, at 4 (2018), https://www.aph.gov.au/Parliamentary_Business/Committees/Senate/Economics/IntellectualProperty2018/Submissions.

[58] *See also* Trade Marks Act 1995 (Cth) § 122A(3) (Austl.) (providing that for the purposes of determining whether a person is "permitted to use the trade mark" under section 122A(1)(c)(iii)–(iv), the relevant party should "disregard how that permission arose").

[59] Trade Marks Act 1995 (Cth) § 122A(1)(c)(v) (Austl.) (emphasis added).

[60] *See* Trade Marks Act 2002 § 97A (N.Z.). *See generally* Rob Batty, *Parallel Importing and Trade Mark Use: A Tale of Two Uses*, 25 N.Z. U. L. REV. 467 (2013).

[61] Explanatory Memorandum, Intellectual Property Laws Amendment (Productivity Commission Response Part 1 and Other Measures) Bill 2018 (Cth), para. 21. This is also reflected in section 122A(4) of the Trade Marks Act 1995 (providing that for the purposes of assessing "significant influence" the relevant party is to "disregard how that influence arose").

structuring its business affairs so that the Australian subsidiary or distributor is, or later becomes, the registered owner of the Australian mark.[62] A common example of such a practice involves a foreign manufacturer assigning its registered Australian mark to a local distributor, on the condition that the distributor sources its goods exclusively from the manufacturer, and that upon termination of the distribution agreement the mark is to be reassigned to the manufacturer.[63] It was on the basis of such a conditional assignment that, in the Federal Court case of *Fender Austl. Pty Ltd. v. Bevk*,[64] the Australian exclusive distributor of U.S.-made Fender guitars was able to restrain the parallel importation of genuine Fender guitars into Australia. This sort of outcome would no longer be possible under section 122A, given the foreign manufacturer would invariably be exercising substantial, ongoing influence over the business activities and use of the mark by the Australian distributor/registered owner.[65]

Second, the effect of section 122A(2) is to expand the notion of "consent" in section 122A(1)(c) to include "conditional consent." That is, where under a license agreement the registered owner (or another "relevant person") consents to the licensee applying the mark to goods, provided that the licensee complies with certain conditions set out in the agreement, "consent" remains established for the purposes of section 122A(1)(c). Looked at the other way, nothing now turns on whether the licensee has breached conditions in the license agreement for the purposes of the application of the defense. This overturns the outcome of the Full Court of the Federal Court's 2012 decision in *Paul's Retail Pty Ltd. v. Sporte Leisure Pty Ltd.*[66] In that case, an Indian licensee of registered Australian marks was entitled to apply the marks to clothing in India for sale in India. The licensee was approached by a Pakistani company to supply it with branded clothes, and agreed to fulfill this order in breach of the territorial restriction in the license agreement. Since it could no longer have been said that the marks had been applied with the consent of the registered owner, the former section 123 did not assist the Australian importer, which had acquired the Pakistani goods via a Singaporean intermediary. Under the new section 122A(1)(c), the registered owner would be deemed to have

62 Explanatory Memorandum, Intellectual Property Laws Amendment (Productivity Commission Response Part 1 and Other Measures) Bill 2018 (Cth), para. 23.

63 *See* MARK DAVISON & IAN HORAK, SHANAHAN'S AUSTRALIAN LAW OF TRADE MARKS AND PASSING OFF 735–36 (6th ed. 2016).

64 25 F.C.R. 161 (Austl.) (1989).

65 Similarly, it was thought that on the facts of Transp. Tyre Sales Pty Ltd. v. Mont. Tyres Rims & Tubes Pty Ltd., 93 F.C.R. 421 (Full Fed. Ct.) (Austl.) (1999), the overseas manufacturer's assignment of its registered mark to its Australian distributor after the manufacturer's application of the mark to its tires prevented the defendant from relying on the former section 123(1) to import tires after the date of the assignment (although this was not argued before the court). It is now clearly the case that an importer can rely on the new section 122A(1)(c) in these circumstances, since this requires attention to be paid to whether the mark was applied by a "relevant person" (e.g., the registered owner) *at the time of the application*, rather than the time of the prima facie infringing act.

66 202 F.C.R. 286 (Austl.) (2012).

given consent to the licensee's application of the mark.[67] Importantly, the impact of the new section 122A(2) goes well beyond breaches of geographical restrictions in license agreements. It will also mean that the application of marks to production overruns (as illustrated in Section II), or to goods of different qualities to those stipulated in a license agreement, would also now deemed to be applications with consent for the purposes of section 122A(1)(c).[68] Indeed, the government does not appear to contemplate any limit to the sort of conditions that can be taken into account.[69] In these circumstances, it needs to be emphasized that permitting the parallel importation of goods does not deprive the trademark owner of a remedy, since it will always have an action against the licensee for breach of contract.

Third, in a remarkable change to the law, the application of the defense no longer turns solely on the factual question of whether or not the mark was applied to the goods by or with the consent of a relevant party. Rather, the defense now turns on the *reasonableness* of the defendant's conduct. Specifically, the combined effect of section 122A(1)(b) and (c) means that the defense will apply if the defendant, before undertaking any activity that constitutes "use" of the mark (which includes importation of marked goods, and extends to every act of sale and advertising), makes "reasonable inquiries in relation to the trade mark" and, on the basis of those inquiries, comes to a reasonable conclusion that the mark was applied by or with the consent of one of the listed parties. That is, the defense can potentially apply even where the mark was not, in fact, applied by or with the (conditional) consent of one of the listed parties.[70]

The problem that the "reasonable inquiries" elements of section 122A seek to overcome is that it may be impossible for a parallel importer to be absolutely certain that the goods are, in fact, legitimate. All that the importer can do is make reasonable inquiries as to whether the trademark had been applied by or with the consent of one of the parties listed in paragraph (c), and act on that information in a reasonable manner. As IP Australia has explained, without such a provision parallel importation would remain "unacceptably risky" and that the supply of

[67] The new section 122A would also lead to a different outcome based on the facts in Paul's Retail Pty Ltd. v. Lonsdale Austl. Ltd., 294 A.L.R. 72 (Full Fed. Ct.) (Austl.) (2012) (discussed *supra* note 44), assuming that the marks applied to the goods sold to the licensee in China in breach of the territorial restriction had been substantially identical to the marks registered in Australia.

[68] *See* Law Council of Australia, Intellectual Property Committee, Submission to IP Australia on Draft Legislation: Intellectual Property Laws Amendment (Productivity Commission Response Part 1 and Other Measures) Bill and Regulations 2017, at 5–6 (2017), http://ipaustralia.libguides.com/ld.php?content_id=38408550.

[69] *See* Explanatory Memorandum, Intellectual Property Laws Amendment (Productivity Commission Response Part 1 and Other Measures) Bill 2018 (Cth), para. 26.

[70] This has the potential to lead to a different outcome to that reached in QS Holdings Sarl v. Paul's Retail Pty Ltd., 92 I.P.R. 460 (Fed. Ct.) (Austl.) (2011) (defendant found liable for the sale of counterfeit goods, where the defendant had no opportunity to argue under the former section 123 that it had conducted itself reasonably in the circumstances by dealing with a reputable supplier and that its dealings with the counterfeit goods were innocent). *See also* Jared Owens, *Sportswear Chain Paul's Warehouse Was a "Victim" of Foreign Fake Ring*, The Australian, Sept. 15, 2011, at 3.

parallel imports to Australian consumers would remain stifled, thus undermining the government's policy.[71] What might constitute "reasonable inquiries" is to be left to the judiciary, but the government's view is that:

> Requesting and receiving a certificate of authenticity from the supplier would be sufficient in most circumstances. However, the extent of the inquiries will be determined by the facts of the situation. For example, where the supplier is widely known or suspected to supply counterfeit goods or where the goods are being offered at suspiciously low prices or through dubious trade channels, more searching inquiries may need to be made, such as contacting the trade mark owner to confirm consent. Conversely, by way of example, if the goods are purchased from a retailer widely known to be the licensed distributor of the trade mark owner at the normal price of genuine goods in the relevant market, then no further inquiries may be needed.[72]

By making the application of the defense turn on the reasonableness of the defendant's inquiries and conclusions, the defense is far-reaching. It is possible that it will mean that goods that a reasonable importer would consider to be legitimate, but which are in fact counterfeit, can be imported into and circulate in Australia.[73] However, it needs to be appreciated that the new defense does *not* provide an ongoing license to import and sell counterfeit goods. The reason for this is that an importer will engage in multiple acts of "use," at different points in time, for the purposes of section 122A(1)(b). The act of importation will constitute the first act of "use," and every subsequent sale will also constitute a new "use" of the mark, as will every subsequent advertisement of the goods. If the trademark owner learns, after the act of importation, that the importer or retailer is continuing to advertise and sell goods to which the mark was not, in fact, applied by or with the consent of a party listed in section 122A(1)(c), the owner can bring this information to the attention of the importer/retailer. Provided that the quality of the information is such that a reasonable person in the importer/retailer's position would, at that point, no longer be able to conclude that the mark was applied by or with the consent of a listed party, paragraph (c) no longer applies. That is, an importer/retailer's persistence after adequate notice will mean that such a party cannot, from that time forward, rely on the defense. Further, although any acts by the importer/retailer before this time will not constitute trademark infringement, the owner can always pursue actions against the makers of the counterfeit goods or those who supplied

[71] IP Australia, *supra* note 50, at 3.

[72] Explanatory Memorandum, Intellectual Property Laws Amendment (Productivity Commission Response Part 1 and Other Measures) Bill 2018 (Cth), para. 15.

[73] Subject, of course, to any regulatory requirements as to safety and fitness for purpose with which any goods sold in Australia must meet. *See, e.g.*, Competition and Consumer Act 2010 (Cth) pt. 3-3 (Austl.).

them to the Australian importer. To the extent that this information might be difficult to obtain, an owner can seek a *Norwich Pharmacal* order[74] from the Federal Court against the Australian importer/retailer.[75] This order can compel a party to disclose the identity of the supplier or maker of goods and, crucially, can be made against a party that is entirely innocent of any wrongdoing.[76]

IV. A New Way Forward?

Australia's new trademark exhaustion regime is admittedly complex, and is likely to give rise to a number of operational uncertainties, at least in the short term. Apart the from the fact that section 122A introduces new concepts that will need to be fleshed out by the courts,[77] it remains unclear how the defense intersects with the Customs seizure regime contained in Part 13 of the Trade Marks Act.[78] It is also unclear whether an importer/retailer protected by the defense up to the point in time it is put on notice that the goods are not legitimate might nevertheless be liable for passing off or contravention of the statutory prohibition on engaging in misleading or deceptive conduct during this period, and what remedies a court would be prepared to award.[79] Despite this, it is clear that Australian law now affords the highest degree of protection to parallel importers and resellers of secondhand goods of any major jurisdiction. A trademark owner's rights are now exhausted in a wide range of circumstances, with few qualifications, and the law is now structured so as to give parallel importers and resellers confidence that they can lawfully engage in their acts based on the knowledge available to them. Looked at from a comparative legal perspective, Australia has bucked the global trend toward increasingly narrow exhaustion rules that impose substantial restrictions on the parallel importation and resale of goods, as described in Section I.

The Australian experience is worth considering not simply because of the specific terms of the new section 122A defense. At a broader level, it provides a useful springboard for a more fundamental reconsideration of how exhaustion rules *could* apply in other jurisdictions—particularly those that accept the economic benefits in prioritizing competition and enhancing net consumer welfare over

[74] *See generally* Norwich Pharmacal Co. v. Customs and Excise Comm'rs, [1974] A.C. 133 (H.L.) (appeal taken from Eng.).

[75] *See* Federal Court Rules 2011 (Cth) div. 7.3 (Austl.).

[76] *See generally* Burrell & Handler, *supra* note 17, at 617.

[77] For example, courts will need to determine when an influence is "significant," how broadly to read the notion of "consent subject to a condition," and what constitutes "reasonable inquiries."

[78] The problem is that if an owner provides the Comptroller-General of Customs with a notice objecting to the importation of goods infringing a registered trade mark under section 132, the Comptroller-General must, under section 133(2), seize goods bearing that trademark (or a substantially identical or deceptively similar variant) "unless he or she is satisfied that there are no reasonable grounds for believing that the notified trade mark is infringed by the importation of the goods."

[79] *See generally* Burrell & Handler, *supra* note 17, at 503, 512, 529–31.

enabling price discrimination. This is because the Australian approach is based on different ways of thinking about exhaustion, and about whose interests should be prioritized in formulating exhaustion rules, when compared with other jurisdictions. Three such ways are worth briefly exploring in this concluding Section.

First, the Australian approach is informed by a clear principle about the proper *scope* of registered trademark law. This is that the rights of registered owners should not be expanded to allow them to control the trade in their own marked goods in an attempt to address the full range of issues thrown up by parallel importation and commercial resale. The Australian approach is based on the fundamental premise that registration laws should prevent conduct that would disrupt the source-identification function of the owner's mark. Logically, such conduct must involve a defendant using the mark, or a sufficiently similar variant, on *the defendant's* goods. Dealing in the mark owner's goods does not disrupt this function. This means that any attempt to deal with issues such as the importation and sale of repackaged or modified goods, or goods with MQDs to those supplied to the local market, within the registered trademark system will involve *expanding* an owner's rights beyond those to which the owner is entitled to protect the source-identification function of its marks.

This is not to say that such expansions are unjustifiable. However, they come with significant risks, since they necessarily involve setting up specific conditions on the conduct of parallel importers and resellers, noncompliance with which will result in their dealings with an owner's goods becoming infringing. Not only is this a blunt legal technique to use[80] but it also puts a premium on formulating "conditions" that are not overprotective of mark-owner interests[81] and are not worded so vaguely that they provide insufficient guidance to would-be importers and resellers as to what constitutes legitimate conduct.[82] In short, the potential problem with the conditions-on-use-based approach is that, as the Productivity Commission recognized, it simply asks the registered trademark system "to do too much."[83]

Australia has made a conscious decision to go down a different path. Rather than seeking to address issues of repackaging, modifications, and MQDs by expanding the scope of registered trademark rights, it leaves issues of potential "unfair competition" to other legal regimes that are better suited to addressing these issues. Specifically, affected owners can always bring actions for passing off or for

[80] *See* ROTHNIE, *supra* note 5, at 40.

[81] *See, e.g.*, WORKING PARTY REPORT, *supra* note 30, at 78 (Recommendation 22D(4)).

[82] The European Union affords the clearest example. *See* Directive (E.U.) 2015/2436 of the European Parliament and of the Council of Dec. 16, 2015 to Approximate the Laws of the Member States Relating to Trade Marks, 2015 O.J. (L 336) 12, art. 15(2) (permitting an owner to control the further commercialization of its goods if there are "legitimate reasons" to do so). However, the problem can also arise if a jurisdiction attempts to craft a more specific rule. *See, e.g.*, Trade Marks Act 1998 § 29(2) (Sing.) (infringement to deal with legitimate goods if their condition has been changed or impaired and the defendant's use "has caused dilution in an unfair manner of the distinctive character of the registered trade mark").

[83] PRODUCTIVITY COMMISSION, *supra* note 7, at 396.

contraventions of statutory prohibitions on engaging in misleading or deceptive conduct, or on making misleading representations that goods are of a particular standard, quality or composition, or have had a particular history or previous use.[84] These actions do not rely on the a priori identification of permitted categories of conduct for importers and resellers. Rather, they place the onus on the mark owner to demonstrate that the importer or reseller's conduct is, in all the circumstances of the particular case, likely to mislead consumers. A particular advantage of this approach is that it is not all-or-nothing: a court can tailor remedies to ensure that, provided that the defendant does not market the owner's goods in a misleading manner (e.g., by the use of appropriate disclaimers), the practice of parallel importation and resale of legitimate goods can continue.[85] The Australian approach should, at the very least, prompt further debate about whether it balances the interests of owners and importers more effectively than the conditions-on-use-based approach adopted in the registration systems of other jurisdictions.

Second, the Australian approach to exhaustion reflects carefully developed thinking as to what types of commercial activities relating to the importation and resale of branded goods should be *incentivized*. It is notable that reform of Australia's exhaustion rules was the by-product of a number of inquiries led by economists, who emphasized the economic benefits in enhancing competition so that Australian consumers could gain access to lower-priced branded goods, and recommended that the law needed to be structured so as to remove as many disincentives to parallel importation as possible.[86] This is most obviously reflected in the fact that the new section 122A defense permits parallel importation even where the mark was applied with only the "conditional" consent of the owner or another relevant person, and requires only that the importer/reseller engage in "reasonable inquiries" in relation to the goods in question and come to a reasonable conclusion that they are genuine. These features recognize that a key problem faced by parallel importers is that precise information about the goods sought to be imported (e.g., whether or not they were made or distributed in breach of restrictions in license agreements) will only ever be available in documents that neither the importer nor any intermediary from which the importer purchases the goods is ever likely to obtain access to. Whereas the former law was drafted so restrictively that it ended up adding substantial costs to the operations of importers of legitimate goods,[87]

[84] Competition and Consumer Act 2010 (Cth) sch. 2, §§ 18(1), 29(1)(a), 29(1)(c) (Austl.).

[85] *See* Rothnie, *supra* note 5, at 40–42 (discussing Consumers Distrib. Co. Ltd. v. Seiko Time Can. Ltd., [1984] 1 S.C.R. 583 (Can.) and Sony K.K. v. Saray Elecs. (London) Ltd., [1983] F.S.R. 302 (Ch.) (Eng.)).

[86] It is also notable how little influence the views of brand-owner representatives had over these inquiries, and the subsequent reform process run by IP Australia and the Australian Senate. *See generally supra* note 50.

[87] *See, e.g.*, Costco Wholesale Australia Pty Ltd., Submission 31 to the Productivity Commission, Intellectual Property Arrangements: Issues Paper (2015), https://www.pc.gov.au/__data/assets/pdf_file/0004/194494/sub031-intellectual-property.pdf.

and possibly forced some importers to abandon their practices entirely,[88] the new Australian defense provides a structural incentive to importers to engage in their activities, based on their reasonable inquiries and resultant conclusions.

Less obviously, the Australian approach creates a range of incentives that might benefit the *mark owner*. A defense that requires the importer/reseller to have made "reasonable inquiries" could well encourage them to take more far-reaching steps than they have in the past to satisfy themselves as to the genuineness of the goods in question, such as going further than asking for certificates of authenticity from a supplier. More directly, the Australian approach provides a strong incentive to owners to be more vigilant in monitoring their license and distribution agreements for breaches.[89] This would seem to be a more effective long-term strategy of addressing the problem of goods being made or circulating in breach of license restrictions than focusing on the activities of the importers and retailers of the goods. In addition, the Australian approach might create an incentive to owners to rethink their use of "global" brands if local quality differences are so important. That is, it might encourage owners to use different sub-brands for their goods when sold with MQDs in different jurisdictions. A common complaint of trademark owners is that the parallel importation of identically branded goods from country X into country Y undercuts its market for those goods in Y, such that it is compelled to raise its prices to a potentially unviable level in X or exit the market there. The use of different sub-brands in X and Y would overcome this problem. It would also potentially lead to better-informed consumers who, as they move from one jurisdiction to another, gain clearer information about the quality differences between the owner's goods in different markets.[90]

Third, the Australian experience shows a different way of thinking about *risk allocation* as between the various parties involved in manufacturing, distributing, and importing/reselling branded goods. What is striking about most approaches taken around the world to parallel importation and the resale of secondhand goods is that they place much of the risk on the importer/reseller. These parties bear substantial costs in taking reasonable steps to verify the genuineness of the goods with which they seek to deal but, even then, matters outside the scope of such parties' reasonable knowledge can make the act of importation/resale infringing, leaving them liable for damages. The new Australian approach changes this. By making the legality of the act of parallel importation or resale turn on the defendant's "reasonable belief" as to the genuineness of the goods, this allows for a more equitable

[88] *See* LAW COUNCIL OF AUSTRALIA, INTELLECTUAL PROPERTY COMMITTEE, SUBMISSION TO COMPETITION POLICY REVIEW: ISSUES PAPER 2–3 (2014), https://treasury.gov.au/consultation/c2014-cpr-issues-paper.

[89] This is particularly important since it is only by the owner bringing accurate information to the attention of Australian importers/resellers that the goods with which they are dealing are not, in fact, genuine that the protections afforded by the section 122A defence will cease to apply.

[90] *See* Burrell & Handler, *A Requiem*, *supra* note 19, at 122.

allocation of risk as between importers/resellers and owners. While importers/resellers will still need to undertake due diligence, owners no longer have the opportunity to seek windfall damages against "innocent" importers/resellers.[91] Instead, owners will need to need to look to other parties to recoup their losses, as well as continuing to monitor the flow of their goods into foreign markets. The advantage of the Australian approach is not only that it makes the act of parallel importation less risky, but also that it ensures that enforcement is targeted against parties that might be described as the real wrongdoers (i.e., the counterfeiters of goods, or those parties in breach of license and distribution agreements higher up the supply chain). Ensuring that actions cannot be taken against importers and resellers that have conducted themselves reasonably also prevents exhaustion rules from overcompensating for the challenges that trademark owners might face in identifying counterfeiters and in enforcing breaches of contractual arrangements in countries where manufacture is outsourced, where the rule of law might run thin.[92]

Clearly, a WTO member's position on trademark exhaustion will need to reflect that member's thinking as to what rules best balance a range of competing economic policy considerations. However, it needs to be remembered that restrictive exhaustion rules are not inevitable. Rules that expand the scope of a registered trademark owner's rights to enable it to restrain the practice of parallel importation, even in the absence of any consumer deception—thereby providing strong disincentives to the importation and resale of legitimate branded goods—represent a conscious choice to privilege a mark owner's interests over those of others. It might well be that such a choice is not in fact in that member's best economic interests.[93] Australia's new, highly liberal approach to trademark exhaustion shows what is possible when different perspectives, and a different set of values, are prioritized.

[91] As such, this measure has more in common with criminal offence provisions relating to the selling of branded goods that do not apply where the defendant had no reason to suspect the genuineness of the mark, or believed on reasonable grounds that its use was not infringing. *See, e.g.*, Trade Marks Act 1998 § 49 (Sing.); Trade Marks Act 1994, c. 26, § 92(5) (U.K.).

[92] *See* Burrell & Handler, *A Requiem*, *supra* note 19, at 127.

[93] For example, it is common for defenders of restrictive exhaustion rules to point to the harm that would be caused to specific industries (e.g., the pharmaceutical industry) if the liberalization of such rules undercut the ability of owners to engage in price discrimination and the ability to control the circulation of goods across borders. Such an approach ignores the question of whether more liberal rules represent the best economic policy across all industries, and a preferable approach would seem to be for those groups likely to be affected by more liberal rules to lobby for industry-specific legislative "carve-outs" to preserve their position, based on robust economic evidence.

PART IV
COMPARATIVE STUDIES OF LIMITATIONS

10

Creative Destruction of the Civil Law Tradition

Lessons from Chinese Trademark Law

Haochen Sun

Introduction

Chinese judges today are playing a leading role in the global protection of intellectual property (IP) rights. With China's judiciary handling more IP lawsuits than any other jurisdiction, their work is prominent not only for its quantity but also for its quality. While acting to safeguard IP owners' private interests, Chinese judges have also in their rulings effectively protected public interests by creatively breaking through the confinements of certain statutory provisions.

This chapter demonstrates how Chinese judges have *proactively* protected the public interest by boldly deviating from the civil law tradition governing the Chinese legal system. Chinese judges have gone beyond the confinements of the civil law tradition to recognize new fair-use exemptions not permitted by Chinese trademark statutes. While the Chinese Trademark Law allows only for the descriptive use of a trademark by members of the public, Chinese judges have decided in several cases that nominative use should be legally permitted and protected in the public interest. Through such creative rulings, Chinese judges have faithfully followed the public interest objectives of IP protection contained within the Agreement on Trade-Related Aspects of Intellectual Property Rights (TRIPS Agreement).[1] As the most important IP treaty, the TRIPS Agreement encourages IP protection that "promote[s] the public interest in sectors of vital importance to [treaty members'] socio-economic and technological development."[2]

[1] Agreement on Trade-Related Agreements of Intellectual Property Rights, art. 13, Apr. 15, 1994, Marrakesh Agreement Establishing the World Trade Organization, Annex 1C, 1869 U.N.T.S. 299, 33 I.L.M. 1197 (1994) (hereinafter TRIPS Agreement).

[2] *Id.* art. 8. Art. 7 of the TRIPS Agreement states the public interest objectives as follows:

> The protection and enforcement of intellectual property rights should contribute to the promotion of technological innovation and to the transfer and dissemination of technology, to the mutual advantage of producers and users of technological knowledge and in a manner conducive to social and economic welfare, and to a balance of rights and obligations.

Haochen Sun, *Creative Destruction of the Civil Law Tradition* In: *Charting Limitations on Trademark Rights.* Edited by: Haochen Sun and Barton Beebe, Oxford University Press. © Haochen Sun 2023.
DOI: 10.1093/oso/9780198871248.003.0011

The chapter further discusses how Chinese judges have developed *creative* legal methods to ascertain the myriad public interests implicated in limitations on trademark rights. Through an in-depth study of their rulings in cases dealing with nominative uses of trademarks, it considers the ways in which Chinese judges have found that public interests such as robust market competition should be protected.[3]

Section I of the chapter compares the different roles played by judges in civil law and common law jurisdictions, focusing on China and the United States, respectively. Section II discusses a range of rulings in cases involving trademarks wherein Chinese judges have deviated from the civil law tradition in order to protect the public interest. Section III considers the legitimacy of this legal practice, arguing that Chinese judges have proactively protected the public interest and developed creative legal methods in doing so. Drawing on a comparison with the judicial practices adopted in the United States, this part of the chapter further presents jurisprudential justifications for affording civil law judges greater autonomy to protect the public interest through trademark law.

I. Differing Roles of Judges in the Common Law and Civil Law Traditions

A. Judges in the U.S. Common Law System

In common law jurisdictions, judges play a more significant role in shaping the legal system than their counterparts in civil law jurisdictions. First, they have law-making power, creating doctrines for dealing with legal matters in many areas of the law. For example, in most states in the United States, the basic legal rules of contracts, property, and torts do not exist in statute, but only in common law.[4] Many statutes are interpreted against the backdrop of the pre-existing common law after legislatures have codified the relevant common law doctrines into the statutes.[5]

Id. art. 7; *see also* Peter K. Yu, *The Objectives and Principles of the TRIPS Agreement*, 46 HOUS. L. REV. 979, 1007 (2009) (pointing out that an official guide to interpreting TRIPS states that Article 7 was "intended to strike a balance that more widely promotes social and economic welfare").

[3] *See infra* Section III.B.

[4] *See generally* OLIVER WENDELL HOLMES, JR., THE COMMON LAW (1891) (describing judge-made law in contracts, torts, and property).

[5] As the U.S. Supreme Court explained in *United States v. Texas*:

> Just as longstanding is the principle that "statutes which invade the common law ... are to be read with a presumption favoring the retention of long-established and familiar principles, except when a statutory purpose to the contrary is evident." In such cases, Congress does not write upon a clean slate. In order to abrogate a common-law principle, the statute must "speak directly" to the question addressed by the common law.

507 U.S. 529, 534 (1993) (quoting Isbrandtsen Co. v. Johnson, 343 U.S. 779, 783 (1952) and Mobil Oil Corp. v. Higginbotham, 436 U.S. 618, 625 (1978)).

Second, judges follow the principle of *stare decisis*, which dictates that rulings made by higher courts are precedents for lower courts to follow.[6] In this sense, precedents serve a controlling function in subsequent lower court cases involving similar circumstances.[7] The lawmaking and precedent roles work in tandem, making each more powerful and durable in practice.[8]

The autonomy afforded common law judges in shaping legal systems has helped to establish them as "culture heroes," studied and remembered for their impact on development of the law.[9] Several justifications have been put forward for their judicial autonomy. For instance, some argue that common law judges merely address the legislative inconsistencies and insufficiencies that inevitably arise from rapidly changing social circumstances,[10] whereas others contend that they serve as an important check on legislatures, being empowered to invalidate unconstitutional laws.[11]

Whichever argument is most apt, a clear decrease in judicial autonomy can be observed when common law judges deal with IP cases. IP is an area of law in which statutes have prevailed in common law jurisdictions.[12] The Statute of Monopolies (1624)[13] and the Statute of Anne (1710)[14] gave birth to IP rights as a distinctive category of legal rights in the common law world.[15] Since the passage of these statutes, statutory protection has been omnipresent in IP law[16] except in certain niche areas such as trade secrets and rights of publicity.[17]

Although IP statutes dominate, judges in common law jurisdictions still enjoy considerable autonomy in shaping IP protection systems. In the United States,

[6] *See* John C. Gray, The Nature and Sources of the Law 211 (Roland Gray ed., 2d ed. 1921) (1909).

[7] *See* Oona A. Hathaway, *Path Dependence in the Law: The Course and Pattern of Legal Change in a Common Law System*, 86 Iowa L. Rev. 601, 622–23 (2001).

[8] *See generally id.* at 604, n.12 (citing sources that illustrate how American common law is "path dependent" on past judicial decisions).

[9] *See* John Henry Merryman & Rogelio Pérez-Perdomo, The Civil Law Tradition: An Introduction to the Legal Systems of Europe and Latin America 34 (4th ed. 2018).

[10] *Id.* at 39–40.

[11] *Id.* at 34.

[12] *See, e.g.*, Shyamkrishna Balganesh, *Stewarding the Common Law of Copyright*, 60 J. Copyright Soc'y U.S.A. 103, 108 (2013)(hereinafter *Stewarding the Common Law*) ("As a purely historical matter, copyright's origins are entirely statutory."); Shyamkrishna Balganesh, *The Pragmatic Incrementalism of Common Law Intellectual Property*, 63 Vand. L. Rev. 1543, 1544 (2010) (hereinafter *The Pragmatic Incrementalism*) ("Intellectual property is today thought to be principally of statutory origin.").

[13] 21 Jac. 1 c. 3 (Eng.), https://www.legislation.gov.uk/aep/Ja1/21/3/contents.

[14] Copyright Act 1710, 8 Ann. c. 21 (Eng.), *repealed by* Copyright Act 1842, 5 & 6 Vict. c. 45.

[15] *See* Brad Sherman & Lionel Bently, The Making of Modern Intellectual Property Law: The British Experience, 1760–1911, at 207 (1999).

[16] *See, e.g.*, Wheaton v. Peters, 33 U.S. 591, 655–56 (1834) (citing Donaldson v. Beckett 4 Burr. 2408 (H.L.) (1774) (appeal taken from Eng.)) (noting that an author's cause of action for copyright claims was "taken away by the statute of 8 Anne" and that "remedy must be under statute"); Balganesh, *Stewarding the Common Law*, *supra* note 12, at 108 ("Ever since [the Statute of Anne], the principal source of law for copyright has remained legislation.").

[17] *See* Balganesh, *The Pragmatic Incrementalism*, *supra* note 12, at 1554–64 (summarizing common law intellectual property regimes that arose in common law).

codifications of IP principles and rules have fostered the judiciary's shaping power primarily in the three following ways, thereby creating a partnership between judges and legislators in strengthening IP protection.

First, IP statutes in the United States have preserved judges' autonomy to adapt codified doctrines according to new circumstances. The fair-use doctrine epitomizes this preserved judicial autonomy. As a judge-made doctrine,[18] fair use was not codified by the U.S. Copyright Act until its 1976 revision.[19] Section 107 of the U.S. Copyright Act contains a non-exhaustive list of four fair-use factors and empowers judges to reach decisions based on those four factors or any other relevant factors.[20] The legislative history of this section reveals an intention to make such a broad and flexible system available to the judiciary.[21] A relevant House Committee Report stated that codification of the fair-use doctrine was merely a restatement of past judicial experiences and was not intended to "freeze the doctrine in the statute."[22] Rather, judges "must be free to adapt the doctrine to particular situations on a case-by-case basis."[23] The transformative use concept subsequently developed and applied by judges is an example of the judicial autonomy preserved by the 1976 codification. Although section 107 makes no mention of transformative use, the U.S. Supreme Court has held that the more transformative the use of a work is, the less significance should be afforded other factors weighing against fair use.[24] U.S. courts have subsequently applied the concept in numerous copyright cases,[25] adapting copyright law to govern uses of works that are aided by new technologies.[26]

Second, where statutes have not codified IP protection rules, judges still have full autonomy to create and develop new doctrines.[27] In U.S. trademark law, the

[18] *See* Harper & Row Publishers v. Nation Enters., 471 U.S. 539, 550 (1985) ("As early as 1841, Justice Story gave judicial recognition to the [fair-use] doctrine").

[19] Haochen Sun, *Overcoming the Achilles Heel of Copyright Law*, 5 Nw. J. Tech. & Intell. Prop. 265, 283 (2007) ("It was not until 1976 that this judicially-made doctrine was given express statutory recognition in the U.S. Copyright Act.").

[20] *See* 17 U.S.C. § 107.

[21] *See* Niva Elkin-Koren & Orit Fischman-Afori, *Rulifying Fair Use*, 59 Ariz. L. Rev. 161, 176 (2017) (quoting H.R. Rep. No. 94-1476, at 66 (1976) and citing S. Rep. No. 94-473, § 106 (1975)).

[22] H.R. REP. No. 94-1476, at 66 (1976), *as reprinted in* 1976 U.S.C.C.A.N. 5109, 5679.

[23] *Id. See also Harper & Row*, 471 U.S. at 561 ("The drafters resisted pressures from special interest groups to create presumptive categories of fair use, but structured the provision as an affirmative defense requiring a case-by-case analysis."); Campbell v. Acuff-Rose Music, Inc., 510 U.S. 569, 577 (1994) (holding that the task of interpreting fair use "like the doctrine it recognizes, calls for case-by-case analysis").

[24] *Campbell*, 510 U.S. at 579.

[25] *See* Barton Beebe, *An Empirical Study of U.S. Copyright Fair Use Opinions, 1978–2005*, 156 U. Pa. L. Rev. 549, 604–5 (2008) (finding that 41.2% of 119 district court opinions and 81.4% of circuit court opinions invoked the transformative use doctrine since *Campbell*); Haochen Sun, *Copyright Law as an Engine of Public Interest Protection*, 16 Nw. J. Tech. & Intell. Prop. 123, 134 (2019).

[26] *See* Sun, *id.* at 134 (2019).

[27] Frederick Schauer, *Is the Common Law?*, 77 Calif. L. Rev. 455, 455 (1989) (book review) ("[C]ommon law rules are not made by legislatures; they are created by courts simultaneously with the application of those rules to concrete cases.").

statutory codification of judicial limitations on the powers of trademark owners in the Lanham Act is substantial but incomplete, meaning that some provisions authorize the continued judicial development of trademark law.[28] Some commentators therefore view the Lanham Act as a delegating statute allowing greater common law development of defenses.[29] In defenses to trademark infringement, there is significant evidence of judicial creativity. For example, as one of the fair-use defenses available to defendants who use a trademark for speech purposes, nominative use has been described as a judge-made variation on the statutory fair-use doctrine enshrined in copyright law.[30] Similarly, the parodic fair-use defense was enshrined in trademark legislation following the 2006 reforms that developed the doctrine of dilution, but has been the subject of judicial attention for much longer than the relevant statutory reform.[31]

Third, judges also enjoy considerable autonomy in making reasoned decisions regarding IP laws interwoven with constitutional norms and the public interest. For instance, judges have provided free speech protection in cases involving nominative uses of trademarks; these cases act as proxies for First Amendment protection in trademark law, similar to fair use in copyright law.[32] By making these interventions, U.S. judges have taken important steps to prevent trademark protection from undermining freedom of expression. Judges in the United States have introduced limitations protecting parodic uses of trademarks, which are seen as an important form of expression.[33] When successful, parodies can powerfully convey "a political statement, social commentary, commercial speech, a bawdy joke, ridicule of a brand name, criticism of commercialism, or just plain humor for its own sake."[34] U.S. courts have emphasized the importance of preventing infringement lawsuits from stifling parody because, despite parody creating an association with a mark, it is clear that parodic use is satirical when done effectively.[35] There is therefore less need in such cases for judges to balance free speech values against the risk of consumer confusion.

B. IP Adjudication in China's Civil Law System

Pursuant to the civil law tradition, civil law judges interpret and follow statutory provisions. Unlike their common law counterparts, they are not entitled to develop new

[28] *See* Michael Grynberg, *The Judicial Role in Trademark Law*, 52 B. C. L. Rev. 1283, 1307 (2011).

[29] Graeme B. Dinwoodie, *Developing Defenses in Trademark Law*, 13 Lewis & Clark L. Rev. 99, 137–38 (2009).

[30] William McGeveran, *Four Free Speech Goals for Trademark Law*, 18 Fordham Intell. Prop. Media & Ent. L.J. 1205, 1215–17 (2008).

[31] Dinwoodie, *supra* note 29, at 144.

[32] *Id.* at 121–22.

[33] *See Campbell*, 510 U.S. at 579.

[34] Gary Myers, *Trademark Parody: Lessons from the Copyright Decision in* Campbell v. Acuff-Rose Music, Inc., 59 Law & Contemp. Probs. 181, 181 (1996).

[35] *See, e.g.*, Louis Vuitton Malletier v. Haute Diggity Dog, LLC, 507 F.3d 252, 267 (4th Cir. 2007).

legal doctrines through the judicial process. Although civil law systems cannot survive without some judicial discretion, as contradiction is inevitable owing to legislation being unable to anticipate future circumstances,[36] it is different from the judicial discretion available under common law. Civil law judges do not enjoy the discretion to change the law, but they do have the discretion to characterize facts according to the law, interpret the law, and interpret rules under the law.[37] Moreover, they are afforded far less influence and power than their common law counterparts, a situation that derives from the idea in civil law that laws should be made only by the legislature and from the consequent rejection of the principle of *stare decisis*.[38] As civil law judges can look only to legislation when making decisions, and are incapable of binding future judges to the principles on which they reach those decisions, their role is substantially more modest than that of judges in the common law tradition.[39]

In the civil law tradition, judges can be viewed as expert clerks or operators of a machine built by the legislature, and ultimately as civil servants performing an important but uncreative function.[40] As a result, they are not studied or celebrated in the same way that common law judges are.[41] There is little advantage or competitive edge to be gained from studying their previous decisions, and they are unlikely to be remembered individually for their role in the historical development of certain legal doctrines.[42]

China follows the civil law tradition.[43] The major sources of Chinese IP law are the Copyright Law,[44] the Patent Law,[45] and the Trademark Law,[46] three national

[36] Roberto G. MacLean, *Judicial Discretion in the Civil Law*, 43 La. L. Rev. 45, 49 (1982).

[37] *Id.* at 50, 54 ("When a judge is faced with a particular set of facts, he has the choice of placing those facts under one legal category or another ... There are some codes which attempt to be as precise and exact as possible concerning the methods of interpretation to be used, such as literal interpretation, logical interpretation, and exegetical interpretation. But, always it is the judge who must choose among the many methods available... A general survey of the Louisiana Civil Code, for instance, provides numerous examples of [particular] rules allowing the exercise of judicial discretion. In the first place, the judge in some cases must determine whether an agreement or obligation is or is not against the public order or the public good.").

[38] Merryman & Pérez-Perdomo, *supra* note 9, at 36.

[39] *Id.* at 36–37.

[40] *Id.*

[41] *Id.*

[42] *Id.* at 37.

[43] Jacques deLisle, *A Common Law-Like Civil Law and a Public Face for Private Law: China's Tort Law in Comparative Perspective, in* Towards a Chinese Civil Code: Comparative and Historical Perspectives 353, 362 (Lei Chen & C. H. van Rhee eds., 2012) ("Chinese law has retained a civilian cast, reflecting China's affinity toward—and multiple receptions of—civil law influences and the civil law tradition.").

[44] Zhonghua Renmin Gongheguo Zhuzuoquan Fa (中华人民共和国著作权法) (Copyright Law of the People's Republic of China) (promulgated by the Standing Comm. Nat'l People's Cong., Nov. 11, 2020, effective June 1, 2021) 348 Standing Comm. Nat'l People's Cong. Gaz. 9.

[45] Zhonghua Renmin Gongheguo Zhuanli Fa (中华人民共和国专利法) (Patent Law of the People's Republic of China) (promulgated by the Standing Comm. Nat'l People's Cong., Oct. 17, 2020, effective June 1, 2021) 347 Standing Comm. Nat'l People's Cong. Gaz. 717.

[46] Zhonghua Renmin Gongheguo Shangbiao Fa (中华人民共和国商标法) (Trademark Law of the People's Republic of China) (promulgated by the Standing Comm. Nat'l People's Cong., Apr. 23, 2019, effective Nov. 1, 2019) 339 Standing Comm. Nat'l People's Cong. Gaz. 595.

statutes passed by the National People's Congress. Supplemental to these statutes are a range of administrative regulations enacted by the State Council. Therefore, Chinese judges are expected to interpret and apply the statutory provisions contained in these legal documents in deciding cases. They cannot go beyond statutory provisions to create new legal bases for deciding cases. Such lawmaking power belongs to the National People's Congress and the State Council. Nor are judges' rulings binding upon later cases.

The treatment of descriptive fair use epitomizes the civil law character of China's IP protection system. For example, the Chinese Trademark Law[47] did not recognize descriptive fair use of trademarks until its third amendment was introduced in 2013.[48] Prior to that amendment, Article 49 of the Implementing Regulations of the Chinese Trademark Law[49] provided exceptions "for the use of common names, logos, or models conferred by a trademark or the quality, principal raw materials, functions, uses, weight, quantities, geographic names, or other features that are explicitly expressed by the registered trademark."[50] Although this wording covered many descriptive uses of registered trademarks, some were potentially excluded, such as the use of surnames or the names of individuals or organizations.[51]

A lack of autonomy has often restrained Chinese and other civil law judges from protecting the public interest in the IP field. Consider the example of the Google Library case. A French court in 2009 held that the Google Digital Library, which reproduces books in full and makes extracts available without authorization from the copyright owners, does not fall under the "brief quotation" exception available under French law despite the value it offers the public.[52] In Germany, a Hamburg court concluded that Google was liable for copyright infringement for displaying thumbnail images in search results, as no existing fair dealing exception covered such conduct.[53] As China also follows the civil law tradition, Chinese judges,

[47] Zhonghua Renmin Gongheguo Shangbiao Fa (中华人民共和国商标法) (Trademark Law of the People's Republic of China) (promulgated by the Standing Comm. Nat'l People's Cong., Aug. 30, 2013, effective May 1, 2014), art. 59, 305 STANDING COMM. NAT'L PEOPLE'S CONG. GAZ. 713 (2013).

[48] *See* George Fu & Cathy Wu, *The Balancing of Fair Use and Exclusivity—Trademark Rights under the Chinese Trademark Law: A Third Amendment Perspective*, 104 TRADEMARK REP. 1241, 1242 (2014).

[49] Zhonghua Renmin Gongheguo Shangbiao Fa Shishi Tiaoli (中华人民共和国商标法实施条例) (Implementing Regulations of the Trademark Law of the People's Republic of China) (promulgated by St. Council People's Rep. China, Aug. 3, 2002, rev'd by St. Council People's Rep. China, Apr. 29, 2014, effective May 1, 2014), art. 49, *translated in Implementing Regulations of the Trademark Law of the People's Republic of China*, WIPO LEX, https://www.wipo.int/edocs/lexdocs/laws/en/cn/cn342en.pdf (last visited Jan. 31, 2022).

[50] Fu & Wu, *supra* note 48, at 1243 ("For a long time, Article 49 of the Regulations was cited as the main legal basis for the fair use defense.").

[51] *Id.*

[52] Rami Olwan, *The Adoption of the American Fair Use in Gulf States: A Comparative Analysis of Authors' Exceptions in Common Law and Civil Law Countries*, 38 EUROPEAN INTELL. PROP. L. REV. 416, 422–23 (2016).

[53] *Id.* at 423.

similar to their counterparts in France and Germany, were also bound by Chinese copyright statutes, which contain no provisions dealing with the specific question of whether reproductions of copyrighted works by digital libraries constitute fair use.[54] These decisions demonstrate that in the civil law tradition judges are unable to expand the list of permissible copyright exceptions to protect the public interest. The law therefore must swiftly adapt to technological changes, which can be difficult to achieve.[55]

II. Chinese Judges' Creative Construction of Trademark Statutes

In this section, I unearth a major judicial development in China that deserves a closer look by the global IP protection community. This development presents crystal-clear evidence showing that Chinese judges have deviated from the civil law tradition in order to protect the public interest in a range of rulings in cases involving fair uses of trademarks.

In contrast to the Chinese Trademark Law's narrow coverage of descriptive fair use, the limitations on trademark rights under the trademark laws of the European Union and United States broadly cover both descriptive use and nominative use exemptions. The nominative fair-use exemption permits the use of another's trademark to refer to the trademark owner's goods and services for the purposes of criticism, news reporting, and/or comparison.[56] For example, U.S. courts have allowed newspapers to use the name of a music group as a trademark to solicit public opinion on that group,[57] and the European Court of Justice permitted a company to use the Gillette trademark to indicate that the blades it produces are compatible with Gillette handles.[58]

Upon its 2013 amendment, the Chinese Trademark Law was extended to cover descriptive uses. Article 59 prescribes the following:

> [t]he holder of the exclusive right to use a registered trademark shall have no right to prohibit others from properly using the generic name, graphics or models of a commodity contained in the registered trademark, or such information as

[54] Haochen Sun, *Copyright Law as an Engine of Public Interest Protection*, 16 Nw. J. Tech. & Intell. Prop. 123, 139–41 (2019) ("While the U.S. courts settled the Google Library disputes based on the public interest, the Chinese courts gave scant consideration to the public interest in their rulings.").

[55] *See, e.g.*, Anupam Chander, *How Law Made Silicon Valley*, 63 Emory L. J. 639, 677 (2014) (describing the how a European Electronic Commerce Directive was less useful than similar American laws because they were less adoptable).

[56] *Id.* at 1248.

[57] 971 F.2d 302, 308–09 (9th Cir. 1992).

[58] Case No. C-228/03, Gillette Co. & Gillette Grp. Fin. Ltd. v. LA-Lab'ys Ltd., E.C.R. I-2337 (2005).

> directly indicates the quality, main raw materials, functions, purposes, weight, quantity or other features of the commodity, or the names of the geographical locations as contained therein.[59]

However, neither the third amendment nor the latest fourth amendment of 2020 provides a better definition of descriptive fair use.[60] The Trademark Law therefore remains silent on whether the legality of a descriptive use depends on the absence of any likelihood of consumer confusion.[61] In this context, the Chinese courts have made conflicting judicial decisions, which demonstrates the importance of revising the Chinese Trademark Law to harmonize the relevant legal rules.[62] Some courts have opined that the likelihood of consumer confusion bars a finding of descriptive use. For example, in a 2002 guideline, the Beijing High Court initially itemized four factors that permit a finding in favor of descriptive use: 1) the use of another's trademark is done in good will; 2) another's trademark is not used as a trademark; 3) the purpose of the use is to describe one's own products or services; and 4) the use of another's trademark will not create consumer confusion.[63] However, in 2006, the Beijing High Court deleted the fourth factor from the descriptive use test, and its subsequent judicial decisions have not considered potential consumer confusion.[64]

Although the Chinese Trademark Law allows for descriptive use alone, the Chinese courts have relied on nominative use in deciding cases without any statutory basis. In such cases, the courts have protected the interests of consumers and businesses by holding that the nominative use of a trademark can be fair despite not being an existing statutory exception to infringement.

In *Shanghai Maisi Investment Co. v. Victoria's Secret*,[65] for example, the defendant sold authentic Victoria's Secret products purchased from a third-party company.[66] It also used Victoria's Secret's registered trademarks in its various business activities. When Victoria's Secret sued the defendant for trademark infringement, the defendant invoked the fair-use defense, asserting that the products it sold were

[59] *Trademark Law of the People's Republic of China*, WIPO Lex 18, https://www.wipo.int/edocs/lexdocs/laws/en/cn/cn195en.pdf (last visited Jan. 31, 2022).

[60] *See* Fu & Wu, *supra* note 48, at 1244.

[61] *See id.* ("The doctrine does not, however, justify the deliberate use of another party's mark as a trademark.").

[62] *See, e.g., id.*

[63] *Id.*

[64] *Id.*

[65] Shanghai Maisi Touzi Guanlli Youxian Gongsi Yu Weiduoliya de Mimi Shangdian Pinpai Guanli Gongsi Qinhai Shangbiao Quan, Bu Zhengdang Jingzheng Jiufen Shangsu An (上海麦司投资管理有限公司与维多利亚的秘密商店品牌管理公司侵害商标权、不正当竞争纠纷上诉案) (Shanghai Maisi Inv. Mgmt. Co. v. Victoria's Secret Store Brand Mgmt. Co. (A Trademark Infringement and Unfair Competition Appeal Case)) 2017 Sup. People's Ct. Gaz. 8 (Shanghai Higher People's Ct. Case No. 104, Feb. 13, 2015) (China).

[66] *Id.*

legally purchased from another company and that its use of the trademarks in the course of their sale therefore constituted a fair use under Chinese trademark law.[67]

The Shanghai High Court, which heard the case, expressly recognized the nominative use of a trademark as a defense against the allegation of infringement because such use is intended to indicate the source of goods to consumers and to help them make purchase decisions.[68] However, it also noted that such use should be restricted to the extent necessary to indicate the source of the goods.[69] Otherwise, the use would amount to an infringement of trademark rights.[70]

The Court found that the defendant had used the Victoria's Secret trademarks on signs, walls, counters, the name tags of store staff, VIP cards, and background screens in a fashion show and had publicly declared that its store was a Victoria's Secret outlet.[71] These uses had misled members of the consuming public, causing them to erroneously believe that the defendant was a licensee of Victoria's Secret.[72] The Court further found that the use of the trademarks in the defendant's online advertising was intended to promote its own franchise operations,[73] and therefore went beyond what was necessary to indicate the source of the goods.[74]

In *Nippon v. Shanghai Zhanjin Trading Co.*,[75] the defendant was sued for its unauthorized use of the NIPPON trademark in selling Nippon and other branded paints on Taobao.com, one of the largest e-commerce platforms in China.[76] The Shanghai First Intermediate Court ruled in favor of the defendant on the basis of nominative use, holding that such use of a trademark is legal as long as the user has not caused consumer confusion or harmed the legitimate interests of the trademark owner.[77]

The Court observed that the trademark had been used in a picture to present Nippon products to consumers, together with pictures of other branded paint products.[78] As to the layout of the defendant's webpage, the main section presented information on the products of various brands, including pictures,

[67] *Id.*
[68] *Id.*
[69] *Id.*
[70] *Id.*
[71] *Id.*; *see also* Zhu Rui, *Victoria's Secret Wins Trademark Lawsuit*, China Rep. Intell. Prop. (Dec. 10, 2014), http://english.cnipa.gov.cn/transfer/2017-10/20171023201945550610.pdf.
[72] *Victoria's Secret*, Shanghai Higher People's Ct. Case No. 104.
[73] *Id.*
[74] *Id.*
[75] Li Bang Tuliao (Zhongguo) Youxian Gongsi Su Shanghai Zhan Jin Maoyi Youxian Gongsi Deng Shangbiao Quan Shu Qinquan Jiufen Yi An (立邦涂料（中国）有限公司诉上海展进贸易有限公司等商标权权属、侵权纠纷一案) (Nippon Paint (China) Co. v. Shanghai Zhanjin Trading Co. & Zhejiang Taobao Network Co. for trademark infringement disputes), Bedia Fabao Magic No. CLI.C.6243684 (Shanghai First Interm. People's Ct., May 24, 2012).
[76] *Id.*
[77] *Id.*
[78] *Id.*

names, prices, and sales records.[79] Accordingly, the relevant public would normally believe that the NIPPON trademark was being used to offer information on the trademark owner's paint products rather than presenting the product seller's trade name, trademark, or business style.[80] This sort of nominative use, according to the Court, conveys information on the trademark owner's products.[81] It does not disrupt the function of the trademark in indicating the source of those products and would not cause any confusion about that source in the minds of relevant consumers.[82]

These two judicial rulings show how judges have deviated from the Chinese Trademark Law by going beyond its provisions to create new limitations on trademark rights. A large number of other relevant rulings have also made such a deviation, legalizing nominative fair use as a limitation in the Chinese trademark protection system. My search of Alpha, a legal database, showed that, as of December 2018, Chinese judges had applied nominative fair use to settle 101 trademark cases, and a recent search of Beida Fabao showed that, from January 2019 to November 2020, Chinese judges did so to settle 98 cases.[83] The Chinese Supreme Court has selected nine of these decisions as typical IP rulings and published the aforementioned *Victoria's Secret* ruling in its *Gazette*.[84] Through this publication, the Supreme Court not only indicated its agreement with the *Victoria's Secret* ruling but also selected it as a guiding case for lower courts.[85]

Similar deviations from the civil law tradition have also occurred in Chinese copyright law. By going beyond the exhaustive list of twelve fair use requirements under Article 22 of the 2010 Copyright Law, some judges have endeavored to recognize new fair uses in the public interest. In *Beijing Sogou Information Service Co., Ltd. v. Wenhui Cong*,[86] Sogou, one of China's largest search engine service

[79] *Id.*
[80] *Id.*
[81] *Id.*
[82] *Id.*
[83] BEIDA FABAO, http://www.pkulaw.cn/ (searching for "nominative fair use" (指示性合理使用) on Jan. 23, 2021.
[84] Shanghai Maisi Touzi Guanlli Youxian Gongsi Yu Weiduoliya de Mimi Shangdian Pinpai Guanli Gongsi Qinhai Shangbiao Quan, Bu Zhengdang Jingzheng Jiufen Shangsu An (上海麦司投资管理有限公司与维多利亚的秘密商店品牌管理公司侵害商标权、不正当竞争纠纷上诉案) (Shanghai Maisi Inv. Mgmt. Co. v. Victoria's Secret Store Brand Mgmt. Co. (A Trademark Infringement and Unfair Competition Appeal Case)) 2017 SUP. PEOPLE'S CT. GAZ. 8 (Shanghai Higher People's Ct. Case No. 104, Feb. 13, 2015) (China).
[85] *See* Susan Finder, *China's Evolving Case Law System in Practice*, 9 TSINGHUA CHINA L. REV. 245, 248 (2017) ("Cases published in the monthly SPC Gazette (最高人民法院 公报) which take two forms: selected judgments (裁判文书选登) and cases (案例) generally totaling 20–30 annually. The first type are cases decided by various trial divisions of the SPC and reflect their views on certain issues, while the second are model cases submitted by the local courts (through the provincial high courts), which have been reviewed by various divisions of the SPC. The cases, which have been edited, contain a summary of the important points of the case (裁判摘要).").
[86] Beijing Sougou Xinxi Fuwu Youxian Gongsi Yu Cong Wenhui Qinfan Xinxi Wangluo Chuanbo Quan Jiufen Shangsu An (北京搜狗信息服务有限公司与丛文辉侵犯信息网络传播权纠纷上诉案) (Beijing Sogou Info. Serv. Co. & Cong Wenhui, infringement of information network

providers, was sued for copyright infringement for employing web caching technology as part of its free search engine service.[87] The Beijing First Intermediate Court ruled that Sogou's web caching constituted a new type of fair use under the 2010 Chinese Copyright Law because it promotes the public interest, although web caching does not fall within any of the twelve fair use exemptions enumerated by Article 22.[88] This decision was selected as one of the *Top Ten Most Creative IP rulings by Beijing Courts* in 2013,[89] and has been widely commented upon by IP scholars.[90]

Similarly, the Guangdong High Court has opined that it is legitimate and plausible to go beyond Article 22's exhaustive list of fair use exemptions on the grounds of protecting the public interest.[91] In *Guangzhou NetEase Computer System Co., Ltd. v. Guangzhou Huaduo Network Technology Co., Ltd.*,[92] it ruled that judges can consider whether the live streaming of video games constitutes a fair use in the public interest even though such an activity is not listed as a fair use exemption under Article 22.[93] This ruling was selected by the Chinese Supreme Court as one of the 50 typical IP rulings decided in 2019.[94] Therefore, it provides guidance to the lower courts in dealing with copyright fair-use cases.[95]

dissemination rights dispute appeal case), 2013 Yizhong Min Zhongzi 12533, Beida Fabao Magic No. CLI.C.90025660 (Beijing First Inter. People's Ct. Dec. 10, 2013).

[87] *See* Haochen Sun & Johnny Xuyang Han, *Requirements for Recognizing a New Type of Fair Use Under PRC Copyright Law*, *in* Annotated Leading Copyright Cases in Major Asian Jurisdictions 257, 259 (Kung-Chung Liu ed., 2019).

[88] Beijing Sogou Info. Serv. Co., 2013 Yizong Min Zhongzi 12533.

[89] Xuesong Zhang & Yanrong Li, *The 2013 Top Ten Most Creative IP Rulings by Beijing Courts*, Beijing High People's Ct. (Apr. 26, 2014). http://bjgy.chinacourt.gov.cn/article/detail/2014/04/id/1283339.shtml.

[90] *See, e.g.*, Luo Dongchuan, Landmark Copyright Cases in China 208 (He Jiong trans., 2019).

[91] Tianxiang He, *Transplanting Fair Use in China? History, Impediments and the Future*, 2020 U. Ill. J. L. Tech. & Pol'y 359, 382–84 (2020).

[92] Guangzhou Wangyi Jisuanji Xitong Youxian Gongsi Su Guangzhou Huaduo Wangluo Keji Youxian Gongsi Qinhai Zhuzuo Quan Ji Bu Zhengdang Jingzheng Jiufen (广州网易计算机系统有限公司诉广州华多网络科技有限公司侵害著作权及不正当竞争纠纷) (Guangzhou Netease Comput. Sys. Co. v. Guangzhou Huaduo Network Tech. Co. for copyright infringement and unfair competition disps.), 2015 Yue Zhifa Min Chu Zi 16, Beida Fabao Magic No. CLI.C.10200131 (Guangdong Higher People's Ct., Y.M.Z. No.137, Oct. 24, 2017) (China).

[93] *See* Tianxiang He, *supra* note 91, at 384.

[94] *Top 10 Intellectual Property Cases and 50 Typical Intellectual Property Cases in Chinese Courts in 2019*, Supreme People's Ct. People's Rep. China (Apr. 21, 2020, 3:41 PM), http://www.court.gov.cn/zixun-xiangqing-226511.html.

[95] Note, *Chinese Common Law? Guiding Cases and Judicial Reform*, 129 Harv. L. Rev. 2213, 2213 (2016) ("Since 2010, China's highest court has converted fifty-six judicial opinions into what are intended to be de facto binding decisions that courts 'at all levels should refer to ... when adjudicating similar cases.'").

III. Deciphering Chinese Judges' Deviations from the Civil Law Tradition

Do Chinese judges' deviations from the civil law tradition amount to illegitimate judicial activism? Or do they amount to legitimate judicial creativity in protecting the public interest where IP statutes are silent? In this section, I argue that these judicial practices should be regarded as the creative destruction of the civil law tradition for the purpose of protecting the public interest through IP law. Chinese judges' expansive interpretations of fair use limitations constitute legitimate judicial activism because they have resulted in both the proactive and creative protection of the public interest.

A. Proactively Protecting the Public Interest through Creative Methods of Statutory Interpretation

In deciding the cases discussed in Section II, the judges concerned faced a dilemma over whether they should merely apply the textual meaning of the relevant statutory provisions at the expense of the public interest or liberally interpret those provisions in the public interest. In fact, judges around the world have oftentimes been bedeviled by this dilemma. The law is replete with ambiguous legal terms such as "public interest,"[96] as it uses language to convey its meanings to the public.[97] As Professor Saul Levmore wrote, "[a]mbiguity can be intentional or unintentional; it can derive from misunderstandings about language, from simple mistakes, from a failure to plan ahead, or from the impossibility of seeing very far ahead."[98]

Given the inevitable existence of loopholes in the law, the dilemma faced by Chinese judges is by no means unique to them, and nor is it the result of discrepancies between the civil law and common law traditions. In fact, such a dilemma universally poses hard legal cases for judges, regardless of whether they practice in civil law or common law jurisdictions. Strict adherence to existing legislation risks denying protection to technologies that offer substantial public benefits. For instance, it is currently unclear whether the use of copyrighted material in training

[96] *See* Haochen Sun, Technology and the Public Interest 8 (2022) (pointing out that "'the public interest' is one of the most perplexing concepts").

[97] *See* Felix S. Cohen, *Transcendental Nonsense and the Functional Approach*, 35 Colum. L. Rev. 809, 836 (1935) ("A definition [in law] is in fact a type of insurance against certain risks of confusion. It cannot, any more than can a commercial insurance policy, eliminate all risks. Absolute certainty is as foreign to language as to life. There is no final insurance against an insurer's insolvency. And the words of a definition always carry their own aura of ambiguity. But a definition is useful if it insures against risks of confusion more serious than any that the definition itself contains."). *See also* Christopher L. Kutz, Note, *Just Disagreement: Indeterminacy and Rationality in the Rule of Law*, 103 Yale L. J. 997, 1004 (1994) ("Vagueness is an ineradicable feature of our everyday language, and its pervasiveness in the law is the most commonly invoked reason for thinking that the law is indeterminate.").

[98] Saul Levmore, *Ambiguous Statutes*, 77 U. Chi. L. Rev. 1073, 1077 (2010).

datasets for artificial intelligence constitutes fair use, but the categorical rejection of such use would cripple the technology's potential and prevent myriad potential applications.[99]

For some judges, statutory ambiguities and limitations are seen as a starting point from which they have an opportunity "to make good law as they see it, to offset interest group effects, or to protect fragile minorities."[100] Critics might argue that this practice is undemocratic and suggest that judges should instead assign statutes "the understanding usually associated with that language at the time the statute was enacted[.]"[101] However, IP law is an area of law particularly prone to technological advancements that render original legislative intentions outdated. Furthermore, in cases of simple language ambiguities, proponents of the activist approach have argued that legislatures always have the option of choosing between precise and imprecise language; ambiguity is therefore a direct invitation for the courts to interpret a statute creatively.[102] As Justice Cardozo aptly observed, "[t]he rules and principles of case law have never been treated as final truths, but as working hypotheses, continually retested in those great laboratories of the law, the courts of justice."[103]

In the cases discussed in Section II, judges proactively protected the public interest when strictly following certain statutory provisions would have caused injustice and harm to the public interest. By deviating from the civil law tradition, these judges correctly applied and interpreted those rigid statutory provisions in light of the public interest. Another of the primary causes of deviation from the civil law tradition by Chinese judges is the absence of a basis within dispositive provisions of the Trademark Law for making decisions that serve the public interest. In the absence of applicable provisions, the courts could arguably be required to dismiss novel applications of trademark rights out of hand. A rigid understanding of trademark law can therefore deny the public's enjoyment of the benefits derived from freedom of commerce and healthy market competition.

In addition to affirming the prime importance of the public interest principle in the trademark judicial process, Chinese judges have also shed new light on how to apply that principle to determine the scope of the public interest in practice. They have developed a broad "public interest standard" to encompass a range of public interests related to fair uses of trademarks.

With respect to nominative fair use, Chinese judges have also identified ways to ascertain the scope of public interest associated with trademark protection. First,

[99] Benjamin L. W. Sobel, *Artificial Intelligence's Fair Use Crisis*, 41 COLUM. J. L. & ARTS 45, 61, 80 (2017).

[100] *See* Levmore, *supra* note98, at 1077.

[101] *Id.* at 1077–78, 1081.

[102] *See* Arthur S. Miller, *Statutory Language and the Purposive Use of Ambiguity*, 42 VA. L. REV. 23, 23–24 (1956).

[103] BENJAMIN N. CARDOZO, THE NATURE OF THE JUDICIAL PROCESS 23 (1921).

the Chinese courts have explicitly recognized a nominative use exemption, albeit without any statutory basis to do so under the Chinese Trademark Act. In *Toyota v. Zhejiang Geely*,[104] for example, the defendant, Chinese car manufacturer Geely, had used the Toyota trademark in its promotional materials to show that its car engines incorporated technology licensed from Toyota.[105] Although the Beijing Second Intermediate Court upheld Geely's contention that such use was legal, it was unable to base its ruling on a finding of nominative fair use.[106] Instead, it merely held that Geely's use of the trademark conformed to normal business practice,[107] which is by no means a legal rule under the Trademark Law.

Second, the Chinese courts have defined nominative use as a legitimate trademark rights limitation in cases involving internationally famous trademarks. For example, in *Caterpillar, Inc. v. Ruian Changshen*,[108] the defendant's automobile filters had been affixed with the defendant's registered mark "C" and "FORCATERPILLAR."[109] The Shanghai Pudong New District Court noted that filters are unique and indispensable components of automobiles and that because different filters match different cars, it is important for manufacturers to help consumers by identifying which filters they need.[110] However, it also stated that such use of a mark must be in good faith and strictly limited to a reasonable scope, thus leading to its finding in this case that the use had exceeded what was necessary, as the defendant had emphasized Caterpillar's mark while making its own difficult to locate.[111] Doing so had thus confused customers as to the filters' origin and did not constitute fair use.[112]

[104] (Riben) Fengtian Zidong Che Zhushi Huishe Su Zhejiang Jili Qiche Youxian Gongsi Deng Qinfan Shangbiao Quan Ji Bu Zhengdang Jingzheng jiufen An Pingxi (（日本）丰田自动车株式会社诉浙江吉利汽车有限公司等侵犯商标权及不正当竞争纠纷案评析) ((Japan) Toyota Motor Co., Ltd. v. Zhejiang Geely Autombile Co., Ltd., etc., on trademark infringement and unfair competition disputes) ER ZHONG MIN CHU ZI 06286 (Beijing Second Inter. People's Ct. 2003), *unofficially reproduced in* Zhongguo Zhishi Changquan Lushi Wang (中国知识产权律师网) (CHINA INTELL. PROP. LAW. NET) (Dec. 21, 2006), http://180.76.51.122:8080/html/fgsb/20061221/122644.html. For an English-language description of the key facts and holding, see Mark O'Neill, *Toyota Loses Logo Suit in China*, S. CHINA MORNING POST (H.K.) (Nov. 25, 2003), https://www.scmp.com/article/435868/toyota-loses-logo-suit-china.

[105] CHINA INTELL. PROP. LAW. NET, *supra* note 104.

[106] *Id.*

[107] *Id.*

[108] Kate Bi Lei Su Changsheng Lu Qing Qi Shangbiao Su An (卡特彼勒诉长生滤清器商标侵权纠纷案) (Caterpillar v. Changsheng Filter Trademark Infringement Case), ER ZHONG MIN ZHONG SHENG 78286 (Shanghai Pudong New Dist. Ct. 2007), *unofficially reproduced in* Zhongguo Zhishi Changquan Lushi Wang (中国知识产权律师网) (CHINA INTELL. PROP. LAW. NET) (Aug. 24, 2007), http://180.76.51.122:8080/html/sfsb/20070824/123097.html.

[109] *See* Fu & Wu, *supra* note48, at 1250.

[110] *Id.*

[111] *Id.*

[112] *Id.*

B. Thinking through Judicial Practice in the United States

Chinese judges' deviation from relevant trademark statutes can, as I argue in the preceding section, be justified as a creative destruction of the civil law tradition for the purpose of protecting the public interest. In this section, I argue that the judicial practices adopted in the United States also lend strong support to Chinese judges' creative destruction of the civil tradition. In the United States, there has been increasing movement away from the traditional emphasis on judge-made principles and toward the statutory protection of IP rights. This process has involved greater codification of existing principles, making statutes the predominant source of IP law. Although this may suggest that the distinctions between common law and civil law adjudications described in Section I will be brought into doubt, there is still room under the new approach for broad judicial autonomy.

There are several reasons for the increased tendency toward the codification of IP principles and doctrines. The primary reason is that Congress is considered to be the best-positioned institution to introduce new developments, both in terms of legitimacy and capability.[113] Unelected federal judges are often scrutinized for their role in the lawmaking process and are further limited by the facts before them, whereas the legislature is not subject to such scrutiny and is considered "more capable of calibrating policies to address the needs of the citizenry as a whole."[114]

Other reasons include the growing complexity of subject matter and relevant markets. For instance, whereas copyright law was originally aimed primarily at regulating books, maps, and charts, modern day copyright law must regulate "such diverse types of works as books, newspapers, magazines, fine art, movies, recorded music, and computer software."[115] This growing diversity has in turn resulted in a more complex set of competing interests and copyright entitlements.[116] As copyrights become more valuable, the incentive to fine-tune the law and the pragmatic need to balance the interests of relevant parties increase.[117] The detailed exemptions introduced during copyright codification, for example, have provided far more guidance to industries about what they can and cannot do with copyrighted works.[118]

U.S. legal reforms have codified IP protection principles and rules into statutes as comprehensively and thoroughly as civil law IP protection systems have done. However, one key remaining difference lies in the varying degree of autonomy that judges possess in the United States compared to their counterparts in civil law

[113] Grynberg, supra note 28, at 1283, 1300–01.
[114] *Id.*
[115] *See* Liu, *supra* note 87, at 129.
[116] *Id.* at 129–30.
[117] *Id.* at 130.
[118] *See id.* at 133 (arguing that the regulatory approach to copyright law provides clearer guidance to interested parties than the judicial, property-rights-based approach).

jurisdictions such as China. Despite the aforementioned changes to the legislative mechanism of U.S. IP law, U.S. judges enjoy a considerably greater degree of judicial autonomy, as demonstrated in Section I. The regulatory approach is limited in that it ensures that reform is slow-moving, and it is also limited in responding to changes or public-interest concerns that emerge as technologies or industries develop.[119] Even under a regulatory model, the limitations of legislation mean that there is still an influential role for judges to play within the U.S. system of IP protection. In this context, judges can act to fill legislative gaps or interpret existing provisions in light of new issues. This role does not necessarily undermine, and is not independent of, the regulatory approach, as judicial action can "remain interstitial and coexist with legislative enactments in an area."[120]

There are jurisprudential justifications for affording greater judicial autonomy to shape IP protection systems through deciding cases, not only to judges in common law jurisdictions such as the United States but also to their counterparts in civil law jurisdictions such as China. To be specific, these jurisprudential justifications allow judges in both common law and civil law jurisdictions to enjoy a greater degree of autonomy in protecting the public interest through their application of IP laws to legal disputes.

First, judges should be equipped with sufficient autonomy in protecting the public interest to fill the loopholes in IP statutes. As the basic ingredient of statutes, language itself is often fraught with ambiguity. As long as the law relies on language to convey its prescriptions, the problem of ambiguity will persist.[121] Legislation often employs words or phrases that are subject to extensive debate during adjudication. For instance, in *Continental Can Co. v. Chicago Truck Drivers*,[122] the court was required to consider the exact meaning of "substantially all," with one party arguing that the phrase referred to a simple majority, and the other arguing that it should be interpreted as meaning at least 85%.[123] In cases where such imprecise language is used, searching for legislative intent can be a fruitless pursuit.[124]

Second, the inability of legislators to foresee future situations makes it impossible for them to enact laws that are capable of regulating all legal matters that might occur after legislation has been passed.[125] Whereas technology is dynamic,

[119] *See* Balganesh, *Stewarding the Common Law*, *supra* note 12, at 104; *see also* Balganesh, *The Pragmatic Incrementalism*, *supra* note 12, at 1569.

[120] Balganesh, *The Pragmatic Incrementalism*, *supra* note 12, at 1595.

[121] *See* H. L. A. Hart, The Concept of Law 127–28 (2nd ed. 1994) ("Whichever device, precedent or legislation, is chosen for the communication of standards of behavio[]r, these, however smoothly they work over the great mass of ordinary cases, will, at some point where their application is in question, prove indeterminate; they will have what has been termed an *open texture*.") (emphasis in original); *see also* Haochen Sun, *supra* note 19, at 304.

[122] 916 F.2d 1154 (7th Cir. 1990).

[123] *Id.* at 1155.

[124] *See* Miller, *supra* note 102, at 25.

[125] *See* Hart, *supra* note 121, at 128 ("[H]uman legislators can have no such knowledge of all possible combinations of circumstances which the future may bring. This inability to anticipate brings with it a relative indeterminacy of aim."); Wesley Newcomb Hohfeld, *Some Fundamental Legal Conceptions as*

legislation is static, and the costs and efforts required to update it cannot reasonably be expended year-in and year-out to keep pace.[126] This situation poses challenges throughout IP law. For instance, the global reach afforded trademarks by the Internet may require courts to take note of evolving factual circumstances and recognize broader geographic rights for unregistered marks than foreseen by legislation that originated in the pre-Internet era.[127] Moreover, the rapid development of artificial intelligence has IP attorneys worldwide asking whether patent law or copyright law is equipped to handle the technology.[128]

In response to this dilemma, Justice Cardozo has suggested that judges should strictly follow precedent and apply the law in easy cases, but apply the law liberally in hard cases by balancing competing considerations, including the paramount value of social welfare.[129] Public law such as constitutional law regularly prioritizes social welfare, and perhaps private law such as IP law should more frequently apply social welfare as a guiding principle for reinterpreting and remaking its rules.[130]

Third, judges must have sufficient autonomy to develop creative interpretations of the nature and scope of the public interest implicated in IP protection. The public interest is a difficult notion to define, and efforts to do so are frequently met with criticism.[131] The topic has been derided as semantic chaos, and assertions of public interest have often been dismissed as nothing more than whatever the speaker believes to be desirable policy.[132] The notion of public interest also suggests that a policy designed to serve this goal should attempt to offer benefits to all members of a given society, but, in practice, owing to the existence of competing interests, the public is more likely to refer to a majority or simply to the many.[133]

Applied in Judicial Reasoning, 23 YALE L. J. 16, 30 (1913) ("The strictly fundamental legal relations are, after all, *sui generis*; and thus it is that attempts at formal definition are always unsatisfactory, if not altogether useless."); Haochen Sun, *supra* note 19, at 305 ("[T]he letters of the law, no matter how general or specific they are, do not provide definite and exhaustive answers in order to sidestep any future legal pitfalls.").

[126] *See* Dan L. Burk, *Patent Reform in the United States: Lessons Learned*, REGULATION, 20, 21 (Winter 2012–13).

[127] *See* Grynberg, *supra* note 28, at 1326.

[128] *See, e.g.*, Renee White, *Medical AI: Can Patent Law Keep up with the Trajectory of Innovation?*, GRIFFITH HACK (Apr. 30, 2019), https://www.griffithhack.com/ideas/insights/medical-ai-can-patent-law-keep-up-with-the-trajectory-of-innovation; Nina Fitzgerald et al., *An In-Depth Analysis of Copyright and the Challenges Presented by Artificial Intelligence*, ASHURST (Mar. 11, 2020), https://www.ashurst.com/en/news-and-insights/insights/an-indepth-analysis-of-copyright-and-the-challenges-presented-by-artificial-intelligence/.

[129] CARDOZO, *supra* note 103, at 150 ("[W]hen a rule, after it has been duly tested by experience, has been found to be inconsistent with the sense of justice or with the social welfare, there should be less hesitation in frank avowal and full abandonment.")

[130] *Id.* at 150–51 ("We have had to do this sometimes in the field of constitutional law. Perhaps we should do so oftener in fields of private law where considerations of social utility are not so aggressive and insistent.").

[131] *See, e.g.*, William A. Galston, *An Old Debate Renewed: The Politics of the Public Interest*, 136 DÆDALUS, Fall 2007, at 10, 11 (2007).

[132] *Id.*

[133] Bruce Douglass, *The Common Good and the Public Interest*, 8 POL. THEORY 103, 110 (1980).

The term is also highly contextual, changing along with social and moral values, meaning that something deemed to be in the public interest today may not be so in ten years' time.[134]

The difficulty of defining the public interest is also evident in IP law. For instance, in copyright law, the public interest is sometimes treated as synonymous with the current law as enacted or, more often, with a specific policy or reform goal being put forward by an interested party.[135] Commentators have argued that since the inception of copyright law there has been an underlying tension between the interests of authors and the interests of the public at large.[136] Copyright law has traditionally treated the rights of authors as synonymous with the public interest.[137] This perspective is based on the idea that a right of public access to works is valuable only if there are works worth accessing.[138] More recently, however, the public interest has increasingly been used as a proxy for the interests of users, often being invoked in favor of free access to copyrighted works for personal use.[139]

Trademark law, too, has experienced a balancing of competing interests, with both sides arguing that their position serves the public interest. For instance, in *New Kids on the Block*,[140] Judge Kozinski held that nominative fair use was essential for free speech, as "[m]uch useful social and commercial discourse would be all but impossible if speakers were under threat of an infringement lawsuit every time they made reference to a person, company or product by using its trademark."[141] However, some commentators have argued that other public interests should be protected over free speech. For instance, despite the free speech value of parody, it has been argued that some uses of brand names add nothing to the humorous element of a product, and therefore amount to nothing more than free riding "to take advantage of the senior brand."[142]

[134] Jane Johnston, *Whose Interests? Why Defining the "Public Interest" Is Such a Challenge*, CONVERSATION (Jan. 22, 2019), https://theconversation.com/whose-interests-why-defining-the-public-interest-is-such-a-challenge-84278.

[135] Rebecca Giblin & Kimberlee Weatherall, *If We Redesigned Copyright from Scratch, What Might it Look Like?*, *in* WHAT IF WE COULD REIMAGINE COPYRIGHT? 1, 3–5 (Rebecca Giblin & Kimberlee Weatherall eds., 2017).

[136] GILLIAN DAVIES, COPYRIGHT AND THE PUBLIC INTEREST 235 (2d ed. 2002).

[137] Giblin & Weatherall, *supra* note 135, at 5.

[138] *See* Neil Turkewitz, *Inside Views: Copyright And The Public Interest: Not Necessarily Competing Forces*, INTELL. PROP. WATCH (July 7, 2015), https://www.ip-watch.org/2015/07/07/copyright-and-the-public-interest-not-necessarily-competing-forces/.

[139] Giblin & Weatherall, *supra* note 135, at 5–6.

[140] 971 F.2d 302 (9th Cir. 1992).

[141] *Id.* at 307.

[142] Maria Solis, Trademark Dilution & Copyright Infringement 5 (Aug. 25, 2018) (unpublished manuscript) (available at author's SSRN account, https://papers.ssrn.com/sol3/papers.cfm?abstract_id=3306431).

Conclusion

China has long had a reputation for blatantly infringing IP rights. The country's failure to curb counterfeiting has caused severe financial damage to foreign companies and earned it the unenviable moniker "king of the global counterfeit trade."[143] Several disputes have arisen between China and other countries based on its faulty protection of IP, not least the ongoing trade war with the United States[144]

In contrast to the prevailing view, however, this chapter reveals a positive dimension to the Chinese IP protection system. Through their creative judicial rulings, Chinese judges are creating a new reputation for China's trademark law, that is, as an engine of public interest protection. The chapter shows that through their creative destruction of the civil law tradition, Chinese judges have made important contributions to protecting the public interest. When interpreting the nature and scope of limitations on trademark rights, they have made appropriate deviations from the civil law tradition to proactively protect the public interest. In doing so, they have developed creative legal methods to ascertain the myriad public interests implicated in limitations on trademark rights.

[143] Lily Kuo, *China is Still King of the Global Counterfeit Trade*, QUARTZ (Apr. 16, 2013), https://qz.com/74942/china-is-still-king-of-the-global-counterfeit-trade/.

[144] *See, e.g.*, Peter K. Yu, *A Half-Century of Scholarship on the Chinese Intellectual Property System*, 67 AM. U. L. REV. 1045, 1075 (2018) ("One major incident that attracted considerable policy and scholarly attention in this phase was the U.S.-China WTO dispute over the lack of protection and enforcement of intellectual property rights under the TRIPS Agreement. This dispute marked the first time the United States used the mandatory WTO dispute settlement process to address the massive piracy and counterfeiting problems in China.").

11

Limitations of Trademark Rights in Major Asian Jurisdictions

Kung-Chung Liu[*]

Introduction

Amid rapid economic growth in Asia, the protection of intellectual property (IP) has become increasingly important.[1] However, there is a shortage of comparative literature on Asian IP laws, and there is even less dealing with Asian trademark laws.[2] Given the size and importance of Asia's bustling trademark landscape, this chapter is dedicated to trademark laws in the major Asian jurisdictions of China, India, Japan, Korea, Malaysia, the Philippines, Singapore, and Taiwan. Based on a survey of the Asian trademark landscape, the chapter explores four crucial limitations on trademark rights in these jurisdictions: international exhaustion, prohibition of abuse of trademark rights, fair use, and unique defenses against the award of damages. It also examines two new limitations on trademark rights that have been adopted in some of the major Asian jurisdictions.

* This author would like to thank Dr. Zheng Shufeng for collecting materials and data on China. Special thanks also to Dr. Huang Hui and Professor Byungil Kim for providing case law on parallel import in China and Korea respectively. All online materials were last accessed in January 2023.

[1] *See generally* Annotated Leading Patent Cases in Major Asian Jurisdictions (Kung-Chung Liu ed., 2017); Annotated Leading Copyright Cases in Major Asian Jurisdictions (Kung-Chung Liu ed., 2019); Annotated Leading Trademark Cases in Major Asian Jurisdictions (Kung-Chung Liu ed., 2019).

[2] In addition to Parallel Imports in Asia (Christopher Heath ed., 2004), there is only another volume that deals with Asian trademark laws, namely Annotated Leading Trademark Cases in Major Asian Jurisdictions, *supra* note 1. One chapter in the 2016 volume *The Law and Practice of Trademark Transactions* focuses on the Asian context. *See* He Guo, *Chinese Trademark Law and Trademark Transactions: A Law in Transition in the Global Economy*, *in* the law and practice of trademark transactions: a global and local outlook 485 (Jacques De Werra et al. eds., 2016).

Kung-Chung Liu, *Limitations of Trademark Rights in Major Asian Jurisdictions* In: *Charting Limitations on Trademark Rights*. Edited by: Haochen Sun and Barton Beebe, Oxford University Press. © Kung-Chung Liu 2023.
DOI: 10.1093/oso/9780198871248.003.0012

I. Asian Trademark Landscape

A. From Counterfeiters to Trademark Users and Promoters

Major Asian jurisdictions are fast transforming from counterfeiters to trademark users and promoters owing to the economic growth that recognizes the importance of trademarks. In the past two decades, trademark applications and registrations have increased considerably in these economies.

For example, in China, 7.837 million trademark applications were filed in 2019, which is around 100 times more than the number of trademark applications filed in Germany in the same year[3] and far exceeds those of all other nations combined. Of these, 6,406,000 were registered; a sixfold increase from the 1,004,897 registered in 2012.[4] By 2020, China's total registered trademarks reached 30.17 million.[5] Similarly, in India, the number of trademarks registered increased nearly fivefold between 2013 and 2018, from 67,796 to 316,798, respectively.[6]

In the city-state of Singapore, trademark applications calculated based on the total classes of designated goods have risen steadily, from 36,801 in 2012 to 58,898 in 2021.[7] Trademarks registered calculated based on the total classes of designated goods exhibit a similar trend, increasing from 27,088 in 2012 to 48,078 in 2021.[8]

Japan, Korea, Malaysia, and Taiwan have also seen increases in applied and/or registered trademarks. Japan had 185,163 trademarks registered in phsical year 2021, compared to 99,896 in 2014.[9] In Korea, trademark applications increased from 147,667 in 2013 to 270,421 in 2021, and the number of trademarks registered increased from 119,255 in 2016 to 136,629 in 2021.[10] In Malaysia, trademarks registered reached 34,304 in 2021, increasing from 26,979 in 2013[11]. Taiwan's

[3] Deutsches Patent-und Markenamt Jahresbericht 2019, https://www.dpma.de/docs/dpma/veroeffentlichungen/jahresberichte/jahresbericht2019.pdf

[4] *See Shangbiao Shuju* (商标数据) [Trademark Statistics], Chinese Trademark Office of Nat'l Intell. Prop. Admin., http://sbj.cnipa.gov.cn/sbtj ; *Zhishi Chanquan Tongji Jianbao* (知识产权统计简报) [Intellectual Property Statistics Reports], Chinese Nat'l Intell. Prop. Admin., https://www.cnipa.gov.cn/col/col87/index.html

[5] Ibid.

[6] In India, the number of registered trademarks has increased as follows: 67,796 (2013), 41,583 (2014), 65,045 (2015), 250,070 (2016), 300,913 (2017) , and 316,798 (2018). The number of registered trademarks decreased in 2019 and 2020 due presumably to Covid-19 pandemic. See *Annual Reports*, The Office of the Controller General of Patents, Designs, Trademarks and Geographical Indications, Department for Promotion of Industry and Internal Trade, Ministry of Commerce & Industry, Gov't of India, http://www.ipindia.nic.in/annual-reports-ipo.htm

[7] Statistics, INTELL. PROP. OFFICE OF SINGAPORE, https://www.ipos.gov.sg/who-we-are/statistics

[8] Ibid

[9] *See Preliminary Statistical Data on Applications, Requests and Registrations*, Japan Patent Office, https://www.jpo.go.jp/e/resources/statistics/syutugan_toukei_sokuho/index.html

[10] *See Annual Report*, Korean Intellectual Property Office, https://www.kipo.go.kr/en/HtmlApp?c=60114&catmenu=ek07_01_01_15

[11] *See Statistic—Application & Registration*, The Official Portal of Intell. Prop. Corp. of Malaysia, http://www.myipo.gov.my/en/statistic-application-registration/#toggle-id-2

registered trademarks reached 87,992 in 2017 and increased to 94,725 in 2021.[12] Overall, in these economies,[13] the appetite for trademark application or registration is showing no signs of subsiding.[14]

Probably the only major Asian jurisdiction showing any immunity to this "trademark fever" is Hong Kong. Its number of trademark registrations decreased from 34,043 in 2014 to 32,554 in 2021.[15]

B. Making Best Global Brands

In 2000, according to marketing consultancy Interbrand's Best Global Brands report, only five brands from Asia ranked among the world's 100 most valuable. These were: Toyota (ranked 15th), Sony (18th), Honda (20th), Samsung (46th), and Panasonic (54th).[16] In 2022, there were thirteen: Samsung (5th), Toyota (6th), Honda (26st), Hyundai (35th), Sony (39th), Nissan (61), HSBC (65), Nintendo (68), Xiami (84), Huawei (86), Kia (87), Panasonic (91st), and Canon (97st).[17] Having extensive experience in original equipment manufacturing (OEM) Asian economies and companies are now becoming brand savvy. As we have seen, the numbers of registered trademarks in these countries are increasing, and associated litigation is also on the rise.

II. International Exhaustion

A typical limitation on trademark rights, the exhaustion doctrine stops the trademark right holders from interfering with the later fate of the trademarked products once they are put on the market by the trademark right holders or with their consent. The scope of exhaustion can be national, regional, or international in scope. The World Trade Organization's Agreement of Trade-Related Aspects of Intellectual Property Rights (the TRIPS Agreement) provides flexibility for

[12] *See* TAIWAN INTELL. PROP. OFFICE, 2018 TIPO ANNUAL REPORT (2021), https://www.tipo.gov.tw/tw/cp-177-483190-adbf7-1.html

[13] There is also clearly a trademark hype in Macau. The number of application of trademark registration reached 10,000 in 2013 and has since been on the rise until 2019: 10,084 (2013); 12,287 (2014); 13,140 (2015); 11,507 (2016); 13,135 (2017); 16,474 (2018), and 15,391 (2019). *See Statistics*, ECONOMIC BUREAU, GOV'T OF THE MAC. SPECIAL ADMIN. REGION, https://www.dsedt.gov.mo/en_US/web/public/pg_ip_sd?_refresh=true

[14] Concerns over the Asian trademark fever has been voiced by Kung-Chung Liu & Shufeng Zheng, *Asian IP Law: An Area of Rising Importance*, 69 G. R. U. R. INT'L 249 (2020).

[15] *See* https://www.ip-prd.net/en/trade-marks/index.html

[16] *See Best Global Brands Previous Years*, INTERBRAND, https://www.interbrand.com/best-brands/best-global-brands/previous-years/2000

[17] *See Best Global Brands 2019 Rankings*, INTERBRAND, https://www.interbrand.com/best-brands/best-global-brands/2019/ranking

members to decide on the scope of their exhaustion regimes.[18] International exhaustion has become a common limitation of trademark rights in major Asian jurisdictions in the past two decades, mostly due to judicial decisions. Recognizing "how restrictive most jurisdictions' laws on exhaustion have become"[19] may be true elsewhere but is certainly not the case in major Asian jurisdictions.

A. Statutory Recognition of International Exhaustion

1. Singapore

Singapore supports international exhaustion to an extent greater than any other major jurisdiction. In characterizing the city-state's pro-parallel import approach, it has been stated that, "policy makers in Singapore leave no stones unturned when it comes to legitimizing parallel imports," with the exception of pharmaceutical products.[20]

After gaining independence in 1965, Singapore continued to apply the colonial-era Trade Marks Ordinance 1938. This ordinance allowed international exhaustion provided that the quality of the imported product was not materially different from that of the product put on the Singapore market. The Trade Marks Act 1998 follows that tradition. It stipulates that a registered trademark is not infringed by the use of the trademark in relation to goods which have been *put on the market*, whether in or outside Singapore, under that trade mark by the proprietor of the registered trademark or with his express or implied consent (conditional or otherwise), unless the condition of the goods has been changed or impaired after they have been put on the market; and the use of the registered trademark in relation to those goods has caused dilution in an unfair manner of the distinctive character of the registered trademark (section 29).[21]

The High Court of Singapore used the public international law principle of territoriality to limit the application of the international exhaustion principle in the case of *Pan-West (Pte.) Ltd. v. Grand Bigwin Pte. Ltd.* (2003), requiring a "subsidiary or associated company" relationship between the Singaporean trademark owner and the foreign trademark owner whose products have been parallel-imported.[22] However, international exhaustion cannot be contracted out or made conditional

[18] Art. 6 of the TRIPS Agreement stipulates "For the purposes of dispute settlement under this Agreement, subject to the provisions of Articles 3 and 4 nothing in this Agreement shall be used to address the issue of the exhaustion of intellectual property rights."

[19] Michael Handler, Chapter 9 in the present volume.

[20] Ng-Loy Wee Loon, *The Exhaustion Doctrine in Singapore: Different Stroke for Different IP Folks*, *in* Research Handbook on Intellectual Property Exhaustion and Parallel Imports 185, 190 (Irene Calboli & Edward Lee eds., 2016).

[21] Trademark scholars would principally agree that it would be almost impossible to prove that actual dilution did happen. This is exactly the reason why "causes dilution" of the Federal Trademark Dilution Act of 1995 in the United States was revised in 2006 to "is likely to cause dilution."

[22] 4 S. L. R. (R) 755 (Sing.) [2003]. *See also* Ng-Loy Wee Loon, *supra* note 20, at 192.

by the trademark owner due to the phrase "conditional or otherwise" in the Trade Marks Act.[23] Therefore, in cases where a foreign trademark owner is different from the Singaporean trademark owner and imposed prohibition on the subsequent movement of the products, such as "Not for resale outside Thailand," the parallel import of such products into Singapore is still legal.[24]

In *Samsonite v. An Sheng* (2017), the High Court adopted a liberal interpretation of the term "put on the market" in section 29(1) of the Trade Mark Act as referring to the situation where an independent third party has acquired the right of disposal of the goods bearing the trademark, which must simultaneously allow the proprietor of the trademark to realize the commercial or economic value of the trademarked goods, and deprives them of the right to control the subsequent exploitation of the goods. Such an act includes, but is not limited to, a sale of the goods by the proprietor to the third party. It does not include preparatory acts such as offers for sale.[25]

2. Taiwan

The Taiwanese Supreme Court has recognized the international exhaustion principle since 1992, and Taiwan's Trademark Act of 1930 finally codified this principle in 2012. Article 36(2) of the Trademark Act stipulates:

> Where goods have been put on the domestic or foreign market under a registered trademark by the proprietor or with his consent, the proprietor is not entitled to claim trademark rights on such goods, unless such claim is to prevent the condition of the goods from being changed or impaired after they have been put on the market or there exist other legitimate reasons.

However, trademark rights are territorial in nature, and the same mark device can be registered and owned by different right holders. Will putting goods under a registered trademark on the market of country A by one trademark holder or with his consent exhaust the trademark rights of another trademark holder in country B? The IP and Commercial Court of Taiwan has in several decisions taken the strict position that the international exhaustion principle only applies when the trademark holders in country A and in country B are one and the same.[26] The reasoning was where domestic and foreign trademark rights on the same mark belong to

[23] Ng-Loy Wee Loon, *supra* note 20, at 191.

[24] *Id.*

[25] Samsonite IP Holding Sarl v. An Sheng Trading Pte Ltd [2017] S. G. H. C. 18, para. 100. For analysis, *see* David Llewelyn et al., Cases, Materials and Commentary on Singapore Intellectual Property Law 520–27 (2018); Susanna Leong, *International Exhaustion in Singapore: Broad Interpretation of "Put on the Market", Yet Offer for Sale Excluded*, *in* Annotated Leading Trademark Cases in Major Asian Jurisdictions, *supra* note 1, at 117.

[26] Min Shang Shang Zi No. 14 (Intell. Prop. and Comm. Ct. Jan. 24, 2017) (Taiwan) (2016) and Min Zan Zi No. 2 (Intell. Prop. and Comm. Ct. Apr. 22, 2019) (Taiwan).

different right holders, then judging from the perspective of equity consideration, domestic trademark holder has not acquired any consideration for foreign goods with the same mark that are entering the domestic market. Therefore, the exhaustion effect as a result of the first sale by the foreign trademark right holder should not apply to the domestic right holder. Consequently, the trademark proprietor mentioned in Article 36(2) must means that its domestic and foreign trademark holders are one and the same when the goods with the mark device was first sold.[27]

In a 2019 decision, the Supreme Court took a more flexible view on the relationship between domestic and foreign holders of the same trademark. It suffices if they "have licensing or other legal relationship." The Court stated that:

> when the trademark right holder registers or licenses others to register the same mark device and the resultant trademark rights are different ones under the principle of territoriality, different trademark holders from different countries should be subject to the same exhaustion, so long as they have licensing or other legal relationship. After all, the mark device is the same and the exclusive rights in essence are derived from the same right holder.[28]

On the issue of the conditions under which the international exhaustion principle is to apply, the Supreme Court ruled in 1993 specifically that "the products have not been processed, remodelled or changed and are sold in original package". It reasoned that since the source of the goods is legitimate, which will not damage the reputation of the trademark owner or its licensee, the monopolization of the market will be prevented, intra-brand price competition enhanced, consumers' interest in paying reasonable prices assured, and therefore parallel import of genuine goods should be considered as being consented to by the trademark owner.[29] This decision has had a lasting influence on decisions of the IP and Commercial Court. For example, in 2015 the Court ruled that "the exception to exhaustion happens when products were tampered with, which objectively affects relevant consumers' buying willingness or the acceptable price level."[30]

B. Exhaustion Principle Developed by Case Law

Trademark statutes in Japan, Korea, Malaysia, and China contain no provisions on parallel importation. In India there is such a provision, but it does not explicitly

[27] Min Zan Zi No. 2 (Intell. Prop. and Comm. Ct. Apr. 22, 2019) (Taiwan).

[28] Tai Shang Zi No. 397 (Sup. Ct. Jan. 16, 2020) (Taiwan) (2019), which was followed by Min Shang Su Zi No. 29 (Intell. Prop. and Comm. Ct. Feb. 10, 2020) (Taiwan) (2018).

[29] Tai Shang Zi No. 5380 (Sup. Ct. Oct. 8, 1993) (Taiwan).

[30] Min Shang Shang Zi No. 17 (Intell. Prop. and Comm. Ct. Apr. 30, 2015) (Taiwan) (2014).

mention the kind of exhaustion principle that applies. In these jurisdictions therefore the international exhaustion principle was adopted through case law.

1. Japan

While lower courts in Japan have repeatedly held that parallel importation of genuine goods does not infringe trademark rights, the Japanese Supreme Court had not recognized the legality of parallel importation until 2003.[31] It stated that parallel importation is justifiable under three conditions: 1) the trademark has been legally affixed to the imported goods by a trademark right holder or their licensee in a foreign country; 2) the trademark right holders in the foreign country and in Japan are the same person or have a relationship wherein they can be regarded as legally or economically identical to each other; and 3) the trademark right holder in Japan is able directly or indirectly to control the quality of the imported goods.

However, in contrast to the Singaporean High Court as discussed in the preceding section, the Japanese Supreme Court held that parallel-imported products may not violate the granting clauses of the trademark licensing agreement by, for example, reaching beyond the licensed territory (production areas), or subcontracting production without the trademark owner's approval. If they do violate such an agreement, they are impairing the quality control function of the trademark and therefore illegal. The Japanese Supreme Court did not discuss the legality of other complicated issues such as refilling products or modifying or transforming their shape or appearance.[32]

2. Korea

In Korea, treatment of parallel importation of genuine goods and international exhaustion has undergone a major shift. Parallel importation was originally prohibited by the Korean Customs Service. However, public outcries prompted the Korean government to amend the public notice of the Fair Trade Commission and Customs Act regulations to permit parallel importation with effect from November 1995.[33] Subsequently, the Korean Supreme Court allows and the prevailing scholarly view supports parallel importation, so long as it is not likely to harm the functions of trademark and cause domestic customers to mistake the source or the quality of the goods bearing the trademarks.

[31] Saikō Saibansho [Sup. Ct.] Feb. 27, 2003, 2002 (Ju) No. 1100, 57 SAIKŌ SAIBANSHO MINJI HANREISHŪ [MINSHŪ] 125 (Japan). For analysis, *see* Masabumi Suzuki, *Justifiability of Parallel Import of Genuine Goods and Trademark Infringement by Imports Produced in Breach of a Licensing Agreement in Japan, in* ANNOTATED LEADING TRADEMARK CASES IN MAJOR ASIAN JURISDICTIONS, *supra* note 1, at 155.

[32] Suzuki, *supra* note 31, at 163–64.

[33] Byungil Kim, *Exhaustion and Parallel Imports in Korea, in* PARALLEL IMPORTS IN ASIA 73, 78 (Christopher Heath ed., 2004).

Under the Korea Customs Service *Public Notice on Customs Service Practice for the Protection of IP Rights*, parallel import of non-counterfeit goods into Korea does not infringe the trademark if the foreign and the domestic trademark holders are identical or deemed identical due to having an affiliate relationship (i.e., holding 30% or more of the shares and being the largest shareholder of the other) or an import agency relationship. The *Notice* goes on to provide that the exclusive licensee can still prevent parallel import if it domestically manufactures the goods. The *Notice* also allows parallel import when the foreign and the domestic trademark holders are not identical and the domestic trademark holder or an exclusive licensee imports or sells genuine goods manufactured in foreign countries (including genuine goods manufactured with permission of the foreign trademark holder).[34]

The Korean Supreme Court has laid down the criteria for permissible parallel importation. Firstly, imported goods must be genuine. Secondly, the foreign trademark holder and the domestic trademark holder must be the same or have a special relationship. Thirdly, goods imported by a parallel importer must be of the same quality as goods distributed by a domestic trademark holder or an exclusive licensee.[35] However, in contrast to Singapore, Taiwan, and Japan, a trademark owner who manufactures and sells branded goods within South Korea can block parallel imports from another country.[36]

In a 2002 decision, the Supreme Court decided on the extent to which a parallel importer can use the trademark of the parallel-imported goods in its marketing activities. It held that the use of the Burberry trademark on signboards, flyers, wrapping paper, shopping bags, business cards, and other advertising materials of the parallel importer did not constitute trademark infringement as it did not lead to confusion over the source and quality of the goods. However, the Court also held that the use of the trademark on signboards outside the parallel importer's store or on business cards should be prohibited under unfair competition law to the extent that such use would lead to consumer confusion as to the identity of the seller.[37]

3. India

Following the British Trade Marks Act 1938, India's trademark legislation and case law are quite liberal in permitting parallel import.[38] The Act continued to apply up to the Trade Marks Act 1999, which adopted the same liberal parallel import

[34] Won Bok Lee & Kyoung-Shin Park, *Scope of a Parallel Importer's Permissible Use of a Trademark in Marketing Activities in Korea, in* Annotated Leading Trademark Cases in Major Asian Jurisdictions, *supra* note 1, at 165, 172.

[35] *Id.* at 172–73.

[36] This is arguably based on the Public Notice just mentioned. *See* Kim, *supra* note 33, at 79.

[37] Supreme Court [S. Ct.], 99 Da 42322 (S. Kor.) (Sept. 24, 2002). For analysis, *see* Lee & Park, *supra* note 34, at 171–75.

[38] Sonia Baldia, *Exhaustion and Parallel Imports in India, in* Parallel Imports in Asia 163, 169 (Christopher Heath ed., 2004).

regime. Section 30(3) Trade Marks Act 1999 is similar to the Singaporean law on exhaustion. However, different from the Singaporean law which adopts expressly the international exhaustion principle, Indian legislation does not explicitly mention the kind of exhaustion principle (international or national) that should apply.

In a leading case, *Samsung Electronics Co. Ltd. and another v. Kapil Wadhwa and others*, pending confirmation by the Supreme Court of India, the Division Bench of the Delhi High Court held in 2012 that India adopts the principle of international trademark exhaustion. The Division Bench also listed circumstances that may give rise to an exception to this principle. These were differences in quality (wherein the physical condition of the goods has been changed or impaired), services and warranties, advertising and promotional activities, packaging, and language of literature provided. The Division Bench also instructed the parallel importer in that case to prominently advertise in its showroom that the products had been imported from abroad, and that after-sale service would not be provided by the trademark owner in India but rather by the parallel importer itself.[39]

4. Malaysia

Just two decisions deal expressly with parallel import in Malaysia, both by the High Court. The first decision, *Winthrop Products Inc & Sterling Drug (M) Sdn Bhd v Sun Ocean (M) Sdn Bhd & Anor*,[40] accepted international exhaustion but without actually using the term. The Court pointed out that trademark rights serve to prevent deception as to the source of goods and do not give rights to control dealings with goods. Legal ownership of the trademark does not enable the owner or the registered user to ensure that products made elsewhere (e.g., in the United Kingdom or United States) are not sold within Malaysia. When parent or subsidiary companies decide to manufacture the same product under the same trademark, they must be regarded as having given implied consent to the use of the trademark among them. The owners of the products therefore acquire the absolute ownership of the goods including the right to sell them in any part of the world in the same condition in which they were disposed of. It is observed that "The case leaves open the opportunity of infringement occurring if the same trade mark is owned by different companies without any common ownership at some level."[41] This is exactly the issue of the second decision by the High Court, *Tien Ying Hong Enterprise Sdn Bhd v Beenion Sdn Bhd*,[42] which found no relationship between a trademark owner in Malaysia, from whom the defendant bought products, and the actual

[39] Arul George Scaria, *International Exhaustion of Trade Mark Rights in India*, *in* ANNOTATED LEADING TRADEMARK CASES IN MAJOR ASIAN JURISDICTIONS, *supra* note 1, at 129, 136–37.

[40] 2 M. L. J. 317 [1998].

[41] John Chong, *Exhaustion and Parallel Imports in Malaysia*, *in* PARALLEL IMPORTS IN ASIA 130 (Christopher Heath ed., 2004).

[42] 2 CLJ 469 [2011].

manufacturer of the products who was the lawful owner of the mark at dispute in Japan. Therefore, the defense of exhaustion by the defendant failed.[43]

5. China

In China, a few provincial court decisions have dealt with parallel importation of genuine goods. However, the term "exhaustion," whether domestic or international, was not used by the courts until 1999.[44] In the 1999 case *Shanghai Lihua Co. Ltd. v. Guangzhou Economic and Technological Development Zone Commercial Import and Export Trading Co*,[45] the Guangzhou Intermediate People's Court rejected the defense of parallel import by the defendant who imported soaps made in Thailand into China, finding that the defendant failed to prove that the products concerned had come from the trademark holder in China or was licensed by the plaintiff. Other decisions emerging around 2009 assess the legality of parallel importation from the perspective of the functions of trademark. For example, the Changsha Intermediate People's Court in the 2009 *Michelin Group v. Tan Guoqiang and Ou Can* case emphasized the "product quality and reputation of product provider" guarantee function. It rejected the trademark infringement defense of parallel import because although the tires were genuinely made by the plaintiff in Japan, they lacked the 3C security certificate and certification which are mandatory for import into China. Therefore, their sale jeopardized the trademark owner's "product quality and reputation of product provider" guarantee function.[46]

The Shanghai Second Intermediate People's Court in the 2012 *Victoria's Secret Store Brand Management Co. Ltd. v. Shanghai Jintian Clothing Co. Ltd.* case first confirmed that the products in question were from the parent company of the plaintiff and were therefore genuine. The Court then concluded that the defendant's use of the Victoria's Secret trademark in tags, hangers, wrapping bags, and flyers was part of the selling activity and did not lead to confusion as to the source of the products among the public and allowed the parallel import.[47] The decision was included by

[43] Lim Heng Gee, *The Exhaustion Defence to Trade Mark Infringement and Parallel Importation in Malaysia*, *in* ANNOTATED LEADING TRADEMARK CASES IN MAJOR ASIAN JURISDICTIONS, *supra* note 1, at 142.

[44] For example, Xiang Yu advocated that the adoption of international exhaustion principle of trademark rights, and that the principle should not be definitely stipulated by law, rather than by the People's Supreme Court. *See* Xiang Yu, Exhaustion and Parallel Imports in China, *in* PARALLEL IMPORTS IN ASIA 38 (Christopher Heath ed., 2004). In contrast, Huang Hui argues for domestic exhaustion and disallows parallel import. *See* HUANG HUI (黄晖), SHANGBIAO FA (商标法) [TRADEMARK LAW] 184 (2d ed. 2016).

[45] Shanghai Lihua Youxian Gongsi Su Guangzhou Jingji Jishu Kaifaqu Shangye Jinchukou Maoyi Gongsi (上海利华有限公司诉广州经济技术开发区商业进出口贸易公司) [Shanghai Lihua Co. Ltd. v. Guangzhou Economic and Technological Development Zone Commercial Import and Export Trading Co.], Sui Zhong Fa Zhi Chu Zi No. 82 (Guangzhou Interm. People's Ct. 1999) (China).

[46] Miqiling Jituan Zonggongsi Su Tan Guoqiang, Ou Can (米其林集团总公司诉谈国强、欧灿) [Michelin Group v. Tan Guoqiang and Ou Can], Chang Zhong Min San Chu Zi No. 0073 (Changsha Interm. People's Ct. Apr. 24, 2009) (China).

[47] Weiduoliya de Mimi Shangdian Pinpai Guanli Youxian Gongsi Su Shanghai Jintian Fushi Youxian Gongsi (维多利亚的秘密商店品牌管理有限公司诉上海锦天服饰有限公司) [Victoria's Secret Store Brand Management Co. Ltd. v. Shanghai Jintian Clothing Co. Ltd.], Hu Er Zhong Min Wu (Zhi) Chu Zi No. 86 (Shanghai 2d Interm. People's Ct. Apr. 23, 2013) (China) (2012).

the Supreme People's Court in its Gazette (2013, No. 12), indicating endorsement of the decision.

The Tianjin High People's Court in the 2013 *Les Grands Chais de France v. Muti International Trade (Tianjin) Co. Ltd.* case discussed the source-indicating and quality guarantee functions of trademarks. It concluded, in that case, that the source-indicating function was not damaged and no source confusion was caused as the wine that the defendant imported into China was produced by the plaintiff, purchased from its distributor in the United Kingdom, and imported without any form of repackaging. The Court further concluded that the guarantee function was not compromised, as the imported wine was intact in quality.[48] The Beijing High People's Court in the 2015 Köstritzer black beer case also allowed parallel imports for exactly the same reasons.[49]

III. Prohibition on Abuse of Trademark Rights

No abuse of rights is a basic legal principle in civil law jurisdictions that at least can be traced to Article 226 of the German Civil Code.[50] Courts have extended the principle to the realm of trademark in Japan, Korea, and China.

A. Japan

In Japan, courts have traditionally applied the doctrine of no abuse of rights anchored in Article 1(3) of the Japanese Civil Code in a restrictive way to patent infringement cases. However, in the Kilby case of 1997, the Japanese Supreme Court allied with the IP High Court (IPHC) and endorsed the applicability of the no abuse of right principle to the exercise of a clearly invalid patent.[51] In 2014, in a series of three cases involving Samsung and Apple, the Special Division[52] of the IPHC ruled that the seeking of injunctive relief and damages exceeding the fair,

[48] Faguo Da Jiuku Gufen Gongsi Su Muti Guoji Maoyi (Tianjin) Youxian Gongsi (法国大酒库股份公司诉慕醍国际贸易(天津)有限公司) [Les Grands Chais de France v. Muti International Trade (Tianjin) Co. Ltd.], Jin Gao Min San Zhong Zi No. 24 (Tianjin High People's Ct. Dec. 17, 2014) (China) (2013).

[49] Daxiyang C Maoyi Zixun Youxian Gongsi Su Beijing Sihai Zhixiang Guoji Maoyi Youxian Gongsi (大西洋C贸易咨询有限公司诉北京四海致祥国际贸易有限公司) [Atlantic C Trade Consulting Co. Ltd. v. Beijing Four Seas Zhixiang International Trade Co. Ltd.], Gao Min (Zhi) Zhong Zi No. 1931 (Beijing High People's Ct. May 12, 2015) (China).

[50] Art. 226 of the German Civil Code (Prohibition of chicanery) provides "The exercise of a right is not permitted if its only possible purpose consists in causing damage to another."

[51] Ichiro Nakayama, *Recognizing the Abuse of Rights Defense and the Invalidation Defense, in* Annotated Leading Patent Cases in Major Asian Jurisdictions, *supra* note 1, at 20, 26 .

[52] Also known as the Grand Panel, which is consisted of five judges with one from each of the four divisions plus the president of the IPHC to swiftly render unified opinions of the IPHC.

reasonable, and nondiscriminatory (FRAND) royalty by a standard essential patent (SEP) patentee bound by the FRAND commitment to issue a license to any willing licensee constitutes abuse of right.[53]

As a contrast, in Japan, "the doctrine of abuse of right is more often used and adopted in cases concerning infringement of trademark rights."[54] In 1982, the Kobe District Court recognized the abuse of trademark rights when a trademark owner invoked a mark contrary to the public's association of it as from a different origin.[55] In the Popeye muffler case of 1990, the Japanese Supreme Court upheld an abuse of right defense. In that case, the Popeye mark had been registered and transferred to the plaintiff without authorization from the copyright holder of the Popeye cartoon, a U.S. company. The defendant marketed mufflers bearing trademarks consisting of the letters "Popeye" with authorization from the copyright holder. The Court held that the exercise of trademark right against the defendant would constitute an abuse of right because the plaintiff's freeriding on the Popeye cartoon character would harm the fair order of competition.[56]

In a 2017 decision, the Japanese Supreme Court recognized a new form of abuse of right defense. Article 47(1) of the Trademark Act of 1959 gives registered trademarks indisputable validity if no requests for invalidation have been filed within five years of registration. However, the owner of an unregistered, well-known trademark accused of infringement after the expiration of the five-year timeframe is still entitled to an abuse of trademark right defense except in extenuating circumstances. Such a defense will not render the registered trademark useless; rather, the registered trademark can still be exercised against persons other than the well-known mark holder.[57]

B. Korea

The Korean Supreme Court in an *en banc* decision in 2012 stated that "if it is obvious that the patent will likely be invalidated, the court should not allow injunctive relief against infringement to prevent patent abuse unless there are special circumstances, even if an invalidation action against a patented invention is still

[53] Masabumi Suzuki, *Enforcement of FRAND-encumbered SEPs, in* Annotated Leading Patent Cases in Major Asian Jurisdictions, *supra* note 1, at 241, 256.

[54] Masabumi Suzuki, *Japan, in* SEPs, SSOs and FRAND–Asian and Global Perspectives on Fostering Innovation in Interconnectivity, 192 n. 5 (Kung-Chung Liu & Reto Hilty eds., 2019).

[55] Christopher Heath, *Exhaustion and Parallel Imports in Japan, in* Parallel Imports in Asia 59 (Christopher Heath ed., 2004).

[56] Saikō Saibansho [Sup. Ct.] July 20, 1990, Showa 60(o) 1576, 44 Saikō Saibansho minji hanreishū [Minshū] 876 (Japan). *See* Masaharu Miyawaki, *Unregistered Well-Known Trademark Owner Accused of Infringement in Japan: Abuse of Right Defence After the Five-Year Invalidation Period, in* Annotated Leading Trademark Cases in Major Asian Jurisdictions, *supra* note 1, at 302, 309.

[57] Saikō Saibansho *supra* note 56. *See* Miyawaki, *supra* note 54, at 309.

pending."[58] In the same vein, the Korean Supreme Court confirmed the application of the abuse of rights doctrine to prevent a third party from exercising trademark rights for the purpose of unfair profit, knowing that his mark was confusingly similar to an unregistered well-known mark.[59]

In another en banc decision on January 29, 2012, the Court held that even before the invalidity of a trademark is confirmed, where there is a clear case of invalidity, an injunction action or a damages claim based on said trademark will not be permitted as it constitutes a misuse of rights, barring any special circumstances.[60] Until this recent decision, the Korean Supreme Court was of the view that even where there is a ground for invalidating a trademark, the court seized of an infringement case may not rule on the invalidity issue until the invalidity decision is confirmed.[61]

C. China

The Supreme People's Court has condemned the abuse of trademark rights by the owner in several decisions since 2014. In the case *Wang Suiyong v. Hangzhou Yintai Century Department Store Co. Ltd.*, the Court held that the exercise of the exclusive right of a trademark registered in bad faith against the good faith user constituted abuse of trademark rights.[62] In another case, the Court found that the plaintiff, a civil servant in charge of trademark affairs at the Administration for Industry and Commerce, had acted against good faith by registering a similar trademark to the mark at issue and suing the defendant without ever putting the registered trademark to commercial use.[63] In 2015, the Supreme People's Court elaborated that:

> One of the functions of the Judiciary is to regulate the relationship between social economy and persons through the application of law, to facilitate market

[58] Supreme Court [S. Ct.] 2010 Da 95390, Jan. 19, 2012 (S. Kor.). For analysis, *see* Byungil Kim, *Recognizing the Abuse of Rights Defence and the Invalidation Defence, in* ANNOTATED LEADING PATENT CASES IN MAJOR ASIAN JURISDICTIONS, *supra* note 1, at 33, 37.

[59] *Supra* note 58; *see* Jong-Kyun Woo, *Trade Marks and Related Rights, in* INTELLECTUAL PROPERTY LAW IN KOREA, 121 (Byungil Kim & Christopher Heath eds., 2d ed. 2015).

[60] The Korean Supreme Court 2010 Da 103000. *See* Aera Kim, Republic of Korea: Supreme Court's en banc decisions holding that the civil courts may dismiss patent/trademark infringement actions if it is evident the patent/trademark is invalid, AIPPI, https://aippi.org/enews/2012/edition27/AeraKim.html

[61] Lee & Ko, *En Banc Decision from the Supreme Court Ruled that the Infringement Court May Rule on the Invalidity of a Trademark*, INTELLECTUAL PROPERTY, Winter 2012/2013, at 1, http://www.leeko.com/newsl/leeko/2012winter/eng/pdf/ip.pdf.

[62] Wang Suiyong Su Hangzhou Yintai Shiji Baihuo Youxian Gongsi (王碎永诉杭州银泰世纪百货有限公司) [Wang Suiyong v. Hangzhou Yintai Century Department Store Co. Ltd.], 2014 Min Ti Zi No. 24 (Sup. People's Ct. Aug. 14, 2014) (China).

[63] Shao Wenjun Su Ningbo Guangtian Saikesi Yeya Youxian Gongsi (邵文军诉宁波广天赛克思液压有限公司) [Shao Wenjun v. Ningbo Guangtian Saikesi Hydraulic Co. Ltd.], 2014 Min Ti Zi No. 168 (Sup. People's Ct. Oct. 30, 2015) (China).

competition based on merits, and to promote social Zeitgeist of honesty and credibility. Any behaviour that violates the purposes or spirits of legislature, aims at infringing legitimate interests of others, acquiring and exercising rights in bad faith, or disturbing fair market competition, shall be deemed as abuse of rights and cannot claim protection and support of the law.[64]

IV. Fair Use

In the major Asian jurisdictions, trademark fair use has had a mixed reception. While it is being gradually adopted in copyright laws,[65] it is not widely accepted as an overarching trademark infringement defense to protect the public interest,[66] and remains mostly within the ambit of academic discourse. This is unfortunate, as the surge in trademark applications and registrations in major Asian jurisdictions could lead to trademark congestion and even depletion of registerable trademarks. Courts should feel empowered to adjudicate more permissively the fair-use defense.[67] In the following sections, two sub-categories of fair use are discussed: comparative advertisement (Section IV.A) and criticism and parody (Section IV.B).

A. Comparative Advertisement

In China, Japan, Korea, and Taiwan, statutory trademark law does not deal with the issue of comparative advertisement. However, if not misleading, it is generally allowed.[68] Since its 2004 amendment, section 28(4) of Singapore's Trade Marks Act allows fair use of others' trademarks "in comparative commercial advertising or promotion." However, this concession is not unlimited. In *Allergan, Inc v. Ferlanz Nutra Pte Ltd*, the High Court held that it does not apply to misleading comparative advertisement.[69]

Section 29(8) of India's Trade Marks Act 1999 allows comparative advertising that does not take unfair advantage of and is not detrimental to the distinctive character or reputation of others' marks. However, Indian courts have deviated from English law tradition and diluted the malice requirement in tortious disparagement

[64] Lin Dongliang Su Juqiang (Guangzhou) Jixie Youxian Gongsi (林东梁诉鉅强(广州)机械有限公司) [Lin Dongliang v. Juqiang (Guangzhou) Machine Co. Ltd.], 2015 Min Ti Zi No. 49 (Sup. People's Ct. Sept. 30, 2015) (China).

[65] For more, *see* Liu & Zheng, *supra* note 14, at 8–9.

[66] U.S. Lanham Act (15 U.S.C. 1125) § 43(c)(3) stipulates an overarching fair-use exception to dilution liability.

[67] Barton Beebee & Jeanne Fromer, *Are We Running Out of Trademarks? An Empirical Study of Trademark Depletion and Congestion*, 131 Harv. L. Rev. 945, 1040 (2018).

[68] Christopher Heath, The System of Unfair Competition Prevention in Japan 189 (2001).

[69] Allergan, Inc v. Ferlanz Nutra Pte Ltd 4 SLR 919 [2016]. For analysis, *see* Llewelyn et al., *supra* note 25, at 518.

actions, providing an effective remedy to parties aggrieved by comparative advertising. Further, Indian courts have developed a generic disparagement tort, where unnamed traders can bring an action in situations where rival products are generically disparaged without a particular trader or trademark being named. This has severely limited the possibility of comparative advertising in India.[70]

B. Criticism and Parody

The parody defense does not often appear in statutory laws in Asian jurisdictions, and it has rarely been successfully accepted as a defense to trademark infringement by the courts. This may have to do with traditional Asian values of respect and could also stem from sensitivities related to accusations of counterfeiting by Western nations.

In China, neither statutory trademark law nor case law recognize parody.[71] A 2011 case involved the French tire company Michelin, famous for its *Red Guide*, a hotel and restaurant guide. The company registered the word device "Michelin" for tires, printing, and travel service in China. The defendant published in its English magazine *That's Shanghai*, a 2010 *Micheling* Shanghai Guide, stating "We have put forward a Shanzhai (transliteration of the Chinese two-word character '山 寨' meaning counterfeit, imitation, or parody products and events) version of Michelin for all French restaurants in Shanghai." In its defense, the defendant alleged that its mark differed from the Michelin trademark device through the addition of "g" at its end, and also that the guide was intended only "for amusement." This argument was rejected by the Shanghai Second Intermediate People's Court, which found a likelihood that the conduct would cause consumer confusion.[72]

We find no cases of parody being used as a defense to trademark infringement in Japan. The issue of parody arises in several cases in relation to trademark registration, such as *Kuma v. Puma* and *Shi-Sa v. Puma*, but courts have mainly focused on the issue of likelihood of confusion.[73]

In Taiwan, Article 36(1) of the Trademark Act recognizes specifically enumerated cases of fair use of others' trademarks which do not include a parody defense.

[70] Calcutta High Court Hindustan Unilever v. Reckitt Benckiser 57 PTC 78 (Cal) (2014). For more, *see* Arpan Banerjee, *Trademark Rights-Infringing Comparative Advertising in India, in* ANNOTATED LEADING TRADEMARK CASES IN MAJOR ASIAN JURISDICTIONS, *supra* note 1, at 315.

[71] For critique see Haochen Sun Chapter 10 in the present volume.

[72] Miqilin Jituan Zonggongsi Su Shanghai Hezhou Guanggao Youxian Gongsi (米其林集团总公司诉上海和舟广告有限公司) [Compagnie Generale Des Etablissements Michelin v. Shanghai Hezhou Advertising Co. Ltd.], 2011 Hu Er Zhong Min Wu (Zhi) Chu Zi No. 5 (Shanghai 2d Interm. People's Ct. 2011) (China).

[73] *See* MIMI MIYAGAWA, COPYRIGHT/TRADEMARK—SPEAKING FREELY ABOUT PARODY (2016), https://aippi.info/wp-content/uploads/2016/09/PS-11_Presentation_Mitsuko-Miyagawa_2016-09-28_web-version.pdf; Aoshima Emi, *Parody Trademark Case*, YUASA AND HARA, https://www.yuasa-hara.co.jp/lawinfo/1447

The IP Court in a 2011 administrative case involving Hermès rejected a parody defense based on the U.S. case *Louis Vuitton Malletier v. Haute Diggity Dog, LLC*[74] on grounds that trademark regimes in Taiwan and the United States are different, as were the facts of the two cases.[75] However, in a 2014 criminal decision involving Chanel, the IP and Commercial Court admitted parody as a fair-use defense and explained that an admissible trademark parody must "possess entertaining factors such as humor, sarcasm, or criticism, convey a contradictory message compared to the original symbol, and be balanced against the public interest in avoiding consumer confusion and the public interest in freedom of expression." The Court concluded that even though the defendant's symbol was humorous and entertaining in nature, it had failed to prove what contrasting image or contradictory message it was trying to convey. Therefore, no contribution to culture or societal values was made, and the Court found only freeriding on the established commercial value of Chanel.[76]

India provides the only clear exception to this trend of not accepting parody. In 2010, Tata brought a suit in the High Court of Delhi against Greenpeace International. The defendant had developed a "Pac-Man" style video game entitled "Turtle v. Tata," inviting players in the role of turtles to eat as much healthy food as possible while simultaneously evading "TATA demons." The one-man bench held that this use of the trademark was non-commercial and for the purpose of parody, fair comment, and criticism, and did not result in trademark infringement.[77]

V. Unique Defenses Against the Award of Damages

In Asia, there are some unique defenses against the award of damages after establishment of trademark infringement. There is a general "no trademark use" defense in China, while in Japan there is a specific non-award of damages defense against a claim for lost royalties if the defendant can successfully prove the impossibility of any damage sustained by the trademark right holders. Both are rooted in the tort law principle of no damages if no actual harm or loss is suffered.

[74] 507 F.3d 252 (4th Cir. 2007)

[75] 2011 Xing Shang Su Zi No. 104 (Intell. Prop. and Comm. Ct. Nov. 24, 2011) (Taiwan). The decision was upheld by 2012 Tai Zi No. 391 (Sup. Admin. Ct. Feb. 23, 2012) (Taiwan).

[76] 2014 Xing Zhi Shang Yi No. 63 (Intell. Prop. and Comm. Ct. Nov. 6, 2014) (Taiwan), which was not appealable. For critique of the two decisions by the TIPC, *see* Yachi Chiang, *Establishing a Parody Defence Standard within the Framework of Taiwan's Trademark Act, in* Annotated Leading Trademark Cases in Major Asian Jurisdictions, *supra* note 1, at 198, 206–07.

[77] When India first introduced in § 29(4) of Trade Marks Act of 1999 the statutory concept of "dilution," it counterbalanced the protection of well-known marks by allowing under the "due cause" condition the protection of free speech-related fair use, including fair comment, parody, and criticism. For more, *see* Renuka Medury, *Denominative Use of Other's Trade Mark to Draw Attention to That Other's Activity Can Constitute Prima Facie "Due Cause" under Section 29(4) of the Indian Trade Marks Act, in* Annotated Leading Trademark Cases in Major Asian Jurisdictions, *supra* note 1, at 187.

A. China

The Chinese Trademark Law did not establish a "no use, no compensation by damages" defense principle until 2013. Article 64(1) of the current Trademark Law provides:

> Where the holder of the exclusive right to use a registered trademark claims for damages, and the alleged infringer counterclaims that the right holder has never used the registered trademark, the people's court may require the right holder to provide evidence of its actual use of the registered trademark during the past three years prior to the lawsuit. The alleged infringer shall not be liable for damages if the right holder is neither able to prove its actual use of the registered trademark during the past three years prior to the lawsuit, nor able to prove other losses suffered as a result of the infringement.

This provision was added to address the rise of trademark speculators who file trademark applications for the sole purpose of reselling them, and who ask for high damages in a lawsuit if someone uses identical or similar marks.

Furthermore, in a 2015 decision, the Shanghai High People's Court ruled that if a trademark owner without the sincere intention of using their trademark files a series of lawsuits just to profit from the damages, their expenses for lawsuits should not be compensated as "reasonable expenses for stopping the infringing act" prescribed by the Trademark Law.[78]

B. Japan

Traditionally, lost royalties were guaranteed as minimum damages in Japan until the Supreme Court held in 1997 that infringers could avoid such liability if they successfully alleged and proved the impossibility of any damage to the trademark right holders.[79] However, the Supreme Court allowed this defense under the facts unique to the case. Specifically, the registered trademark was never used and had no capability to attract customers, and it was obvious that the use of the mark

[78] Guangzhou Shi Zhinanzhen Huizhan Fuwu Youxian Gongsi Su Youyiku Shangmao Youxian Gongsi yu (广州市指南针会展服务有限公司诉优衣库商贸有限公司) [Guangzhou Compass Exhibition Service Co. Ltd. v. Fast Retailing Trading Co. Ltd. (Uniqlo)], 2015 Hu Gao Min San Zhi Zhong Zi No. 97 (Shanghai High People's Ct. 2015) (China). For analysis, *see* Li Chen, *The De-linkage and Re-Linkage Between Trademark Use and Damages in China, in* Annotated Leading Trademark Cases in Major Asian Jurisdictions, *supra* note 1, at 351.

[79] Saikō Saibansho [Sup. Ct.] Mar. 11, 1997, 1994(o)1102, 51 Saikō Saibansho minji hanreishū [Minshū] 1055 (Japan). For more analysis, *see* Ichiro Nakayama, *Trademark Damages Defence Based on Non-Occurrence of Damage in Japan, in* Annotated Leading Trademark Cases in Major Asian Jurisdictions, *supra* note 1, at 361.

similar to the registered mark made no contribution to the alleged infringer's sales. To date, given the narrow scope of this defense, it has succeeded only in a handful of cases.[80]

VI. New Limitations on Trademark Rights

A. Compulsory Trademark Licensing

The TRIPS Agreement explicitly prohibits World Trade Organization (WTO) members from issuing compulsory trademark licenses.[81] However, given the diverse, competing interests in trademark scenarios, it has been contended that there might very well be scenarios in which compulsory trademark licensing is not only justified but also imperative. One such scenario involves use of the trademark of a patented vaccine made under compulsory license in a pandemic.[82] In 2013, China's Supreme People's Court found trademark infringement by a housing developer which used the registered trademark of the plaintiff as the title of the apartment buildings the developer has built, awarded damages, and yet refused to issue an injunction to stop the continued use of the infringing title of the apartment buildings. This was due to the fact that residents of the development did not know of the infringing use when they moved in, and also that the infringing name was approved by the local government as a place name and conceived of by locals as the same. It was held the residents could continue to use the trademark after their payment of RMB100,000 in damages, essentially purchasing a de facto compulsory license of the trademark.[83]

[80] Nakayama, *supra* note 79, at 370.

[81] Art. 21 (Licensing and Assignment) of the TRIPS Agreement stipulates: "Members may determine conditions on the licensing and assignment of trademarks, it being understood that the compulsory licensing of trademarks shall not be permitted and that the owner of a registered trademark shall have the right to assign the trademark with or without the transfer of the business to which the trademark belongs."

[82] Kung-Chung Liu, *The Need of and Justification for a General Competition-Oriented Compulsory Licensing*, 43 Int'l Rev. Indus. Prop. & Competition L. 679 (2012).

[83] Guangzhou Xinghewan Shiye Fazhan Youxian Gongsi Su Tianjin Shi Hongxing Fangdichan Kaifa Youxian Gongsi (广州星河湾实业发展有限公司诉天津市宏兴房地产开发有限公司) [Guangzhou Star RiverReal Property Development Co. Ltd. v. Tianjin Hongxing Real Estate Development Co. Ltd.], 2013 Min San Zhong Zi No. 3. (Supreme People's Ct. 2013) (China). For analysis, *see* Huaiwen He, *Finding Infringement but Refusing to Grant Permanent Injunction Under Chinese Trademark Law, in* Annotated Leading Trademark Cases in Major Asian Jurisdictions, *supra* note 1, at 208.

B. "Well-Known" Trademarks Not Listed by the IPO Need to Prove Their Well-Known Status

The continual strengthening of the protection for well-known marks has been a feature of international trademark development in the post-TRIPS era. However, for market latecomers seeking a new trademark registration, there is no clear way to determine if a particular mark is well-known. Without this certainty, the applicant cannot calculate the risk of having the trademark application rejected or foresee legal liabilities caused by the confusion surrounding or dilution of a well-known mark. Some jurisdictions in Asia such as Japan, Korea, and Taiwan have established different ways of listing well-known marks. China also did so, but in an abusive way described below that eventually led to its own demise.

In 1996, China embarked upon "active and wholesale approval of well-known marks" and publication thereof, which led to widespread fraud among trademark officials and applicants. From 1996 to October 2010, some 4485 well-known marks were recognized and publicized by the Trademark Office, and this figure does not reflect those recognized and publicized by the Trademark Review and Adjudication Board and courts.[84] The abuse resulted in the 2013 amendment to Article 14(5), prohibiting manufacturers and business operators from using a description of "well-known trademarks" on products, packages or containers of products, on advertisements, or in exhibitions or commercial activities. Article 53 states that violation of this provision is subject to an RMB100,000 fine. This swing to the opposite extreme of not mentioning "well-known trademarks" at all, typical of China's paradigm shifts, is on the one hand not justified as it abridges the freedom of commercial speech, and on the other does not satisfy the market latecomers' need in knowing and avoiding the infringement of well-known marks.

In this regard, Japan has provided a mitigation mechanism. Since 1959, the owner of a registered, well-known mark has been allowed to register similar marks as defensive marks, without needing to use them on goods or services (Article 64 of the Japanese Trademark Act). This pre-empts dishonest competitors. The Japanese National Centre for Industrial Property Information and Training provides in Japanese and English an online well-known trademark search service. This service allows users to search for data on trademarks registered as defensive marks and registered trademarks recognized as well-known or prominent in objection decisions, trial decisions, and judgments. After more than sixty years of practice, the Patent Office currently recognizes 1228 well-known marks in the application process for defensive marks.[85] Such listing is of legal effect but provides no context, timeframe, or reasons for recognizing a well-known mark.

[84] *See* Kung-Chung Liu et al., *The Use and Misuse of Well-Known Marks Listings*, 40 Int'l Rev. Indus. Prop. & Competition L. 685, 697 (2009).

[85] *Japanese Well-known Trademark Search*, Japan Platform for Patent Info., https://www.j-platpat.inpit.go.jp/t0400

The Korean IP Office began maintaining and updating its *Foreign Trademark Directory* in 1995. The directory comprehensively listed trademarks of international or domestic fame. For trademarks included in the directory, often the IP Office did not require evidence of well-known status to save time and effort when opposing or rejecting trademark applications. Recently, the directory has become the *Booklet of Trademarks Which Are Frequently Infringed*, and it also now includes domestic marks. The IP Office continuously updates this booklet "based on the number of raids against counterfeits for the past two to three years."[86]

Upon suggestion of this author, the Taiwan IP Office has maintained since 2010 a well-structured online database summarizing cases in which well-known marks have been recognized in the last five years. Currently, the database contains 3,384 cases. The database is all-inclusive, incorporating all decisions about well-known marks made by the IP Office during rejection, opposition, and invalidation procedures, and by courts of all instances, the competition authority, Fair Trade Commission, and the administrator of domain names. Most importantly, the database provides relatively detailed reasons for recognizing a well-known trademark.[87]

Listing of well-known marks by the Japanese Patent Office, the Korean IP Office, and the Taiwan IP Office can have both limiting and relieving effects for well-known trademark owners. It is limiting because well-known trademark owners bear the burden of proving the renown of their marks if these marks are not on the list. It is a relief because once their marks are on the list, they bear no such burden. Other jurisdictions are advised to reflect on the usefulness of this Asian practice .

Conclusion

Asia has a thriving trademark landscape, making trademark law the most ideal area of IP for Asian economies to work toward harmonization and integration with some pan Asian arrangements. The study of this chapter shows that major Asian economies are not neglecting the importance of limitations of trademark rights while building their respective trademark regimes. Moreover, they have even developed some new limits on trademark rights that might lend some light to the rest of the world.

[86] Woo, *supra* note 59, at 126. However, no English materials on this topic can be found on the websites of Korean IP Office and its affiliations.

[87] *Jin 5 Nian Zheming Shangbiao Minglu Ji Anjian Huibian* (近5年著名商標名錄及案件彙編) [Directory and Case Compilation of Well-Known Trademark of the Past 5 Years], TAIWAN INTELL. PROP. OFFICE, https://topic.tipo.gov.tw/trademarks-tw/lp-566-201.html

12

The Constitutional Basis for Trademark Parodies in India and South Africa

Arpan Banerjee[1]

Introduction

Trademarks are often considered the least controversial of all intellectual property (IP) rights[2] given their roots in the noble objectives of consumer protection and prevention of deception. Unlike copyright and patents, the rudiments of a trademark system existed in ancient non-Western civilizations.[3] Economists view trademark protection as beneficial for developing countries.[4] A noted legal scholar has even described trademarks as a "pro-competitive monopoly."[5]

Today, while traditional assumptions about the noncontroversial nature of trademark law still largely hold true, the expansion of dilution and tarnishment doctrines has led to a sharp increase in conflicts surrounding trademark monopolies and the public interest. A good example of this lies in the use of trademarks in the course of parody. Trade-Related Aspects of Intellectual Property Rights (TRIPS) Agreement trademark provisions are thought to be applicable in the sphere of trade, but corporations have also sporadically approached courts to prevent use of their trademarks in noncommercial contexts.[6] In certain instances,

[1] This chapter draws from a paper presented at the NYU–HKU Conference on Limitations on Trademark Rights, Hong Kong University Jan. 8, 2019. I thank the organizers for inviting me to participate in the conference and for their hospitality. I also thank the other participants for their inputs.

[2] *See, e.g.*, Richard T. De George, *Intellectual Property Rights*, *in* The Oxford Handbook of Business Ethics 408, 419 (George G. Brenkert & Tom L. Beauchamp eds., 2010); Justin Malbon, Charles Lawson & Mark Davison, The WTO Agreement on Trade-Related Aspects of Intellectual Property Rights: A Commentary 275 (2014). Jim Harper, *U.S. Patent and Trademark Office: FAIL*, Cato Institute (2009), https://www.cato.org/publications/techknowledge/us-patent-trademark-office-fail (last visited Apr. 13, 2020); John E. Jr. Vick, *Intellectual Property Aspects of NAFTA and GATT: An Update*, 2 Tex. Intell. Prop. L. J. 131, 137 (1993).

[3] *See, e.g.*, Russ VerSteeg, *Ancient Egyptian Roots of Trademarks*, 63 The Antitrust Bulletin 283 (2018).

[4] For instance, in one of his most influential articles, the Nobel-winning economist George Akerlof justified the utility of "brand-name goods" by using the example of adulterated rice sold in Indian bazaars vis-à-vis packaged products in American supermarkets. George A. Akerlof, *The Market for "Lemons": Quality Uncertainty and the Market Mechanism*, 84 Q. J. Econ. 488–500 (1970).

[5] Gustavo Ghidini, Intellectual Property and Competition Law: The Innovation Nexus 80 (2006).

[6] *See* Edson Beas Rodrigues jr., The General Exception Clauses of the TRIPS Agreement: Promoting Sustainable Development 237–65 (2012).

Arpan Banerjee, *The Constitutional Basis for Trademark Parodies in India and South Africa* In: *Charting Limitations on Trademark Rights*. Edited by: Haochen Sun and Barton Beebe, Oxford University Press. © Arpan Banerjee 2023.
DOI: 10.1093/oso/9780198871248.003.0013

trademark tarnishment claims appear to have been invoked as quasi-defamation actions in conflict with constitutional free speech safeguards.

The use of constitutional law principles to decide trademark cases has divided scholars. One school of thought is skeptical of using the "external" aid of constitutional jurisprudence to remedy the potential chilling effect of trademark expansionism. Instead, it favors clearer interpretation of "internal" trademark norms.[7] A contrasting view argues that "constitutionalization" is a way "to bring intellectual property closer to the people again, to humanize the subject by binding it to the basic values of our juridical system: fundamental rights and human rights."[8]

In countries whose constitutions prioritize social justice principles over private rights, the latter view would naturally seem attractive. In addition, there are two, less obvious reasons why constitutionalizing trademark law may be advantageous. First, in certain countries, cases may involve trademark infringement claims being filed alongside tortious injurious falsehood or defamation actions. What Lord Justice Jacob found fairly obvious in an English context—that, after the adoption of E.U. trademark directives, an action for injurious falsehood "merely adds the burden (and costs) of proof of malice" to a trademark infringement claim[9]—may not be so obvious elsewhere. In such situations, resorting to constitutionalization can result in wider principles applicable not just in trademark actions, but also other tortious actions. Second, trademark jurisprudence is growing increasingly complex. Many countries lack specialist judges, lawyers, and teachers well-versed in its complexities. If a trademark case is decided with reference to basic constitutional rights, it can possibly serve as a more durable and accessible precedent. For example, a watertight compartmentalization between parody, satire, and criticism in IP cases not always easy to achieve.[10] In Europe, trademarks have been described as "a horrendously difficult area of IP law,"[11] E.U. trademark legislation as "terrible,"[12] and European Court of Justice case law as inconsistent.[13] In countries lacking IP expertise, constitutional free speech principles can sometimes be used to reduce technical complications in trademark dilution cases, while still maintaining jurisprudential robustness. This chapter discusses a precedent in which both these advantages are apparent: an order of the Justice S. Ravindra Bhat of the Delhi High Court in *Tata v.*

[7] Robert Burrell & Dev Gangjee, *Trade Marks and Freedom of Expression—A Call for Caution*, 41 I.I.C. 544 (2010).

[8] Christophe Geiger, *Reconceptualizing the Constitutional Dimension of Intellectual Property—An Update*, *in* Intellectual Property and Human Rights (Paul Torremans ed., 4th ed. 2020).

[9] Cable & Wireless Plc v. British Telecommunications Plc F.S.R. 383 (Ch.) 385 (Eng.) [1998].

[10] For example, a website in India, teez.in, currently sells a t-shirt with the words "Diet Joke," mimicking the logo of Diet Coke. It is not easy to strictly characterize this expression as a parody or satire or criticism. See *Diet Joke Funny Parody Women's T-shirt*, TEEZ, https://www.teez.in/products/diet-joke-womens-t-shirt (last visited June 14, 2020).

[11] *The Next Ten Years of IP Law in the European Court of Justice*, *in* 10 Intellectual Property Law and Policy 63 (Hugh Hansen ed., 2008) (remarks by Hugh Laddie).

[12] *Id.*

[13] *Id.* at 63–64 (remarks by Robin Jacob and Hugh Hansen).

Greenpeace.[14] In this case, the court relied on a decision of the South African Constitutional Court popularly known as the *Laugh It Off* case,[15] paving the way for an overarching free speech defense in cases involving the protection of reputation, both in a trademark and wider tortious context. The chapter consists of three parts. First, I discuss the facts and decision in *Laugh It Off*. I then discuss *Greenpeace* and its application of *Laugh It Off*. Lastly, I refer to cases decided after *Greenpeace* in which courts have adopted an approach starkly different to that taken by Justice Bhat, and reflect on the potential significance of the final decision in *Greenpeace*.

I. The *Laugh It Off* Case

The *Laugh It Off* case tested the dilution (tarnishment) provision of South Africa's trademarks statute[16] against the free speech provision of the South African Constitution.[17] The case arose from the sale of t-shirts parodying well-known trademarks. One such t-shirt lampooned the popular beer brand Carling Black Label (using multiple registered trademarks). The t-shirt read:

> Africa's lusty, lively exploitation since 1652
> White
> *Black Labour*
> Guilt
> No regard given worldwide.

[14] (178) D. L. T. 705 (India) (2011) (hereinafter *Greenpeace*).

[15] Laugh It Off Promotions CC v. South African Breweries International (Finance) B. V. t/a Sabmark International & Freedom of Expression Institute Z. A. C. C. 7, para. 17 (S. Afr.) [2005] (hereinafter *Laugh It Off*) 199.

[16] According to the provision, the rights acquired by registration of a well-known trademark are infringed if there is an unauthorized use in the course of trade in relation to goods or services, if such identical or similar mark is likely to take unfair advantage of or be detrimental to, the distinctive character or the repute of the registered trademark, notwithstanding the absence of confusion or deception. Trade Marks Act 1993, § 34(1)(c) (S. Afr.). The case was described as being concerned "not with blurring, but with tarnishment," as "the source of the respondent's disquiet is the offending use of its marks, in relation to noncompeting goods, and yet in a manner that creates unfavourable associations and unsavoury connections, which carry the likelihood of tarnishing the repute of its marks." Minister of Home Affairs v. Fourie (1) S. A. 524 (CC), para. 42 (S. Afr.) (2006).

[17] The provision (S. Afr. Const., 1996 §16) states:

(1) Everyone has the right to freedom of expression, which includes–
   (a) freedom of the press and other media;
   (b) freedom to receive or impart information or ideas;
   (c) freedom of artistic creativity; and
   (d) academic freedom and freedom of scientific research.

(2) The right in subsection (1) does not extend to
   (a) propaganda for war;
   (b) incitement of imminent violence; or
   (c) advocacy of hatred that is based on race, ethnicity, gender or religion, and that constitutes incitement to cause harm

When Carling Black Label and associated trademarks owner South African Breweries International discovered the production and sale of the t-shirt, it sent the manufacturer cease and desist letters.[18] When the manufacturer did not comply, South African Breweries filed a trademark infringement suit citing the dilution provision of the South African Trade Marks Act.[19] It argued that the likely prejudice or detriment required under the provision was evident as the message on the t-shirt was likely to "erode the exclusiveness of the mark" and decrease sales.[20] South African Breweries was eventually pitted against not just the t-shirt manufacturer but also the Freedom of Expression Institute, a non-government organization (NGO) intervening as amicus curiae. Their five concurrent arguments were as follows. First, the anti-dilution provision did not oust the constitutional right to comment on or lampoon a trademark.[21] Second, although no proof of actual loss is required under the provision, a trademark owner must establish the likelihood of detriment to the repute of the trademark and this was not apparent in the case at hand.[22] Third, the use of the trademark amounted to a parody and was permissible.[23] Fourth, the test for interpretation of the message should be to consider the impression upon a "national customer of average intelligence, viewing the marks as a whole or looking at the dominant features of each mark."[24] Fifth, although the t-shirt was for sale it also expressed a social statement, and this expressive function should be constitutionally protected.[25]

At first instance, the Cape High Court ruled in favor of South African Breweries. The court held that the t-shirt carried a likelihood of detriment to the distinctive character of the trademark, as it suggested exploitative and racially discriminatory practices by the brewer.[26] The court felt that since the t-shirt was being sold for commercial gain, it could not be contended that its message was protected by free expression, and the message actually bordered on hate speech.[27] On appeal, the Supreme Court of Appeal upheld the order. The court acknowledged that trademark rights were not absolute and ought to be balanced with freedom of expression.[28] However, it concluded that the t-shirt's message was likely to create a "particularly unwholesome, unsavory, or degrading association" with the mark in the minds of consumers, and thus materially tarnish the reputation of the

[18] (1) S. A. 144 (C. C.), paras. 4, 7, 9, 12 (S. Afr.) (2006).
[19] *Id.* paras. 2–3, 12.
[20] *Id.* paras. 14, 51, 57.
[21] *Id.* para. 22.
[22] *Id.*
[23] *Id.* paras. 25, 61.
[24] *Id.* para. 60.
[25] *Id.* para. 62.
[26] *Id.* para. 15.
[27] *Id.* para. 15.
[28] *Id.* para. 18.

trademark.[29] The court rejected a freedom of speech defense as it felt that there were alternative avenues for expressing a message about "black labor" without appropriating the trademark.[30] The court did not find the message to amount to a permissible parody on the basis that it did not comment on the trademark, and thus found that the dilution provision had been breached.[31]

On appeal to the Constitutional Court of South Africa, the decision was reversed. Justice Dikgang Moseneke observed that the Constitution of South Africa excluded only three categories of expression from protection: those concerning war propaganda, imminent violence, or hate speech. Thus, the default position for speech not falling into those categories is that it is protected speech.[32] Hence, courts ought not to convert dilution claims ("usually controlled by powerful financial interests") into a monopoly adverse to the constitution's free speech safeguards, and should carefully weigh the interests of a trademark owner vis-à-vis the right to free expression of a trademark user.[33] Justice Moseneke opined that merely because an expressive act stirred discomfort or contravened morals, this did not by itself amount to tarnishment. The constitution protected degrading expression and such expression ordinarily enjoys protection as fair use.[34] The dilution provision, felt the justice, required the trademark owner to establish a likelihood of "substantial economic detriment," and an expressive act must not be curtailed if the harm is unrelated to the commercial value of the trademark.[35] Here, Justice Moseneke did not find a likelihood of commercial harm as there was no evidence of a real possibility of beer sales declining or likely future detriment, and the reach of the offending use was small (only a few hundred t-shirts were sold).[36] The justice did not specifically comment on whether the message on the t-shirt amounted to a parody, but stated that the mere characterization of an expression as parody is not decisive of what is fair use.[37]

Nine other justices of the court agreed with Moseneke, out of whom Justice Albert Sachs delivered a separate judgment. Notably, Justice Sachs remarked that the Supreme Court of Appeal had failed to appreciate the parodic use by the t-shirt and placed too much importance on the profit made from sales of the t-shirt;[38] that a commercial element does not remove free speech protections available to a trademark user;[39] that the probability of beer drinkers taking the t-shirt message

[29] *Id.* para. 21.
[30] *Id.* para. 23.
[31] *Id.* para. 25.
[32] *Id.* para. 47.
[33] The judge held that what is "fair" depends on the facts of each case, considering "importance of the purpose, nature, extent and impact of the limitation of free expression invoked against the claim of infringement." *Id.* paras. 48–50.
[34] *Id.* para. 55.
[35] *Id.* paras. 54, 56.
[36] *Id.* paras. 57–58.
[37] *Id.* para. 66.
[38] *Id.* para. 75.
[39] *Id.* para. 86.

seriously or regarding it as hate speech was low;[40] that the activity was a "take-off, not a rip-off";[41] that the activity was also not a commercial activity masked as free speech;[42] that parody is not a separate defense to trademark use but merely forms a single element of a larger analysis;[43] and that an overzealous application of trademark law can have a chilling effect on the free circulation of ideas and stifle legitimate debate.[44] He concluded by stating:

> A society that takes itself too seriously risks bottling up its tensions and treating every example of irreverence as a threat to its existence. Humor is one of the great solvents of democracy. It permits the ambiguities and contradictions of public life to be articulated in non-violent forms. It promotes diversity. It enables a multitude of discontents to be expressed in a myriad of spontaneous ways. It is an elixir of constitutional health.[45]

In South Africa, scholars perceived the decision's main significance to be in accepting trademark parodies as a form of social commentary qualifying for constitutional protection,[46] and in favoring a restrictive interpretation of trademark rights in such cases.[47] The judgment was rightly described as "prescribed reading for students, not only in South Africa, but overseas."[48] A noted scholar supported the decision on the basis that it was "necessary for big business to be brought down to size."[49]

Among views critical of the judgment was one arguing that the court had failed to "create a new category of fundamental rights" that included IP rights.[50] According to this argument, property rights are included in the Constitution of South Africa under its Bill of Rights.[51] The South African Constitutional Court, in an earlier case, observed that many constitutions did not explicitly recognize IP rights as constitutionally protected property rights.[52] Yet, various scholars have submitted

[40] *Id.* para. 99.
[41] *Id.* para. 102.
[42] *Id.*
[43] *Id.* para. 82.
[44] *Id.* para. 106.
[45] *Id.* para. 110.
[46] Thea Illsley, *How to Tell a Take-Off from a Rip-Off: Trade Mark Parody and Freedom of Expression in South Africa*, 22 S. Afr. J. on Hum. Rts. 119, 125 (2006).
[47] B. R. Rutherford, *Trade-mark Protection and Freedom of Expression*, 18 S. Afr. Mercantile L. J. 355, 367 (2006).
[48] Wim Alberts, *The Future of Trade Mark Dilution in South Africa*, 2006 J. S. Afr. L. 212 (2006) 223.
[49] George Devenish, *We Are Amused: Laugh It off Promotions CC v SAB International (Finance) BV t/a Sabmark International*, 122 S. African L. J. 792, 802 (2005).
[50] Mikhalien Du Bois, *Intellectual Property as a Constitutional Property Right: The South African Approach*, 24 S. Afr. Mercantile L. J. 177 191–92 (2012).
[51] S. Afr. Const. 1996 § 25(1) (stating: "No one may be deprived of property except in terms of law of general application, and no law may permit arbitrary deprivation of property.").
[52] Ex parte Chairperson of the Constitutional Assembly: In re Certification of the Constitution of the Republic of South Africa, (4) S. A. 744 (C. C.), para. 75 (S. Afr.) (1996).

that IP rights are within the scope of South Africa's constitutional property rights provision, and the Constitutional Court has not made an explicit statement to the contrary.[53] Here lies an intriguing parallel with India. The right to property in India is constitutionally protected, but it does not enjoy the status of a fundamental right. In practice, this has created "a hierarchy between rights."[54] Private property rights have been viewed by both judges and lawmakers as "a check on social revolution rather than an instrument of change."[55] Yet, even in South Africa, despite property rights being included in the Bill of Rights, scholars hold that courts are obliged to strike a balance between private property rights and the public interest, and interpret constitutional rights in a broader social and political context.[56] In *Laugh It Off*, the Supreme Court of Appeal observed that trademarks were "property, albeit intangible or incorporeal," and this did not change just because trademarks were "the result and part of a 'capitalistic' economy."[57] However, the court added that IP rights were not accorded "special protection" by the constitution and "their enforcement must be constitutionally justifiable."[58] The Constitutional Court cited these observations approvingly.[59] There appears to be a similarity in how India and South Africa conceive of IP rights within the broader constitutional framework, and this helps us appreciate Bhat's application of *Laugh It Off* in *Greenpeace*.

II. The *Greenpeace* Case

Greenpeace tested the tarnishment provision of India's trademark statute vis-à-vis its constitutional free speech provision, which is a fundamental right. While the wording of India's trademark tarnishment provision is similar to that of South Africa,[60] India's constitutional free speech provision is worded somewhat

[53] *See generally* Du Bois, *supra* note 50.

[54] Anindita Mukherjee, The Legal Right to Housing in India 20 (2019). *See also* A. K. Ganguli, *Right to Property: Its Evolution and Constitutional Development in India*, 48 J. Ind. L. Inst. 489 (2006).

[55] *See generally* Tom Allen, *Property as a Fundamental Right in India, Europe and South Africa*, 15 Asia Pacific L. R. 193 (2007).

[56] *Id. See also* A. J. van der Walt, Constitutional Property Law 23–26 (2005).

[57] Laugh It Off Promotions CC v. South African Breweries International Z. A. S. C. A. 76, paras. 10–11 (S. Afr.) [2004].

[58] *Id.* para. 11.

[59] Z. A. C. C. 7, para. 17 (S. Afr.) [2005].

[60] Trade Marks Act 1999 § 29(4) (India). The provision states:

A registered trade mark is infringed by a person who, not being a registered proprietor or a person using by way of permitted use, uses in the course of trade, a mark which—

(a) is identical with or similar to the registered trade mark; and
(b) is used in relation to goods or services which are not similar to those for which the trade mark is registered; and
(c) the registered trade mark has a reputation in India and the use of the mark without due cause takes unfair advantage of or is detrimental to, the distinctive character or repute of the registered trade mark.

differently.[61] A comparison between *Laugh It Off* and *Greenpeace* shows that both cases were decided on a broader conception of the freedom to parody in a democratic society, making these technical differences less relevant. However, a significant difference between them concerns the use of a tortious defamation claim to supplement the trademark infringement claim. In *Laugh It Off*, Justice Sachs, referring to English law, noted that IP rights were "essentially rights against appropriation, not rights against unfair criticism," and that the latter was "regulated, if at all, by the law of injurious falsehood and defamation."[62] But neither defamation nor injurious falsehood appear to have been pleaded in the case. In comparison, *Greenpeace* involved both a defamation and trademark infringement claim.

The facts of *Greenpeace* were as follows. Tata, one of India's largest and best-known corporations, was a 50% shareholder in the Dhamra Port Company Limited (DPCL), named after the Dhamra River in the state of Odisha. DPCL was awarded a contract by the Odisha state government to build and operate a port bordering the Dhamra River. While Tata had secured environmental clearances for the project, Greenpeace alleged that the project would endanger the nesting and breeding of the olive ridley turtle, an endangered species. Greenpeace started a campaign against the project, a highlight of which was a game on its website called "Turtle v. Tata." Modeled on the arcade game "Pac-Man," it required a player to help a turtle gobble up as many dots as possible without bumping into the four "Tata demons." The demons resembled Tata's logo (a T within a circle) and were called Tinku, Matty, Natty, and Ratty (the latter alleged by Tata to be a reference to its chairman, Ratan Tata).[63] The Tata group sued Greenpeace for trademark infringement via tarnishment, as well as defamation (of both the group and its chairman).

On the trademark infringement claim, even though India's tarnishment provision requires infringing use to be in the course of trade and Tata acknowledged that Greenpeace's use was not in the course of trade, Tata nevertheless argued that the provision covered speech and expression other than that in the course of trade.[64] Tata also argued that Greenpeace's use of the Tata logo in a demonizing way showed malicious intent.[65] On the defamation claim, Tata argued that Greenpeace's claims of environmental damage were malicious and untrue, and that an injunction was

[61] India Const. art. 19(1)(a) and (2). The provisions, in relevant part grant all citizens the right to "freedom of speech and expression" and limit this right by stating that it shall not:

> affect the operation of any existing law, or prevent the State from making any law, in so far as such law imposes reasonable restrictions on the exercise of the right conferred by the said sub clause in the interests of the sovereignty and integrity of India, the security of the State, friendly relations with foreign States, public order, decency or morality or in relation to contempt of court, defamation or incitement to an offence.

[62] (1) S. A. 144 (CC), para. 110 (S. Afr.) (2006) (citing Michael Spence, *Intellectual Property and the Problem of Parody*, 114 L. Q. Rev. 294 (1998)).

[63] *Greenpeace* 178 D. L. T. 705 (2011), paras. 7–8.

[64] *Id.* para. 15.

[65] *Id.* para. 11.

warranted. It argued that the right to free speech could not be construed as a license to publish defamatory matter.[66] Greenpeace countered the trademark tarnishment claim by arguing that the provision only covered commercial use, and that its game did not fall in that category.[67] Further, Greenpeace argued that "reasonable fair criticism, comment, and parody" were permitted.[68] Placing reliance on *Laugh It Off*, Greenpeace argued that IP rights were subject to the right to free speech.[69] Greenpeace countered the defamation claim by citing expert reports on the possible environmental impacts of the project,[70] and invoked the free speech provision of India's Constitution as an overarching defense applicable to both the trademark infringement and defamation claims.[71] Greenpeace further argued that its message was "honest, with justifiable reasons on a matter of public importance."[72] It cited favorable Indian precedents involving the criticism of public figures and matters of public interest.[73] It also cited the classic English case of *Bonnard v. Perryman*, which held that courts ought to be circumspect in granting injunctions in cases involving the right to free speech.[74]

Tata's use of both defamation and trademark infringement claims were of considerable significance. In the event of a ruling that India's tarnishment provision did not cover uses outside the course of trade, Tata could still rely on the defamation claim. In that event, Greenpeace's use of the constitutional right to free speech to counter both claims may have given rise to a dichotomous situation, whereby the Indian Constitution protected a message for being a trademark parody but not for being defamatory. Bhat, the sole judge hearing the case, rejected Tata's defamation claim by upholding the *Bonnard v. Perryman* rule. He stated that the court would "invariably not grant an interim injunction to restrain the publication of defamatory material as it would be unreasonable to fetter the freedom of speech before the full trial takes place, where each of the parties can argue in detail with the help of additional evidence."[75] Bhat also gave short shrift to Tata's trademark infringement claim. Going by a textual reading of India's tarnishment provision, he concluded that its drafters intended it to be applicable in situations involving commercial use of the marks.[76] To this extent, Bhat's decision was unremarkable.

66 *Id.* para. 10.
67 *Id.* para. 21.
68 *Id.* para. 27.
69 *Id.* para. 24.
70 *Id.* paras. 34–36.
71 *Id.* paras. 20–27.
72 *Id.* para. 21.
73 *Id.* paras. 22–23. *Greenpeace* cited an Indian Supreme Court decision (involving the censorship of a film) where the court had emphasized the right to free speech in a political context (S. Rangarajan v. P. Jagjivan Ram, 2 S. C. C. 574 (India) (1989)). Greenpeace also cited a Delhi High Court decision (involving a prominent politician who had sought to restrain the publication of an allegedly defamatory book) where the court had similarly emphasized the public interest in allowing criticism of public figures (Khushwant Singh v. Maneka Gandhi, A. I. R. Del 58 (India) (2002)).
74 *Id.* para. 22 (citing Bonnard v. Perryman 2 Ch. 269 (Eng.) [1891]).
75 *Id.* paras. 28–32.
76 *Id.* para. 40.

However, Bhat then engaged with *Laugh It Off*, praising Sachs's opinion as "very perceptive and insightful" and quoting from it extensively.[77] The passages quoted referred to the question of parodic trademark use, as well as the broader issue of balancing private rights with constitutional free speech provisions. Bhat then clubbed together the issues of defamation and trademark infringement and considered the wider implications of the right to free speech. He felt that a trademark could be an object of parody and criticism (again citing the example of *Laugh It Off*), and a court should neither "anoint itself as a literary critic ... nor ... don the robes of a censor" in such cases.[78] Instead, a court should merely monitor the boundaries of free speech "and in exceptional cases, issue injunctions," following *Bonnard v. Perryman*.[79] Finally, exactly as Sachs had done in *Laugh It Off*, Bhat ended with observations on the importance of "free speech and its salutary catalysing effect on public debate," and of tolerating "caricature, lampoon, mime parody and other manifestations of wit."[80] Thus, whereas Tata had strategically used the twin claims of trademark infringement and defamation, and harped on both the use of the logo and the allegations of environmental damage, Bhat concluded by arguably blurring the technical differences between the two claims and emphasizing the right to free speech.

A. Relevance

Greenpeace is now a decade old. Scholars have already used this case to illustrate, among other things, the role of human rights as "extrinsic limits" to IP rights,[81] the balance of convenience in issuing injunctions in trademark cases involving expressive activity,[82] political activism in the form of "antibranding,"[83] and the use of corporate power to "control the semiotic landscape."[84] Nevertheless, there are strong reasons why the case should be revisited. To begin with, the litigation is, surprisingly, still pending. Official records, along with an exchange of emails with Greenpeace's lawyers, reveal that the Tata corporation has contested the court's order. The parties still await a final decision by the Delhi High Court.[85] In the

[77] *Id.*

[78] *Id.* para. 42.

[79] *Id.*

[80] *Id.* para. 43.

[81] RODRIGUES, *supra* note 6, at 255.

[82] Rajam Neethu, *Reconceptualizing the "Fair Use" Under European and Indian Trademark Law*, 31 DELHI L. REV. 211 (2014).

[83] Sonia Katyal, *Trademark Cosmopolitanism*, 47 U. C. DAVIS L. REV. 875 (2013).

[84] Lawrence Liang, *Fair Use of Cinematograph Films and Sound Recordings: Finding the Solution in the Amendment*, 5 N. U. J. S. L. REV. 687, 698 (2012).

[85] The law firm representing Greenpeace informed me: "The trial is complete in the case and it is pending final hearing before the Delhi High Court." Email from Sneha Jain, Saikrishna & Associates to the author (Apr. 15, 2020) (on file with the author).

event of an adverse ruling, a corporation with deep pockets like Tata certainly has the resources to drag the case to the Indian Supreme Court on further appeal, as might Greenpeace which is reportedly being represented pro bono. It is interesting to note that, in 2015, the Indian government canceled Greenpeace's license to receive foreign donations, purportedly for "prejudicially affecting the public interest and economic interest of the state."[86] In 2018, the organization's bank accounts in India were frozen. Although the freezing order was later struck down by a court (on the technicality of a delay),[87] Greenpeace was compelled to shut most its offices in India and lay off staff.[88] Hence, behind the scenes, there are developments that heighten the stakes involved.

Another reason why revisiting *Greenpeace* is helpful (and this is where judicial guidance from the Supreme Court would be welcome), is the intervening rise in Internet meme culture. In popular culture usage, the term "meme" dates back to at least the 1990s. In his 2000 book *Culture Jam*, the activist Kalle Lasn prophetically observed: "[M]eme warfare has become the geopolitical battle of our information age. Whoever has the memes has the power."[89] Today, meme culture has been amplified by social media websites and apps like Facebook, Twitter, Instagram, and WhatsApp. Academic and journalistic commentary on the legal implications of memes have justifiably revolved around the use of copyright-protected images.[90] However, there have been a handful of instances where famous trademarks have also been the subject of viral, often unflattering memes.

For example, in 2017, when United Airlines infamously evicted a passenger on an overbooked flight using brute force a few years ago, Internet users flooded social media with parody advertisements. One meme featured a photograph of the bloodied passenger next to United's logo and slogan "Fly The Friendly Skies"—both registered trademarks.[91] Another modified the company's former logo (a mix of blue and red lines), replacing the red lines with bloodied handprints.[92] The same year, a meme attracting much attention comprised a video of a WWE match in which President Donald Trump had participated, with the face of a wrestler being

[86] Vijaita Singh, *Greenpeace India's Registration Cancelled*, THE HINDU (Sept. 4, 2015), https://www.thehindu.com/news/national/greenpeace-indias-registration-cancelled/article7613184.ece.

[87] Greenpeace v. Union of India, Writ Petition 47822 of 2018 (Karnataka H. C.) (Feb. 14, 2019).

[88] Srijan Shukla, *In the Dock for "Fund Fraud", Greenpeace Scales down India Campaigns*, THEPRINT (Feb. 4, 2019), https://theprint.in/india/governance/in-the-dock-for-fund-fraud-greenpeace-scales-down-india-campaigns/189135.

[89] KALLE LASN, CULTURE JAM 123 (2000).

[90] *See, e.g.*, Jaya Harrar, *#copyrightdirective and the #deathofmemes*, LAWYER MONTHLY (Nov. 1, 2018), https://www.lawyer-monthly.com/2018/11/copyrightdirective-and-the-deathofmemes; Thomas F. Cotter, *Memes and Copyright*, 80 TUL. L. REV. 331 (2005); Giacomo Bonetto, *Internet Memes as Derivative Works: Copyright Issues under EU Law*, 13 J. INTELL. PROP. L. & PRACTICE 989 (2018); Lorelei Laird, *Do Memes Violate Copyright Law?*, A. B. A. JOURNAL (Sept. 1, 2016), https://www.abajournal.com/magazine/article/do_memes_violate_copyright_law.

[91] John Lim, *12 Most Savage Memes and Responses to United Airlines' Passenger Fiasco*, SAYS (Apr. 12, 2017), https://says.com/my/fun/united-airlines-meme.

[92] *Id.*

punched by Trump replaced with the CNN logo. Trump retweeted the meme, adding the hashtag #FraudNewsCNN.[93] More recently, the COVID-19 pandemic prompted a host of Corona beer memes. A mock news report claimed that the company had changed the name of its beer, photoshopping "Ebola" on existing Corona bottles in the brand's distinctive font.[94] Others used slogans alongside Corona bottles, such as "HEALTH WARNING ... Do Not Drink," and "Available Now With Extra Virus."[95] Incredibly, because of an algorithmic faux pas, the term "Corona beer virus" began to rank highly in Google searches.[96]

In situations like these, corporations rarely threaten Internet users with trademark infringement lawsuits—possibly because they believe the law would not be on their side, that trying to police social media is futile, or that threatening Internet users could lead to a public relations disaster. While the reputation of the Corona brand may have taken a hit, the company's strategy was to "hunker down" until the social media storm subsided.[97] However, sometimes highly objectionable content is made using corporate logos. For example, in an elaborate hoax, users of the notoriously far-right website 4chan continuously tweeted a fake Apple advertisement claiming that the company's new iPhone was enabled with "wave-charge" technology allowing it to be recharged in a microwave oven. Many iPhone owners inadvertently damaged their phones as a result.[98] In another egregious example, 4chan users mass-tweeted a fake Starbucks advertisement offering African Americans a complimentary drink with the hashtag #FreeBlackCoffee. The stunt was organized in protest against a statement made by the CEO of Starbucks apologizing to two African Americans who were discriminated against at a Starbucks outlet.[99] To cite another example, Kellogg's was assailed with racist memes after withdrawing advertising from the far-right news website Breitbart. One such meme featured the letters "KKK" using the Kellogg's logo typeface. Another altered a box of Honey Nut Cheerios to read "Honey Nut Gestapos," adding an image of a Gestapo officer

[93] Alana Abramson, *Trump Just Tweeted a Video of Him Punching CNN in the Face*, Time (July 2, 2017), https://time.com/4843303/donald-trump-twitter-cnn-video

[94] *"Now With Extra Virus": Memes Go Viral as Online Searches Soar For "Corona Beer Virus,"* CBS Los Angeles (Feb. 28, 2020), https://losangeles.cbslocal.com/2020/02/28/coronavirus-corona-beer-virus-cdc-meme.

[95] Bruce Y. Lee, *Coronavirus Is Not The "Corona Beer Virus," What People Are Googling*, Forbes (Jan. 30, 2020), https://www.forbes.com/sites/brucelee/2020/01/30/coronavirus-is-not-the-corona-beer-virus-what-people-are-googling.

[96] *Id.*

[97] Jeff Beer & Jeff Beer, *Why Corona Beer's Silence Is the Best Possible Response to Coronavirus Memes and Discussion*, Fast Company (Apr. 3, 2020), https://www.fastcompany.com/90471294/why-corona-beers-silence-is-the-best-possible-response-to-coronavirus-memes-and-discussion.

[98] Karma Allen, *Fake Microwave Charging Ad Enrages iOS8 Users*, CNBC (Sept. 24, 2014), https://www.cnbc.com/2014/09/24/fake-microwave-charging-ad-enrages-apple-ios8-users.html.

[99] Mayukh Sen, *4Chan Hoax Claims Starbucks Is Giving Free Coffee Coupons to Black Customers*, Vice (Apr. 19, 2018), https://www.vice.com/en_us/article/zmgkjw/starbucks-hoax-coupon-4chan-pol-politically-incorrect.

and transforming the brand's cartoon bee into a "Zyklon Bee" hunting for Jews.[100] Switching to a different ideology, art activists from the anti-advertising movement "Brandalism" plastered the streets of Paris with mock advertisements during the U. N. Climate Change Conference in 2015. The Volkswagen logo was used with the tagline "We're sorry that we got caught," referring to the emissions scandal involving the company, while an advertisement for Mobil, also using its logo, stated "We knew about the impact of fossil fuels but publicly denied it."[101]

The progressive political sentiments driving Brandalism distinguish its trademark appropriation tactics from those of 4chan users. However, the *Greenpeace*, *Laugh It Off*, and various other cases[102] show that corporations might still be unhappy over such portrayals and consider trademark infringement claims. If and when the ongoing weaponization of memes triggers serious trademark litigation, precedents like *Greenpeace* and by extension *Laugh It Off* could be tested anew. The meme culture of today did not prevail when these cases were decided yet, much like today's memes, both involved "culture jamming"—an attempt, as characterized by Lasn, to "uncool" the "image factory" of powerful corporations and brands.[103] For this reason, *Greenpeace* and *Laugh It Off* can still be regarded as judicial canon in the context of future trademark meme litigation.

Finally, *Greenpeace* is worth revisiting because the case, in many ways, tells Justice Bhat. Now a judge of the Indian Supreme Court, Bhat heard a number of important IP decisions while serving at the Delhi High Court—the forum of choice for most high-value IP disputes in India. While Bhat has been credited with "creating a strong and sophisticated body of IP jurisprudence," he possessed no IP experience prior to becoming a judge.[104] According to one view, this ostensible deficiency has been advantageous to the development of IP jurisprudence in India, as Bhat has apparently resisted "a blind adherence to IP formalism."[105]

Bhat's non-specialist, autodidactic approach toward IP is evident in a 2018 article in which he uses the Constitution of India as the key to unraveling IP rights. He begins by discussing the fundamental rights granted directly or indirectly by the Constitution and a complementary set of welfare obligations imposed by it upon

[100] Nick Rose, *The War Between Breitbart and Kellogg's Has Spawned #BreitbartCereals*, VICE (Dec. 2, 2016), https://www.vice.com/en_us/article/z48nj5/breitbartcereals-goes-viral-during-cereal-culture-wars.

[101] Danny Lewis, *Hundreds of Fake Ads Protest Paris Climate Summit's Corporate Sponsors*, SMITHSONIAN MAG. (Dec. 2, 2015), https://www.smithsonianmag.com/smart-news/hundreds-fake-ads-protest-paris-climate-summits-corporate-sponsors-180957434.

[102] *See, e.g.*, Esso v. Association Greenpeace France, Cour d'appel (C. A.) (regional court of appeal) Paris, 4e ch., 04/12417 (Fr.) (Nov. 16, 2005). The case arose over the use of "STOP ESSO," "STOP E$$O," and "E££O" in a campaign by Greenpeace. For more examples, *see* RODRIGUES, *supra* note 6.

[103] LASN, *supra* note 89, at xvi.

[104] Shamnad Basheer, *Specialised Courts (III): Commercialising the High Courts?*, SPICYIP (Feb. 17, 2016), https://spicyip.com/2016/02/specialised-courts-iii-commercialising-the-high-courts.html.

[105] *Id.*

the state, referred to as Directive Principles.[106] Bhat reminds us that the right to property—a crucial fundamental right—was deleted from the Constitution in the 1970s.[107] This was the result of a controversial intervention by then Prime Minister Indira Gandhi, who also succeeded in amending the constitutional preamble to declare India a socialist republic. Bhat notes that, despite no longer being a fundamental right, the Constitution still protects rights over property.[108] He then cites a Supreme Court judgment, on agricultural land, where the Court observed that the term "property" includes "intangibles like copyrights and other intellectual property and embraces every possible interest recognized by law."[109] Putting two and two together, Bhat concludes that courts ought to protect IP rights and promote innovation, but should "not treat the protection of IP rights as absolute" as "such rights can be made subservient to the larger public interest."[110]

In essence therefore, Bhat's approach toward IP jurisprudence is that of constitutionalization with a social welfare bias. Thus, in a high-value pharmaceutical patent dispute, Bhat weighed "the public interest in granting an injunction" against "the public interest in access for the people to a life-saving drug," and concluded that "the balance has to be tilted in favor of the latter."[111] In another pharmaceutical patent case, Bhat cited the fundamental right to health and a directive principle on health care.[112] He then frowned upon the tendency of IP disputes being "confined in the 'silo' of assertion and negation of private rights and their enforcement, despite (at times) larger implications to the general public in terms of outcomes."[113] Bhat's decision in *Greenpeace*, and his embrace of *Laugh It Off*, represent the apogee of his constitutionalizing approach in a trademark context. Bhat clearly used the Indian Constitution's free speech provisions as a catch-all provision that would aid defendants in both trademark infringement and defamation cases. To this extent, *Greenpeace* has additional uses as a precedent when compared with *Laugh It Off*.

Greenpeace has since been cited as a precedent in a number of Indian trademark cases. However, the results have not always favored defendants. For example, the shoe company Bata was inserted in a Bollywood song mocking powerful Indian businessmen because it rhymed with Tata ("Whether Birla or Tata, Ambani or Bata . . . In their own interests, all have exploited the country"). Bata sued for defamation and trademark infringement before the Delhi High Court. The defendant

[106] S. Ravindra Bhat, *Innovation and Intellectual Property Rights Law—an Overview of the Indian Law*, 30 I. I. M. B. Mgm't Rev. 51, 52 (2018).
[107] *Id.* at 52.
[108] *Id.* (citing India Const. art. 300A, which states: "No person shall be deprived of his property save by the authority of law.").
[109] *Id.* (citing K. T. Plantations v. State of Karnataka, 9 S. C. C. 1, para. 110 (India) (2011)).
[110] *Id.* at 61.
[111] Hoffmann-La Roche v. Cipla, 148 D. L. T. 598 para. 86 , (India) (2008).
[112] Bayer v. Union of India, 78 PTC 521, para. 117 (India) (2019).
[113] *Id.*

cited both *Greenpeace* and *Laugh It Off*, but Bata was still awarded an injunction.[114] The court observed that the filmmakers had used the mark for "not only entertainment but also commercial gains."[115] Eventually, the Indian Supreme Court directed the filmmakers to insert a disclaimer, observing that the lyrics were "in poor taste and ... could have been avoided."[116] Thus, the judiciary adopted exactly the role that Bhat had desisted from—that of a literary critic and censor.

In a recent case, a YouTube influencer alleged to have made disparaging remarks about a brand of hair oil was sued for injurious falsehood and trademark infringement before the Bombay High Court. Again, a reliance on *Greenpeace* did not aid the defendant. The Court directed the defendant to take down the video and observed: "Social media influencers, whether their audience is significant or small, impact the lives of everybody who watches their content. They do have a responsibility to ensure what they are publishing is not harmful or offensive."[117] The defendant had argued that his use of the trademark was not in the course of trade, but the court held that this was immaterial in a tortious injurious falsehood claim, and even in a trademark infringement claim where there was no honest use of the mark (which the court felt was the case).[118]

Conclusion

The judicial trends post-*Greenpeace* are cold comfort for parodists and meme creators who use trademarks. Trademark tarnishment actions may eventually jeopardize parodies if the provision is used in noncommercial contexts or if social media influencers, like filmmakers, are regarded as commercial entertainers. Furthermore, if trademark tarnishment, defamation, and injurious falsehood claims are strictly compartmentalized (which may, in fact, be desirable in many cases), the shield of noncommercial use may be an insufficient one for defendants. It thus becomes imperative for the final judgment in *Greenpeace*—whether emanating from the Delhi High Court or the Supreme Court—to clarify a large number of gray areas. Arguably, an approach where the constitutional right to free speech is given primacy, and treated as an overriding safeguard in both trademark infringement and other tortious actions, is advisable. In cases where trademark owners are legitimately affected through the use of false or hateful propaganda (such as in the 4chan examples mentioned earlier), such a constitutionalizing approach would still work. Both the South African and Indian constitutions explicitly

[114] Bata v. A. M. Turaz, (53) P. T. C. 536 (India) (2013).
[115] *Id.* para. 30.
[116] Bata v. Prakash Jha, 1 S. C. C. 729 (India) (2013).
[117] Marico v. Abhijeet Bhansali, Indlaw Mum 41, para. 28 (India) (2020).
[118] *Id.* paras. 24–25.

limit the right to free speech (as do most other constitutions of the world) and IP rights have been recognized in both countries as akin to property rights. Thus, should the court writing the final opinion in *Greenpeace* be wary of replicating Bhat's constitutionalization approach, it ought to remember that such an approach can equally serve as a license and a leash.

13

Trademark Parody under Japanese Trademark Law

Finding the Fine Line in Japanese Humor

Christoph Rademacher and Roberto Carapeto

Introduction

Trademark parodies are not a particularly new phenomenon,[1] though with the continued development of digital marketing and e-commerce, the relevance of this discussion has been growing on a global scale. One noticeable trend is that well-known international brands have become the target of "regional" or "domestic" parodies. Consumers usually see trademark parodies as fun marketing tools that evoke a lighthearted and cheerful image of a well-known mark. Of course, trademark owners attempt to maintain a high degree of protection regarding their marks around the world; they usually look at parodies differently and are concerned about the potential consumer confusion or trademark dilution that parodies might cause.

Like other major jurisdictions, Japan has been the venue for a number of trademark parody disputes. This chapter highlights the two main problems noted in the growing body of Japanese case laws. First, courts seem to have embarked on developing a somewhat inconsistent substantive standard. Second, in the context of parodies, the Japanese trademark community seems to commingle registration with infringement. This chapter reviews the underlying provisions of Japanese trademark laws and connects the dots between the most significant trademark parody decisions made by Japanese courts and the Japan Patent Office (JPO).

[1] *See, e.g.*, Robert J. Shaughnessy, *Trademark Parody: A Fair Use and First Amendment Analysis*, 72 Va. L. Rev. 1079 (1986); Annette Kur, *Borderline Cases of Trademark Protection—A Study in German Trademark Law on the Eve of Amendment*, 485 I. I. C. 500–01 (1992).

Christoph Rademacher and Roberto Carapeto, *Trademark Parody under Japanese Trademark Law*
In: *Charting Limitations on Trademark Rights*. Edited by: Haochen Sun and Barton Beebe, Oxford University Press.
© Christoph Rademacher and Roberto Carapeto 2023. DOI: 10.1093/oso/9780198871248.003.0014

I. Japan, Parody, and Legal Issues

This discussion of parody in Japanese trademark law begins by defining the word "parody" in Japanese society and language. One of the most widely used Japanese dictionaries, the *Kōjien*, defines parody as "a form of literary work; a literary work that imitates the style and rhyme scheme of a well-known literary work and changes its content to make it ridiculous and satirical."[2] The *Kōjien* alludes to Japanese *kaeuta*[3] and *kyoka*[4] as forms that constitute examples of parody in Japanese culture, but it also refers to a broad range of other artistic forms, such as paintings and photographs. The *Daijirin*, another leading Japanese dictionary, defines "parody"[5] as "a literary work that retains at a glance the characteristics of a famous existing work or the style and rhyme scheme of another person, but expresses something completely different, and is reworked to give a sense of satire or comedy." Aside from mentioning theater, music, art, and film as media forms in which parody is used, it refers to Japanese *kyoka*, *kaeuta*, and *hon-kadori*[6] as specific examples of parody.

The above definitions seem to be quite similar to the Western understanding of parody. For example, the *Cambridge English Dictionary* defines parody as "writing, music, art, speech, etc. that intentionally copies the style of someone famous or copies a particular situation, making the features or qualities of the original more noticeable in a way that is humorous." Both "Western" and Japanese parody thus require the same elements, such as (1) reference to a well-known work (2) while changing the content and maintaining the same style and (3) with the new content having a satirical or funny connotation. That said, a closer reading indicates that while both Japanese dictionary definitions point to specific examples of traditional Japanese works that fall under the umbrella category of a parody,[7] there is no Japanese term that contains the same lexical range. The need to borrow the Western term "parody" indicates that no traditional word for the umbrella concept in the Japanese language has been established. Similarly, terms such as "satire" or "pastiche" also do not have an equivalent in the Japanese language. Given the linguistic absence of parody in the Japanese language, it is perhaps not too surprising that Japanese intellectual property (IP) law does not carry specific references to parody.

[2] Shinmura Izuru, Kojien 2407 (7th ed. 2018).

[3] A parodic song that is written and sung with lyrics other than those originally attached to the song while keeping the melody and rhythm as unchanged as possible.

[4] *Kyōka* is a kind of Japanese poetry that is related to parodic versions of Japanese "short poems" ("*tanka*") that possess a metric of 5-7-5-7-7 syllables.

[5] Akira Matsumura, Daijirin 2247 (4th ed. 2019).

[6] *Honkadori* is a style of Japanese poetry, where one or two phrases of famous old poems are incorporated into a new and original composition. The incorporated parts of the poem should work as a background to create a multilayered expressive effect.

[7] There are other possible examples, such as the "monomane," a Japanese form of mimicry used for entertainment.

A. Parody and Copyright Law

Aside from trademark law, the IP discipline that prompts most discussion on the balance between IP protection and parody is copyright law.[8] Japanese copyright law does not provide for a general fair-use exemption. Instead, it lists a number of specific purposes for which the effects of copyright protection are limited. Parody is not included in such a list of explicit limitations. Rather, courts have referred to the right to quote provided under Article 32 of the Japanese Copyright Act when balancing copyright protection and parody.

The most authoritative precedent within the realm of copyright and parody is a 1980 Supreme Court decision that assessed copyright infringement in the context of a photo montage that aimed to raise awareness of the environmental dangers of over-tourism.[9] The Supreme Court admitted that criticism would be a permissible purpose for quotations under the applicable text of the Copyright Act and that the photo montage's production and publication must be considered copyright infringement "if it is possible to directly perceive the essential characteristics of the other person's photograph from this montage photograph."[10] While the court recognized that the montage at issue expressed "ideas and feelings different from" the original photograph,[11] such a difference in purpose was not significant enough to overcome the direct perception of the essential elements that pushed the montage picture outside the permissible range of quotation.

The Supreme Court's decision created a very difficult standard for works of parody, holding that only those works of parody that identify an original work in a sufficiently light or indirect way may be considered quotations under copyright law.[12] Japanese courts in Japan have to follow precedential decisions by the Supreme Court,[13] and—in the absence of legislative action—only the Supreme Court would have the authority to modify the standard under which parodies qualify for the quotation exception under Article 32 of the Copyright Act. In light

[8] For a more detailed discussion of the concept of parody in Japanese copyright law, *see* Christoph Rademacher, *Cultural Impact on Copyright Exceptions: Parody in Germany and Japan*, *in* THE CAMBRIDGE HANDBOOK OF COPYRIGHT LIMITATIONS AND EXCEPTIONS 343 (Shyamkrishna Balganesh et al. eds., 2020).

[9] Saikō Saibansho [Sup. Ct.] Mar. 28, 1980, Sho 51 (O) No. 923, 34 SAIKŌ SAIBANSHO MINJI HANREISHŪ [MINSHŪ] 244.

[10] *Id.*

[11] *Id.*

[12] The Supreme Court's decisions triggered significant criticism amongst Japanese commentators; *See, e.g.*, Tatsuhiro Ueno, *Inyō o meguru yōken-ron no saikōsei [Reconstructing the Theory of Requirements on Quotation]*, *in* CHOSAKUKENHŌ TO MINPŌ NO GENDAITEKI KADAI: HANDA MASAO SENSEI KOKI KINEN RONSHŪ [CONTEMPORARY ISSUES IN COPYRIGHT LAW AND CIVIL LAW: WRITING IN HONOR OF PROF. MASAO HONDA] 307 (Akira Moriizumi, Hōgakushoin ed. 2003); NOBUHIRO NAKAYAMA, CHOSAKUKENHŌ [COPYRIGHT LAW] 399(3rd ed. 2021); Toshiaki Iimura, *Saibanrei ni okeru inyō no kijun ni tsuite [About the Standards for Quotation in Court Cases]*, 26 ANNUAL OF COPYRIGHT LAW, 91 (1999).

[13] For a brief note on the power of precedence in Japan, *see* Colin A. Jones & Frank S. Ravith, The Japanese Legal System, West Academic, at 273 (2020).

of the strict requirements set by the Supreme Court, it is not surprising that not many defendants accused of copyright infringement have even tried to raise and substantiate a parody defense.

B. Parody and Freedom of Expression

The Japanese Constitution protects the freedom of expression in Article 21.[14] Enforcement against trademark parodies must observe the balance between trademark protection and constitutional guarantees. Trademark parody can often be presented as an expression of personal opinions, such as a work of art or political speech. Although only marks used in commerce are currently relevant in the context of trademark law, the general understanding in Japanese academia is that commercial expressions are also entitled to some level of constitutional protection.[15]

The freedom of expression, as a constitutionally guaranteed civil liberty, is a right that should be strongly protected in a modern democracy, and any kind of restriction must be carefully assessed.[16] Permissible restrictions of the freedom of expression could be based on an overarching objective of promoting "public welfare" (*Kōkyō no fukushi*) or on "intrinsic constraints" of the constitutional order (*Naizai-teki seiyaku*). It is not entirely clear which of the two concepts would serve as a justification for limiting free expression in the context of trademark law.[17] That said, since the Constitution itself contains a number of explicit restrictions on rights based on "public welfare," there is no objection to interpreting a possible restriction on the freedom of expression also in the trademark law context based on the supremacy of "public welfare."

[14] Art. 21: *Freedom of assembly and association as well as speech, press and all other forms of expression are guaranteed. No censorship shall be maintained, nor shall the secrecy of any means of communication be violated.*

[15] Nobuhara Obinata, *Chiteki zaisan-ken to hyōgen no jiyū [Intellectual Property Rights and the Freedom of Expression], in* NAZE HYŌGEN'NOJIYŪ KA—RIRON-TEKI SHIZA TO GENKYŌ E NO TOI [WHY FREEDOM OF EXPRESSION? QUESTIONS ABOUT THE THEORETICAL PERSPECTIVE AND THE CURRENT SITUATION], 166–67 (Shōjirō Sakaguchi et al. eds., 2017). Japanese scholars on constitutional law have not entered any explicit discussions of the implications of trademark law on freedom of speech. However, there are discussions on the freedom of speech and "commercial expressions." Prof. Masami Ito, former dean of the Faculty of Law at the University of Tokyo and former judge at the Supreme Court of Japan, has argued that "purely commercial expressions" are "not related to the free market of ideas" and therefore "it is more appropriate to regard its regulation as an economic regulation, given that it has little relevance to autonomy or individual self-realization." See MASAMI ITŌ, KEMPŌ [CONSTITUTIONAL LAW] 312 (3rd ed. 1996). However, more recently, scholars have also argued that in the present age the types of commercial expressions are diversified and perform various social functions, which is why it has become difficult to determine whether commercial expressions are purely for commercial purposes or not. *See, e.g.*, TOSHIHIKO NONAKA ET AL., KEMPŌ [CONSTITUTIONAL LAW] 360–61 (5th ed. 2012).

[16] Kaoru Satō, *Shōhyō Parody [Trademark Parody]*, 4 KOKUSAI KŌKYŌ SEISAKU KENKYŪ [INTERNATIONAL PUBLIC POLICY STUDIES] 155 (1990).

[17] NONAKA ET AL., *supra* note 15, at 258; NOBUYOSHI ASHIBE, KEMPŌ [CONSTITUTIONAL LAW] 337 (7th ed. 2019).

Japanese law recognizes three overarching principles that any restrictions to constitutional rights must comply with: the principle of superior position (*Yūetsu-teki chii no gensoku*), the principle of prohibition of prior restraint (*Jizen yokusei no kinshi gensoku*), and the principle of clarity (*Meikaku-sei no gensoku*).[18] Among these principles, superior position might play a particular role in hindering the enactment of a clear statutory provision on parody in Japanese trademark law.[19] Any explicit limitation of the expression of parody touches on the freedom of expression, and any such limitation must pass a strict constitutional test.[20] For example, any explicit statutory provisions or administrative interpretations stating that trademark parodies would infringe on trademark rights will likely be considered unconstitutional. Therefore, conflicts between the interests of a parody and trademark owners should involve an analysis of the constitutional freedom of expression guaranteed by the Constitution.[21]

Although constitutional arguments have not been directly cited in trademark parody-related case law, this interpretation might be an underlying reason for the current line of rather lenient decisions. Both the JPO and Japanese courts have increasingly accepted the registration and the use of trademark parodies. This begs the question of why copyright law has maintained its rather restrictive approach when it comes to parody.

II. Parody and the Japanese Trademark System

The current Trademark Act was promulgated on April 13, 1959 and enacted on April 1, 1960.[22] An amendment in 1991 introduced the protection of service marks.[23] In 1996, Japan became a signatory of the Trademark Law Treaty and introduced the protection of three-dimensional trademarks.[24] The Japanese government introduced regional collective trademarks as a basis for geographic indications in 2006.[25] The most recent significant amendment to the Trademark Act occurred in 2014 with the introduction of additional non-traditional trademarks.[26]

[18] KOJI SATŌ, KEMPŌ [CONSTITUTIONAL LAW] 403 (3rd ed. 1990).

[19] The "Theory of Double Standard" is historically the predominant standard for constitutional review under the Principle of Superior Position. Accordingly, spiritual freedom is an indispensable right for the political process of a constitutional democracy, and therefore it occupies a position that is superior to mere economic freedom. Therefore, in the constitutional review of laws regulating human rights, any legislation limiting spiritual freedom must be examined according to a stricter standard. *See* NOBUYOSHI ASHIBE & KAZUYUKI TAKAHASHI, KENPŌ [CONSTITUTIONAL LAW] 100 (3rd ed. 2002).

[20] TAKERU EHARA ET AL., RONKŌ KENPŌ-GAKU II (JINKEN-RON) [ARTICLES ON CONSTITUTIONAL THEORY (HUMAN RIGHTS THEORY)] 257–61 (1993).

[21] SATŌ, *supra* note 18, at 455.

[22] Act No. 127 of Apr. 13, 1959.

[23] Amendment Act No. 65 of 1991 (Revision of the Trademark Act).

[24] Amendment Act No. 68 of 1996 (Revision of the Trademark Act).

[25] Amendment Act No. 55 of 2006 (Revision of the Trademark Act).

[26] Amendment Act No. 36 of 2014 (Revision of the Trademark Act).

The Japanese trademark system adopts a "first-to-file" principle. The trademark owner's exclusive right to a trademark comes into force upon completion of trademark registration at the JPO. However, trademarks do not have to be currently in use (either in Japan or overseas) to be eligible for registration in Japan.

Within Japanese trademark law, there is no provision that explicitly mentions the concept of parody. That being said, an analysis of whether parodic use is permissible under Japanese trademark law may touch on other doctrinal tests established in trademark law, such as dilution, similarity, or the likelihood of confusion.

A. Anti-Dilution Provisions

Trademark dilution is a trademark law concept explicitly recognized in certain jurisdictions, such as the United States, that provides the owner of well-known trademarks with the right to prevent others from using such well-known marks even in ways that would have little connection to the trademark owner's mark and that would constitute no risk of consumer confusion.[27] While Japan's trademark law does not explicitly protect marks against dilution, it does recognize enhanced protection for well-known marks (*Chōmei Shōhyō*) pursuant to Article 4(1)(x) of the Trademark Act. Accordingly, the JPO must refuse an application for trademark registration if it is identical to or similar to a well-known trademark of another person used for the same or similar goods or services, even if the registration is sought for a different class. Further, Article 4(1)(xix) directs the JPO to refuse registration of marks that are well known among consumers in Japan or abroad if there is a risk of a likelihood of confusion and if the applicant is filing the application with an "unfair intention," such as an intention to gain an unfair profit or to cause damages to the well-known mark's owner. While these provisions resemble anti-dilution protection, the JPO applies them to analyze similarity or the likelihood of confusion, including but not limited to the context of trademark parodies.[28]

[27] 15 U. S. C. § 1125(c). For a relatively current review of the effects of trademark dilution doctrine in the United States *see, e.g.*, Kenneth L. Port, *The Commodification of Trademarks: Some Final Thoughts on Trademark Dilution*, 46 HOFSTRA L. REV. 669 (2017).

[28] The lack of explicit provisions on dilution and trademark parody may be one reason for Japan's relatively flexible approach to parody marks: the more famous a mark is, the more attractive it is for parodying. Furthermore, if the senior mark is sufficiently famous, allowing consumers to understand that the parodied mark is a parody of the famous senior mark, such consumers might be rather unlikely to confuse the different sources of goods.

B. Similarity of Trademarks in Japanese Law

The most important determination governing trademark parody in Japan is the determination of similarity. Courts and the JPO analyze the similarity of marks by referring to the pronunciation, concept, and appearance of the marks at issue.

Pronunciation refers to the pronunciation of the entire trademark and to the pronunciation of any characters used therein. Japanese practice usually assumes that Japanese consumers will be able to recognize the correct pronunciation of English and Japanese words written in Roman alphabetical characters. Despite such assumptions, many owners of trademarks written in Roman alphabetical characters also file such marks as they are pronounced in Japanese kana characters to ensure that the proper pronunciation is protected.

An inquiry into the **concept** of marks will review the meaning inferred from a mark as perceived by the average consumer. In the case of a trademark spelled out in a foreign script, such as the English words "black cat," for example, these words would conjure the image of a feline animal black in color in the minds of the relevant average Japanese consumer. The German words "schwarze katze" or the Spanish words "gato negro" would, however, presumptively not spark the same image of a feline in the average consumer's mind. Thus, such German or Spanish terms can be recognized as coined words without any specific meaning. Consequently, the owner of a trademark for "schwarze katze" or for "gato negro" would probably not be able to exclude a third party from registering other trademarks, which causes people to imagine a black cat. Therefore, it is not uncommon for trademark owners to seek registrations of Japanese translations of original foreign-language marks.

Appearance refers to a mark's actual visual appearance. It is important to note that while Western jurisdictions would register Japanese characters as "figures," Japanese trademark law considers such characters as "words" in the same way as words written in the Roman alphabet.[29]

Courts and the JPO consider two marks similar on some level if they are similar in terms of any of these three relevant elements. Commentators have observed that the JPO's examination practice puts a particular emphasis on the similarity of "pronunciation," while courts consider "appearance" and the situation of the market to be on the same level as pronunciation.[30] Recent empirical research has also indicated that courts, or the JPO, find marks similar if two of the three elements are

[29] Japanese trademark practice treats characters that most Japanese people would be unable to read, such as Hindi, Korean, or Thai characters, as figures.

[30] HIROMICHI AOKI, ATARASHĪ SHŌHYŌ TO SHŌHYŌ-KEN SHINGAI [NEW TRADEMARKS AND TRADEMARK INFRINGEMENT] 39 (2015); KANJI KUDŌ, JITSUREI DE MIRU SHŌHYŌ SHINSA KIJUN NO KAISETSU [EXPLANATION OF THE TRADEMARK EXAMINATION GUIDELINES THROUGH ACTUAL CASES] 196 (5th ed. 2006).

considered similar.[31] Such research also confirmed the ongoing trend of giving a particular deference to the similarity of pronunciation. Concurrently, if another element is considered to be particularly characteristic of the trademark at issue, the similarity of such elements would also trigger the two marks to be considered similar.[32]

The Supreme Court decided the first leading case on similarity under modern Japanese trademark law in 1968.[33] The underlying dispute involved the assessment of the similarity between the composite mark "Hyouzan" (in Japanese "氷山") that showed Japanese Kanji letters in front of an iceberg background and the composite mark "Shouzan" (in Japanese "しょうざん") that showed hiragana letters with no particular concept. Both marks were applied to goods concerning sewing thread.

The JPO initially found the trademarks similar because of their similarity in pronunciation. The Supreme Court ultimately reversed this ruling, finding that the similarity between the marks should be decided by assessing whether there is misdirection or confusion based on the impression given to consumers resulting from appearance, concept, and pronunciation. The Supreme Court pointed out that when only one of the three elements (appearance, concept, and pronunciation) is similar and the other two elements are considerably different, the trademark is unlikely to cause any confusion about the origin of the goods. In such situations, the marks should not be considered similar.

The Supreme Court decided another case on trademark similarity in the context of infringement in 1997.[34] The court stressed that when determining similarity between trademarks for identical or similar products, market factors related to the transaction and the use of the trademarks are important to consider, given the impression and association that the appearance, concept, and pronunciation of the marks may evoke between the trader and consumer. Therefore, even if there is similarity in one or more of the three elements, there should not be a finding of similarity if there are significant differences in other elements or if other market factors remove the risk of confusion.[35]

[31] Takuto Hirasawa, *Shōhyō-ken shingai soshō ni okeru shōhyō no ruiji-sei yōken no jisshō-teki kenkyū [An Empirical Study on the Requirement of Similarity of Trademarks in Trademark Infringement Litigation]*, *in* 57 Chiteki zaisan hōseisakugaku kenkyū [Intellectual Property Law and Policy Studies] 1 (Oct. 2020).

[32] For example, the IP High Court found the marks "Tenshi no Suiitsu" (in kanji and kana) to be similar to "Angel Sweets" (in Roman characters) and "Enzeru Suiitsu" (in kana characters). "Tenshi" is the original Japanese (kanji) word for angel. The court found the marks dissimilar in pronunciation and appearance, but characteristically similar in concept. *See Chiteki Zaisan Kōtō Saibansho [Intellectual Prop. High Ct.]* Jul. 2, 2009, Hei 21 (gyō ke) No. 10052.

[33] Saikō Saibansho [Sup. Ct.] Feb. 27, 1968, Sho 39 (gyo) 110, 22 Saikō Saibansho minji hanreishū [Minshū] 399.

[34] Saikō Saibansho [Sup. Ct.] Mar. 11, 1997, Hei 6(o) 1102, 51 Saikō Saibansho minji hanreishū [Minshū] 1055.

[35] Based on such revised and more flexible tests, the Supreme Court found no similarity between the plaintiff's "Kozo" (in Japanese) trademark and the defendant's "Kozo Sushi" (in Japanese) and "KOZO SUSHI" trademarks, as the court decided that the fame of the trademarks and specific circumstances of the sushi-related business effectively rendered the trademarks as dissimilar.

When discussing similarity, note that the Japanese Trademark Act does not have an explicit definition of "confusion." Instead, the concept is derived from Article 4(1)(xv), which provides one possible reason for refusing trademark registration. Accordingly, courts will find a likelihood of confusion upon showing a clear risk that the trademark in question may be associated by the average consumer with the goods or services of another person's business.[36] The notion of confusion tends to be predetermined by the underlying similarity analysis performed either by the JPO or the court.

A mark can only be recognized as a parody if it is sufficiently distinct from the original mark. In reality, however, confusion can occur, even when the mark is rather dissimilar from the original. This is particularly true in the context of trademark parodies.[37]

III. Parody Trademarks and Trademark Prosecution

A. Overview of Relevant Grounds for Rejection

As mentioned above, there is no clear provision regulating trademark parody under Japanese trademark law. Therefore, if a parodist desires to register a trademark at the JPO, the JPO must confirm the registrability of that parodic mark by applying the following provisions to justify rejecting registration:

- Negative effect on public policy (Article 4(1)(vii))
- Similarity to a famous mark (Article 4(1)(x))
- Similarity to another mark (Article 4(1)(xi))
- Likelihood of confusion (Article 4(1)(xv))
- Unfair purposes, such as free riding on the goodwill of a famous mark, and intentions to dilute the distinctiveness or to impair the reputation of a famous mark (Article 4(1)xix))

Although these different provisions seem to overlap somewhat arbitrarily, the JPO applies them as two distinct sets of provisions. First, Article 4(1)(xi) stipulates a general rule regarding conflicts with prior applications and registrations used in connection with the same or similar designated goods. The general rule under Article 4(1)(xi) again has two threshold inquiries: the analysis of similarity between goods and services and that between the marks. In evaluating the similarity of

36 SHOEN ONO & SHUNJI MIYAMA, SHIN SHŌHYŌ-HŌ GAISETSU [NEW INTRODUCTION TO TRADEMARK LAW] 164 (3rd ed. 2021).

37 Kaoru Satō, Shōhyō Parody [Trademark Parody], 4 KOKUSAI KŌKYŌ SEISAKU KENKYŪ [INTERNATIONAL PUBLIC POLICY STUDIES] 151 (1990).

goods or services between two or more marks, the JPO relies on the "Examination Guidelines for Similar Goods and Services," which prescribe "Similar Group Codes" (or SGC) for goods and services within the Nice Classification. A reading of the SGCs will determine the similarity of goods and services (for example, jewelry (Nice class 14) is deemed to be a similar good to furniture (Nice class 20) because they both fall under the SGC 20A01).[38] The analysis of similarity between the marks was conducted by comparing the three factors introduced above.

The other set of provisions (Article 4(1)(x), (xv), and(xix)) is generally directed to resolve conflicts with famous marks. They also defer to the general rule on similarity, as they apply the same general practice to determine similarity. Article 4(1)(x) aims to prevent the registration of marks that are similar to a well-known or famous mark that is being used for identical or similar goods and services. The main difference from the general rule is that when invoking Article 4(1)(x), the senior trademark does not necessarily need to be registered. Article 4(1)(xv) aims to prevent the registration of marks that are similar to a well-known or famous mark and that raise a likelihood of confusion. This provision seeks to prevent the dilution of the senior marks and does not require the same level of similarity of goods and services that Articles 4(1)(x) or 4(1)(xi) do. Article 4(1)(xix) aims to prevent the registration of marks that are similar to a well-known mark, in Japan or abroad, when the trademark application might generate unfair profits from its use or cause damage due to the dilution of the origin of the goods or services or damage to the reputation of the trademark.[39] Unlike Article 4(1)(x), refusal of registration under Article 4(1)(xix) is also possible if the senior mark is well known only outside Japan, as long as the applicant mark is likely to be used for any unfair purposes. Additionally, the similarity threshold pursuant to Article 4(1)(xix) is comparable to that under Article 4(1)(xv). Under Article 4(1)(xix), the analysis focuses on the indication of unfair purposes, whereas the analysis under Article 4(1)(xv) focuses on the likelihood of confusion regarding the origin of goods or services.[40]

B. Similarity of Trademarks

As mentioned above, the JPO and Japanese courts assess the similarity of marks by comparing pronunciation, appearance, and concept. An applicant's mark will be rejected for being similar to a famous mark or to another mark if the registration of the applicant's mark would cause confusion as to the goods' origins if the two trademarks in question are used in connection with the same or similar goods.

[38] JPO, *Ruiji shōhin ekimu shinsa kijun [Examination Guidelines for Similar Goods and Services]*, Jan. 2019, at 1–9.
[39] Takeshi Kotani, Shin shōhyō kyōshitsu [New Trademark Classroom] 394 (2013).
[40] *Id.* at 395–96.

The Supreme Court stated that it is necessary to consider the actual circumstances of trade in areas where trademarks are inserted to comprehensively consider the overall impressions, memories, and associations perceived by consumers.[41] As for the "circumstances of trade," this would mean the actual conditions of trade that are constant in relation to the designated products of the trademarks in discussion.[42]

C. Likelihood of Confusion

The leading test for determining the likelihood of confusion is a five-factor test that was developed by the Supreme Court in the *Reerudyutan* decision of July 2000.[43] These five factors are: (1) the degree of similarity between the trademark and other party's indication; (2) the degree of fame and originality of said other indication; (3) the degree of relevance between the designated goods of the trademark and goods pertaining to the business of said other person in terms of property, intended use, or purpose; (4) commonality of traders and consumers of the goods; and (5) the attention that is ordinarily given by traders and consumers of designated goods.[44]

D. Negative Effect on Public Policy

A broad catch-all claim against trademark parody is that such trademarks negatively affect public policy and therefore must be rejected pursuant to Article 4(1)(vii). The JPO will consider rejecting a parody trademark due to a negative effect of public policy if the mark's main purpose is to free ride on the customer's attraction to a well-known senior trademark by making the trademark "reminiscent" of that well-known trademark and if the parody mark is likely to dilute the function of indicating the origin of the well-known trademark.

Even if the parody leads to the dilution of a well-known trademark, such dilution is mainly a matter of private interest. Only if the JPO can recognize a blatant intention to free ride on the senior trademark will it conclude that the parody trademark is negatively affecting public policy.

Considering that Article 4(1)(vii) was enacted to address marks that cannot be registered for public interest reasons, commentators have argued that Article 4(1)

[41] Saikō Saibansho [Sup. Ct.] Feb. 27, 1968, Sho 39 (gyotsu) No. 110, 22 SAIKŌ SAIBANSHO MINJI HANREISHŪ [MINSHŪ] 399.
[42] Saikō Saibansho [Sup. Ct.] Apr. 25, 1974, Sho 47 (gyotsu) No. 33, SHINKETSU TORIKESHI SOSHŌ HANKETSUSHŪ 1974, at 443.
[43] Saikō Saibansho [Sup. Ct.] Jul. 11, 2000, Hei 10 (Gyo-Hi) 85, 54 SAIKŌ SAIBANSHO MINJI HANREISHŪ [MINSHŪ] 1848.
[44] *Id.*

(vii) should, in principle, not be applied in private disputes between parties that primarily try to determine to which party a disputed trademark right belongs.[45] Another commentator who has written extensively about parody trademarks has argued that Article 4(1)(vii) should be applied to parody cases only very carefully, reiterating that issues such as parody, dilution, and free riding essentially belong to the category of private disputes and will—irrespective of the outcome—usually not be detrimental to public policy.[46]

E. Cases Regarding the Registration of Parody Trademarks

1. JVC Corporation Case

The oldest trademark parody decision reported in Japan is a JPO trial decision dating from November 7, 1958 regarding the registration of a design mark showing "a bear sitting in front of a phonograph without a cylinder" for class 9.[47] Commentators regarded such a design mark as a parody of JVC's well-known design mark showing "a dog sitting in front of a phonograph with a large trumpet cylinder."[48]

The JPO trial board found that the structure of the JVC design mark of a dog sitting in front of a phonograph was unique and original. While admitting the difference between a "dog" and a "bear," the JPO regarded both marks representing a scene of an animal listening to a gramophone to be structurally similar. The board further considered the status of JVC's mark as a well-known trademark and therefore decided to refuse registration of the "dog" trademark due to a likelihood of consumer confusion. In this early parody trademark decision, the JPO therefore

[45] Satomi Matsuda, *Shiteki ryōiki ni okeru hō 4-jō 1-kō 7-gō no tekiyō ni kansuru kōryo yōso no kentō [Consideration of Factors to Be Taken into Account for Application of Article 4(1)(VII) Of the Act in the Private Sphere]*, 14–165 CHIZAI PURIZUMU [IP PRISM] 11 (June 2016); Ryoko Iseki, *Chosakumono no kyarakutā kara naru shōhyō to shōhyō-hō-jō no kōjoryōzoku gainen [Trademarks Consisting of Characters of Copyrighted Works and the Concept of Public Order and Morals under the Trademark Law]*, 61 DŌSHISHA HŌGAKU [DOSHISHA LAW JOURNAL] 1 (2013).

[46] Takuto Hirasawa, *Shōhyō parodi to shōhyō-hō 4-jō 1-kō 7-gō oyobi 15-gō [Trademark Parody and Trademark Law Article 4(1)(vii) and (xv)]*, 44 CHITEKI ZAISAN HŌSEISAKUGAKU KENKYŪ [INTELLECTUAL PROPERTY LAW AND POLICY STUDIES] 283, 332–33 (2014).

[47] Tokkyochō [JPO] Nov. 7, 1958, Shōwa 32 kōkoku shinpan No. 179.

[48] The JVC parody trademark decision is the only decision rendered by the JPO or by a Japanese court prior to 1998 that commentators have identified as a parody trademark decision. We attribute this somewhat surprising paucity of parody-related JPO and court decisions at least in part to the recognition of parody trademarks by commentators as a relatively new notion in Japan. Toshio Eguchi included the JVC case as a case on similarity in his 1971 trademark law treatise. He did not consider the case as a parody case. *See Toshio Eguchi, Shōhyō-hō kaisetsu (2) [Commentary on Trademark Law (2)], in* GAKU KŌGYŌ SHOYŪ-KEN KENKYŪJO SHUPPAN-BU 145–46 (1971). Only decades later other commentators started taking notice of the JVC decision, likely thanks to Eguchi's treatise, and categorized the decision as a trademark parody case. *See, e.g.*, TOMOYUKI OKAMOTO, SHŌHYŌ PARODI NO KENRI [TRADEMARK PARODY RIGHTS], 20 (2019). Other twentieth-century similarity cases could also fall within the category of trademark parody cases. Given these cases' relatively low impact on the contemporary discussion, we decided to not discuss them in this chapter.

focused more on the uniqueness of the structure and the fame of the JVC trademark than on the degree of similarity between the two marks.

2. Coffee, Cars, and Rock 'n' Roll: Shifting the Analysis (*Boss Coffee v. Bouzu* Case)

The last two decades have yielded a number of decisions regarding the registration of parody trademarks, both by the JPO and the IP High Court, and an overall shift away from fame to similarity. The first noteworthy decision in this context was rendered by the JPO appellate board in 1998.[49]

Boss was established as a trademark for canned and plastic bottled coffee and coffee-flavored beverages sold by Suntory, one of Japan's largest beverage companies. The Boss mark is built around a well-known logo that uses artwork based on the image of American writer William Faulkner. The parody trademark in question replaces the word "BOSS" of "BOSS COFFEE" with the word "BOZU," which is the Japanese word for "monk." The BOZU mark was filed for clothing.

The appellate board of the JPO compared the marks in question and concluded that their appearance had a high degree of similarity, creating a considerable likelihood of confusion between consumers and a risk of association between the marks. While the board explicitly recognized a high level of fame for the BOSS Coffee mark, the core analysis of its opinion focused on the similarity that prompted the decision to cancel the BOZU parody mark.[50]

About ten years after the JPO's BOSS decision, the meanwhile established IP High Court had the opportunity to issue its first parody trademark decision. The underlying dispute was initiated by the famous rock band Rolling Stones, who had filed a post-grant opposition against a trademark application for a mark bearing visual elements similar to the Stones' lips and tongue logo.

The JPO decided in favor of the Rolling Stones and canceled the parody mark under Article 4(1)(xix), finding the parody mark to have attempted to free ride on the Rolling Stones' fame. The JPO also found that the parody mark had a negative effect on public policy.[51]

The parody mark owner appealed to the IP High Court, and the IP High Court overruled the JPO and allowed its registration.[52] The IP High Court explained that the appearance of the two trademarks was not similar, as the tongue displayed in the parody is seen directly from the front and the mark's overall image is rather flat, while the Rolling Stones' trademark has the tongue leaning to the left and also contains shading and other details that give the mark an almost three-dimensional

[49] Tokkyochō [JPO] Oct. 27, 1998, Heisei 10 igi No. 90851.

[50] When assessing the decision of the JPO, readers should note that the owner of the BOZU mark did not file a response to Suntory's cancellation request, prompting the JPO to render a default decision.

[51] Tokkyochō [JPO] Aug. 5, 2009, Igi No. 2008-900243.

[52] Chiteki Zaisan Kōtō Saibansho [Intellectual Prop. High Ct.] Jan. 13, 2010, Hei 21 (gyō ke) No. 10274.

impression. The court concluded that such a difference in appearance would result in marks without enough conceptual resemblance to determine similarity. Thus, even if the trademarks were used for the same products, the differences were enough to ensure that consumers would not associate the trademark with the famous rock band. Therefore, the IP High Court decided to reverse the JPO's decision and maintain the challenged trademark.

About two years after the Rolling Stones decision, the IP High Court had another opportunity to decide on a parody trademark dispute. A Japanese company had been manufacturing and selling single-passenger custom buggies under the trademark "Lambormini," attempting to draw a humorous resemblance to LAMBORGHINI luxury sports cars. Automobili Lamborghini SpA filed an invalidation trial against Lambormini for trademark registration at the JPO. The JPO dismissed the invalidation action and found that the Japanese pronunciations of "Lambormini" and "LAMBORGHINI" were not similar enough to trigger a likelihood of confusion.[53]

On appeal, the IP High Court held that the general impression of the pronunciation and appearance of the two trademarks were similar, pointing to the fact that nine of the ten letters of the parody mark were identical to Lamborghini's trademark.[54] The court further explained that the sounds "mi" (in the parody trademark) and "ghi" (in the cited trademark) sound similar, as they share a common vowel sound. The court acknowledged the more evident differences in the visual component of the two marks, but concluded that the proximity of the pronunciation element was enough for the marks to be considered similar under Article 4(1)(xi).

The court also considered in its reasoning that "LAMBORGHINI" is a famous mark and that the difference in the products (including their price and size) was therefore not relevant for the determination of confusion. The courts further concluded that the parody mark's owner's knowledge of a possible association between the marks was an indication of bad faith and thus allowed an intention to gain unfair profit or cause damage to Lamborghini. Therefore, the court ordered that the parody mark be canceled pursuant to Article 4(1)(xix).

3. The Puma Cases

Famous sports and clothing brands have become the subject of parody in many jurisdictions around the world. In 2010 and 2013, respectively, the Japanese IP High Court decided on two cases initiated by the German sportswear company Puma. The parody marks that were subject to the disputes were the marks "SHISA" and "KUMA."

[53] Tokkyochō [JPO] Aug. 24, 2011, Mukō No. 2010-890092.

[54] Chiteki Zaisan Kōtō Saibansho [Intellectual Prop. High Ct.] May 31, 2012, Hei 23 (gyō ke) No. 10426.

A shi-sa is a guardian lion in Okinawan mythology. An individual from Okinawa had established a small business selling apparel with the SHI-SA indication and had filed for registration of such an indication designated for t-shirts and hats in 2005. The JPO proceeded with the registration, but Puma successfully moved for the invalidation of the mark pursuant to Articles 4(1)(xv) and 4(1)(xix) in 2008.[55] The owner of the SHI-SA mark appealed to the IP High Court, and the IP High Court reversed the decision, finding that the two marks were not likely to cause confusion.[56]

To assess the likelihood of confusion, the IP High Court relied on the five-factor test that was developed by the Supreme Court in the *Reerudyutan* decision of July 2000.[57]

Assessing the most important factor—similarity—the court found that the two marks were not very similar. While certain aspects such as font style, the overall layout of the two marks, and the figure of a four-legged animal jumping from the lower right to the upper left support a finding of similarity, other aspects, such as additional text in the SHI-SA mark below the word SHI-SA and the noticeable decorative differences between the two animals, resulted in the court finding the appearance to be not the primary determinative factor. The pronunciation of the two marks is not similar. Additionally, the court found the third factor of the similarity analysis, the concept of the two marks in question, not similar, given that the PUMA mark stems from an existing cat family, while a shi-sa is just an imaginary animal and local cultural icon. Looking at appearance, pronunciation, and concept, the IP High Court found the two marks not to be similar. Looking at the other *Reerudyutan* factors for the likelihood of confusion analysis, the court found Puma's mark to be famous and original, a certain level of overlap between SHI-SA's designation and Puma's designated goods, and commonality between consumers of goods, albeit pointing out the vast difference in the scale of the operations of Puma and SHI-SA. Finally, looking at the fifth factor, the court found that the attention that buyers of T-shirts and headgear ordinarily paid while shopping would be enough to distinguish between the two marks in question, tipping the balance in favor of denying a likelihood of confusion.

Three years after the SHI-SA decision, the IP High Court assessed the registrability of Kuma, another Puma parody mark. Kuma is the Japanese word for "bear." The owner of the Kuma mark filed the trademark application in 2006. Like the SHI-SA mark, Kuma was designated for class 25, that is, various types of apparel. Undeterred from its unsuccessful endeavors against SHI-SA, Puma filed a cancellation action for KUMA at the JPO in 2011. The JPO again agreed with

[55] Tokkyochō [JPO] Oct. 29, 2009, Igi No. 2007-900349.

[56] Chiteki Zaisan Kōtō Saibansho [Intellectual Prop. High Ct.] Jul. 12, 2010, Hei 21 (gyō ke) No. 10404.

[57] Saikō Saibansho [Sup. Ct.] Jul. 11, 2000, Hei 10 (Gyo-Hi) 85, 54 SAIKŌ SAIBANSHO MINJI HANREISHŪ [MINSHŪ, at 1848. *See* Section III.C.

Puma and found the KUMA mark likely to cause confusion pursuant to Article 4(1)(xv).[58] KUMA appealed to the IP High Court, which decided to uphold the JPO's decision and thereby drew a fine line between KUMA and SHI-SA.[59] As in the SHI-SA proceedings, the main focus of the court's decision was the determination of the degree of similarity between the two marks.

In its analysis, the court noted that both marks used four letters with a very similar font. Both also included the side view of a silhouette of a four-legged animal stretching its front legs leftwards and moving toward the four-letter alphabetic character. Furthermore, the court observed a phonetic similarity between KUMA and PUMA, with only the first letter being different. Finding such a high degree of similarity, the court found that other factors, such as the high fame of PUMA's mark, the overlapping product designation of the marks, and the fact that products carrying both marks were available for sale in close proximity, such as in department stores and shopping malls, supported Puma's claim for cancellation of the KUMA mark due to a likelihood of confusion.

4. *Franck Muller* Case

The IP High Court's decisions with respect to the two Puma parody mark cases presented observers with a relatively clear and visible line between a permissible parody and a mark that would not be eligible for registration due to a too-high degree of similarity. This line got—unfortunately—blurred again by the IP High Court's 2016 *Franck Mueller* decision.

Franck Muller is a famous Swiss luxury watch manufacturer that entered the Japanese market in 1992 and that owns the Franck Mueller trademark. In the case at issue, Franck Mueller's Japanese distributor FMTM DISTRIBUTION LTD sought invalidation of the parody trademark "FURANKU MIURA" (original wording in Japanese as "フランク三浦"). The parody mark had been registered by the Osaka-based watch manufacturer Dinks in 2012 in an effort to safeguard watches that arguably imitated Franck Mueller watches. The JPO followed FMTM's request and decided to invalidate the parody mark, finding the parody mark to be similar pursuant to Article 4(1)(xi) Trademark Act and likely to cause confusion pursuant to Article 4(1)(xv) Trademark Act.[60] The IP High Court disagreed and essentially found that the two trademarks at issue were not similar.[61] The court conceded a similarity of pronunciation. It did, however, find the appearance "clearly distinguishable" and the concept "significantly different." Unfortunately—though not unusual for Japanese case law—the court offered little background for these

[58] Tokkyochō [JPO] Nov. 27, 2012, Hei 23 Oct. 10 Mukō No. 2011-890089.

[59] Chiteki Zaisan Kōtō Saibansho [Intellectual Prop. High Ct.] Jun. 27, 2013, Hei 24 (gyō ke) No. 10454.

[60] Tokkyochō [JPO] Sep. 8, 2013, Mukō No. 2015-890035.

[61] Chiteki Zaisan Kōtō Saibansho [Intellectual Prop. High Ct.] Apr. 12, 2016, Hei 27 (gyō ke) No. 10219.

findings beyond explaining that Kanji characters look different than Katakana characters and that "MIURA" conceptionally relates to a Japanese person while the concept of "MYURA"—in the context at issue—is that of foreign luxury watches.[62] In this context, the court did not explore or discuss the possibility that the parody mark applicant chose "MIURA" because of its conceptional relationship and proximity to the senior mark's "MYURA."

This case received brought attention from Japanese commentators, as not only the trademark itself but the entire product was a parody.[63] Nonetheless, the IP High Court focused only on the similarity of trademarks and the likelihood of confusion, leaving the impression that whether a trademark (or a product) is a parody should not have any specific effect on the assessment of the likelihood of confusion. Furthermore, the court explained that while dilution and free riding are possible causes of action to cancel a trademark registration, not all acts of dilution and free riding cause a likelihood of confusion. Therefore, even if a parody mark owner's business benefits from the senior mark owner's reputation, such an act by itself does not cause confusion.

5. Subsequent Case Law

A review of more recent case law on the validity of humoristic trademark registration highlighted the more forgiving direction regarding similarity and confusion that the IP High Court seems to have cemented, at least for now. In 2019, the IP High Court upheld the trademark registration of Dr. Linn Sakurai by denying the invalidation action by the French fragrance maker diptyque.[64] A brief glance at the marks does leave at least a first impression of similarity. That said, the court focused on the word elements of the depicted marks and found that the elements "Dr. Linn" and "Sakurai" would be sufficiently dissimilar from "diptyque" in terms of pronunciation and concept.

[62] A cursory review of Japanese trademark case law revealed a surprising paucity of discussion on the conceptional relationship/similarity between kanji (such as "三浦") and kana (such as "ミュラー"). Possibly inspired by the unequivocal decision of the IP High Court in Frank Muller, the Tokyo District Court and the JPO held in recent decisions that two marks that had a very similar pronunciation were conceptionally dissimilar, as the registered trademark used kana and the junior mark used kanji. *See* Tokkyochō [JPO] Dec. 25, 2019, Mukō No. 2019-890028, affirmed by Chiteki Zaisan Kōtō Saibansho [Intellectual Prop. High Ct.], Sep. 23, 2020, Rei 2 (gyō ke) No. 10014. The same issue was discussed in a related infringement lawsuit. Again, the infringement court found a lack of conceptional similarity. *See* Tokyo Chihō Saibansho [Tokyo Dist. Ct.], June 17, 2021, Hei 31 (wa) No. 11130.

[63] Tatsuhiro Ueno, *Chomei shōhyō no parodi [Parody of Famous Trademarks]*, 72 PATENTO 67 (2019); Shoichi Ogawa & Takashi Saito, *Parodi shōhyō ni taisuru fu tōroku jiyū no tekiyō kanōsei [Applicability of Grounds for Non-Registration to Parody Trademarks]*, 10 CHIZAI JĀNARU [JOURNAL OF INTELLECTUAL PROPERTY] (2017); Katsuyuki Izumi, *Shūchi shōhyō o parodi-teki ni riyō shita shōhyō no tōroku kanōsei (Furanku miura jiken) [Possibility of Registering a Trademark that Parodies a Well-Known Trademark (Frank Miura Case)]*, SHIN HANREI KAISETSU UOTCHI CHITEKI ZAISAN-HŌ [NEW CASE COMMENTARY WATCH, INTELLECTUAL PROPERTY LAW] (2017) 110.

[64] Chiteki Zaisan Kōtō Saibansho [Intellectual Prop. High Ct.] Feb. 19, 2019, Hei 30 (gyō ke) No. 10129.

About one and a half years later, the IP High Court rendered a similar decision in a dispute between Starbucks and Bull Pulu, a Tokyo-based company operating small shops and stands that sell bubble tea.[65] Again, at first glance, the marks leave the impression that Bull Pulu designed their mark with an intention to free ride on the recognition and fame that Starbucks' well-known mark may offer.

Starbucks asked the court to invalidate Bull Pulu's mark, asserting that not only should the word and mark receive trademark protection but also that protection should be extended to the green circular arrangement of which Starbucks' mark consists. Starbucks offered survey evidence that showed that 80% of the respondents indicated an association between such a green circular arrangement and Starbucks, building the argument that Bull Pulu's mark should be invalidated. The court, however, was not particularly impressed by such evidence and focused its analysis on the similarity of the words displayed in the two respective marks. With that specific focus established, the court found the marks to be different in terms of appearance, pronunciation, and concept. As such, the IP High Court decided that even if the two trademarks were used in the same industry, there was no risk of confusion as to the origin of the goods or services.

IV. Parody Trademarks and Infringement Issues

A. Trademark Infringement and Unfair Competition Law

Article 25 of the Trademark Act provides the trademark holder with the exclusive right to use a registered trademark in connection with designated goods or services. Further, Article 37(1) stipulates that the use of a mark similar to a registered trademark in connection with the designated goods or services, or the use of a registered trademark or a trademark similar thereto in connection with goods or services similar to the designated goods or services is deemed to constitute infringement.

However, one of the main points regarding the practice of trademark infringement in Japan is that when the use of a trademark is done in a manner where the trademark is not working as an "indication of origin," this use would not be considered a "trademark use," and thus, trademark infringement is denied. Additionally, because Japanese trademark law does not clearly stipulate confusion as a requirement for finding infringement, the finding of "trademark use" is extremely important in Japanese practice. Article 26(1)(vi) provides that the trademark right does not extend to "a trademark that is not used in a manner that enables consumers to recognize the goods or services as belonging to a business

[65] *Id.* Sep. 16, 2020, Rei 1 (gyō ke) No. 10170.

of any person." It has become common practice that, if a mark is actually used but not in a manner harmful to another trademark's function to identify the source of origin of goods, infringement should be denied on the grounds that such use does not constitute a use as a trademark.

The Japanese Unfair Competition Prevention Act (UCPA) offers further avenues for trademark owners to enforce their trademark rights against infringing third parties. Article 2(1)(i) and (ii) UCPA provide that the act of using an indication of goods identical or similar to a well-known indication to cause confusion with another person's goods or business or the act of using an indication of goods identical or similar to a well-known indication of goods as one's own indication of goods are deemed as acts of unfair competition. The law defines the term "indication of goods" as "a name, trade name, trade name, trademark, mark, container, or packaging of goods, or any other indication of goods or business in connection with a person's business." Thus, not only the trademark itself, but also the form and packaging are subject to protection under the UCPA.

The most prominent trademark parody infringement case in Japan was argued both as a trademark infringement as well as an unfair competition action.[66] "Shiroi Koibito" ("white lovers" in Japanese) is a langue de chat style biscuit that is considered the most popular souvenir from Hokkaido and is manufactured by Ishiya Seika, a well-known confectionery company. Ishiya Seiko registered a trademark for and used a variation of the registered mark for its Shiroi Koibito package design. In July 2010, Yoshimoto Kogyo, an Osaka-based entertainment company, started selling waffles named "Omoshiroi Koibito" ("Funny lovers" in Japanese) in souvenir shops in the Osaka area using a similar package layout. When Yoshimoto Kogyo started selling this parody product in areas outside Osaka, Ishiya filed an infringement action at the Sapporo District Court, requesting that the court prevent Yoshimoto Kogyo and two other companies from selling Omoshiroi Koibito.

Ishiya argued that it was obvious that "Omoshiroi Koibito" deliberately imitated "Shiroi Koibito," both in terms of pronunciation and packaging. They further argued that even if "Omoshiroi Koibito" could be considered a parody, this level of parody should be deemed trademark infringement, given that it would dilute the fame of Ishiya's trademark. Yoshimoto Kogyo argued that the humoristic intent and various "jokes" included in the mark and packaging were clear enough to ensure that no likelihood of confusion would arise. In the end, the parties settled the

66 Osamu Koyama. *Mohō shōhin to chiteki zaisan-ken — parodī shōhin to shōhyō-ken hogo mondai no kenshō — [Counterfeit Products and Intellectual Property Rights—An Examination of Parody Products and Trademark Protection Issues —]* 44, 45 SAN-KEN RONSHŪ (2013); Yoshiyuki Tamura. *`Shiroi koibito' vs. `Omoshiroi koibito' jiken—shōhyō-hō fusei kyōsō bōshi-hō ni okeru parodi-teki shiyō no toriatsukai— ["Shiroi Koibito" vs. "Omoshiroi Koibito" Case: Treatment of Parodic Use in Trademark Law and Unfair Competition Prevention Law]* W. L. J. HANREI KORAMU [WEST LAW JAPAN CASELAW COLUMN] https://www.westlawjapan.com/pdf/column_law/20130415.pdf. *See also* Tatsuhiro Ueno, *supra* note 64, at 76.

case, and Yoshimoto Kogyo agreed to change the package layout and restricted its sales to the Kansai region.

B. Other Possible Causes of Action

A trademark owner might also be able to pursue an action against a parody based on publicity rights infringement or civil law tort.

The Japanese Supreme Court recognizes the "right of publicity"[67] as the right to make exclusive use of customer attraction when the name or portrait of a person has the power to attract customers to promote products, such as the names and portraits of entertainers. According to the court, the right of publicity will be infringed upon when the following conditions are met:

(1) When the portrait itself is used independently as an object of appreciation;
(2) When a portrait is affixed to a product for the purpose of differentiating the product; and
(3) If the portrait is solely for the purpose of using the power of attraction of the portrait to attract customers, such as using the portrait as an advertisement for a product.

Despite courts recognizing the right of publicity and commentary, suggesting that such rights could be applicable in the context of trademarks,[68] we did not find a Japanese court case that addressed this issue. Nonetheless, using the image of a well-known person might qualify as a permissible trademark parody, and at the same time infringe the right of publicity.

Within the scope of general civil liability, even if a trademark parody free riding on someone else's well-known trademark does not constitute a separate violation of IP law, such as trademark infringement or violation of the UCPA, it might be possible to claim passing off under the general rule of tort based on Article 709 of the Civil Code. However, there is a general understanding that unless there is clear damage arising from infringement, it would be difficult for a trademark owner to prevail based on such a general tort law claim.

Finally, the Japanese Trademark Act provides for the criminal punishment of trademark infringement. An interesting characteristic of the system for criminal procedures in trademark matters is that, due to the nature of consumer protection inherent in the protection of trademarks, criminal procedures might be commenced even without a complaint by the trademark owner. That said, the Japanese

[67] Saikō Saibansho [Sup. Ct.] Feb. 2, 2012, Hei 21 (Uke) 2056, 66 SAIKŌ SAIBANSHO MINJI HANREISHŪ [MINSHŪ], at 89.

[68] Tatsuhiro Ueno, *supra* note 64, at 79

practice of criminal procedures for trademark matters usually demands a clear showing of intent to infringe on the trademark. In the case of parody trademarks, the use of senior trademarks is usually clearly intentional, and trademark owners have resorted to criminal procedures to pursue trademark parody matters.[69]

Conclusion

As this chapter shows, Japanese trademark law does not have any specific legal provisions addressing trademark parody. Therefore, users and commentators looking for guidance largely rely on the body of case law on the similarity and likelihood of confusion from trademarks that might fall within the category of parody developed over the last decades.

Recapping such case law, the JPO looked at parody as a relevant point in a somewhat holistic similarity analysis only at an early moment. In more recent cases, such as cases that occurred by and around 2010, courts started to focus on free riding when assessing similarity, at least in decisions in which they found similarity. However, considering recent case laws that commenced with the 2016 *Franck Mueller* decision, courts have started to focus solely on similarity and the likelihood of confusion.

The emphasis on the likelihood of confusion makes it difficult for owners of famous brands to combat the registration of parody marks. In reducing the relevant analysis to trademark similarity and the likelihood of confusion, courts have arrived at what we perceive as an overly high standard for similarity and have established an unfortunate practice of ignoring other factors that may be incidental and relevant in assessing parody mark registration. Courts in other countries tend to factor the humoristic yet reputation-exploiting element of parody into similarity analyses. The concept factor that is part of the Japanese test of trademark similarity would also allow Japanese courts to place greater relevance on the possible exploitation of the senior mark's reputation. Yet, and in our view, regrettably, recent case law chose to employ a more technical approach that ignores the real conceptual similarity from which parody trademark owners often attempt to benefit.

[69] For instance, in 2013, Starbucks used criminal provisions and convinced the prosecutor's office of Chiba prefecture to press charges against a night-life entertainment shop using a parody mark "GIRL'S STAR BAR" on grounds of suspicion of trademark infringement. (*See Sutaba kokuji no kanban keiji yōgi no kaisha yakuin shorui sōken Tōgane-sho [A Company Director Suspected of Posting a Sign that Closely Resembles Starbucks is Sent to the Togane Police Station]* (CHIBA NIPPO Mar. 9, 2013), https://www.chibanippo.co.jp/news/national/126498). In 2016, the Osaka Police department acted against the sellers of several NIKE and ADIDAS parody products, resulting in the arrest of thirteen individuals (*See* Tomo Kuwamura, *"Owarai no machi" de ōkō suru parodī shōhin oboetemasuka? "Shiroi koibito' naranu 'omoshiroi koibito"... akushitsuna pakurika sōdaina share ka [Do You Remember the Rampant Parody Products in the "City of Comedy"? "Shiroi Koibito" and "Omoshiroi Koibito"... A Malicious Parody or a Grand Joke?]* (SANKEI SHIMBUN Jan. 11, 2017), https://www.sankei.com/article/20170111-GXNYXRQ6LFIOVCXKHCNAGJUNR4/).

The impact of this development is exacerbated by the notion that almost all decisions involve the registration of parody marks. We do think that the constitutional guarantee of freedom of expression warrants a relatively forgiving approach to the use of humoristic adaptions to registered trademarks in the context of infringement analysis. We also think that marks like SHI-SA that are not obviously motivated by the intent to exploit another brand's reputation deserve registration. However, as foreign scholars who teach comparative IP law at Japanese law schools, we find that the currently applied standard is making Japan a jurisdiction in which it is too easy to register parody trademarks, and we hope that the pendulum will swing back and that courts will again take a more holistic approach to parody trademark registration in the future.

Index

For the benefit of digital users, indexed terms that span two pages (e.g., 52–53) may, on occasion, appear on only one of those pages.